Feet on Earth,
Head in Heaven

Feet on Earth, Head in Heaven

The Challenge of Living in Two Worlds

NORMA JEAN DUNCAN, MBBS FFARCS

RESOURCE *Publications* · Eugene, Oregon

FEET ON EART, HEAD IN HEAVEN
The Challenge of Living in Two Worlds

Copyright © 2012 Norma Jean Duncan. All rights reserved. Except for brief quotations in critical publications or reviews, no part of this book may be reproduced in any manner without prior written permission from the publisher. Write: Permissions, Wipf and Stock Publishers, 199 W. 8th Ave., Suite 3, Eugene, OR 97401.

Scriptures taken from the Holy Bible, New International Version®, NIV®. Copyright © 1973, 1978, 1984, 2011 by Biblica, Inc.™

Resource Publications
An Imprint of Wipf and Stock Publishers
199 W. 8th Ave., Suite 3
Eugene, OR 97401

www.wipfandstock.com

ISBN 13: 978-1-62032-565-0

Manufactured in the U.S.A.

This book is dedicated to Marcelle Leahy who filled a special role in my Christian journey, and in my heart, and who now rests in the loving arms of her Creator.

I would like to thank the following people for their help in my search for God: Rev. Barry and Louise Bryant for welcoming me into their home for Bible study many years ago; Judith and Rev. Stephen Barrett for their example of living faith, their teaching, and friendship; the many, many other Christians who have been an inspiration to me in their walk with God.

I would also like to thank Carolyn Baxter for her steadfast interest and help throughout the writing of this book; Jan Anderson for her editing skills so cheerfully given; Rev. Colin Chamberlain, retired NSW Baptist minister, for his help and encouragement in completing the writing of the book.

Contents

Preface | ix

1. Personal Testimony | 1
2. Journey Back to God | 19
3. The Glory of God | 34
4. Hello, Hello ... Anyone There? | 46
5. The Most Excellent Way | 63
6. Ask Me Anything But That | 88
7. Love, Punishment, and Blessings | 106
8. How to Love and Delight God | 131
9. Off the Starting Blocks and Into the Race | 141
10. Has the Church Forsaken Its First Love? | 156
11. The Bible and Tradition | 194
12. Submission | 218
13. Sexuality and the Church | 242
14. Terminal Illness | 256
15. Non Believers | 276
16. Out of Darkness into Light | 300
17. Picking Up the Pace with Jesus | 316

Appendix: The Difference Between Buddhism and Christianity | 321

Bibliography | 325

Preface

I CAME LATE INTO God's presence as a product of the secular world. Overall I found the ways of the church close up were a marked contrast for the better and individuals within the organization worthy of great respect. The church is the body of Christ and mostly behaves that way. There is no doubt civilisation has benefited and continues to benefit from Christianity; it is always there in the background and comes to the fore whenever the human spirit is hard pressed. Nevertheless, in this book I have at times criticised the organisation of the church, as well as actions taken by individual Christians. I haven't enjoyed being critical and have done so only because God has put it on my heart to write this way. I hope that the airing of many topics pertinent to everyday Christian life will encourage fellow Christians to aspire to the standards of our Holy God. I also pray that those non-believers who have recoiled from their Creator in disgust, because of the wrong actions of the organised church or individual Christians, will read this book and realise their urgent need to look past human failings to see the God who loves them and yearns for their return.

1

Personal Testimony

My testimony is a stark illustration of spiritual blindness and God's perseverance to overcome such blindness. It is based on a direct revelation of his love, which spiritually and practically turned me around 180 degrees. I was born again in August 2004 after a lifetime searching for him. By then I had wandered up almost every blind spiritual alley there is, but managed by his grace to find the way home eventually. There is a milling throng in all those dead ends and I am hoping by hearing about my Christian journey others will find the way out also.

I was brought up in a typical nominally Christian family. We had a social conscience and tried to do the right thing. Sometimes, especially at Christmas, we went to church; we thought there was probably a God somewhere. Often when I felt my life was out of control, which was most of the time, I prayed to this nebulous God even though I wasn't at all sure he was there—yet paradoxically I believed in the power of prayer. I attended almost every denomination of Christian church there is. I did a three year Bible study course but I made no apparent spiritual progress and I knew it—now I can see it was extremely valuable because it was the groundwork God laid for my future. It was the promise in two Bible verses that kept me searching and praying:

In Matthew 7:8 Jesus said, "For everyone who asks receives; he who seeks finds; and to him who knocks, the door will be opened."

Jesus repeated his promise in Revelations 3:20, "Here I am! I stand at the door and knock. If anyone hears my voice and opens the door I will come in and eat with him and he with me."

Feet on Earth, Head in Heaven

After nearly a fifty year search, in August 2004, God in his grace opened that door and I was overwhelmed by the quality and depth of his love, "my word that goes out from my mouth: It will not return to me empty, but will accomplish what I desire and achieve the purpose for which I sent it." (Isa. 55:11).

My conversion came about after a friend died of cancer. At the time the diagnosis was made we were acquaintances but as we walked together over the fifteen months of her illness we became friends. She was a person of great integrity and very stoical and uncomplaining. I was "cut up" as I watched her general deterioration and increasing weakness and understood the inevitability of her death. I prayed feverishly many times a day that God would minimize her suffering and he certainly did this. During the entire time she remained comfortable with very little medication and only needed the stronger drugs by injection in the last six hours of her life. At the same time I was constantly surprised that despite her ill health we would have very happy times together during which the ever present "hanging sword of Damocles" didn't seem to matter. There seemed to be a very positive loving presence around us such that I said to her in puzzlement on a number of occasions, "You know it seems like there are three of us here not just the two of us." Following that very strange statement we would both just look at each other as she obviously felt this too, but didn't have any more of a clue than I had as to what it was all about, and neither of us realized who this Presence was.

A month after she died a professional acquaintance told me of his experience when he looked after a dying friend. In order to explain my delayed appointment with him I had told him only that I had been busy caring for a friend who had recently died of cancer, but other than that I hadn't discussed any details with him at all. While I listened for some time to him recounting his story, I had the uncanny feeling he was saying exactly the same things I would have said to someone else about my experience. The only significant difference was that although he described exactly the same love surrounding his situation he did not seem to feel this love as a Presence. Shortly before his friend died the friend had said, "It is all about love you know, there is nothing else." I had assumed my experience could be explained by a very positive rapport between two psychologically compatible people, but by the end of this man's conversation I realized my friend and I, and these other two people, had been surrounded and supported by something far more universal than that.

For the first time I saw the love of God for my friend, for me, and for every other person. Paul offered this prayer for the Ephesians: "I pray that you, being rooted and established in love, may have power, together with all the saints, to grasp how wide and long and high and deep is the love of Christ," (Eph. 3:17–18). Two thousand years later this intercessory prayer of his was answered for me. As I walked away from the man who had told his story, I felt ten feet tall. It wasn't until over a year afterwards that I understood that the third presence was Jesus; I had found the pearl of great price. I really came backwards through the recognition of God and his love, to repentance and the forgiveness of the cross. I realized I had failed throughout my life to worship a holy and loving God who had made me in his image for himself. I am forever aware of the enormity of my offence, and humbled by the unmerited sacrifice that has excused me. As I continue my walk with Jesus, the initial glimpse of his love has become an expanse that has no limits.

As one of the slowest of starters, by recounting my story I am like the psychiatrist, who treated his patient with an inferiority complex by giving him the name and address of "someone who is definitely inferior to you." In other words if I can find God almost anyone can. Personally, I take comfort in the story of the hare and the tortoise. Like the tortoise, despite the poor start I am determined to put in a best-effort finish. It is never too late, now is the time to start living and experiencing the marvelous earthly quality of eternal life available to those who strive to serve God, "now is the time of God's favor, now is the day of salvation." (2 Cor. 6:2).

WHAT IS THE PROBLEM?

There has always been a restless anxiety in humankind, a sense of urgency to find something vital we cannot identify but know is missing, and like an itch we cannot scratch it drives us to find relief. The less fortunate pursue worldly solutions like money, fame, and power only to find these things act like accelerants to this smoldering sense of loss. It is only when we seek God and restore communication with him that our soul is satisfied and we find peace. Though made in the image of our Creator, we took on the image of evil. God didn't change; we did. When we rebelled against God and decided we knew better than he did, we took ourselves away from our Creator, and his power and perfection.

In the beginning he breathed his life into us. It is amazing that in our arrogance we couldn't see that our breath, which means all of our life and living, is totally derived from God. We seized a spurious independence we didn't have when we cut ourselves off from our life source. His perfection is complete; it is life, wisdom, love, light, power, holiness, righteousness, and justice. We cut ourselves off from all this when we turned away from God. Without his wisdom we find it almost impossible to discern right from wrong, without embracing his love we are self absorbed, without his power we are helpless, without his holiness we are evil, without his righteousness and justice we hardly care about the disgusting level to which we have sunk.

Like sheep in distress we bleat about our sorry state, but like humans we defend our right to continue in it while blaming everyone but ourselves. Isaiah described our stubborn refusal to open our hearts to God and be healed by him. Even those of us who see the better way, the way it was in the beginning and long for it, without healing we are no longer fit to be with God. We are in a desperate and hopeless situation that only the divine intervention of Christ can address. He is the only way for us to return to our Creator and satisfy the yearning in our soul.

Many of us dither around putting off the day when we will get serious about God. It is such a hard thing to do, it requires much concentrated thought; you can't have a split focus and hope to come up with clear thoughts about God. We can leave it too late and even when others can see our time is running out we tell ourselves we will do it tomorrow. I agonize over the good-living people I see doing this. I see the warnings God gives them. They come unscathed through major illnesses and "Evel Knievel" car crashes, and still don't heed the warning. I have seen dementia overtake some so that although still alive they are incapable of making any decisions. Incredibly many people just don't give their salvation enough priority. Just as the unprepared virgins who ran out of oil for their lamps arrived late and were shut out of the wedding banquet, these unprepared people will also be locked out of heaven and hear the same words, "I tell you the truth, I don't know you." (Matt. 25:12). What will it take for people to give their eternal life its necessary priority? I don't know, but if there is a way God will find it, and in the meantime I can and do pray for them. A friend prayed for me for at least two years before I was born again, so that is a huge incentive for me to pray for others.

Personal Testimony

LIVING LIFE WITH A SPIRITUAL PERSPECTIVE

Life in the earthly and spiritual sense has progressed on a bumpy road, but having accepted that I have been made righteous in the sight of God by the death of Jesus, I am now reconciled to God and my relationship with him is restored. I can see life is a spiritual journey, and as I travel the road I don't take my eyes off Jesus—I don't want to and I can't afford to. I know that of myself I am nothing, but in God I am everything. I seek strenuously to dwell in God's presence, to do his will every day and to recognize the daily ministry he sets before me. Jesus gives us the power to come back from our mistakes, so I try to leave my failures behind and always to go forward. Whatever I achieve is in his power.

In the following pages I have written about the highlights, the difficulties, and struggles I have faced in the everyday application of an emerging faith. I feel I need to do this while it is all still fresh in my mind, even though I still have a long way to go. I have often wrestled with some spiritual issue enveloped in a fog of confusion bordering on despair, only to eventually see a very clear and obvious answer. Hopefully relating this movement from confusion to clarity will help others. Although often encouraged by other Christians there were times when I felt daunted by their faith and spiritual strength. Now that a few years have passed I realize doubt is normal—as we read in Exodus, even Moses had difficulty at times trusting God. I have mentioned some of the mistakes I have made as well as what has worked for me. Much of it may not be relevant to anyone else because we are individuals and God treats us as such. Even so he often teaches us not only by our own experiences, but by the experiences of others.

He will do for everyone what he has done for me. He will "open the floodgates of heaven and pour out so much blessing that you will not have room enough for it." (Mal. 3:10). At the same time Jesus tells us it is not always easy and we should first pause and consider the cost we will incur if we follow him. We need to be prepared for that cost and what form it commonly takes and why it costs. Here is how he described it: "If anyone would come after me, he must deny himself and take up his cross and follow me." (Matt. 16:24). The changes in becoming more like Christ can feel like vivisection at times as the Holy Spirit carves out the evil areas in our lives. Some service is a pleasure, as writing this book is for me, while some is heart wrenching and full of hard slog, sacrifice, sorrow, and strain. It hurts to deny oneself in favor of someone else, and with Jesus we suffer with and for others, but God makes provision for all this, "For just as the sufferings of Christ flow over into our lives, so also through Christ our comfort overflows." (2 Cor. 1:5).

How does God inspire such supreme devotion in his followers? It is because when we find him, we find treasures that cannot be adequately described, but only experienced. The writers of the Scriptures have managed to give us a glimpse of them to get us started. One such instance is Job's description of the wisdom of God. He names the earth's precious gems and says they cannot be exchanged for it, or compare with it in any way.

The first and immediate change I noticed in myself was a growing peace of mind. "Peace I leave with you; my peace I give you. I do not give to you as the world gives. Do not let your hearts be troubled and do not be afraid." (John 14:27). A big change in my thinking is that I no longer concern myself a lot with tomorrow. I don't worry constantly as I used to, because now every facet of my life and all my activities are in God's hands. In particular I have a "too hard" basket God keeps for me and I have learnt to wait patiently for him to sort the items out. Sometimes a resolution is almost instantaneous while some issues have been sitting in the basket for years. It is not my worry. He will show me when and what to do, if anything. My concern is to dwell closely with him so that I don't miss his reply when it comes.

Recently, allied to this, I have learned to rest in God. Because I am by nature a very anxious and impatient person this was very hard for me—I always want to rush out and solve every problem yesterday. God tells us many times when we live in his will with the purpose of promoting his kingdom that he is the problem solver not us. Also, my ego was dependent on earthly purpose and activity, so God kept me restricted through ill health for several years until I found my purpose and value only in him. This was so hard.

As Jesus takes more and more ground from Satan in my life, benefits like love of others and forgiveness are becoming easier so my mind is more tranquil. When trouble affects a relationship I find myself increasingly distanced from all the turmoil, although not necessarily from the people concerned. I no longer need or want to argue my case, but turn immediately to God in prayer for guidance. Now I know the joy of heaven even in sorrow. Nothing the world can offer us is worth forfeiting this indescribable joy of being with God.

Learning that in the hard times God is working for my spiritual good was a huge breakthrough. As a result I have lost much bitterness, paranoia, and anger. A life locked in negativity is a living contradiction to God's love. I can enjoy the blessings; I can be thankful for the discipline—especially after it's over! I agree with Peter when he said that we can rejoice in trials because in this way our faith, which is more valuable than gold, is progressively refined and made more resilient.

Increasingly I see the quality in the things of God, the rubbish in the things of man. More and more I find that many of the harmful things that used to entrance me have lost their attraction. The glittery packaging with which Satan deceived and lured me just looks tawdry. I thought I wanted to be like some of the people featured in the Sunday papers—rich enough not to have to work, with an easy lifestyle of glamour and popularity. Now unless I see God is part of the scene it is repugnant. My perception of the gap between what God stands for and offers humankind, and what Satan stands for and offers humankind is growing ever wider, and I know there is no way to survive in both camps. It is the gap between heaven and hell that the rich man who denied the beggar Lazarus understood too late.

Everything I try to do for God flows back to me in abundance on a wave of his marvelous love; why wouldn't I do it? God doesn't need a thing from me but I want to be a delight to him and not an offence. I want to line up somewhere behind Jesus. Daily I see vividly the ever-present miracle of the magnificence, beauty, and intricacy of Creation. I am part of unfolding miracles every day as my prayers small and large are answered. I try not to give God advice on how to solve a problem I lay before him, but still I do it. Then it often makes me laugh at the innovative solution when God steps in, because it is different and so much better than I envisaged. His horizons even in everyday problems are so much bigger than mine. He never works in one direction at a time—rather the result is multidirectional, somewhat like watching fireworks.

A fellow Christian illustrated this point when she told me about one of her earliest childhood memories. She said she was very young and remembers being in a room in her home looking up to what seemed like her very large parents. Her father was quite upset and it was because of money. Her mother said to him, "God has always provided for us, so why do you think he would stop now?" God gave these words to her mother to give to her father and comforted both of them; the listening child never forgot, and now grown up, she continues to tell the story to countless others. It is a significant and poignant story because it was understood and remembered by a little child who was probably thought to be too young to benefit. As Jesus said, spiritual truths are sometimes hidden from intellectuals but understood by children. God didn't just reassure the father about his concern. He generated a message of comfort which may well reach thousands as it continues to be told long after the worried father himself has entered the Kingdom of Heaven.

I've learnt the mindset I need in order to allow room for God to continually amaze me. Many times a Christian tells a tale about a problem they had prayed about that ended well, but they fail to see God's hand in the good result. This is illustrated by the well-known story of the man who was working on a roof, lost his footing and found himself spread-eagled, and slipping down the tiles. He prayed frantically, "God save me! God save me!" he continued to slip when suddenly his fall was arrested by a nail that caught in his belt and held him. He then prayed, "It is okay God you needn't worry, a nail has caught me by my belt." He never knew the joyful surprise of knowing God had answered his prayer.

Even when we have faith that he will answer, the way he does is often surprising. Jesus was physically with the disciples for three years teaching them, but he still surprised them. Similarly we are told his words amazed the crowds who came to listen to him. If we are not open to being repeatedly astonished by God we are stuck in a rut, we will underperform, and we will miss out on a lot of the joy we are promised.

One of the biggest challenges to my faith is watching the seven o'clock news. There are some items I can't watch and I have to turn the television off. The suffering in the world would overwhelm me without faith and almost does so at times even so. Many times I find myself saying, "Why God, why? Where were you?" This is a cry that has echoed down the ages and may seem to have gone unanswered. Yet we can see God does care and has answered, because God himself has said, "let justice roll on like a river, righteousness like a never-failing stream!" (Amos 5:24). The defense of justice underpinned Jesus's entire ministry, for him it was a top priority and many of his verbal disputes were on that basis. In the Beatitudes he was specific in his promise, "Blessed are those who hunger and thirst for righteousness, for they will be filled." (Matt. 5:6).

The death of Jesus put these promises on track and his return will cause justice to triumph, but meanwhile watching the state of the world while waiting for him is hard. If I can keep my faith despite this anguish, then like Job, I don't need to ask this "why" question and right now can say with him, "My ears had heard of you but now my eyes have seen you."

(Job 42:5). Job saw God with his own eyes; we can see him with the eyes of our heart. As Paul points out in Romans 8:24, hope realized requires no faith at all, whereas it is faith-testing and therefore faith-building to believe on a promise when the circumstances point the other way. When we do so, we reach the very pinnacle of faith and this is why Abraham is seen as the man of faith in the Bible. I can cope with the seven o'clock news when I think of Abraham and God's many promises to us in the Scriptures.

I know I will always be walking closely with the great sovereign God of love, mercy, and justice, who was faithful in fulfilling his words to me—"he who seeks finds." He leads me on, drawing me ever closer to him. I know one day I will clearly see face to face the Savior who died for me and the God who never gave up on me.

THE CONVERSION EXPERIENCE AND ITS AFTERMATH

When we first see God burst with power into our lives he gets our full attention as we experience a very real personal moment of awareness of him. It is something we never forget. Many Christians describe this as a moment of great joy as they receive the best news they have ever been given—the same good news of great joy the angels announced to the shepherds at Jesus's birth. With this joy there is often deep shock and shame as we feel confronted by our blindness and the love of God that we have consistently abused. He appears to us in many ways including through the Scriptures, other people's words, our thoughts, dreams, and visions, but all bring an intense awareness of his being. He speaks personally to all of us, bringing a certainty that he is the only God, the Almighty God who has always known us and loved us, and this knowledge demands our complete allegiance. It is very precious to us and we can't let the memory of it fade, and for ever after there is a special place in our minds marking the event. For all of us it is a turning point and life is never the same afterwards. Often there is an immediate change visible to others in the way we conduct our lives.

Paul's conversion is a thrilling story because it is so direct, so personal, and so dramatic. He caused great turmoil and distress for those Christians living in Jerusalem. Then sanctioned by the high priest, he started out on his journey from Jerusalem with the express purpose of persecuting the Christians in Damascus. To his associates and Christians alike he was a force to be reckoned with, or so it seemed until God intervened. Then in an instant he was terrified, blind, and helpless. As he drew near to Damascus a light from heaven suddenly surrounded him and he fell to the ground. From within this light a voice spoke to him, "'Saul, Saul, why do you persecute me?' 'Who are you, Lord?' Saul asked. 'I am Jesus, whom you are persecuting,' he replied." (Acts 9:4–5). You could call this the reality check of all time. After three days a very reluctant and fearful Ananias obeyed God's instructions and laid hands on Paul. Then his sight was restored and he was filled with the Holy Spirit. Paul then astonished the people when he began preaching in the synagogues that Jesus is the son of God.

It was a total about face and not surprisingly, just as he had hunted down Christians, he himself became hunted. The Jews in Damascus and the Grecian Jews tried to kill him. It seemed everyone wanted a piece of Paul. When he came to Jerusalem he tried to join the disciples, but they suspected treachery and were all afraid of him. No one wanted to know him; life must have been very confusing. Confusion can happen today to new Christians as secular friends think the newly converted are weird and the church sees all the flaws of those who have not yet begun to take on the likeness of Christ.

Paul then went further afield preaching and enjoyed a time of peace. Subsequently he had one of the most tumultuous and persecuted lives recorded in the Bible, as through him God brought salvation to the Gentiles. His conversion story and life story is enthralling, marked by drama and the outpouring of the glory of God. As a result we hold Paul in great respect, admiration, and gratitude, but in his writings Paul himself never stopped ascribing the glory to God.

All Christians share some parts of Paul's story and also have the opportunity to make known the glory of God by spreading the gospel. Like his story ours starts with a "before", then a testimony that marks the turning point, followed by the persecutions, the respites, the "time out", the fatigue, the isolation, and the frustration at the slow spiritual progress in self and others. Only relatively few people are called to a life like that of Paul, but his description of his life is how we all feel at times when we are embroiled in the struggles of our own journey, because we all have times where life seems too hard. If we follow Christ we will suffer, but we can join Paul in agreeing it is when we are hard-pressed that we are strong in Christ. We also share the treasures Paul knew—the joy of being brothers and sisters of Jesus, and the indescribable quality of life when we dwell in God's presence, and know his power, his love, and his peace.

Just as Peter described God's elect as "strangers in the world," (1 Pet. 1:1), so Paul had his mind and heart in heaven but had to live with his feet on earth and do God's will here—the devil's playground. From this conflict he repeatedly gave two messages to the churches he planted: to rejoice in the one and to persevere in the other. When Paul was having time out in jail he was irrepressible as he witnessed in triumph, as illustrated in this famous verse, "Rejoice in the Lord always. I will say it again: Rejoice!" (Phil. 4:4). Regardless of his circumstances, when it came to rejoicing in Jesus, Paul just wouldn't shut up. The attitude these words reflect is all the more amazing because he wrote from jail when he was in chains, and probably had little in the way of comfort, food, company, or sanitation.

THE CHRISTIAN RACE

Paul wrote the most inspiring verses exhorting us to persevere. His favorite imagery is that of striving to run a race with all his might with his eyes always fixed on the victor's prize at the end, "I have fought the good fight, I have finished the race, I have kept the faith. Now there is in store for me the crown of righteousness," (2 Tim. 4:7-8). His disappointment is palpable in this verse: "You were running a good race. Who cut in on you and kept you from obeying the truth?" (Gal. 5:7).

We need that essential ingredient of perseverance because we are running no quick sprint but a marathon race, and the finish line is uphill. There are the downhill stretches and the water handed to us as refreshment on the way, but much of it is overwhelming fatigue, blisters, and pain while others seem to bump us out of the way as they run effortlessly past us or over us. It can seem pointless and hopeless. Heartbreak Hill at the end is both the worst and the best as we grind up that hill that seems impossible and endless in our own strength, but is neither when Jesus is with us.

In the Olympics we see the runners a moment before they enter the stadium aware of nothing but a fog of weakness, isolation, and pain, as they wobble around on the track with buckling knees. Then as each one enters the stadium the crowd spots them coming through the gate and erupts in a roar of welcome. In an instant the body language and expression of the runner is transformed by pure delight as spirit and body are lifted on this wave of recognition and support. Each runner realizes in amazement he has got to the finish line and that all through the race everyone has been following his progress and willing him to keep going.

Our reception in heaven will be even better. Travelling with us is Jesus, he'll get us up the hill and we will see God, who has drawn us all our lives to him by his inexpressible love for us. Jesus brings each repentant prodigal son safely home on this final leg of the journey—it is the culmination in each person of what Jesus died for. It is his triumph and his glory, and our joy. In the cheering crowd surrounding us will be the great figures of the Bible we have read about, other Christians, the angels, and our loved ones. All heaven roared with joy when we turned back to God, and the eyes of heaven have been glued on our progress ever since and preparation made for our welcome home, "For this son of mine was dead and is alive again; he was lost and is found." (Luke 15:24). We are also told the greater our struggle has been to stay in the race, the greater the reception we will be given.

REMEMBER BUT MOVE ON

Our moment of conversion is only the beginning and must lead on to the race. For some people it becomes a camping site and our testimony can become a cause for competition and pride. We all really love it when we are selected from the throng and given positive personal recognition in some way. In this case there is a danger we will wear the story of our first real awareness of God as a badge of holiness and thus use it to start building our house upon the sand of man's praise. Flattered by the personal revelation instead of humbled by it, we bask in the recognition but forget the grace. Like every precious thing God gives us it has to be used to his glory, which means it has to be followed up by a life expressing our relationship with Jesus. Otherwise, it becomes a monument not to triumph but to the tragedy of what might have been. Our testimony is in the past, so in a sense can fixate us there, instead of boosting us into the future. Many of us linger there when we should be forging ahead, or we stop altogether. We allow ourselves to be overcome by the distractions of life and fail to progress on our spiritual journey

Paul gave his testimony to Festus and King Agrippa after his arrest by the Jewish authorities. He described his life in parts: first before

Personal Testimony

his conversion, next Jesus's appearance and words to him on the road to Damascus, and then his life afterwards. Although he quoted Jesus's words to defend himself in order to try to gain his release from prison, his overarching higher purpose of spreading the gospel was very obvious. Agrippa, challenged by the gospel Paul presented, told Paul he could not expect him to be persuaded in such a short time. Paul replied, "Short time or long—I pray God that not only you but all who are listening to me today may become what I am, except for these chains." (Acts 6:29). In Paul's reply there was so much passion for the gospel and concern for his accusers. He never slackened or lost the plot.

The road to Damascus was both a turning point and a beginning for Paul. From there he worked selflessly, ceaselessly, and sacrificially without complaint and full of praise in a life dedicated to God. Following his example, we rightly tell others our testimony of when God through his personal love and grace first arrested our attention. It is accepted as routine evangelism that every Christian can and should do. But there has to be a meaningful "after" to our story; there should be clear evidence of Jesus in our lives and the huge changes his presence brings about in us. People should see a change in our attitude and behavior for the better. They should see Jesus in us. Of what value is recounting a vision, a dream, or any other revelation from a spiritual armchair, when instead we should have been galvanized into action like Paul? Those who knew us before and after won't be impressed at all if they see no evidence of the gospel working in our lives. Rather it will be a total turnoff because our words are only validated by our behavior.

For some time the personal testimony of love God gave me made me feel very comfortable and I basked in the warmth of it. However, I have become aware it was not given to me for this reason alone, but also to pass on, not just by describing it in recounting the tale, but by living it. It is sobering because it was about love and I thought I would have scored quite well in loving others, but as time goes by and the Holy Spirit shows me more and more I've had to move away from that idea. It is just as well God in his wisdom and mercy doesn't take us too far too fast with this self-knowledge or we would never get up off the canvas. Being convicted by the Holy Spirit feels as I imagine it would feel to suddenly find oneself naked in a public place. This discomfort doesn't last long because the purpose of the Holy Spirit is always to bring us back to God, to restore our relationship with him—a guilt-free relationship based on his love for us in Jesus.

Feet on Earth, Head in Heaven

A woman who had had a close association with the church for decades gave a moving description of a vision she had had about compassion. This was her testimony and underpinned her conversion. She went on to describe another meeting she had had with a man whose lifestyle had been suddenly turned upside down for the worse following loss of health and independence. The woman presented him as a humorous grumpy figure and criticized his negative attitude, and we, the Christian audience, joined in the joke. Not only did we all show an amazing lack of sensitivity, but we were without excuse because we had just heard a life-changing lesson on compassion. It was tragic that this woman could be so affected by a revelation, which she obviously still considered one of the most important things to have ever happened to her, and yet at least on this occasion was not able to incorporate true heartfelt compassion into her response to someone in need. Similarly, we in the audience warmed to the story of her revelation, but not to the man who should have benefited by it. We should have been putting up our hands to find out how we could help him or people like him. We all fail to make the connection at times. We should continually return to our conversion experience to see what God is trying to tell us. Having understood, we should then concentrate on the hard part, which is getting his message into our hearts and from there we should act on it.

Some Christians never have any landmark conversion experience, rather they start without fanfare and grow steadily into their faith. How our journey starts must depend on many circumstances unique to each person, but we all end up at the same place. I wonder if the people who have wandered the furthest from their God-appointed path have the most dramatic kick off—literally. The further we are away from God the greater our pride, our rebellion, and false self-sufficiency. Paul was charging away in exactly the wrong direction with great zeal. In the Scriptures he bears forever the shame of his despicable act when he stood by and abetted the cowardly mob-stoning of Stephen, who by contrast so shone as the Christian ideal. Paul needed the "baseball bat" treatment to arrest his flight from God, whereas those not far off course may only need a nudge—although probably no one escapes the bat altogether, because even the best of us are so far away from him. The manner of our conversion experience may also be related to the ministry required of us on the remainder of our journey. The faith Paul needed would have been constantly fed by his memory of the events on the Damascus road and Jesus's words to him there.

Personal Testimony

Those without conversion stories may be envious of those with, and the late arrivals like me regret the service and spiritual maturity that can't be made up. But through the story of the thief on the cross we are told all this is beside the point. Our righteousness in Jesus is absolute whether we acquire it as a child or on our deathbed. It is all in God's timing, all by his grace, and all to his glory. Children born into Christian families may be more often in the non-dramatic group. There are all degrees in between. In whatever manner we come, there is no room for complacency. We need to be sure we hit the ground running, and in the right direction as soon as possible.

Some of those without a conversion experience may not be saved. Many who miss out on salvation are the "good-living decent people," who wander along aimlessly unsuspecting and unprotected until Satan picks them off. In this group in great danger are the nominal Christians who dwell in a Christian crowd following the church traditions, while never comprehending the eternal truths, or the need for "a baptism of repentance through the forgiveness of sins." (Mark 1:4). They have religion in their heads but do not have God in their hearts. I was there; I know what it is like. It is tragic, and we in the organized church need to reach out to this large section of the congregation more strenuously than we do. If we look at how Jesus tackled this same problem he did it by speaking very plainly with personal challenge, and certainly didn't "pussy foot" around, or count the number of people coming to listen to him.

Although the strength drawn from the social structure of the church is a good thing, it can masquerade as faith, or keep faith small. This is particularly a disadvantage for those growing up in the church or having a long-term association with church life. We can have false confidence in our faith when we are in these sheltered confines amongst other believers. I have found even a holiday away from these supports is a challenge, even though most of my life was spent in secular surroundings. I get the same feeling I get when I watch a colony of ants intent on some project, while completely unaware of the big picture and their place in it. When I am out there in the world at large it can seem like "business as usual" in this changed environment without God, where money and power rule, and I find myself wondering if I am the one person marching out of step with a rational world. Going into unfamiliar places and environments should first test and then strengthen faith. Staying afloat spiritually in secular society reminds me of Peter trying to walk on water; like him we may need rescuing.

OTHER REVELATIONS

No Christian misses out on the thrill of the Holy Spirit shining a spotlight on God's truths. How often does a Bible text we have read many times previously suddenly tell us something new and stunning? We can't wait to tell someone else but unfortunately we are often met with bewilderment. That doesn't matter because God has his own personal agenda for everyone. When others tell us something that has thrilled them we may be similarly underwhelmed because we are not where they are. Maybe down the track we will remember and the light will dawn. Because the Bible is the revelation of God's glory we will never come to the end of the joy of unearthing its treasures.

God also gives us other special revelations apart from the Bible that are similar to that of our conversion experience. They teach us by giving us his perspective on some situation or they can direct, comfort or alert us. He speaks in words, pictures, dreams, and emotional impacts, "God also testified to it [salvation] by signs, wonders and various miracles, and gifts of the Holy Spirit distributed according to his will." (Heb. 2:4). By way of illustration I will recount such a message from God that my mother and I shared.

She was in her sixties at the time and in one of the hardest phases of her life. She was in constant pain with crippling rheumatoid arthritis; her lifestyle had just changed from one of status, money, and married life to that of being divorced and living in rented accommodation on the government pension; through no fault of her own, she was involved in an acrimonious court battle, which lasted several days; close supporters were few. Her spirits were at rock bottom one night when she arrived home from the day's court proceedings. She went and lay down on her bed feeling physically cold through and through and emotionally desolate. She then felt something like a breeze pass over her and described a sensation of being blissfully warm and secure, "like being under a bird's wing in amongst the down." She recognized this was of God and because of the miraculous nature of the event we both loved to discuss what had happened. But it wasn't until twenty five years later, and about four years after her death, that God revealed the full story to me. Not so long after my "born again" experience I was sitting in a midweek service. The pastor read out Psalm 91, "he who dwells in the shelter of the Most high will rest in the shadow of the Almighty. I will say of the Lord, 'he is my refuge and my fortress, my God, in whom I trust.'" … "He will cover you with his feathers, and under his wings you will find refuge; his faithfulness will be your shield and rampart." (Ps. 91:1, 4). As soon as I heard the words I immediately recognized my mother's experience and was overjoyed.

It is impossible for a finite mind to really fully grasp something like this. God made these promises and wrote these words in David's time, and then carried them out at just the right time, in the life of one person among the billions on earth, some three thousand years later. This is power, this is faithfulness, and this is love of the divine kind. In the years surrounding God's revelation to my mother her life was marked by much suffering, but also by huge spiritual progress, so that she counted this part of her life as the best and the most blessed.

It is so fantastic when God manifests himself like this in our lives. However we have to take care not to chase or manufacture experiences for their own sake, or wait idly on the next one. We can rest assured these wonderful things will keep happening, usually when we least expect it, and often when we are in greatest need, but we have to get on with putting effort into the rewarding but less colorful activities like daily Bible study, obedience, and serving others. There is a danger we can become addicted to seeing God move in our lives in miraculous ways, while not bothering to move in it ourselves.

SUMMARY

Humankind is dissatisfied with the unhappy state of the world as well as the finality of death. Only the knowledge of God can address these problems and it is God himself who enables our hearts to believe. God wants everyone to return to him, but why some people never seem to understand or relate to the revelation of himself in Christ is a mystery only he can answer. For our part we need to exercise the free will he has given us to search diligently and unceasingly until we find him. He has promised many times in the Scriptures, if we do so, we will be successful. This was certainly the case for me.

The details of conversion testimonies are as varied as the people who experience them. This is because God knows us intimately and is so personal in his approach. Even so the pattern is the same. When converted, we become intensely aware of God's love and perfection. By contrast our own lack of holiness is stark and the realisation of the mercy, grace, and power of his forgiveness through the cross of Christ is initially overwhelming. From there we move into a life with Christ, where we live in the Spirit with him. In this way we approach the presence of God. We become intimately aware of him as he speaks to us personally, and our lives increasingly conform to his will.

Conversion brings about a permanent radical change in perspective. There are the new challenges of conforming to God's will and this is often extremely painful. If we persevere God rewards us with increasing faith in him and with his peace. We are surrounded by his love and we constantly live with the joy of the knowledge of his purpose of salvation for us. Despite the trials and sorrows, life becomes worth the living, now and forever.

2

Journey Back to God

"The fear of the Lord is the beginning of wisdom, and knowledge of the Holy One is understanding." (Prov. 9:10). God tells us he will give us this wisdom and understanding: "I guide you in the way of wisdom and lead you along straight paths." (Prov. 4:11). These paths are the Bible, Jesus, and the Holy Spirit. In this way we progress in our love and reverence for God. In Isaiah we read about Jesus and the Holy Spirit, "The Spirit of the Lord will rest on him—the Spirit of wisdom and of understanding, the Spirit of counsel and of power, the Spirit of knowledge and of the fear of the Lord" (Isa. 11:2).

GETTING STARTED

We succeed in our life by giving ourselves completely over to God's will. This is our spiritual journey and to progress on it is the purpose of living. The Bible tells us we can make a start by being reconciled and saved to God through Jesus. We then become Christians. It is so simple and summarized in John 3:16: "For God so loved the world that he gave his one and only Son, that whoever believes in him shall not perish but have eternal life." Christ tells us he is not just one way of several ways we can get to God, but the only way—"I am the way and the truth and the life. No one comes to the Father except through me." (John 14:6). Christianity is not complicated and should never be seen to be. Jesus said it can be understood by the mind of a child.

Accepting salvation means repenting of the evil in us and offloading it onto the cross of Christ, loving him, serving him, and staying so close that we never lose sight of him. The initial decision brings indescribable joy to the person concerned and it doesn't stop there, but reverberates through both heaven and earth as it is shared by Jesus himself, by the angels, and by other believers. The salvation of each and every one of us is a cosmic event marked by momentous joy in heaven every time a sinner repents.

Once we set out on the Christian journey the next step is becoming more like Jesus and it can only happen when we are with him. The Scriptures leave us in no doubt that even our apparently righteous acts are evil compared to the holiness of God and place us irretrievably distant from him. We are from a very early age liberally endowed with dissent, anger, jealousy, bitterness, lack of compassion, elitism, and nepotism. As we go along our spiritual journey, this flawed thinking and the negative reaction patterns, which come so naturally to us, are overcome. We become more like God intended us to be and then our quality of life soars above our troubled earthly existence as he brings us his love, joy, and peace. This change continues only as our relationship with Jesus deepens, which allows the Holy Spirit to work more effectively in us. It takes years and is never complete, but we are told if we have a deep desire for the knowledge of God, then we will continue to move closer to his image.

The in-dwelling of the Holy Spirit answers our own spiritual thirst, but also spills out from us to revive others. These inner changes of becoming more like Christ should translate into the exemplary behavior that characterizes faith and biblical principles in action. For us to be credible it must be the Holy Spirit who talks for us and Jesus who shines forth in us. If we just accept salvation and leave it at that, then we will live a very shallow life, and all people will see and hear is the mess Satan has made of us. No one will benefit, or want to be like us, or believe we have found something of value, or want what we have. We have found the Kingdom of God—the treasure, the pearl of great price, and by looking at us people should know it and want it too. We have to be convincing when we tell them no price is too great to pay for this treasure. Once it is ours, the only really effective way for us to guard it is to progress faithfully on our own spiritual journey.

This progression for the better is sometimes a peaceful and gradual change and as such is not hard for us, or others affected by us. In fact it is very enjoyable. Jesus leads us not only in these good times but also through struggle and pain. Unfortunately human nature is such that we are more likely to respond to God during negative events than during positive ones and so God uses these difficult milestones in our path to promote our spiritual maturity. They are likely to be stresses over which we have little control and which challenge our faith. They are all too familiar and include such things as illness, grief, unemployment, injustice, and violence. The result is that approaching and passing a milestone is more often likely to be difficult and painful, rather than easy and pleasurable. When we experience very stressful situations we can either take the usual earthly shortcuts, which lead to unsatisfactory long-term solutions, or we can wait until we get God's message and the problem is solved his way. He brings about spiritual change for the better, but while it is happening the effects on us can be of seismic proportions, almost destroying us and those around us. So when we get to a milestone we sometimes decide it is too hard and opt not to press on rather than experience the pain involved in passing it. We opt for the chronic long-term pain of life at a distance from God rather than the acute short-term pain involved in going through the lesson needed to move closer to him. Giving up is not the answer, rather we must persevere and claim the reward God gives us when we succeed. The harder it is, the greater the reward and this can mean a quantum leap in spiritual growth, a giant step closer to him.

THE LORD DISCIPLINES THOSE HE LOVES

Not to be unrealistic, I have found God does take us right down to the wire. Our milestones are often our spiritual Achilles heel, our areas of weakness, the worldly things we are most dependent upon, our gods that stand in the way of the one true God. In practical terms we may lose the person we are besotted with or depend on too much; or lose our money, which gave us security; or our intellect with which we solved our problems; or our health, which gave us independence; or our ego, which propped us up. Losing our earthly treasures is often the only way God can get our attention. If he can't communicate in a whisper I have found he will use a baseball bat, and if necessary, straight between the eyes. Fortunately, if we give our life to God he takes us at our word and will go to any lengths to save us.

The difficulties we encounter on our journey should not come as a surprise, because in the Scriptures we are warned to expect pain, but that it is for our own good and because God loves us. It is vital to our success to remember this. Otherwise, based on past painful experiences at the hands of our fellow man, it often feels a lot more like hate than love; it feels more like God is trying to destroy us than save us. We need to remember what a loving and encouraging God we worship and to keep going: "Those whom I love I rebuke and discipline. So be earnest, and repent." (Rev. 3:19). As well, God is very definite in his reassurance that he will not test us beyond our endurance, "God is faithful; he will not let you be tempted beyond what you can bear." (1 Cor. 10:13). Nor do we suffer alone, God suffers with us.

After we have reeled under the suffering of the milestone and staggered past it, he will restore us and promote us. It is painful on the Potter's wheel, but after the discipline of God we rise to greater spiritual heights. Contrast this with Satan who often gives us what we think we want and in the process crushes the life out of us. It is not possible to pass a milestone with Jesus and not receive amazing blessings. This is because in doing so we follow harder on his heels and dwell closer to God. The joy of this is indescribable. When God told us in the Old Testament about the coming of Jesus he told us what he wants for us, and it is not pain and suffering—far from it, rather in Jesus he will "bestow on them a crown of beauty instead of ashes, the oil of gladness instead of mourning, and a garment of praise instead of a spirit of despair." (Isa. 61:3). Jesus himself reaffirmed his purpose when he promised he would give us life in all its fullness. Life with God is our great eternal destiny. It is worth the pain, and in striving for it we become more like Jesus. He makes it clear that suffering at the hand of God is a reward system, not a punishment system. He has promised his disciples they will sit with him in his place of honor at God's right hand.

MILESTONES ON THE JOURNEY

One of my own early milestones felt like a boxing ring. Pursuit of God was the prize; the opponent was me, and this makes for a very confusing contest. From the vantage point of lying flat on my face most of the time, I was able to examine the canvas from close range in great detail. Battling on was very hard—so that I found myself preferring to just lie there, but this view was so uninspiring that eventually I would rally enough to want to get up, and God in his mercy would get me to my knees and occasionally even fleetingly onto unsteady feet. Then down again I would go and back to the canvas. When down there I would consider my pitiful plight and the unfairness of it all because I was putting in such a tremendous effort to get right with God; I was convinced I deserved so much more. When I got up I would flail around until I managed to land another king hit on myself; then down I'd go again. Finally, I realized beating myself up for failures is futile, and self-pity is futile, and questioning God is futile. It was a momentous milestone. It was only the close view of the canvas and the pain of it all that allowed me to understand what God was telling me. He was telling me to stop struggling in my own strength, but in all things and in all circumstances to rest in him. Looking back I give God heartfelt thanks for my time in the boxing ring, but I am also doing my best not to go back for any return bouts!

As in everything, the secret to success is to rely on God's power, not our own, and when we get to that point in our thinking during a trial we know we will get there. He "is able to do immeasurably more than all we ask or imagine, according to his power that is at work within us," (Eph. 3:20). I now find increasingly that while the battle is raging around me it is easier to hand the burden of the pain of it over to God and rest in his peace. It is what Jesus meant when he said, "my yoke is easy and my burden is light." (Matt. 11:30). As soon as we show we are willing to yoke ourselves to Jesus and we pick up the burden, we can immediately pass it to him. This is a deal only God would think of; it is the realization of the promise of the gift of his peace, which is beyond our understanding.

Once I passed a few milestones and got the hang of it, I found myself eager and straining to get to the next—until I got there of course! In between, in the happy times, I forgot the pain—it is easy to become overconfident! Now I am more realistic and try even harder in prayer and obedience so that I will be better prepared for the next milestone, which will surely come. Our journey is like running in an obstacle race that only ends at the gates of heaven. The operative word is of course "running", as opposed to dawdling, camping out, or retracing one's steps. The pain of successive tests doesn't diminish, each trial stands on its own, and progress often means even harder milestones. I guess that is logical as we approach closer to our Holy God. This means of course the rewards also become greater. No doubt I will have to revisit some places—and more than once, but each time I do so I will be progressing. Any feelings of inadequacy are swept away by God's words of reassurance to Paul, "My grace is sufficient for you, for my power is made perfect in weakness." (2 Cor. 12:9). Paul said he liked being weak because then the power of Christ had full reign. He was confident that when we are willing, God will see to it that our journey is successfully completed: "The one who calls you is faithful and he will do it." (1 Thess. 5:24). If we can only focus on God and give him a free hand we can travel a most amazing journey.

One of Jacob's milestones occurred when he struggled all night with the angel. It is reminiscent of what we do. His is a somewhat puzzling story because we are not told clearly what it was about—although presumably it was about submitting to God's will. This is the same as when we turn on God at our milestone and engage in a battle with him that is both unnecessary and unwinnable. Like Jacob, we have to realize this and make the decision to stop, to submit to God, and to move on with him to the next spiritual place that he has prepared for us. Also like Jacob, we are likely to sustain a permanent injury—hopefully to our pride, but whatever the damage it will be to our spiritual benefit.

A memorable milestone is described in Chronicles, where we read the stirring account of a victory, which King Jehoshaphat enjoyed. It is a reminder to us of what is happening behind the scenes at every milestone in our path. Jehoshaphat was confronted with far superior forces and his small army was in despair. After he prayed, God said to him: "Do not be afraid or discouraged because of this vast army. For the battle is not yours but God's . . . Take up your positions; stand firm and see the deliverance the Lord will give you . . . Do not be afraid; do not be discouraged. Go out to face them tomorrow, and the Lord will be with you." (2 Chr. 20:15, 17). In obedience the Israelites went out towards the enemy singing praises to God. He caused the enemy to destroy each other so they were defeated without the Israelites lifting a finger against them. (Similarly it is not uncommon today to see evil people self-destruct).

These verses about Jehoshaphat can serve as a handbook for us to learn all God wants us to know about getting through trials successfully. He is vitally interested in us and wants to take command of every aspect of our lives to ensure the outcome is according to his will. All he needs is our cooperation. In this story he says even when we are helpless facing disaster, he is with us, and he will prevail. He tells us that after praying and listening to him, we should decide what his will is in the matter, and then take that as our position and stick to it. He wants us to be positive in our faith in him so we will be neither afraid nor discouraged. If we always defer in our lives to him, we know we don't own the trials we face, but God does, and he will be with us and see us safely through. After Jehoshaphat prayed, he appointed men to march at the head of his army singing praise to God for his holiness, and thanks for his enduring love.

Similarly, our job is to pray and move in his will as the Israelites did at that time, and to give thanks in the crisis with praise, because in his love for us God has taken up our cause. Then we wait faithfully on him and see the deliverance he will bring us.

Some years ago I read about a milestone in the life of a servant of Elisha, the prophet. In the book of Kings we are told Elisha repeatedly thwarted the plans of Israel's enemy, the King of Aram. When the King set up ambushes, God would tell Elisha where they were located and he would relay the information through to the King of Israel. One of the Aramean officers was asked by his enraged king to identify the traitor in their own ranks. He protested their innocence and said Elisha even seemed to know the words the King spoke in his bedroom. This was better than a hidden microphone, and the King of Aram decided Elisha had to go. They found out where Elisha was and sent a strong force during the night to surround the city. The next morning, Elisha's servant saw the might of the enemy and went to Elisha in dismay. "'Don't be afraid,' the prophet answered. 'Those who are with us are more than those who are with them.' And Elisha prayed, 'O Lord, open his eyes so he may see.' Then the Lord opened the servant's eyes, and he looked and saw the hills full of horses and chariots of fire all around Elisha." (2 Kgs. 6:16–17). Elisha then prayed that the enemy would be blinded and he led them into a trap. After capturing them they were given a great feast and released. This marked the end of hostilities.

The story about Elisha is certainly not just a very old story with a feel-good ending. It is there for us to read and apply in our own lives. A few years ago I was privileged to do just that. Then, I was involved in a legal battle where a matter of social justice was the issue. My opponent had the favor and support of the government, as well as many millions of dollars in assets. Before I undertook the task I realized this was a "David and Goliath" contest, where I was another "David". But as I pointed out to my skeptical and worried friends, David won when all human logic would have predicted he would lose. Three years passed in legal maneuvering. It was extremely stressful and the legal fees huge, and in every way I was at the limit of my ability to go on. Then there was a tribunal hearing. By the end of the first day of discussions the other party offered a solution, which would in effect have shut down the whole enquiry, or as an alternative, they promised me a contest, which would lead to my failure and financial ruin. My legal team knew I could not match my opponent in any way and were pressuring me to agree to give up. I couldn't see what else I could do and virtually agreed to sign their proposal, but I said I would think about it overnight. While I was travelling in the train to go back to the second day of the hearing I read the story of Elisha. It hit me in a flash that God is always on the side of justice. I knew from the earthly perspective I was something of a joke, a solitary and puny figure fighting a cause without any hope of success. Then with renewed insight I also knew that the hosts of heaven were ranged around me. God was with me, I was in a position not of utter weakness, but one of great strength. When I told my legal team I would not agree to the proposal they were as indignant with me as my opponent was. But I did as God told me to do and "stood firm", which was something of an overstatement because in effect what I did was to get out of his way. The decision to persevere, directly inspired by the story of Elisha, proved to be the right one, and eventually the victory became a matter of public knowledge. This was God's battle not mine, and it always was, "For our struggle is not against flesh and blood, but against the rulers, against the authorities, against the powers of this dark world and against the spiritual forces of evil in the heavenly realms." (Eph. 6:12).

We need to constantly remind ourselves not to underestimate God and never bow to the forces of evil. When we get out of God's way the emotional impact of what we see is beyond human words to describe. The closest description I can give is "amazing" and "marvelous". David knew this exhilaration. He said, "Declare his glory among the nations, his marvelous deeds among all peoples." (Ps. 96:3). God speaks to us today as he did in ancient times, we have only to listen and obey. It is then such a sweet thing to see God work so directly in our lives.

There are a number of things happening at every one of our milestones and it is not all about us. Other people inevitably become involved, like Job's friends, and our conduct affects their spiritual progress. It may be that the main point of our struggle is to help someone else. This is likely if we are in a stressful situation where God wants us to persevere in love and forgiveness, when it would be easier to walk away. We are told to commit ourselves faithfully to him so we can continue to do good, just as he is faithful in his goodness to us.

Paul described his time chained up in jail as time well spent, because it helped others to spread the gospel more courageously. It is typical of God that he often gets a result that is opposite to our best guess. You would have thought seeing Paul in chains would be likely to have been a disincentive to others. Their encouragement came about because God could rely on Paul to witness so well at his milestones that it took away the fear of persecution for these other people and strengthened their faith. Similarly I have reflected on situations where I have been close to the suffering of someone else and realized in retrospect that as a result of their suffering I have benefited greatly spiritually myself. I think we need to remember this when our own suffering seems pointless. The Christian martyrs who died for their faith probably had no idea at the time what a huge encouragement their suffering would be to the faith of billions of people coming after them.

Because we are part of God's support team for our fellow Christians our concern should not just be for ourselves and our own milestones. It is when the battle at their milestone is at its fiercest, when the outcome is hanging in the balance, that they need us most. When things are blackest, we all often doubt God's goodness or power and ask "why", and so this is one way we know when a friend or acquaintance is under heavy fire. Their "Why" is a rallying call to alert us to be as supportive as possible. Unfortunately, because of our own self-absorption, we don't want to hear their angry, self-defeating cry, or be near them during their struggle to accept the will of God. The more we hear "why" from a fellow Christian at their milestone and the more their behavior offends our delicate Christian sensitivities, the more desperate is their battle. We often react by distancing ourselves, or telling the other person directly or indirectly that they should stop wallowing in self pity, pull themselves together, and have faith—all the things they are struggling to do. Not very insightful! We need to take Jesus's perspective and come alongside them in his strength with his love. It is the quality of our own faith and compassion that limits our ability to respond.

"WHY, WHY, WHY?"

It is not just the beginners who talk along these lines and ask "Why, why, why." Although God seems to regard any communication from us as better than none at all and tolerates our "Whys", by harping this way we are not acknowledging God's glory. The common "Why" reaction is typified in the book of Job as he fought so hard in his battle against evil—and we think we've got problems! His milestone—at stake for him was his faith in the justice of the God he worshipped and loved. Unlike him, we know the answer to his questions because we have been told of the conversation between God and Satan that preceeded Job's suffering. God delighted in Job and praised him to Satan, "There is no one on earth like him; he is blameless and upright, a man who fears God and shuns evil." (Job 1:8). Satan said Job's faith in God was because God had bribed him with blessings and if these were withdrawn then Job would lose his faith. God disagreed, and said no matter what ill fortune Satan could bring on Job, he would remain faithful. And he did.

Yet Job asked God many times why he was suffering. When God later appeared to Job, he said, "Who is this that darkens my counsel without knowledge?" (Job 38:2)—and this about a man whom God had described in such glowing terms! It just highlights the unfathomable patience and love of God that he listens to this same old whine down the centuries. Interestingly, God never gave Job any explanation at all for his sufferings, or answered any of his questions. When Job saw God, he did not ask again any of the burning questions he had been putting repeatedly to his unhelpful friends. Rather, at the sight of God, he could only put his hand over his mouth (Job 40:4). The presence of God was the complete answer to all Job's "Whys" and made all the questions he had saved up and agonized over quite redundant. This is still the answer today because when we are in the presence of God the "Whys" lose their meaning and fade away.

It was touch and go for Job and so it often is with us. Knowing the answer to his "Whys," as I read of his suffering and mental and spiritual torment, the tension inside me rose because I feared he would give up. There was so much at stake and I found myself barracking for Job, saying things to myself like, "Come on Job!", "Don't give up", "Keep going". The thought of him giving up and letting himself and God down was terrible. It would have meant Job would die in defeat, he would have brought sorrow to God, and Satan would have said to God "I told you so". Nothing has changed; the same scenario is played out over and over again today as Satan battles with God for your soul and mine.

Of course the story of Job is there to teach us how to think and behave when like him we find ourselves in great trouble. Focusing on Job's friends is just as important because it is vital we learn from their mistakes. Like Eliphaz and his two other friends, we are falsely very confident in our religious advice to those suffering and we often totally miss the point. God was angry with Eliphaz, so we know he is definitely not someone to copy. In his speeches, Eliphaz most of the time got it quite wrong. He said the innocent and the upright never perish—what about

Abel? He also said it would be of no interest to God if Job was righteous. This is exactly the opposite to the theme of God's conversation with Satan at the beginning of the story. Eliphaz showed he had much religious knowledge, but in failing to correctly apply it to Job he demonstrated that a truth told out of context can be a very persuasive lie. He also wrongly accused Job of condemning himself with his arguments, which was the very thing he was doing himself.

The account of Eliphaz has a frighteningly familiar ring. He went through the full repertoire of mistakes that we make. There is as much to learn from him as there is to learn from Job. Eliphaz failed his own spiritual opportunity at Job's milestone because he himself moved further from God, not closer to him. Also, when we use his approach it can be the last straw for the person at their milestone who, unlike Job, might lose the battle. Job was obviously worn down by the self-righteous advice of his friends. No doubt Satan was delighted with them. Rather we should acknowledge pain, and give love and support, both emotional and practical. We don't have to understand the reason for someone else's milestone. Like Job's friends we are usually unable to do so, but the sufferer does need to know we understand the pain they are going through. We need to ask them what practical help we can give them and they need to hear a sympathetic rallying cry from us. No matter how we word it, they should get this message: "Come on you can do it! Don't give up! Keep going!" At the core of the mistakes Eliphaz made was the fact that his attitude to Job was not loving, rather he was arrogant and self righteous.

Christians often baulk at the better approach because they fear it fosters criticism of God and self pity, but in fact it does the opposite because it is love—and love always heals. It buoys the person up, helps their faith and keeps them going. Unfortunately, well-meaning enthusiastic Christians want to give a sermon on faith and how worthwhile pain is to our spiritual development. When a person is battling to hold on to their faith it is so obvious that telling them to have faith is ridiculous; when they are at the height of anger with God it is equally ridiculous to tell them to say "thank you"; a person on the rack doesn't want to hear how lucky they are spiritually to be suffering. It might be true, it might be good advice, but it is no use telling them to do the very things that at that time they are unable to do. There is an appropriate time to talk like this, but it takes the wisdom of God to know when it is. If we approach them with love and understanding then we will hear him tell us when that is, or maybe it will be meant for someone else to do. Basically it is God, not us, who will take a sufferer to the spiritual places where they will achieve all he wants for them. Our job is to support them and help them to persevere with Jesus so they can get to those places. We don't want our ignorance and arrogance to cause God to be angry with us as he was with Eliphaz.

SPIRITUAL MATURITY

This process of progressing in spiritual maturity is a huge struggle, because we have to move in our thinking, attitudes, and behavior from the ways of the flesh to the ways of the Spirit and this is often not addressed formally in a supportive way by the church. We are taught the broad principles, but not the practicalities. This is partly because progress often comes through experience and therefore instruction from the Holy Spirit, rather than from instruction from other people.

The gap between theory and practice in the established members of the church is one of the commonest reasons for new Christians to stop church attendance and for atheists to justify the blasphemy of their disbelief. At the same time there often seems to be zero tolerance to the obvious mistakes of the newcomer. It is easy to forget the difficulty a problem posed for us, so that later on when someone else is in that place we tend to dismiss them lightly with indifference and glib reassurances, or worse still judgment and condemnation. The result may be such deep disillusionment that the newcomer loses faith and is set back on their journey. So no matter how far we have come, as we progress we have an obligation to be supportive and understanding, especially to those behind us, but also to those ahead of us.

The writer of the book of Hebrews expresses his frustration when he alludes to the confused thinking and behavior of Christians and their lack of progress. He accused them of being slow to learn, so that far from being the teachers they should have been, they still needed someone to teach them "the elementary truths of God's word all over again. You need milk not solid food!" (Heb. 5:12). When our faith is in its infancy we all need spiritual milk and without it can't make the transition to solid food. Without help in making this natural progression we may either drop out altogether, or stay as spiritual babies, and fail to fulfill God's will for us. To stretch the analogy—even those who have graduated to solid food at times can't tolerate a complete diet, but have to fall back on milk as well.

So although the concept is most relevant to new Christians it never ceases to be relevant to everyone.

If Paul, a giant of Christian teaching, had trouble moving Christians along so they could realize their full potential in Christ, it is no wonder our leaders today are similarly burdened. They must often feel like Paul, frustrated at the underperformance of their parishioners. It should not be left to the leaders alone to shoulder this burden, it is the duty of the whole congregation. How it is handled is critical. When I have underperformed or seen others do so, a common reaction of the mature Christian seems to reflect frustration and a mindset of "battle fatigue" or "burn out", rather than one of love, patience, and understanding. We are told we will mature if we train ourselves to distinguish good from evil. This instruction gives helpful advice, but there is only one way to do it. The immature Christian needs to do his utmost to become more like Jesus, and the more mature Christian needs to do the same, while constantly remembering the compassion of Jesus for the repentant sinner. My diet is still heavily supplemented with milk; I am seeing from the perspective of the spiritual dyspeptic. Hopefully, sharing my difficulties will help beginners to keep going and the mature to remember their own early struggles, and thus be more understanding and patient.

We know from the parable of the sower and the seed in Matthew 13:3 that many who accept Christ will give up. To some extent this is inevitable, but how tragic if even one person drops out because their need is not recognized and addressed. Jesus puts such great emphasis on keeping us safe. He describes himself as our shepherd, whose priority is to retrieve the one hundredth sheep that strayed, and to lay down his life for his sheep (John 10:11). We can't just evangelize and then expect the new Christian to slot into Christian ways and the thinking of organized religion with the ease of someone who has spent years in the church, or to withstand the buffeting of Satan as he capitalizes on the flaws of the congregation. It can be worse than mere settling in because organized religion can be cold, and people in it at times promote power, money, and every form of evil in obvious and covert ways.

All Christians need nurturing and especially the newcomers. How do we do that? We have to become more like Jesus, and as fast as possible, so that we are able to quickly recognize and correct error within ourselves. As well, when seeing flaws in others, in the love of God we should do something constructive about it. Jesus showed us how to do this when he told the rich young ruler he worshipped money and this would cost him a place in the Kingdom of God. It was essential for the man to know this even though it was the worst possible criticism. In this story there is some vital information for us to focus on. Before Jesus said a word to the young ruler, "Jesus looked at him and loved him." (Mark 10:21). Unlike Jesus we usually have very mixed motives every time we try to move into the giving of advice. Love, if not absent, is usually not prominent. If we make a conscious effort to put God above everything else, then we put love up there also because he is love. Unfortunately the common reaction is that we forget all about what God wants and factions develop, there is dissent and discord so the whole congregation suffers and is weakened. When this is happening in a church, unless the threat is recognized and fixed in time, Jesus and the Holy Spirit will leave that church, as he warned the church in Ephesus that he would do. We have scored a home goal, and Satan loves that! We are warned he stalks us continuously as a lion stalks its prey, just waiting for a chance to charge in for the kill—and it is a feast indeed if Satan can devour a whole congregation in one go. Ephesus was the high profile church of those first planted, but the rules are the same; Jesus demanded to be their first love, as he was at the beginning.

SUMMARY

Our over-arching purpose in life is to be reconciled to God and to dwell in his presence. Accepting Jesus as our Redeemer enables this and is an event marked by pure joy. None of us knows the details of our future but we can have confidence in a marvelous journey if we go wherever the hem of his garment takes us, "This is what the Lord Almighty says: 'In those days ten men from all languages and nations will take firm hold of one Jew by the hem of his robe and say, Let us go with you, because we have heard that God is with you.'" (Zech. 8:23).

Our insight into the evil entrenched in the world and in us is very limited and quite unrealistic, as is our appreciation of the perfect holiness of God. Our journey with Jesus continually teaches us where we are falling short. Our greatest areas of weakness become milestones on the journey as God heals and changes us. The pain of these milestones is often extreme, and would be unbearable if we did not turn to his love and power. If we persevere, the rewards for us are great as we increasingly become a delight to God and not an offense. Then our will is not continually clashing with his. Also he can more effectively work through us to help and save others. Around us our fellow Christians are on their journey and we need to recognize their struggles, and nurture them, and help them on their way.

Spiritual progress occurs while we travel through our life with the Holy Spirit, always following the light of Jesus. We move from darkness to light, "the people living in darkness have seen a great light; on those living in the land of the shadow of death a light has dawned." (Matt. 4:16). It is not a journey where our achievements count with God; he looks at the state of our heart. When we amaze ourselves by limping over the finish line in heaven then we know, the world knows, and God knows he did it.

3

The Glory of God

THE GLORY OF GOD is the revelation of God's being, nature and presence to the world; it is what we know about him—his creation, love, power, holiness, wisdom, goodness, righteousness, and justice. God designed all of Creation and every living thing in it to reveal and reflect his glory. He will neither give away his glory to anyone nor allow it to be seized. King Nebuchadnezzar found this out. His throne was taken from him when he became proud and arrogant, and chose to forget that God was his only real glory and strength.

Jesus is both God and the revelation of God. It is chiefly through him that we understand God's glory because he "made his light shine in our hearts to give us the light of the knowledge of the glory of God in the face of Christ." (2 Cor. 4:6). Our journey back to God should be characterized by all the things that continually reveal his glory. It must be the priority in our lives as it was in the life not only of Jesus, but also of the apostles, who strove to conduct themselves in thought, word and action, in a manner that unveiled the display of God's glory for all to see. In this way they stood guard over the priceless treasure of God's presence on earth. Jesus's closing words in the Lord's Prayer remind us where glory lies, and many times Paul plainly ascribed glory to God in his letters to the churches.

The Scriptures also speak of man's glory. There are two categories—that of unredeemed man and of redeemed man. The "glory" of the unredeemed encompasses such things as status, youth, beauty, accomplishments, and possessions. Unlike God's Word we age and die just like all other living things and our glory lasts at best as long as we do—and that is in God's hands. We have the other glory, the eternal glory, only when we have Christ in us. "I have given them the glory that you gave me, that they may be one as we are one:" (John 17:22). Through the power of the Holy Spirit his glory grows in us as we become increasingly like him. Our relationship with God through Jesus will be expressed by our faith working in love, and then there will be "glory, honor and peace for everyone who does good" (Rom. 2:10). Sharing the glory of Christ is a promise God has given to all believers. It will become complete in us, and become our crowning glory when he returns.

We see that God can give us glory, but can we give God glory? The angel in Revelations told us to fear God and give him the glory due to him as the Creator of all things. We are meant to "give" only in the sense "give back". This is because the only lasting glory we have is the glory God gives us in Christ, who reclaimed God's purpose in creating us. We "give" God glory or we "bring" God glory by proclaiming, declaring, ascribing, acknowledging, showing, honoring, and reflecting his glory in his work of Creation, and in his plan for the redemption of humankind through the death of Jesus. In declaring the gospel of Christ we are highlighting the glory of God in Christ. As well, we are meant to speak of the evidence of his glory in our lives and the marvelous things he has done for us. Everything we do should be done in such a way that we honor him, "So whether you eat or drink or whatever you do, do it all for the glory of God." (1 Cor. 10:31).

THE GLORY OF GOD REVEALED IN JESUS

The Birth of Jesus

When the angels appeared to the shepherds with the announcement of Jesus's birth, God's glory was displayed visibly as great light. It is no wonder the shepherds were able to see his glory and reacted the way they did because Jesus was God and brought the glory of God to earth. The news of his birth was the embodiment of all we know about God—his holiness in that he cared about the presence of evil, his righteousness in moving against it, his wisdom in the plan for our rescue, his love in that he sacrificed his son to save us, his promised justice through the judgment role of the resurrected Jesus, and his power in that Jesus was victorious over death. This glory was revealed before Christ was even born when the prophets like Isaiah foretold his birth in the Old Testament.

The Life of Jesus

We can think of Jesus as having an innate glory derived from his divinity, "The Son is the radiance of God's glory and the exact representation of his being," (Heb. 1:3). As well he has an acquired glory derived from his whole earthly life culminating in the cross. Nearing the end of his ministry he prayed, "I have brought you glory on earth by completing the work you gave me to do." (John 17:4). He spent his life entirely in God's will while showing an unshakeable faith in him and tirelessly witnessing for him. It is our responsibility to position ourselves spiritually so God can work like this in our lives. Jesus's path to the cross shows us our own path to glory. If we copy the love and dedication of Jesus in everything we do, we too will reveal God's glory. We can only get it right if he is constantly with us, leading us and teaching us the truth through the Holy Spirit in us. It means declaring there is a God, and he is the only God, and by acknowledging everything we believe about him in various ways. We need to worship publicly as well as privately; to be seen to be overflowing with thanksgiving every time he moves in our lives and the lives of others; to be pure of mind; to live in obedience; to do things like turning the other cheek; forgiving; cancelling a social engagement to serve him; giving up a negative hobby; declining invitations to events that degrade humanity. Our motivation in trying to do these things is not to earn the praise of man or work our way to heaven, but to honor our God of glory. In all the practicalities we are saying we know a great personal God of power and love whose whole character is beyond reproach; we are telling the world it is because of his nature—this glory we see in him, that we love him, and want him to run our lives, and there is nothing we wouldn't do for him. In this way, as Christians, we hope to show the glory of Jesus in us and the reflected glory of God. Clearly, this glory of ours is not of ourselves.

When I watch the television program, "Songs of Praise", I can't help but see and feel a very special beauty in each member of the congregation as they sing. They are there in all shapes, sizes, ages, and colors; some could win beauty contests, most certainly couldn't. As I watch them and listen to them worshipping God in song, I feel I am seeing the outpouring of the glory of God. It reminds me of the scene John witnessed when he heard every creature throughout heaven and earth singing to God's glory. Who knows what unseen heavenly choir is accompanying this earthly one?

We were made in God's image, filled with his glory. It is what he longs to see in us—it is how we delight him—what an incentive for us to strain to recapture the image of our Creator by living to his glory!

FAITH

It really boils down to this: if we choose to continue on our way back to God, what is required of us is to declare the glory of God, and the platform for doing this is faith. We are demonstrating the living faith James describes by thanking him equally in the happy times and the sad, by believing his promises no matter how they are strained by the reality of our circumstances at the time, by walking in obedience, and by serving him. We can't do any better than Abraham did. He gained God's promise to him to become the father of many nations because he unswervingly trusted the words God spoke to him.

A more modern example of great faith that acknowledged the glory of God was shown to us in the late 1800s by Horatio Spafford who wrote the well-known hymn, 'It Is Well with My Soul'. His four daughters were drowned in a shipping disaster on a voyage from America to England. He left the States to join his grieving wife in England and wrote the hymn as he passed over the place where his daughters had drowned. Despite his grief there was not even the hint of questioning God. He wrote about the peace with which God had filled his soul and of the blessing of Christ. We see the glory of God in this line: "Praise the Lord, praise the Lord, O my soul!"

We have similar opportunities to point to the glory of God by demonstrating our belief in his goodness when we are bereaved of those we love, and like Spafford struggle with heart-wrenching grief. The same principle applies when we are very ill, and face our own death, and show our trust in him both when he heals us and when he doesn't, but prepares us to take us home. "But you are a shield around me, O Lord; you bestow glory on me and lift up my head." (Ps. 3:3).

We find persevering in faith so hard! Nevertheless, we can be confident like the great men of faith in the history of the church, both because of their example, and because God repeats his promises many times throughout the Bible. He will stop at nothing by way of giving us trials and tribulations in order to bring many to glory, and so get us over the finish line in heaven. But we had better be sure about what we want and be sure our vision is aligned with this vision of what God wants for us, because it is a journey that is not for the faint-hearted.

Some start their journey at breakneck speed after "a road to Damascus experience", while others start early in a Christian family, or come later in the company of Christian friends. Regardless of the nature of the beginning, the single greatest stumbling block is the need for perseverance. Directly and indirectly, this is a recurring theme throughout the Scriptures. We are warned not to give up and so forfeit God's promise of salvation. It was a huge problem in the early days of Christianity as it is today. We need to fix our eyes on God for strength for our journey. He will place mature people ahead of us for our encouragement and expect us to do the same for those coming behind us. Perseverance requires great courage. Often life seems overwhelming, there seems to be no justice, nothing makes sense, we pray fervently for an obvious solution, but troubles increase. It is not long before we start on the "Why theme" and say to God something like: "God, I am trying as hard as I can to do your will but you don't hear me and by the way Lord, that person I know at church is a total hypocrite and unlike me is doing very well! I can't understand why you don't just make my son see sense, get me a job, cure my cancer etc. I have faith God, I know you can do it—why don't you?"

One time when wrestling in prayer I stopped talking to God because he didn't seem to be responding. It was much the same feeling when on the telephone after being put on hold the other party forgets to come back. So I decided to talk to myself instead. In an aside I started saying to myself, "I don't know what more I can do." Before the thought was actually completed two words filled my head and I saw them written across my mind:

"ONLY BELIEVE".

There are a few lessons here: first, you can't talk to yourself, there is no such thing—God always hears; second, the operative words in my statement were "I can do," but God says, "apart from me you can do nothing." (John 15:5); third, our timing is not God's timing—certainly anyone who has ever prayed has no trouble believing this! The fourth point, and the crux of the matter, is that our relationship with God completely rests on faith. That is what he wants from us and it declares his glory. By believing, we are paying homage to the character of God by saying we trust him to work in our best interests. So often we think God is busy elsewhere, not listening, or we are not deserving enough, or a thousand other reasons. This is because we fall into the trap of the earthly perspective. But God has a heavenly perspective and is intent on not only saving our souls, but in transforming us into the likeness of Christ as well. It is also easy to forget it is not all about us, and the quick obvious solution to our problem may not be the best thing spiritually for someone else. Jesus told the disciples they would share his cup of suffering by their service in his name to others.

Surviving dips of faith is a recurring challenge. We shouldn't forget of course as in everything, we only have to be *willing* to believe and God supplies the very thing he requires of us. The importance of our willingness to comply with God's will is illustrated in the story of the disabled man at the pool of Bethesda. Before healing him Jesus first asked him if he wanted to get well. Because Jesus loved the man he wanted to heal him, but he wouldn't act unilaterally, the man had to want this too. The crucial factor about faith is whether we want to believe the truth of the gospel—whether we want to belong to God, or whether we want to rebel against him. When faith fails despite our wanting to be with him, he will never let us go. Not so when there is a deliberate turning away and faith fails, then we are like the ancient Israelites in the desert. With unbelieving hearts they continually went their own way until they finally forfeited the ultimate blessing of resting in God. The consequence to us when our faith fails all depends on whether God holds our heart or not. God doesn't reject us because our faith is weak; he rejects us only if we make a deliberate decision to rebel against him and then fail to repent. If we ask ourselves whether we want to be with God or not, and our answer is an unequivocal "Yes", then we need only rest prayerfully and peacefully in his promises. Surviving faith dips is another aspect of perseverance. All the advice about perseverance in the Bible is given to encourage believers to continually and consciously dedicate themselves to God so they won't decide it is too hard and turn away.

Our faith is very like the electricity supply in a storm, it waxes and wanes and even disappears at times, sometimes for days. When the lights are out and we can't use the appliances we are helpless to restore the power supply ourselves and totally dependent on the provider reconnecting us to the power grid. In the same way, we are dependent on God reconnecting us to him when we blow the faith fuse. In this we can have complete confidence because the Bible is full of God's promises to stand by his people in the good times and the bad, and personal proof of his faithfulness rapidly accumulates in the life of a believer. We shouldn't despair in these dips of faith, so long as we still yearn for God. Jesus assures us, "I give them eternal life, and they shall never perish; no one can snatch them out of my hand." (John 10:28). Here he is saying no power can take us from him against our will. As well, God will actively move to protect us against any such an attempt, "whoever touches you touches the apple of his eye—I will surely raise my hand against them," (Zech. 2:8–9). We are free to leave Jesus at any time, but that would be a unilateral decision on our part because he will never reject us, "All that the Father gives me will come to me, and whoever comes to me I will never drive away." (John 6:37).

Temporary loss of faith has happened to better Christians than most of us will ever be. The disciples lost their faith in the boat during the storm but Jesus didn't write them off, and unlike us they had the advantage of actually being with Jesus in physical form. No doubt it was a sobering learning experience for them and helped to prepare them for the enormous tests of faith that lay ahead. If we are willing, God won't let us rest in a state of false confidence, nor will he let us remain complacent or proud. Instead he gives us a milestone to pass after which we are stronger and more like Jesus.

Nevertheless, once we unreservedly commit to God we yearn for the faith that moves mountains. In happy times we start to feel confident our faith is solid and growing, but then life takes a turn for the worse; we start on the "Why" theme, and what faith we had seems to disappear. At this low point it is helpful to remember that our faith itself is by grace. God tells us we must have faith. Just as we despair it eludes us he then hands it to us gift-wrapped, "For it is by grace you have been saved, through faith—and this not from yourselves, it is the gift of God—not by works, so that no one can boast." (Eph. 2:8–9). We have only to reach out and take it from his hand. In other words we don't have to supply our own faith but simply be willing to accept it from him. It is through Jesus God gives us this faith and causes it to grow, "Let us fix our eyes on Jesus, the author and perfecter of our faith," (Heb. 12:2). So when at times the depth and breadth of our faith eludes us we need only to look to Jesus, the living Word of God, and in this way hang on to our basic belief that the God of the Bible lives and will keep all his promises to us. Then back comes the fullness of faith and the testing time makes it better than before.

So we declare God's glory, however painful the circumstances at the time, by focusing on, and accepting, and persevering in the will of God—all the moving parts that make up faith as a whole. In this way we not only acknowledge God's glory but it is how we ourselves see his glory, "Then Jesus said, 'Did I not tell you that if you believed, you would see the glory of God?'" (John 11:40). Incredibly, we also actually share in this glory when we share in the sufferings of Christ. With God there is always a reward that dwarfs the cost to us. He has inextricably bound together his glory and ours. It is how we become one with God. Why wouldn't we do it?

Faith is catching. To ascribe glory to God we not only have to have faith in his glory, or in other words everything we know about him, but also to demonstrate our faith. One way Jesus revealed his own faith in the power of God was in the miracles he did. The effect flowed on to the disciples, who after seeing his first miracles at Cana in Galilee, put their faith in him. We can't perform miracles but by faith we can be a vehicle of them, and recipients of them, and tell others what God has done not two thousand years ago but right now. Creation has always reflected the glory of God by being a silent witness to him. As the highest order of Creation, man is expected to be vocal in describing God's glory by speaking about him to others.

COMPLETE OBEDIENCE

When we start on our journey we make the conscious decision that from then on God will be supreme in everything. The next thing is to decide how to translate this priority into the practicalities of everyday living, so we both have faith and demonstrate it in action, and thus live our lives to his glory.

Obedience both springs from faith and generates it. By prayer and Bible study we need to be informed about what is correct thinking and behavior, and what is not, so that we are living in obedience to him. It took me a while to see how to do this, but it is quite clear because there is a broad principle here. Our first concern should always be to ensure absolutely *everything* in our lives is squeaky clean. A practical start is to throw out every possession, every habit, and every thought, that as a Christian, we would not like to be included in our biography were it to be printed on the front cover of the Sydney Morning Herald newspaper.

As an example, I went through the books on my bookshelf and threw out anything tacky. In the homes of Christians, I have sometimes noticed the statues of other religions acquired as souvenirs when travelling. They seem awfully like the idols of the ancient Israelites to me. By having them in our possession we are saying they are of value in some way. Even if we have collected them as art, their presence among our possessions could be misunderstood and people may think they are of spiritual value to us. "If in doubt throw it out." We need to have peace of mind that when we "unpack our bags in heaven" there is nothing we would be ashamed of in them; otherwise we will feel a whole lot worse than a drug smuggler caught out by a Customs check.

Isaiah described how the redeemed should live when he described a "Way of Holiness" that would be off limits to those content to pursue evil ways. Paul stressed the importance of this holy life for him when he wrote to the Thessalonians. He said when he had been with them he had been righteous and blameless. This was not only in Paul's best interest, but he explained his behavior would be of great benefit in comforting and supporting them in their faith.

To give back glory to God we have to reveal his nature in our own spiritual development, and this should flow through and be obvious in every involvement we have with other people. It makes no difference what we are doing, whether we are engaged in worshipping God directly in prayer, or mowing the lawn, or having a party. In prayer we should model ourselves on the tax collector, not the Pharisee; when mowing the lawn we should do so at a time when we don't wake the whole neighborhood; at a party we should remain sober, drug free, and not engage in negative talk or behavior. The opposite to this, which is to deny the glory of God, is the essential nature of sin. Then our hope is lost, because God abandons us to our depravity when we don't put him first.

By obedience we show we believe God has our best interests at heart; it is faith in action. Everything we think, feel, say, or do that is not from him runs counter to his glory and has to go. Note it is not *nearly everything* that has to go but *absolutely everything* to which the Holy Spirit alerts us. The things we personally can't get in God's perspective are taboo. Some of these things are different in different people. One person may be unable to limit alcohol intake, another may succumb to problem gambling at a race meeting. The former should not drink alcohol at all, while other Christians can take it in moderation if they want to do so; those with a weakness for gambling should stay away from race tracks while others are safe to go. If we comply, we reveal God's glory. As time goes by and we mature, the Holy Spirit shows us more and more things that grieve him that we need to change. This doesn't mean we will eventually have nothing recreational left. God will open up other more enjoyable areas of entertainment for us. In this way our old self dies, the rubbish falls away and we become more like Jesus, and therefore more able to do God's will, and this pays tribute to his glory.

The story of Achan is a stark illustration of how God feels about us when we deliberately defy him and withhold even one thing just for ourselves. Achan's "one thing" cost him his life. Before the battle leading up to the fall of Jericho, Joshua had warned the Israelites that if they took away anything from the enemy they would in effect be stealing from God, and this would bring destruction on themselves and Israel as a whole. Achan disobeyed and kept forbidden spoils of war hidden in his tent, and God was outraged. In their next battle the Israelites were defeated, and God told Joshua that until they rectified their disobedience he would continue to desert them. When Joshua identified Achan as the culprit he took him, his whole family, and possessions, and destroyed them all.

A parallel in my life may seem laughingly trivial by contrast but nothing is too small to be relevant. Jesus told us details count with God. He taught the parable of the servant who had made a good return on a small sum of money entrusted to him by his master. As a result the master then rewarded him with the much greater responsibility of taking charge of ten cities. So don't feel too embarrassed for me as I relate this short story.

I realized my love of Country and Western music with the "somebody done somebody wrong theme," was taking me to a place of negative thinking and God is never to be found in such a place. Many people of course may benefit from the other themes of love, and caring, and humor in Country and Western music, but I always wound up in a negative mindset so in my case it had to go. At the same time, I acknowledge for others it may be positive.

It is by admitting a treasured possession is not what God wants for us and by going through the pain of removing it from our lives that we honor our God of glory. So although it could be said comparing the story of Achan to my response to Country and Western music may seem like comparing the sublime to the ridiculous, I really believe making such comparisons is what Bible study is about. It is about personally engaging the Bible in our lives so it tells us individually how to live in this day and age.

It is interesting we take immediate notice of God's promises to believers but mostly assume all the descriptions of the sinners and their precarious state doesn't apply to us. We should look closely at every warning and condemnation in the Bible to make sure God is only talking to us, and not also about us. The story of Achan has many facets but it is only an interesting story from ancient times until the Holy Spirit shows us the Achan in ourselves. The Holy Spirit not only shows us great and marvelous truths in the Bible but also individualizes the message so it is especially for us at the right time and right place on our journey. It is the Holy Spirit who translates these great stories and makes them relevant at a practical level to each person. Then we see the milestone, and in God's strength respond, and move on to bigger and better spiritual places. Not only that—God is never in our debt. When I have given up something because I have felt prompted to do so, it has only been a matter of time before God gives me something better. In this instance he replaced a love of Country and Western music with a greater enjoyment of listening to Classical Music, which I used to find deadly dull.

In describing the connection between God's initiative in helping us to move in his will and our own response, we have heard the saying "100 percent grace and 100 percent effort." We can understand and be comfortable with God's grace because we have an all powerful, all wise, all good, and all loving God who has made it abundantly clear by the death of Jesus that he will go to any lengths to promote us. We can, without a backward glance, leave that part of the equation in God's hands. But what do we do about making our response appropriate? This is where it gets tricky. We certainly need to act in purity because we are dealing with a perfectly Holy God. Perhaps the only pure response of which we are capable is to strive to give God our whole heart, and then to step back to give Jesus a free hand, because the second we get a bright idea of our own we wander from the true path. The emphasis is on the word "whole". If we withhold even a small part of ourselves just for ourselves, it is like nailing one foot to the floor and expecting to be able to move forward.

When as new Christians we are first convicted by the Holy Spirit we are often left feeling we may be God's biggest challenge so far, and even wonder what he can do with us. Doubt of course is the opposite of faith and is one of Satan's biggest weapons with which he acquaints us from the beginning. We can counter this attack by getting the start right by unreservedly giving to God everything we are and everything we have. What follows brings us to our knees in adoration as he shows us on the one hand what we are, and on the other hand what we can be.

Immediately we accept Jesus as our Redeemer we have an assurance of salvation. Without detracting from the enormity of this gift, it should mark a new beginning in life where we are no longer slaves to our innately sinful nature, "if the Son sets you free, you will be free indeed." (John 8:36). This means we are free in every way—free from the penalty of death and free from our dependence on the negativity in our life to which we are addicted. We have a choice either to lounge around at the start or begin on a spiritual journey with Jesus leading us into this freedom. Unfortunately many choose the former. Not only is this a great personal loss but we are not revealing the glory of God. If others can't see his glory in our Christian life they won't be attracted to him; rather, they are likely to be driven away. In our natural state we behave literally like the bull in a spiritual china shop—we are all zeal and no wisdom. We have a clear choice either to live godly lives or to live as enemies of Christ, focused on earthly things and steeped in shame.

SUMMARY

The purpose of our life is to reveal the outpouring of the glory of God. It is by our faith expressed in a sanctified life that we do this, "This is to my Father's glory, that you bear much fruit, showing yourselves to be my disciples." (John 15:8). How do we get this faith? To the willing heart God gives the very thing he says we have to have. It is free because Jesus already paid for it.

God's demands on us are always for our good, and will take us to his heart, as Jesus tells us in this beautiful prayer of his: "I have given them the glory that you gave me, that they may be one as we are one: I in them and you in me. May they be brought to complete unity to let the world know that you sent me and have loved them even as you have loved me." (John 17:22–23).

4

Hello, Hello . . . Anyone There?

TO BE EFFECTIVE IN guarding the treasure of the gospel of Christ we must live in God's presence and move in his will. We can only do so by constantly talking with him and we don't find this easy. Prayer often seems difficult at least at some time for everyone and it seems no one is quite satisfied with their ability to pray. The disciples of both John the Baptist and Jesus had the same problem and asked to be taught.

When praying, I often feel a sense of remoteness as though I am having a one-way conversation, even though I know God is there, and I find myself wishing I could test the line for technical faults. Often when we try to pray there seems to be a huge gap between us and God that we cannot close. This is possibly one of the reasons why there are so many formats for worship, and so many different denominations all trying to bridge this gap in a different and hopefully better way. Talking about God often seems a lot easier than talking to him. Behind the illusion of the remoteness of God is the irrelevance of the senses we normally use in our relationships, such as sight, hearing, and touch. Prayer is so different; it is a dialogue between the spirit of man and the spirit of God. Not surprisingly, this different way of relating takes a lot of practice, but if we are willing to live for God, then he will enable us in prayer not just to contact him, but also to enter his full embrace.

TALKING TO GOD AS IT WAS MEANT TO BE

In the book of Genesis there is a description of God's relationship with man before Adam and Eve were banished. It is all the more poignant because it comes after Adam and Eve had sinned and were feeling convicted and confused, but before their confrontation with God. There is this simple sentence: "Then the man and his wife heard the sound of the Lord God as he was walking in the garden in the cool of the day," (Gen. 3:8). These words portray an intimate relationship between God, and Adam and Eve, the way we are meant to communicate. Then we had this intimacy, it is what God and humankind yearn for, what we were made for, what we lost at the Fall, and it will take the second coming of Jesus for us to get it back. But God has said, "Never will I leave you; never will I forsake you." (Heb. 13:5). Our meeting place to receive the fulfillment of these words and the comfort of God's presence is in prayer.

Prayer is communicating with God. We need to be in unbroken communication with him, which means our whole life should be a continual prayer. Paul said, "pray continually;" (1 Thess. 5:17). By his lifestyle Jesus taught us this constancy in prayer and there are many, many references to this fact. He prayed when things for him were relatively calm and in times of deep distress; he prayed with the disciples, in crowds, in solitude, in deserts and on mountain tops; he prayed for his disciples present and future, for those suffering and for himself; he prayed in the day and in the night and sometimes all night. Prayer was his sustenance and delight.

We communicate with each other in many different ways. There is direct speech, telephone, email, webcam, body language and acts of service—to name a few. Sometimes we need to be formal, sometimes informal, sometimes serious, and sometimes light-hearted. We tailor our communications according to the circumstances and it is the same when we talk to God; we can express ourselves in off-the-cuff informal snatches of conversation as well as formal worship; with words or without. So the form of the communication varies, but some aspects of good communication never change. Even in business communication we need always to be truthful, respectful, and considerate. In personal communication it is particularly the attitude of our heart that underpins our approach. If our attitude is good the communication is positive, if it is bad it would be better not to have opened up a dialogue at all. God does have requirements we must fulfill in order to approach him successfully in prayer. All these requirements are fulfilled in a general sense when, as in everything, God has our heart. When we give him our heart when we pray, then anything goes. This is why in his lead-up to the Lord's Prayer in Matthew 6:5–8, Jesus warns us against hypocrisy—against outward show to impress others or inward show to impress ourselves. God is angered by the prayer of a hypocrite who lives to serve himself, while protesting his own holiness before God, "When you spread out your hands in prayer, I will hide my eyes from you; even if you offer many prayers, I will not listen . . . wash and make yourselves clean. Take your evil deeds out of my sight! Stop doing wrong, learn to do right! Seek justice, encourage the oppressed." (Isa. 1:15–17).

GOD'S REQUIREMENTS FOR US TO BE HEARD

Pray in God's Will

Our prayers have to be in line with God's will as we see from the Lord's Prayer, "your will be done on earth as it is in heaven." (Matt. 6:10). John tells us: "if we ask anything according to his will, he hears us." (1 John 5:14). Similarly, implicit in the following promise Jesus gave his disciples is that we have to pray in God's will, because we pray in the name of Jesus, who not only reconciled us to God, but always did his will: "I tell you the truth, my Father will give you whatever you ask in my name." (John 16:23). So a prayer asking God to give a pesky neighbor a heart attack won't work: "when you ask, you do not receive, because you ask with wrong motives," (Jas. 4:3). God made it very clear he won't respond to us when we are in rebellion against him. On one occasion, the Israelites had attacked the Amorites against his command and lost the battle. As a result God paid no attention to their weeping and left them unaided for many days. Similarly we will stay at our milestone for many days if we persist in praying in our will and not God's.

Once I asked a professional acquaintance who was a Christian of high standing in his church and the community for help in a matter of community justice. He declined to help because it conflicted with the interests of a friend, also of high standing in the same church and community. He closed our meeting with a prayer, wherein he asked God to change my mind, so I would let the matter drop. It was a lost golden opportunity to ask God to increase my understanding so I would do what he wanted, whether to go on or to stop. As it was, the man's prayer was that his own will would prevail and God's will did not rate a mention. This anecdote is not to show the Christian standing of this person was necessarily invalid—in fact there is overwhelming evidence to the contrary (and of course this is a judgment call for God alone), but rather to show praying in our will rather than in God's is such a trap.

We know of two major occasions when Jesus was faced with the option of moving outside God's will and doing as he wanted. First, early in his ministry he was tempted directly by Satan in the desert. Then, at the end of his ministry he was in anguish over God's will in Gethsemane, but even then he said, "yet not my will but yours be done." On both occasions God sent an angel to strengthen him. When God overrules us he is aware of how hard it is for us. He doesn't just say, "No" and walk away. He stays with us and supplies what we need to overcome the suffering incurred by his decision. So "No" is not the end of the matter, he wants us to keep talking to him.

By looking at Jesus's example, if we are doing our best to live wholeheartedly in the will of God, we see a "No" from God is a reward not a punishment. The reward may be immediate or delayed until heaven, it may be seen or not seen, but it is there. He rewards us because he loves us, and because we have faith and believe he is always working for our best interests. If we want "Yes" every time then we are speaking to the wrong party—Satan will bribe us as surely as he tried to bribe Jesus. It is our soul that is at stake. We have to make up our mind just as clearly as Joshua did. He chose to serve the Lord regardless of the difficulties he was facing.

Humility

We need to do a reality check on ourselves before we pray—or better still, ask the Holy Spirit to do it for us, because Jesus tells us to be humble in prayer. He contrasted the prayer of the Pharisee and the tax collector. In his prayer, the Pharisee thanked God he was better than others, including the tax collector who was praying nearby, and he extolled his own good works. "But the tax collector stood at a distance. He would not even look up to heaven, but beat his breast and said, 'God, have mercy on me, a sinner.'" Here Jesus assures us a prayer spoken with true humility results in our being justified and exalted by God. That is a promise I certainly don't want to miss.

Forgiveness

In the Lord's Prayer, Jesus tells us a definite requirement for God to welcome us is that we have first forgiven everyone—is that all!!?? As I am now, this statement of Jesus taken alone would mean I would never pray. In things like this that I aspire to, but am unable to do without hypocrisy, I have to adopt this approach: "Dear Lord, help me to forgive John, Joe, and Mary, and all those people I still hold in unforgiveness and change my heart to be like yours." I trust him to do that, in fact it is already getting noticeably easier. I do quake somewhat though, at the thought of the milestones I will have to pass on the way to finally get there. In my very early days as a Christian, for some weeks I blithely asked for humility; it seemed the pious thing to do. I didn't realize how proud I was and got the baseball bat treatment. I was still on a milk diet, but this was solid food, and I almost choked on it. It is a lesson I won't forget. Before we ask for spiritual progress in a particular area we need to be as realistic about ourselves as possible—either that or batten down the hatches.

Righteousness

James tells us we need to be righteous when he gives us this advice, "The prayer of a righteous man is powerful and effective." (Jas 5:16). That statement seems a bit of a worry at first because we know, when measured against God's perfection, that no one is righteous. But God has made provision for this because if we ask, he allows us to claim the righteousness of Jesus. I think James also means, if we truly belong to Christ, we will be striving to honor him by moving in our lives towards the goal of his righteousness.

PRAYERS THAT TEACH US HOW TO PRAY

The Lord's Prayer

It is interesting Jesus usually spoke in parables requiring study to understand his message, whereas he framed the Lord's Prayer as an example on how to pray in plain language. Apart from the fact the Pharisees couldn't make political mileage out of it, this clarity seems to imply prayer is a problem for everyone, and also it is so important he wanted immediate clear understanding. This prayer is not only marvelous in its own right, but serves as a pattern of the basic steps for us to use to frame our prayers.

Our approach to God: First we focus on God and our words should honor him, "hallowed be thy name." We are to state categorically that we bow to God's will, "thy kingdom come, thy will be done", and placed at the beginning it confirms our relationship with him comes before our needs.

Pray for ourselves: Jesus tells us to pray for ourselves—for forgiveness, for the gift of the day ahead of us, and for our basic needs. We are to ask for protection against falling into sin and for deliverance from the evil forces that surround us.

Praise God: We are to praise God as the mighty, sovereign Creator, "for Thine is the kingdom the power and the glory."

It is a prayer of Christian unity and shows us we are meant to pray for others—"*our* Father"; "give *us*"; "forgive *us*"; "lead *us*"; "deliver *us*".

As an aside, it is interesting to note it is not recorded anywhere in the Scriptures that Jesus prayed in tongues. It was said to me once in a Bible class that as I did not pray in tongues, I was not saved, and I have also heard this opinion taught from a pulpit. People who hold this opinion believe when the Holy Spirit is in a person that prayer will automatically be spoken in tongues. They conclude if prayer is not in tongues, then the Holy Spirit is absent, and so the person is not saved. This denies Jesus's promise to give us the Holy Spirit once we believe, "Having believed, you were marked in him with a seal, the promised Holy Spirit," (Eph. 1:13). Jesus certainly had the Holy Spirit throughout his ministry and yet he never prayed in tongues himself. He spoke of the immensely important changes that would take place spiritually on earth as a result of his death, particularly in regard to the Holy Spirit indwelling in those who are saved to God, but he never mentioned speaking in tongues. The way Paul writes about it later in his letters it seems clear it is a gift. God gives it to some Christians and to others he gives other gifts. I also think Satan sends the spiritually immature presents which closely mimic the real thing, and then they become a trap because we place our spiritual security in them instead of in Christ himself.

Feet on Earth, Head in Heaven

Daniel's Prayers

The prayers of the great men of the Old Testament like Nehemiah and Hezekiah and Daniel can teach us so much about how we should view prayer. In prayer Hezekiah pleaded for an extension to his life based on life-long obedience. God responded by giving him an extra fifteen years.

Gabriel's appearance to Daniel paints a marvelous picture of the importance God places on the prayers of believers and the respect with which he receives them. It is tragic for us when we entertain any negative views on prayer that run contrary to God's word.

The background to Daniel's prayer was his heartache over the desolation of Jerusalem at the hands of the Babylonians. So in prayer he worshipped God and pleaded in great humility with him. He admitted rebellion against God had resulted in the righteous punishment of Israel and based his pleas for rescue on God's covenant with Israel. While Daniel was still praying, Gabriel appeared before him and said, "I have now come to give you insight and understanding. As soon as you began to pray, an answer was given, which I have come to tell you, for you are highly esteemed." (Dan. 9:22–23).

There are at least four things here worth noting—God's answer was instantaneous, known in heaven as soon as Daniel opened his mouth; the answer was then relayed to Daniel before he had finished asking; Gabriel says as a result Daniel will have insight and understanding; finally Daniel was told these three things came about because "you are highly esteemed."

Most of us will never attain the godliness of Daniel, but that doesn't seem to be a prerequisite to our receiving the same response from God when we pray, as we can see by an account of another meeting Daniel had with a messenger from God. This time the message was about prophesies spanning the time to the second coming of Christ: "Since the first day that you set your mind to gain understanding and to humble yourself before your God, your words were heard, and I have come in response to them." (Dan. 10:12). Note our prayers are heard and answered "since the first day," which means from the beginning of a fully committed journey.

Even when we are still in a pretty foul state we can know this same intimacy with God through prayer that Daniel knew—but only if he holds our heart, so that we are cloaked in the righteousness of Jesus; it is up to us. We have to be like Daniel, living and praying in God's will and delivering our prayers to God in the manner he did, and not only pray for our own needs, but like him pray about the concerns of God outside ourselves. Jesus told us to ask God to send people out into the world to spread the gospel. Asking in prayer is a powerful way for us to help further God's will in the world at large.

We don't have to have the spiritual stature of these great men of the Bible to be heard just as surely by God—and that's easy to prove—try it! When it comes to personal requests sometimes we feel guilty, because we falsely see ourselves as seemingly insignificant small people asking for small things, and we feel we are disturbing God with trivialities.

My mother was crippled with rheumatoid arthritis and needed a motorized wheelchair. She was living in a retirement village and wanted to take something to a friend in another unit, but it was raining and she didn't want to get wet. Because of pain and restriction of joint movement, battling with raincoat and umbrella was too hard. She prayed she would stay dry. Later, very excited, she told me she got back to her unit bone dry. I was horrified, I cringed. Fancy worrying God with that! I thought she was lucky not to get a serious rebuff. What I with my self-absorption failed to realize was that because of her disability, getting clothes on and off was very difficult and painful. She knew that and God knew it too. Looking back, I really think her request, her faith behind the request, and her gratitude afterwards would have delighted God; he wants to be part of everything in our lives.

PERSONAL EXPERIENCE OF PRAYER

On some days prayer comes easily to me because God is there on my mind. Intermittently he comes to the forefront of my thinking and then my thoughts turn fully to him, and I talk to him on and off throughout the day. At other times the events of life distract me, and I suddenly realize the day is nearly over, and I have been silent for most of the time. Keeping up a dialogue with God is so uplifting. At times I have been bursting to say something, but can't think of anything. I used to wonder "but what will I say? I've already said that." This is an ideal time to say "thank you"; when we start on that theme there really isn't enough time in the day. Also, we can always pray Scripture directly or in the words of our favorite hymns. The other way to stay consciously in the presence of God is to ask for God to bless the people you pass in the street, or friends and acquaintances as they come to mind. Just saying anything gives the

Holy Spirit an entry, and leads on to conversation with God about the things he specially wants us to discuss with him. Finding something to say is really not a problem. In terms of form and content we make prayer harder than it is.

Jesus told us God knows what we want before we even ask. Paul added that our weakness in prayer is covered by the Holy Spirit, who intercedes for us when we are unable to voice our concerns. What could be easier? At the height of a battle raging around me at one of my milestones, when I am just hanging onto God by my fingernails, the form of my prayer is simply to rest in the thought of God and let the Holy Spirit speak for me. I have been in that place more than once, but only just recently realized this resting is the thing to do. Also it is worthwhile noting even when Satan pries our fingers off God and our grip loosens, God's grip on us remains as secure as ever—no one can snatch us out of his hand.

Not only does the Holy Spirit speak for us but Jesus does also. During his ministry he prayed for all his disciples who would ever be, "My prayer is not for them alone [the disciples with Jesus in his lifetime], I pray also for those who will believe in me through their message." (John 17:20). In other words Jesus prayed for us before we were ever born!

By dying for us he interceded for us when we were under sentence of death and restored our status with God. Now after the resurrection, he sits in heaven at God's right hand as our permanent intercessor. Every time we speak to God we don't come before him in our own strength, but we are part of this powerful prayer team—Jesus, the Holy Spirit and us. God carries us in prayer as in everything else.

Desperation makes us cry out for God and in that state of mind we are happy to give him everything, even our heart. Unfortunately, we often take it back once the crisis is over. One huge indelible insight into prayer occurred for me in a time of great sorrow and distress. It occurred when I was caring for a friend who died of cancer over a period of fifteen months. Because of the medical facts, I knew from the beginning she would not get better. Many times on every day over this period of time, I would find myself spontaneously pleading with God in short desperate snatches of phrases, "God please don't let her suffer," "Please give her a peaceful death." I have seen many people die of cancer over the years but the manner of her death was truly the perfect answer to prayer. She needed only a very small amount of over-the-counter pain killers until her last day when her vital signs began deteriorating quickly. In this terminal phase she developed restlessness and so was given a subcutaneous infusion of medications to make her comfortable. She died six hours later without pain. My prayers for her had been about as crude and raw as is possible, but God heard them and answered. Prayer is as easy as that. I had also asked my friend if she wanted me to be with her when she died, and she said she did. I was grateful this was her decision, because I wanted to be there, and I was there, and I thank God so much for that also.

It is worth noting, at the time I wasn't absolutely sure there was a God at all, so these prayers were not even based on great faith. I suppose that happens all the time when non-believers and doubters suddenly find themselves in a life-threatening situation. Then formal dress is not required. God will receive us, listen to us, and answer us, even when we rush into his presence unheralded, disheveled, wild-eyed, spiritually grubby, and demanding undeserved favors. Perhaps the fact we turn to prayer in these situations shows there is at least some faith there. It is just a stark example of what we know anyway, which is that we are totally undeserving and totally reliant on the mercy of God.

But why wait until we are desperate? We have the all-loving God of Creation keeping up non-stop communication with us, watching and waiting for us to answer him. Incredible as it may seem, God can't get enough of us. It is not God who has the problem answering prayer, it is us.

WHY PRAY?

God does want to give us earthly gifts as well as spiritual ones. So we ask for things relevant to our comfort, whether it is a tangible thing like a better house, or relief from worry over an upsetting problem. Unfortunately, we often only remember to pray after we have made a decision and start getting into difficulties. Far better to ask God for advice before we make any move at all, then we can avoid a lot of trouble. If we do ask him first and trouble still follows then it is comforting to know he is running the program not us, there is some higher purpose, and we are not just in a mess of our own making. James reminds us of this need to ask first and act later; he says this is why we don't get what we want from God. Then we blame him for an adverse result. James also says when a person prays there must be faith. Often we deliver our request to God like a wish, we really believe it is something fanciful and will never happen. We need to believe, and remember, that to God all things are possible, and fortunately he makes allowance for our weak faith. Jesus said faith as small as a mustard seed would move mountains.

GOD ALWAYS ANSWERS PRAYER: "YES," "NO," "WAIT."

God always answers our prayers, "For everyone who asks receives; he who seeks finds; and to him who knocks, the door will be opened." (Luke 11:10). Some prayers God answers before we have properly formulated them, "Before a word is on my tongue you know it completely, O Lord." (Ps. 139:4). When the answer comes it falls into one of three categories, "Yes," "No," or "Wait," and there is often great confusion in our minds as we try to understand his reasons for the answer he gives us. The commonest misconception here is unless God says "Yes," that he hasn't said anything at all.

When God Says "Yes"

We don't have a problem with a "Yes" answer. If God says "Yes" we celebrate and why not? It means he has heard us and moved on our behalf. We are reassured he loves us and this brings us great joy. At a practical level, the problem we had has been solved and this makes us happy. We want to tell others and share the joy with them; it is a great way to support other people with their faith. Remembering to thank him is so important.

When God Answers "Wait"

The second possible answer to prayer is "Wait," and only time can tell us if God is saying "Wait," rather than "No." That is why, while the issue is still pending, we should persevere in prayer. To teach his disciples this principle Jesus told the parable of the widow who refused to accept the judge's inaction on her behalf, until she finally wore him down. Then there was Job, God finally said "Yes" to him after what seemed to him and the rest of us to be an interminable wait. Waiting places us firmly in God's plan not ours, it keeps our focus on him and it strengthens our faith. Sometimes, particularly in health matters such as cancer in loved ones, we think God is saying "Yes," but his answer is really "Wait" before "No". This is probably the hardest scenario of all because our hope is built up only to be dashed. Nevertheless this delay gives us important time to prepare ourselves for the sorrow ahead.

When God Says "No"

"No" is hard to take. It seems so like a rejection and immediately doubts arise. The bigger the denied request, the bigger the doubts. If it is a small thing, as it was a few years ago when I prayed unsuccessfully for the return of my lost mobile phone, we may rationalize that in the scheme of things it is too trivial to God to bother with. Wrong again! If something bothers us then God never ignores us, he always cares and responds. I never found my mobile phone—not because God ignored me, but because he said "No."

When God answers "No" and where the request is about something really important to us—such as a life and death matter, a relationship, or job security, then when God doesn't come through with an immediate unequivocal "Yes," our faith takes a direct hit. There is only one way to recover from "No" and that is to remember the love of God. This is the reason for every time God answers "No" whether we have lodged a small request or a large one. We need to go back to the concept of our spiritual journey and that of others. We have already realized that because of his love for us God's purpose is twofold—to save humankind and in the process to transform us into the likeness of Christ. Regrettably, we know because of the perversity of human nature we will change more often in adversity than in ease.

If we can accept "No" from God when "No" is abhorrent to us, then our faith grows and another milestone is passed, but it won't be without great heartache and suffering. By being accepting and faithful to him, we are giving God glory. This is our highest aim.

Acceptance is the first step in our response, the next is gratitude. First we accept the "No" verdict and then we thank God. Thanks are appropriate because God has answered us and he is working for our good. When God says "No" to me, sometimes the best I can do at the moment is to be accepting. I can't always say "Thank you" and mean it. This is another example of where at times I still need to pray "Thank you" in obedience, while at the same time asking God to change my heart so one day it will be spontaneous.

Feet on Earth, Head in Heaven

The commonest conclusions people draw when God answers "No" is that there is no God, or God at best doesn't care, or at worst hates them, or he is punishing them, or their faith is not strong enough, or they are too unimportant or disgusting. God makes his presence plain so often in our lives and in answered prayer that you don't have to pray for long to realize the first guess is wrong—there is a God. He cared enough to send Jesus to die for us so we can strike out the uncaring and hating explanation. The punishment theory doesn't always stand up either: "he causes his sun to rise on the evil and the good, and sends rain on the righteous and the unrighteous." (Matt. 5:45).This is not to assume God doesn't turn a deaf ear to the rebellious and let them take the consequences, as we see many times in the Bible.

It is said sin in a person's life is the reason for why God answers "No." This would mean because no one is perfect, there would never be any answer forthcoming but "No." The belief system of some denominations is built on the concept that a person is sick because they have a sin in their life, and until they overcome this sin, they won't get better. This was the core of the erroneous argument Job's friends heaped on him. The logical result, if this were true, is that we would all be moribund all the time, given the weight of sin that we all have in us. If the sick person doesn't get better, they are told they have failed spiritually, so it is their own fault; if they get better, they are told they have overcome a sin, which may be false reassurance. It also doesn't explain why some people are born with a physical ailment. Many Christians have prayed through their pregnancy for a healthy baby, but it didn't happen. When the disciples came upon a blind man they assumed his blindness was punishment for the sin of either the man himself or his parents. Jesus said neither was to blame, but that God had a purpose for the man's blindness. This is about as plain a statement as you could get. As long as we are praying in God's will, it takes the blame and responsibility for the "No" answer off us, and places all explanation and responsibility firmly with God.

All the above reasons are factors in our thinking and our response when God says "No" to us or to others, but the most frequently held explanation is probably that the sufferer lacks enough faith. For the sufferer it is so demoralizing because it seems to prove that just when faith is needed most, it fails. Where someone else is the sufferer it is quite a comfortable viewpoint for us, condescending and almost charitable compared to attributing their negative result to their sin. The problem for us is that sooner or later our turn will come and we will have to find the right reason—and we may well only find it after passing a very painful milestone. Blaming a lack of faith when God says "No" is common in healing ministries and is a belief often held by both the healers and the sick alike. This seems so arrogant to me because it is really expressing the view that we know better than God and can dictate to him. It is saying if we want something, whether it is healing or anything else, we should get it. People asking for healing who hold this view can be so devastated by what they consider to be an adverse verdict that they give up, and are not only still sick, but label themselves as spiritual failures as well. That is the last thing God wants. He wants us to grow spiritually when he says "No," not to drop out.

The attributing of blame when healing does not happen after prayer is not an official teaching in most churches, but it is a thought we as individuals find lurking in the back of our mind if we are not careful. It is easier for us to stay resting happily with a small unchallenged faith if we can somehow trace the cause of any problem back to some flaw in the sufferer. Then we know it couldn't happen to us because we are near perfect, and also we don't have to stir ourselves to compassion because the sufferer actually brought it on themselves, whether through sin or lack of faith. We would rather hear a smoker got lung cancer than a non-smoker—as if we ourselves have never done anything stupid.

Jesus said, "Therefore I tell you, whatever you ask for in prayer, believe that you have received it, and it will be yours." (Mark 11:24). This verse like every verse in the Scriptures cannot be taken in isolation. We must always be aware we are here to do the will of God; he is not here to do ours. What we know, because it has been said and implied in many ways in the Bible, is that underpinning any prayer there must be a commitment to pray in God's will and not our own; then this verse represents yet another of God's great promises to us. I have heard people say that because we know God wants the best for us, it must be his will that all people be healthy. Then they conclude that if sufferers remove sin from their lives, or have enough faith, or belong to the right denomination, or go to church twice on Sundays, or whatever, he will heal them. It obviously is his will for us to be in a perfect state and that is why Jesus died, so God could restore Eden. Sickness in its entirety is just one of the many evils in this fallen world with all its suffering. We wait for the second coming to rectify it: "No one living in Zion will say, 'I am ill'; and the sins of those who dwell there will be forgiven." (Isa. 33:24).

Feet on Earth, Head in Heaven

Jesus's healing ministry when he was on earth illustrated his message of God's power, forgiveness, and love. But at times he healed only a small minority of those present. At the pool of Bethesda he healed one man of the many waiting hopefully by the pool. It was the same when he was on the way to Jairus's sick daughter, and the woman with the bleeding touched the hem of his garment and was healed. Although she was part of a milling mass of people who were crowding against him, there is no mention of any other healings at that time—because it was not God's will. When we want healing for ourselves and others God wants us to ask for it. But he also wants us to accept his will, whether he heals us or not.

Faith is being able to take "No" for an answer. Jesus told the disciples though he was about to die despite their pleas to the contrary, they could nevertheless still enjoy God's peace. He said this was so because he had conquered the woes of the world. When unrelieved of trouble, if we can keep our faith by remembering evil cannot triumph over God's progressing plan of salvation, then we will know this peace. Who would have understood this better than the redeemed thief who hung in agony beside Jesus on the cross? His soul was saved but not his life. Regardless of the answer, prayer is the door to God's great gift of peace.

A beloved pastor taught our Bible group that God will only give us something we ask for if we can handle it. For example, if we were living a single life and asked God for an idyllic partner and he gave us one, we would then have the problem of not putting this person before God in our affections. For many of us, that might be hard to do, and for some impossible. Even where our request may seem perfectly reasonable or according to the Scriptures even in general a good thing, it may not be for us. Earthly treasures are dangerous spiritually. God knows our weaknesses better than we do; if he withholds or delays something we want and pray for, it is worth considering this might be the reason. We might eventually grow spiritually strong enough for God to give it to us, or we might not. We have to wait and trust him while doing so.

"No" can seem so cruel. Was God cruel to Jesus in Gethsemane when Jesus pleaded to avoid the cross and God said "No"? Perhaps part of the reason the disciples fell asleep was because they couldn't cope with watching Christ in such anguish. Why didn't God say "Yes"? Jesus was perfect in obedience to God; didn't he deserve a "Yes"? (If it comes down to what we deserve, unlike Jesus we would of course get a "No" every time). In hindsight we see clearly that God was pursuing his purpose of saving humankind and all of Creation, and it took the death of Jesus to achieve this. Even so was Jesus a loser, was he used and abused, a mere stepping stone for God's purpose and then cast aside? On the contrary, God has flooded the Bible with an account of the rewards Jesus inherited, and after his death he was exalted to sit at a place of honor at God's right hand. After the resurrection when he spoke to the women at the tomb, Jesus himself said: "Did not the Christ have to suffer these things and then enter his glory?" (Luke 24:26).

We share in the same good result. When Simeon held Jesus as a child in his arms he prophesied the effect Jesus's life would have for us: he would be "a light for revelation to the Gentiles and for glory to your people Israel." (Luke 2:32). Because of his death and resurrection, when we suffer, we can confidently say with Job that out Redeemer lives.

We can learn so much from the "No" God gave Jesus in Gethsemane. During Jesus's prayer he went to his limit in mental and spiritual suffering, but he accepted God's answer, turned resolutely towards Jerusalem, and without looking back or faltering, he allowed himself to be crucified. Jesus was perfect, sin was utterly repugnant to him, yet for our sake he covered himself on the cross with the total sin of humankind and died under the weight of it. He must have felt a sense of utter self-loathing. Added to this, while in his greatest need, God, who was unable to look upon such accumulated evil, turned his face away from him. Jesus's cry from the cross must be the loneliest, most abandoned cry in history and it came about deliberately out of the love God has for us. When I watch the television news segment, and see some terrible evil as it is being played out today, I realize I am seeing a minuscule part of what Jesus took the punishment for; and it is not over yet. Trying to comprehend the burden of all the accumulated evil from the beginning to the end of civilization is just not possible.

Any reasonable person present with Jesus in Gethsemane would have acquiesced to his prayer for release from crucifixion. Yet his death has had the result that The Savior of the World stands for eternity at the right hand of God in glory. The unthinkable "No" resulted in victory for God, victory for Jesus, and victory for humankind and Creation. In hindsight logic dictates that we all agree with God and change our answer to Jesus's prayer from "Yes" to "No"; it is the "Yes" answer that then becomes unthinkable. As disciples of Christ now it is our turn. If Jesus could take "No" for an answer in Gethsemane for our sake, surely we can take "No" at times in our lives and bear our cross for his sake.

SUMMARY

To pray means to communicate with God, so it is a two-way dialogue. God is always available and never fails to speak to us, listen to us, and answer us. This contrasts with us; we are too busy most of the time doing what we want, so we ignore him. God wants to hear from us—all the time. He always answers prayer; we don't. If God doesn't give us all we ask, we often accuse him of everything from indifference to vindictiveness—everything we are and he is not.

Faith is taking "No" for an answer and thanking God that in his love and wisdom he has made a decision according to his will. If our will is aligned with his, he has promised us many times that after we lay our petitions before him we will receive an answer that satisfies us. And we do—we receive anything and everything that is in our best spiritual interests. Through our acceptance of his decision, even when he denies the earthly component of our request, he always heals our soul. Then we enter his peace.

Prayer takes us into his presence and the beauty of this state is illustrated in Psalm 141:2: "May my prayer be set before you like incense; may the lifting up of my hands be like the evening sacrifice."

5

The Most Excellent Way

WHEN AN EXPERT IN the law asked Jesus to name the greatest commandment I wonder if those present were surprised by his reply: "Love the Lord your God with all your heart and with all your soul and with all your mind. This is the first and greatest commandment. And the second is like it: Love your neighbor as yourself. All the Law and the Prophets hang on these two commandments." (Matt. 22:37–40). The Jews in Jesus's day were brought up under the Old Covenant of the Old Testament where there was a great emphasis on obeying the law and the awful consequences of not doing so. The question reflects this. Jesus's answer not only raised love to the status of a commandment but elevated it above the rest. So they might have been surprised.

If we compare these two commandments with the Ten Commandments in the Old Testament we can see what he means. In the latter there are four commandments related to our duty to God, (Exod. 20:3–11), and six related to our duty to others, (Exod. 20:12–17). All bar one is expressed in the negative. They tell us what not to do, but not what we should do. The two new commandments show us that in order to fulfill the law, all the commandments must operate on the basis of love, and in that way they show us the way forward. Why this emphasis on love? Because God is love, it means to do anything without love is to do it without God. This is why expressing God's love is not an occasional thing, rather we are told to, "Do everything in love." (1 Cor. 16:14). How much easier it is to do this if we always work wholeheartedly for God and not for man, then the impossible becomes possible.

The two greatest commandments are intertwined; by fulfilling one commandment then in part we fulfill the other. It is by loving God that we can recognize every person's unique and equal relationship to God and the love in which he holds them, and that helps us to love them also. Turning it around, in loving others according to God's will, we love God. How can we think to do other than our best for them? We love God; they are beloved of God; if they hurt, God hurts. It is a circle: We love God, so we love others, so we love God, and round it goes. On our journey through life with Jesus, as he takes us successfully past our milestones, God's love in us grows. Divine love perfuses every worthwhile thing in life, and once our eyes have been opened to it, it becomes unthinkable not to give it everything we've got. It is the greatest treasure we guard on earth for God.

How much reason there is to thank and praise God because he has shown us this "most excellent way" of love. Paul describes what he means by this phrase in detail in one of the best known passages in the Bible. I have seen verses from this tract framed and decorating people's living rooms even though they don't know where it comes from and that it is God speaking to them. This marvelous description of God and his love has universal appeal because every human heart is touched and awakened by the perfect love of God. It is worth reading it in its entirety in 1 Corinthians 13:1–8:

> "If I speak in the tongues of men and of angels, but have not love, I am only a resounding gong or a clanging cymbal. If I have the gift of prophecy and can fathom all mysteries and all knowledge, and if I have a faith that can move mountains, but have not love, I am nothing. If I give all I possess to the poor and surrender my body to the flames, but have not love, I gain nothing. Love is patient, love is kind. It does not envy, it does not boast, it is not proud. It is not rude, it is not self-seeking, it is not easily angered, it keeps no record of wrongs. Love does not delight in evil but rejoices with the truth. It always protects, always trusts, always hopes, always perseveres. Love never fails. But where there are prophecies, they will cease; where there are tongues, they will be stilled; where there is knowledge, it will pass away."

In describing the most excellent way of love Paul is describing God, and where it is lacking he is describing transient earthly things. He knew love is the key to the kingdom of God and he wanted to put it in the

The Most Excellent Way

hand of every person. So that the early Christians would have as full an appreciation of God's love as possible, he prayed, "that you, being rooted and established in love, may have power, together with all the saints, to grasp how wide and long and high and deep is the love of Christ, and to know this love that surpasses knowledge—that you may be filled to the measure of all the fullness of God." (Eph. 3:17–19).

The death of Christ had the effect of planting our souls in the love of God. We can choose to send down roots into his heart and establish ourselves there in the most excellent place, or we can move off into a tacky place of our own where we sound as attractive to his ears as a clanging cymbal, gain nothing, and are nothing. We represent nothing of value in our own right; it is only the love of God in us that has the power to transform us into the image of his excellence. If only people really understood the difference—we can live in the love of God, which "never fails," or choose a life of defeat without him.

The word "love" appears in the Bible 551 times. Such emphasis is because "God is love." (1 John 4:8). Love is the paramount attribute in God's nature as described in the Bible and it underpins, directs, pervades, and empowers all his other attributes—God's wisdom, goodness, righteousness, justice, faithfulness, and holiness all operate through love. For us also it outranks everything else, even faith, "And now these three remain: faith, hope and love. But the greatest of these is love." (1 Cor. 13:13). This seems surprising until we realize love and faith are interdependent, and you can't have one without the other because faith is dead faith until it acts in love, and love is ineffective without faith, "The only thing that counts is faith expressing itself through love." (Gal. 5:6).

Even God's vengeance, a last resort delayed by love, affects only those who having crucified his Son remain unrepentant. In the third of the Ten Commandments God says he will punish those who hate him for three or four generations, but show love to a thousand generations of those who love and obey him. These words are an illustration of the balance God has between love and punishment. Extending this symbolism numerically means a difference between punishment and reward of a factor of two hundred and fifty times! What an incentive to us—by loving God we can hand down a legacy of God's love to our descendants for twenty thousand years! This is solid love, we can depend on it. Paul certainly thought so: "For I am convinced that neither death nor life, neither angels nor demons, neither the present nor the future, nor any powers, neither height nor depth, nor anything else in all creation, will be able to separate us from the love of God that is in Christ Jesus our Lord." (Rom. 8:38–39).

Love started with God, not with us and it is an unconditional, selfless, self-sacrificing, active love. We are told he made us with loving care and still loved us while we were sinners. Our rescue is the greatest act of love in history. When we are touched by this love we are overwhelmed by it, we are "undone" and yearn to love him more, and increasingly we seek to dwell in his presence.

God is the source of all love, without him there would be no love in the world. The only "love" we have by nature is self love and its ramifications, which when we make a comparison with divine love, we realize is not love at all. From self love spring promising things like love of family, friends and country, but we impose a condition—we must benefit in some way, even if it is only to ensure the survival of our genes. If we don't benefit, then our love fails; it fades away or goes sour and can even turn into attack. Our love is conditional in every way; God's love is unconditional. Without him we do not know what pure love is and have no capacity for this real love at all, either to receive it or to give it, whether to God or man.

HUMAN LOVE

Mother Love

Of the human loves, "Mother love" seems to be in a category of its own, both in its intensity and in its willingness to sacrifice self. We see it expressed throughout nature. God seems to have a special regard for it as he often refers to it. He describes the coming of Christ in these terms, "As a mother comforts her child, so will I comfort you." (Isa. 66:13). Similarly Jesus, sorrowing over the pride of the people and their rebellion against God, foresaw the impending destruction of Jerusalem and said his anguish was like that of a mother hen trying to gather in her chicks to protect them from danger. The evolutionists would say the obvious practical spin off from mother love is survival of the species; it seems God thought of that—first. Even so, while in the mould of divine love, as we express it, mother love is still tainted by human frailty. As the offspring grow and become increasingly demanding in seeking self-gratification, a mother's love may falter.

Erotic Love

Erotic love is a misnomer. It rises to its greatest intensity during the state of being "in love". While being one of the happiest states to be in, it is a temporary state of sexual attraction based on instinct and hormones, and not love at all, even in the human sense. It is a "love" that can't stand alone for long and needs input from other forms of love to make the transition to a state that will endure. Marriage is one of the ways of expressing the love described in 1 Corinthians 13, but it is not the source of it. However, erotic love does have features in common with divine love in that it is intense, possessive, and exclusive of other such loves. The imagery of the bridegroom, which is used to express Christ's relationship to the church and its people, is described in the New Testament, including by Jesus himself.

Friendship

Friendship is another expression of human love and something we all seek. Without God it is very fragile, but with him it is one of the greatest pleasures he has given us. In extending his love in his own life, Jesus didn't make any of the distinctions we make between people. For him there were no categories that assumed greater love for one person over the other, such as ruler or servant, rich or poor, relative or friend, neighbor or stranger. Jesus clearly said that he considered every person who did God's will to be his closest relative. We also know that in the same way our friends are not necessarily our relatives, it is also true our relatives are regrettably not always our friends. Either way, we nevertheless usually have a special bond with kin. This is of earthly value related to the social structure, our logistical and emotional support system, and hence our earthly happiness and survival. Similarly, for reasons of circumstances, personality, and interests, we are naturally more compatible with some people than others. Families and close friends are one of the great blessings God has given us, but we also need to follow Jesus's lead, because he brings everyone to him in the unity of the love of God.

Paul's interactions with others embodied the attitude and love we should have for everyone regardless of genetics and personal preference. He not only said we should love everyone as brothers and honor them above ourselves, he also lived according to his own advice. Consider how he spoke to the Philippians, "Therefore, my brothers, you whom I love and long for, my joy and crown," (Phil. 4:1). He addressed the Thessalonian Christians in a similar vein. These sentiments are not always well expressed at morning tea after the church service. Through prayer and love our purpose should be to build up our fellow Christians, bring them joy, and thank God for them. Then they can say with Paul, "Your love has given me great joy and encouragement, because you, brother, have refreshed the hearts of the saints." (Phlm. 1:7). Every relationship we have been given by God is meant to be embedded in, and rich with his love, so that it is overflowing with forgiveness, free from judgment and criticism, and dedicated to his glory.

We should enjoy the company of the people God sends to us on our journey and give him thanks for them. Some of us are surrounded by family and friends, some are not. Those people who are relatively alone in the world should take comfort from the fact that a life with fewer distractions from other people can provide a solitude, which opens the way to a closer relationship with God. It is to start earlier than others on the focus we will all have during eternal life with him.

DIVINE LOVE

Selfless Love

One of the core characteristics of divine love is that it is selfless love. This means, when we love each other with this selfless love, we don't see ourselves in the picture at all and our only interest is the wellbeing of the other person. Once we look back at ourselves to check our own interests we have blown it. Immediately we do this we start planning how we can profit by any action we take and if the pay-off is not big enough our love falters and may fail altogether, so that we may decide not to proceed at all. Then we make the same mistake the rich man made when he ignored the beggar Lazarus at his gate. He spent eternity in agony in hell; not a good choice—in fact, a fatal one.

Self-sacrificing Love

Part of the essence of divine love is that it is self-sacrificing and the person who loves his neighbor as himself incurs a cost. Who could have said it better than C S Lewis?:

> "To love at all is to be vulnerable. Love anything, and your heart will certainly be wrung and possibly be broken. If you want to make sure of keeping it intact, you must give your heart to no one, not even to an animal. Wrap it carefully round with hobbies and little luxuries; avoid all entanglements; lock it up safe in the casket or coffin of your selfishness. But in that casket — safe, dark, motionless, airless — it will change. It will not be broken; it will become unbreakable, impenetrable, irredeemable. The alternative to tragedy, or at least to the risk of tragedy, is damnation. The only place outside of heaven where you can be perfectly safe from all the dangers and perturbations of love is hell."[1]

Love cost Jesus both his life and temporary alienation from God. Many people have paid with their life, but most of us with considerably less, and we often consider even a small price is too high. If in spite of deterrents we go ahead, then it costs us and we suffer in some way. When we look to help others we automatically have to stop thinking about ourselves and what we want and we don't like this. Giving worthwhile help takes time, which is so highly valued in modern society; giving may use resources, which we would rather keep and spend on ourselves; in empathizing we suffer ourselves. To be where someone is suffering is not to be in a happy place, but of course with Jesus it is a place of joy. As usual if we are doing well, Satan is frantically beavering away in front of us making a trap he hopes we will fall into—it is the trap of making self sacrifice the end in itself. If we let it become so, we adopt the role of martyr and after a while we even sicken ourselves.

We need to constantly realize that what we do for others we are doing for God. We have to think as David did when he was commanded to make a sacrifice to God for sparing Israel. When Araunah offered to supply the land for the sacrifice at no cost, David was adamant he would pay the full price himself and not make an offering to God which cost him nothing. Similarly we should be generous in helping others because it is a way of thanking God for all the good things he has given us. To do

---

1. Lewis, *The Four Loves*.

it "on the cheap" should be unthinkable. In practice this means if we give a gift then we give something we value (not necessarily monetary value); if we give our time then we give it whether it is convenient or not. There is a "convenience test" for helpers, which sorts the wheat from the chaff and shows the quality of the love behind the help. Many people are willing to help if it is convenient, far less if it is not. We tend to allot a certain amount of our time to others in need, at a time convenient to ourselves, then either make ourselves unavailable outside these convenient constraints, or make an exception with grim determination and a martyred attitude. This is one of the differences between love of the human kind and the self-sacrificing love of God.

Similarly, Jesus was not impressed by the rich men who were putting money into the temple treasury, for although making large donations, they had not dented their wealth. But he was impressed by the impoverished widow who gave very little, but nevertheless gave all she had to live on. As an aside, the opposite sometimes occurs, so that people without a lot of worldly wealth may not put in their share at all, and undervalue the donations of the people they perceive as rich. This can happen when we fail to give thanks for the blessings God has given us and then covet our neighbors' possessions. Whether we are rich or poor, when the magic ingredient of self-sacrificing love is withdrawn from an act of mercy, it is like seeing the color fade out of the dawn. It is the mentality of helping others only if it costs us very little that sees us take the quick and easy way out when someone needs help. We do something that looks good and then we give ourselves a pat on the back. Then Satan scores twice, because it may well not answer the need and will certainly mean we are worse off spiritually than if we had not bothered at all.

As Christians most of us worry that if our life depended on professing our faith, we would renege. We can't imagine ourselves responding like Tyndale, who died at the stake because he wanted to help people understand the gospel by translating the Bible into English. Similarly, many thousands of Christians today suffer torture and death because they are trying to bring the love of God into their communities. They refuse to disown the name of Jesus and they die for it. In the same way we worry about failing in our faith, we also worry about how much easier we sometimes find hating than loving. If we aspire to rising to the heights of self-sacrificing faith and love it means making a determined effort, and if necessary to start small and keep practicing.

Compassionate Love

We speak of the compassionate love of God. In essence his love for us is unconditional, selfless, self-sacrificing, and *active*. Compassion as described in the Oxford Dictionary means "suffering together with another," or "pity that inclines one to spare or to suffer."[2] So it is a "doing" word, it is love in action. Most decent people feel upset when they see or hear something sad affecting someone else. That is empathy and that is a great first step, but it isn't true compassion, which requires us to do something about it. Compassion demands we act.

I have only realized lately, that as in all our God-given talents, the quota of talents for empathy and compassion given to each person is different. There are non-believers who put some believers to shame because they seem naturally so empathic and compassionate. (Of course if such non-believers were empowered with the love of God, they would be even more effective.) It would not be surprising if research in the near future showed a basis for this difference in the neuroanatomy and neurophysiology of the human brain. This consideration is relevant to us in order not to judge those who fall short. If we are relatively non-empathic or uncompassionate then it is obviously something very important we need to pray about. Another way to improve is to serve others in obedience while asking God for more compassion and he will give it to us. Whether God has given us a low supply or a plentiful supply of compassion "talents", we need to look to Jesus and pray for help in returning them with interest. J. C. Ryle, in his commentary on the gospel of Matthew, said the compassion of Christ is mentioned in the Bible more often than any of his other character traits such as his zeal, anger, and thankfulness. In our case our aim is to increase our talents and not take pride in the number God gave us.

An expert in the law asked Jesus what he must do to inherit eternal life. Jesus prefaced his reply by first asking the man what he himself thought and agreed with him when he answered by quoting the two greatest commandments. But the man, with the dawning realization of the implications of the love of God, and that he had fallen short, tried to get off on a technicality, so asked for the definition of the word "neighbor." Like us he was anxious not to help anyone who didn't qualify. Jesus gave him more bad news when he answered with the story of "The Good Samaritan":

2. Little, *The Shorter Oxford English Dictionary*.

A traveler had been attacked, beaten, robbed, and left for dead on the roadside. A priest and a Levite were also travelling on the road, but when they came upon him they crossed over and did not stop. Then "a Samaritan, as he traveled, came where the man was; and when he saw him, he took pity on him. He went to him and bandaged his wounds, pouring on oil and wine. Then he put the man on his own donkey, took him to an inn and took care of him. The next day he took out two silver coins and gave them to the innkeeper." (Luke 10:33–35).

The Samaritan saw the man's need and responded immediately and appropriately by giving him first aid, his time, and his money. He put his own plans aside—he inconvenienced himself and focused completely on the injured man; he didn't allot a certain amount of time and then go home part-way. Apparently it was on a stretch of road well-known for waylaying travelers. To stop and help someone was to risk the same fate. Because Samaritans were considered by Jews to be inferior, the Samaritan had to overcome cultural bias as well—his help was unconditional. So the Samaritan put the interests of the injured man completely ahead of his own. When he set unconditional, selfless, self-sacrificing love into action, he brought to the injured man the fullness of compassion—the divine love of God.

This story is so well-known that it has entered the annals of everyday speech and every Australian knows what is meant by the term "a Good Samaritan," and yet it is amazing how easily we as Christians pay lip service to the sentiment, while our own efforts bear little resemblance to the spirit of the story. The account is so dramatic in itself that we tend to forget the question that triggered its telling. The expert in law asked how he could inherit eternal life. Similarly our eternal life is on the line. How often do we choose by default to be the priest or the Levite in the story, those who passed by on the other side? We can walk into God's kingdom with the Good Samaritan or away from it with the priest and the Levite.

Another time that Jesus spoke directly about compassion was after the woman anointed him for burial and in so doing she incurred the displeasure of the other guests. Jesus spoke up for her, pointing out that she had done what she could by anointing his body in anticipation of his coming death. The man in whose house this event took place, conscious of his standing as a host, had given Jesus hospitality and food probably above what Jesus's earthly status called for, but Jesus was not at all impressed. The woman was totally focused on Jesus, not on herself. No doubt she knew she looked like a fool and she suffered the disdain of the gathering; her gift was worth a lot of money but she gave it freely; she couldn't save Jesus's life but she could pour her love over him as she anointed his head. In her soul she was obviously suffering for him. Jesus recognized all this. He valued her efforts so highly that he promised the story would be told for all time, and so it is. Her actions illustrate the essential ingredient of the love that God values—she gave her heart along with her response. We need to do the same.

GOD AND US, AND LOVE IN ACTION

Divine love is the only love that counts with God because we are not capable of generating love other than self-love. In the same way that our faith in God is by grace, so is our love for him. When we accept Jesus as our Redeemer, he gives us not only the gift of salvation but also the gift of the Holy Spirit. It is this indwelling of the Holy Spirit in us that enables us both to receive and to express God's love.

Even so, while the initiative is God's, a response is required from us to promote this relationship of love. Though the Holy Spirit pours the love of God into our hearts, what we do with it is up to us. We can confine it within ourselves or we can let it flow back to God and to others. Our effectiveness in doing this is a slow process and results from our journey—the milestones we pass and the progress we make. There are no shortcuts. I'm sure we are all filled with sorrow and disappointment when we see the short distance we have come in our response to his love and how far we have to go. We become increasingly aware that our own efforts to love God more are extremely weak at best and pathetic at worst. Increasingly we realize that as Paul told the Galatians we can only boast in one thing, "May I never boast except in the cross of our Lord Jesus Christ," (Gal. 6:14) and we do boast in the cross because it is the visible representation of the power and love of God.

The success of our entire journey depends on our ability to assimilate and express God's love because it is the force that empowers us to do everything that delights him—our worship, prayer life, obedience, forgiveness, and service. If we refer back to considering the greatest commandment in the Law, then based on my experience of being amongst Christians today, I think we may have been right in the first part of the answer, "Love the Lord your God with all your heart and with all your soul and with all your mind." Knowing it and doing it are different matters, of course. But I really don't think disciples of our time, meaning you and me, would score well on the second part of Christ's answer, "Love your neighbor as yourself." In this it seems not a lot has changed over the centuries.

When people were bringing their children to Jesus the disciples objected, but Jesus was indignant and corrected them for their lack of understanding and compassion. We seem to have this huge blind spot for the welfare of other people. It is more than a deliberate choice to put ourselves first in everything, (although we do seem to work tirelessly at this); it is more as though we are often not aware of the needs of others at all. Maybe it is a distortion of our basic instinct for survival. Whatever it is, Jesus tells us it is not only a commandment to love others, but it is the second greatest of all the commandments and incorporates six of the Ten Commandments. Paul says we have more than an obligation to love one another—we have a debt that must not be left outstanding.

Christians and non-Christians alike recognize Jesus was the epitome of unconditional love. This was not only because he died to save us, but because in his ministry he both understood human suffering and moved against it regardless of a person's station in life. Implicit in compassion is this wisdom and understanding that comes from the love of God. It means we have to focus fully on the other person, to identify with them, to take the time and trouble to understand the circumstances of their present situation as well as we can, and then work out the best way to help them. Jesus's life of love was one for us to model our life on, and he expects us to do this, "A new command I give you: Love one another. As I have loved you, so you must love one another." (John. 13:34). His act in washing the feet of his disciples shows the spirit of love and humility with which Jesus served others and which he specifically tells us to follow. Bear in mind the disciples' feet had not been washed first and because they wore open sandals their feet would have been coated with the filth of the dust and excrement of the streets of ancient Jerusalem. If we get rid of our "me" attitude and live our life like Jesus did, we will be blessed by God—he says so, "Now that you know these things, you will be blessed if you do them." (John 13:17). Note the "if".

Love and forgiveness go together. We have been given a lot of advice in the Scriptures on how to grow in love. Jesus tells us our love for God is related to the sense of our own sinfulness and therefore to the realization of our unworthiness to receive the sacrifice he made for us. Well, that shouldn't be hard—but unfortunately it is, and we need this awareness to take us through confession and genuine regret into true repentance. The gospel message is several times called "the gospel of repentance for the forgiveness of sins," both in relation to the preaching of John the Baptist and in Christ's own words to the disciples. God warns us throughout the Bible how he feels about us failing to repent. It is the only way back to him. Admitting to being caught out is not repentance. A statement with the words "I apologize", made to avoid retribution, whether spoken to God or man is not repentance unless it comes from the heart. As in all God requires of us, it is his grace that enables us to repent. Yet again if we manage to respond to him, there is no place for pride. So once we get real about ourselves and repent, we are well on the way to loving God and we can rejoice in our reconciliation with him.

After we repent God immediately forgives us, and this frees him to run our lives and release all his promises to us. We naturally doubt God, we doubt his presence, we doubt his love, and we doubt everything else about him including the forgiven state in which he allows us to stand. It was because he loved us that he forgave us. As a friend in a Bible study group emphasized, it is the conscious acceptance of forgiveness that lifts the burden of evil and so clears the way for us to recognize, believe, accept, and return the irresistible love of God.

This close interrelationship between love and forgiveness is illustrated in the story about the woman who anointed Jesus with oil. Jesus said this of her: "Therefore, I tell you, her many sins have been forgiven—for she loved much. But he who has been forgiven little loves little." (Luke 7:47). In our forgiven state, divine love flows through us into the forgiveness of others and this dampens our attitude of accusation and criticism, which is the repercussion of sin, "Above all, love each other deeply, because love covers over a multitude of sins." (1 Pet. 4:8). This is the case whether it is God's love and forgiveness of us, or our love and forgiveness of others in his name.

Jesus tells us obedience is a necessary part of the love that binds man to God and it is a nice concrete place for the beginner to start. "Whoever has my commands and obeys them, he is the one who loves me. He who loves me will be loved by my Father, and I too will love him and show myself to him." (John 14:21). Jesus didn't make one rule for us and another for himself as we see when he spoke of his impending arrest, "the world must learn that I love the Father and that I do exactly what my Father has commanded me." (John 14:31). Note Jesus says he does *exactly* what he is commanded; near enough is not good enough. Our rebellion, that is our disobedience, has shattered our relationship with God. Obedience, being the opposite, demonstrates where our allegiance lies—not with Satan, not with ourselves, but with God. We continually fail of course, but as usual God stays with us and in his love and mercy forgives us a countless number of times, "he does not treat us as our sins deserve or repay us according to our iniquities." (Ps. 103:10); "I have swept away your offences like a cloud, your sins like the morning mist." (Isa. 44:22). This truly is divine love in action.

Suffering generates love. It is a great paradox but a great truth that the painful milestones on our journey enable us to love God more. In Romans Chapter 5, Paul shows us the human side of this love equation as he traces God's love for us in Christ and shows us the empowering effect his death has in helping us to persevere in our suffering.

During his ministry Jesus showed us by example how to rely on the love of God during suffering. His way was to talk continually and intimately with God in prayer, have faith in the love and goodness of God, live in obedience, and show peaceful acquiescence to his will. When we have no other hope, when we have no recourse but to rely on God, it is then we feel his enveloping love moving in our lives. It is a love we can't deny; it calls forth a response and so our love for him grows. In fact if we just keep putting one foot after the other, which is often all we can do, then during our suffering our love for him positively surges. I have experienced this both with myself and through Christian friends. It was the suffering incurred by the death of a friend that opened my eyes to God's love and claimed my soul. If we make it a time when we focus intently on God rather than on ourselves and our plight, we find we have a heightened awareness of every little move he makes on our behalf. It is then not too hard to give God thanks for his faithfulness to us throughout. When we do this it gives God carte blanche to work all things according to his will. Then victory is assured, another milestone is behind us. Victory for us is a closer walk with Jesus, more of God's presence in our lives and more of God's love flowing through us. It is a precious time of revelation, which we never forget. It is a simple formula: we persevere in wobbling along with our little portion of faith and love for him and he stokes us up with even more faith and more love. Every victory we get under our belt helps us to cement our relationship with Jesus and allows him to speed us on our journey into the presence of God.

Expressing God's love to others is not optional. The Bible leaves us in no doubt about the importance the apostles gave to Jesus's teaching of loving one another. It is the only way we can know God, "Whoever does not love does not know God, because God is love." (1 John 4:8); "And he has given us this command: Whoever loves God must also love his brother." (1 John. 4:21). There, the second of the two greatest commandments is paraphrased and stated again for the dense among us—which, on this subject, is most of us for most of the time. Considering how we live and what these verses tell us should give us great cause for concern.

In sending Jesus to die for us God has given us an example on which he expects us to model our love for each other. This act of divine love in its expression is proactive, deliberate, planned, free, and need-generated; it is a "no holds barred" and "no sacrifice too great" type of love. Its effect has been to overwhelm and disarm countless individuals and so change the course of history.

Loving others is how we make God's love complete in us, so that his love achieves his purpose—which is our salvation, "No one has ever seen God; but if we love one another, God lives in us and his love is made complete in us." (1 John 4:12). John goes on to say it is this complete love in us that gives us assurance of pardon on the Day of Judgment. We can't see God directly, but when we express his love to another we do see him, and so do they. God and his love are synonymous; we can't have one without the other and so loving others is a true indication of our own salvation. It is not surprising we will be judged on this basis, because we have been told that the indwelling of the Holy Spirit is a prerequisite to having perfect love in us and therefore the capacity to love each other with the love of God. The sequence is: God's love for us in Jesus; acceptance of Jesus's sacrifice; our perfect righteousness in Christ; the Holy Spirit in us; God's perfect love in us; our love for God and for others; no punishment; eternity with God; no fear. This means we need only fear judgment if we have failed to love others, because doing so is a true test of God in us.

So it is not just to make other people feel good—our eternal life depends on us getting this right. There is no greater fear than the fear of dying and losing all possibility of ever being with God, of being away from the presence of love and everything that is good. John leaves us in no doubt this is a real possibility when he says, "If anyone says, 'I love God,' yet hates his brother, he is a liar." (1 John 4:20). We can only call God our Father by loving our fellow man. There is no room for misunderstanding here. Jesus tells us how dangerous it is to be called a liar by God. The alternative of ignoring our love for others means we are in effect calling Satan "father," and Jesus calls us a son of hell.

Peter tells us the same thing. First he exhorts us to make every effort to love our brothers and finishes with these words: "Therefore, my brothers, be all the more eager to make your calling and election sure. For if you do these things you will never fall," (2 Pet. 1:10). Indirectly he is saying that without strenuously pursuing the things of God, which is marked by the love of others, we may forfeit salvation.

Living in love is a condition for our prayers to be heard. God is outraged when we come to him having pleased ourselves and neglected to address the needs of others. He is not open to bribery. In Isaiah he tells the Israelites their worshipping rituals are detestable to him because of their rebellion and lack of love for the needy, "Your New Moon festivals and your appointed feasts my soul hates. They have become a burden to me; I am weary of bearing them." (Isa. 1:14). He continues, "learn to do right! Seek justice, encourage the oppressed. Defend the cause of the fatherless, plead the case of the widow." (Isa. 1:17). Instead of "New Moon festivals and appointed feasts", today we might read "Sabbaths, Christmas Days and Easters" and other celebrations. God is no happier with us than he was with the ancient Israelites when we just roll up to church functions in our party dresses to enjoy ourselves, while leaving undone acts of love to help those in need. On one occasion Jesus directed an angry barrage at the Pharisees. He pointed out their hypocrisy of meticulously tithing, while at the same time neglecting the love and justice of God. He said both practices were necessary. At the end of his speech one of the experts in the law answered him, "Teacher, when you say these things, you insult us." (Luke 11:45). Well, he got that right!

PITFALLS OF HUMAN LOVE

It is crucial to position ourselves beside Jesus before we even start to try to live a life of compassion, because for us on our own it is like starting out on a journey through a minefield.

Righteousness is by Faith not Works

The first hidden explosive is avoided by remembering righteousness is by faith not works. Otherwise we may progressively delude ourselves into thinking we can work our way to heaven, and for this reason we put our hand up for every act of service we can find whether God wants us involved or not. Paul warned us of this mistake when he said Israel had not attained righteousness because they pursued it through the work of obeying the law instead of through faith in Christ. It is essential to be busy helping others so long as we are working to God's schedule and not our own. We must realize God's love in us flourishes from faith, not from works. Without this realization we risk becoming heartless workaholics and worst of all we are working our way to hell not to heaven. Hosea puts it this way: "For I desire mercy, not sacrifice, and acknowledgment of God rather than burnt offerings." (Hos. 6:6).

Seek the praise of God not Man

The second trap is avoided when we remember to seek the praise of God not man. Jesus's attitude was black and white about that when he flatly told the Pharisees he wasn't interested in their approval or that of any man. Our relationship with God is diminished if we look to man not God. During Jesus's ministry many leaders believed in him but would not admit to it openly because they valued earthly status more than God's approval. In practice it means persevering in something God has put on our hearts for us to do regardless of how others rate it. It is those people working for God quietly out of the limelight who delight him. Jesus uses the subject of fasting as a way of telling us we are always to shun the open display that looks for earthly praise.

Jesus also taught about avoiding the false praise of man by example when he healed the paralyzed man who had been lowered through the roof to his feet. We are told everyone was amazed and praised God. I find it intriguing that all those people present, the beneficiary as well as the onlookers, understood it was the power of God they had seen in action and didn't presume Jesus had acted in his own power as a man, like the many other sorcerers and magicians who were apparently around in those days. Even today we can become quite sycophantic towards Christian healers. Immediately following on the verse about the danger of preferring the praise of men, we read how Jesus summed it up. He said when anyone looks at him, "he sees the one who sent me." (John 12:45). We mustn't miss this crucial point when we are involved in an act of service—all those present must see not us but God, the One who sent us.

Everyone acknowledged God after the cure of the man lowered through the roof because Jesus himself always made it clear his power came from God. This is an acid test we should apply when our own efforts are acknowledged. Do people praise us or do they praise God? If they praise God, they have got it right, but they will only get it right if we behave and speak as Jesus did. If we have done our best in this regard but they still don't understand, then we probably need to improve our approach, but also to immediately let them know where their praise should lie. And we need to join them in their praise. If we do something positive for someone who then praises God, while leaving us out of the picture, we have ourselves been indirectly praised to dizzy heights. This is because it means that like Jesus, we have done the work God has given us and done it well. What an amazing honor God thought of us, entrusted us to do the task, empowered us, and sent us with Jesus on a mission of love to another of his beloved. It makes me wonder who helped whom; it is as if the roles have been reversed. This is heady stuff indeed and all the more so compared to the fleeting feeling of pride we get when we are praised directly.

God's praise builds us up spiritually and has a lasting effect; the praise of men inflates our ego and drags us down. We can pursue it like an addiction and like any addiction become obsessed with it, our appetite becoming ever more ravenous, causing us to become ruthless in seeking it. Seeing God at work is fantastic, but seeing he has worked by using us just blows our socks off. At times I have stopped short when reflecting on something I have been involved in and I see God's plan laid out from beginning to end. And there I was part of this plan. It can seem unreal. I feel like saying, "Who me? Really?" It doesn't seem to matter whether we had the starring role or a "bit part" in the cast of helpers because it is so obvious that success belongs to the Director. In our gratitude for his plan and for the part we played we need to give our own thanks and praise to him, "If anyone speaks, he should do it as one speaking the very words of God. If anyone serves, he should do it with the strength God provides, so that in all things God may be praised through Jesus Christ. To him be the glory and the power for ever and ever." (1 Pet. 4:11).

True Compassion is Not Conditional in Any Way

Our love and service is so often conditional. The first condition we may impose is a requirement to understand *the cause* of someone's distress. The reason for trying to understand a situation is to be more helpful, but unfortunately, we often use our understanding to judge whether we consider the sufferer's distress to be valid or not. If we can't understand why a person is suffering then we shrug and give it a miss, thankful to get out of any obligation that might have nagged our conscience. It is as though we go into denial by telling ourselves, if there is no obvious neat explanation we can see, then the distress is not valid, and so there is nothing for us to be compassionate about. Instead, we should look at *the fact* of their distress; it makes sense to them and it is not relevant whether it makes sense to us or not. Similarly if someone has an illness we can understand and fear, like cancer, we find compassion easier while people who spend a lifetime with a disability hardly get a passing glance. Even if we can get past that mistake, if we are not careful we impose a second condition, which is to decide whether we can *blame* the person in distress for their troubles and so decide if they deserve help. We require that their suffering is not in any way self-inflicted.

Thus we impose two conditions, first their suffering must be logical to us and second they must be worthy to receive help. Rather than roll up our sleeves and get on with it, we would rather see them fill out a ten-page form in triplicate in order to be sure they qualify for our help. If we see someone scantily clad freezing cold on a park bench in the middle of winter, knowing how they got there is not relevant to our response. This is a stark example; our scenarios are usually much more subtle but no less important.

There are a myriad of other conditions we impose. Whole populations go almost hysterical with emotion when someone famous or beautiful or otherwise idolized becomes ill and dies. We identify with them and bask in reflected glory. Then we will go into hoop-la mode, dress in fancy dress, reach into our pocket, and generally admire each other for the effort we are making. Not so well noticed, if at all, are those on the lower rungs of society, the powerless in aged care, the mentally retarded, the isolated, the unlovely by earthly standards. It is right to help the elevated in society and to enjoy doing so, but the danger is at times it becomes mostly all about us and what makes us feel good. What a contrast Jesus is! How beautiful he is. The many stories of his healing ministry show us he was no respecter of persons; he made none of the distinctions we make—his compassion touched rulers and servants, the clean and the unclean, the famous and the infamous.

Another reason we turn away from people needing our help is that when we see another person in distress it moves us out of our own comfort zone and so disturbs the security we thought we had in the world around us. We see how fragile we all are and how no one is exempt from trouble. We would rather cocoon ourselves in an unreal world than face the reality of the suffering around us. It is a test of faith. We wonder if we can trust God not to let us have a similar problem, and if we do get into strife, can we trust him to bale us out? It is easier to go into denial, turn away, and stay in our relatively happier world where a little bit of faith will do.

There Must be Flexibility in our Response to Really Meet a Need

We should look at our pattern of response. If it is always the same whether it be a casserole, a telephone call, or a cup of coffee then maybe we are more interested in doing what is easy for us, or looks or feels good to us and others, rather than fulfilling the other person's need.

Gary Chapman[3] sees love as a language that he puts in five categories: acts of service, quality time, physical touch, words of affirmation and gifts, and each person has a different emphasis on these categories. This can be a helpful framework because it can guide us to deliver the most appropriate help that is needed in different people. We can minister through the other person's love language to address their spiritual, physical, and emotional needs while taking into account their situation, personality, likes and dislikes. If their love language is physical touch then a loving hug is likely to help them; if it is quality time then we can sit with them and listen to them as they talk; if it is acts of service then shopping, cleaning, or doing the washing might be appropriate; if it is gifts then a book or a bunch of flowers might show them we love them; if they are feeling inadequate in coping with great stress then words of affirmation need to be heard. Often we act according to our own love language and not that of the other person. Then we wonder why they have not benefited. Also we can get together with other helpers, so that instead of an ad hoc approach, there is a co-operative plan.

3. Chapman, *The Five Love Languages*.

The Most Excellent Way

Needless to say, God speaks everyone's love language by perfectly blending all the facets of compassionate love on an individual basis. How often do we feel overwhelmed when he hits the spot with some blessing another Christian would not notice?

Perseverance

Here it is again—perseverance, one of the things we find hardest. We might make an effort once or even twice but if the problem isn't over quickly we find more pressing matters of our own to occupy us. In that case, we commonly start blaming the person for being in a difficult situation, or for failing to resolve it, and by doing this we absolve ourselves from our obligation to continue to help them. This is a problem well-known to the medical profession, who recognize that the patient who fails to respond to treatment risks the ire of the therapist.

The Restricted Approach

Many people think helping our own family, and friends, and the people whom we like and who like us is enough, and anything more is gilding the lily. This restricted approach can be quite enjoyable and we are likely to get a lot of "secondary gains". But we are warned if we love only those who love us, and do good only to those who do the same for us, then we are behaving no better than those who do not follow Christ. Instead we are to make no distinction and to treat everyone, including those who treat us badly, on the same basis of love and mercy with which God treats us. We look to God for our rewards, not man, and he never disappoints us. To know how we are going with this principle, we need to cross off all our outreaches of love and good deeds to family and friends, and then see what is left—for most of us not a lot.

The best I can usually do is to help those about whom I feel neutral (and of course feeling "neutral" is a problem in itself). The times I have helped an enemy (another problem), are few and far between. In the same way, if we are not sure of our motives, we can always pick someone to help whom we find quite disgusting in some way. It is often the trouble people are in that brings about their disgusting state, so we don't need to look far. It is a great reality check because the result is often less flattering to us than we might have thought. Maybe we should look for someone like the man called Legion from the Gerasenes whom Jesus met and cured. He was apparently so disturbed the community chained him up and tried to keep him under guard, but he broke free and roamed naked amongst the tombs and around the country side. I'm certainly not ready for this, or anyway not for a very long time.

Acknowledgement of Suffering

An absolute must if we really want to extend God's love to someone who is suffering, whether it is spiritual, mental, emotional or physical, is to acknowledge to them in some unmistakable way that we know they are suffering. Acknowledgement implies we value them enough to have given thought to them; we believe their problem is genuine and we don't require a certificate to prove it; we extend sympathy and regret their situation; we are available to support and help them in an appropriate way if at all possible. Just simply acknowledging there is a problem, which may be all we can do, is often all someone needs.

We falter in this acknowledgement for two reasons. First, as Christians we rightly try to understand and appreciate just how good God is to us. We try to value all his many blessings starting with salvation. We know that each day he cares for us, and keeps us not only safe but alive, "In his hand is the life of every creature and the breath of all mankind." (Job 12: 10). That we fall far short in our thanks to God is all too obvious to us. However, there can be a distorted expression of this worthy sentiment when we judge people who voice their distress as being thankless and so we become hypercritical. We imply, often not very subtly, they should not be complaining but should be giving thanks. Did Jesus ever tell a sufferer to say thank you for their suffering? It is the callous attitude of "I'm all right, Jack, and so are you, so pull yourself together." We may tell them about someone who is worse off than they are, or who is *really* sick, or after they have informed us they are not well, we triumphantly tell them how well they look—by which we mean to imply they are a hypochondriac. We mistakenly think if we acknowledge their problem we will encourage them to have a thankless attitude to God.

Personally, when I have been in a very hard place, I have felt dragged down and cut off from God when a person has come to me with an attitude and words of denial. It is literally as though all my batteries have flattened—physical, emotional, and spiritual. Conversely, those who have acknowledged my distress with a few words of sympathy have caused self-pity to melt away and I have felt a boost in inner strength. Then I see God more clearly with me. God cares, "If anyone speaks, he should do it as one speaking the very words of God." (1 Pet. 4:11). The one who came to me bringing acknowledgement, came bringing love, while the other came bringing judgment. The only thing that will make the sufferer feel better is to feel the love of God. The one thing he never does is deny we are hurting when we are. Neither should we do this. Acknowledgement is support; denial is attack. Acknowledgement delivered in a positive way is therapeutic; denial is destructive. We can only come as God's messenger if we bring his love.

The second reason we stumble over acknowledgment is because it calls our own faith to public account. Once we agree there is a problem, we may mistakenly feel we have to explain to ourselves, as well as to the other person, how this God of love has let this happen. Of course we are no more able to do so than Job's friends were. It is easier for us to go into denial. Our faith won't grow but we will stay in our comfort zone while their faith of course is put under even greater strain. By acknowledgement we bring our faith to support the sufferer. Acknowledgement says all the following for us: we trust God to help them; nothing is too hard for him; he is working for their good; just as he was with them when things were going well, so he is with them when this is not the case, and he will still be with them after it is over. The love and faith of both sufferer and helper will grow. This is what God wants.

In a television interview I heard a person speak who had gone to help in Nazi concentration camps immediately after the end of World War Two. She said the former prisoners of the camp wanted most of all for their story to be told. For them, acknowledgement of their suffering was paramount and therapeutic. She also told the interviewer the thing she as a helper found hardest to deal with was the banality and denial of those unaffected. I know what she means, because I was once personally involved in a matter of human suffering and injustice, and I remember wanting to see the story written in huge letters across the sky for all to see. It wasn't a matter of revenge. To me this picture represented acknowledgement and with that came validation of the concept of right and wrong, of justice.

Jesus cried out to God from the cross, "My God why have you forsaken me?" It was a cry to God for acknowledgement. Jesus's faith in God's love and power was perfect. Also unlike us he was privy to God's plan and knew why he was called to suffer. So why did Jesus need this acknowledgement? In his humanity, in his suffering and under the burden of our sin, he felt abandoned by God. He needed God to reassure him he was aware and he cared. God did not respond by ignoring Jesus until he pulled himself together. Quite the opposite, almost immediately after these words God answered Jesus's cry and ended his suffering. We need to bring God's reassurance to others when they are suffering and we can't do so without acknowledgement.

Bitterness Drowns Out Compassion

How can we feel sorry for someone else when we think we have been treated even more unfairly ourselves? Then we want to say, "Join the club. Now you know what it feels like." To help them seems a bit like giving money to a person who is richer than we are. If we approach someone with this attitude it is similar to trying to enter the exit ramp on a freeway. We need to obey the sign, "Wrong Way Go Back". It is only by turning around and thanking God for our own life that we can stop making negative comparisons and so are able to lose our bitter and unloving attitude.

SUMMARY

When we speak of the power of God Almighty we are speaking of his love; he is love and he is the source of all love. Through the power of this love we have been redeemed by Christ and reconciled to God, and in this our hope is sure because "Love never fails." (1 Cor. 13:8). It is love continually flowing from the heart of God that sustains everything of real value in the world, it carries man to the heights of his existence—all the acts of selfless, self-sacrificing, unconditional love of which we are capable spring from the perfect love of God.

We have been commanded to love God and each other. These two loves are part of the one whole. Neither is optional, because we are to love God completely. Once touched by his love, once our eyes have been opened, it draws us ever closer and really does become the reason for living, our ever-present goal.

We can't give what we don't have. It is the Holy Spirit given to us by Jesus who fills us with the love of God. Then we need to look to Jesus as our model, so that we actively, continually, and strenuously aspire to his standards. It is a costly love, it cost God his son and it will cost us too. Apart from paying with our transient earthly treasures, compassion and sorrow are soul mates in the heart where Jesus dwells, but so are the priceless treasures of God's love, joy, and peace.

6

Ask Me Anything But That

WE ARE TOLD, "A man's wisdom gives him patience; it is to his glory to overlook an offense." (Prov. 19:11). The wisdom, and therefore the glory, can only come from God. Ability to forgive is the great leveler; it fells the spiritually mighty among us. I wonder if anyone ever quite does it. Certainly it seems to be something we have to come back to over and over again. Sometimes I have thought I have forgiven someone and then after a while I see them or hear about them and all the old negative thinking comes back. There is then nothing for it but to start all over at the beginning of the forgiveness process. I hope God sees a genuine effort to try to forgive as the same as succeeding, otherwise my position would be hopeless. Some of the fiercest battles around milestones on our journey occur because God is altering our hearts to enable us to forgive. Of all the essential spiritual things we can't do in our own strength this seems to lead the rest. Success can only come through the usual combination of the grace of God to empower us and our own effort to co-operate with that grace.

God empowers us through his love in us, without it forgiveness is impossible. It is our failure to love others that causes us to be unable to forgive. I have noticed once I feel this love for someone I no longer have to try to forgive them; forgiveness is no longer an issue, it is just there. Only God can implant this love, no amount of effort on our part will manufacture it for us. When a particular challenge arises we have to turn to God with a willing heart. When we use his love and his wisdom, we will know the joy of success and we will reflect his glory. I had a recent experience where a Christian I respected behaved badly. This caused me much anger and heartache and I prayed a lot about the issues and tried to forgive. Some time later I met this person and to my amazement found love and forgiveness just sitting there in my mind. Since then the forgiveness process is not only complete but the love is continuing to grow. It emphasized to me that it is God who works all things for good and when we struggle to do his will it is his strength that brings success.

Paul showed he had no illusions about himself. He said his own enormous offences against God were cancelled out only because of the unlimited patience of Christ. God's mercy, expressed in his patience towards us, is an expression of his love. Paul's example shows us nobody stands outside this mercy. As in everything we should follow Jesus's example by displaying the same unlimited patience, so that we can forgive someone who seems to us to be the worst possible example of fallen man. We don't naturally have unlimited patience, but we can acquire it if we strain to align our will totally with that of God, and so allow him to fill us up with his love and his mercy.

These following two verses taken together mean by being unforgiving we step out of God's presence: "Anyone who claims to be in the light but hates his brother is still in the darkness." (1 John 2:9); "This is the message we have heard from him and declare to you: God is light; in him there is no darkness at all." (1 John 1:5).

Jesus makes it clear that inherent in unforgiveness is hypocrisy, "You hypocrite, first take the plank out of your own eye, and then you will see clearly to remove the speck from your brother's eye." (Matt. 7:5). Throughout the Scriptures his anger is most clearly expressed when he detects hypocrisy and he condemns it repeatedly.

In the Lord's Prayer Jesus makes us aware our own forgiveness by God is dependent on our forgiveness of others. He says it more than once, "if you do not forgive men their sins, your Father will not forgive your sins." (Matt. 6:15). This is a warning from the one who loves us and redeemed us at great cost. There are no exceptions, no "get-out clauses", it is non negotiable, we have to try our best to do it.

Feet on Earth, Head in Heaven

WHY FORGIVING IS SUCH A HARD THING TO DO

A Broken Heart

If the person who is in dispute with us is much loved and trusted by us, then our heart is wounded and we recoil feeling hurt, vulnerable and betrayed. Nevertheless we must forgive. Trying to think clearly above this sort of distress is very difficult. It is often a hurt we can only bear by giving it to God in prayer, and all the more so if despite our best efforts there is no true reconciliation. Then it is like handing our heart to someone on a plate and having it flung back at us. All we can do is accept that the searing pain of forgiveness withheld is a consequence of the vulnerability love brings. To step back from it is to step back from love and therefore from God. Jesus didn't do so and we follow his lead.

Pride

Pride plays a huge part in unforgiveness. There is no wound as painful as the wound caused by injured pride. Because we are so self-absorbed and consider ourselves to be all important, there is a permanent and pervasive distortion in our perception—even the smallest attack on us seems to deserve capital punishment. If someone should have the temerity to suggest we have overreacted to a perceived slight then our genuinely astonished reply is likely to be, "*What*? They're getting off lightly!" Conversely, if we become aware someone else is upset by something we did, we commonly ask ourselves and others in genuine bewilderment, "What are they on about?"—presuming we pause at all to recognize there is a problem. Because we see ourselves as being so sweet and lovely, while seeing other people clearly aren't, it just seems to be natural justice that their crime should be severely punished while ours should be entirely overlooked. Satan fell from heaven because of his pride, and his fate is an important warning to us because our pride is our Achilles heel, and puts our entire relationship with God at great risk.

Anger

Anger immediately follows hurt pride and dented ego and makes positive communication almost impossible. It causes loss of control and we lose the power of rational thinking and action just when we need it most. We literally "can't think straight." So while we are angry we should pray as much as possible, say as little as possible, and do as little as possible, until our anger has subsided. Anger is not just expressed by frothing at the mouth. There is cold fury, which is expressed in vindictive behavior where we turn our back on the offender, give him "the cold shoulder", ignore him in a group, and generally wish him ill. Hot anger occurs partly because of loss of control whereas cold anger is so cruel because it is thought out and deliberate—if we go there it is a long, long road back.

The Importance of Culture

Community and family culture underpin our pattern of reaction to an offence. I was born in a marvelous country where community justice is built on Westminster law and though faulty may be the best overall. However, I went to a primary school where gang fights were the norm. My parents had to teach my sister and me to defend ourselves even at such a tender age. As I grew up I developed the mindset that if I was attacked in any way I should immediately retaliate, because literally to hesitate was to be lost. Later on in life if someone offended me, then without more ado I would immediately go and "kick their duck house down"—to quote an advisor. This was because I had been taught to do so and it was an approach that worked well at that school. For all of us, there can be a lot of unlearning of old habits in order to do things God's way.

When a Loved One is Hurt

Forgiving someone who has injured us is very hard. Even harder is forgiving someone who has attacked someone we love. We know the victim so well, we know their vulnerability and clearly see their pain, and so we hurt for them; in fact we commonly hurt more than they do. It is a very complex situation. First, it involves our own ego because especially if it is a relative, our own status is often tied up with theirs. In effect an attack on them is an attack on us. This is illustrated in the old cowboy movies when two families are in conflict and close ranks against each other, and right and wrong become irrelevant.

If we have a role in the care of the victim then we also feel guilty and ask ourselves why we didn't do a better job of protecting them from the hurt. This guilt is very relevant where the person harmed was powerless against their attacker—where the victim was a child, disabled, elderly, an animal, or another of God's creatures, and especially if there was physical violence or death. To cope with this we have to face our guilt squarely and forgive ourselves. Otherwise life is not worth living and our negativity spreads to affect those around us as well. Added to our feeling of guilt we see the obscenity of evil and feel horror and outrage. Crimes against humanity such as genocide are in the same category. Grief is added to the mix—personal grief, and sorrow, and despair at the outcome, and at the state of the world. If ever there was a reason to pray this is it. I can't always forgive in these circumstances, but the upside of failure in anything is to turn to God and trust him to sort it all out. This is faith and acknowledges God's glory. And this is progress.

A Dispute is Never Simple

Typically most interactions between people are complicated even in apparently simple scenarios and there is often fault on both sides. It is soon difficult to know who did what to whom or where to start to unravel the mess. So we walk away, or worst of all put our own contribution to one side and see only the error of the other person. Then new injuries are compounded on old. A relationship may never recover, and if we belong to God, he will surely give us a very sobering milestone to pass.

Unforgiveness is a track we don't even want to put a toe on. In our past most of us have not realized the importance of forgiveness or have failed in trying to do so. The result is we have a long list of people we still hold in unforgiveness. I have found no sooner do I have some success and cross someone off the list than another emerges from the shadows of the past. This means there is a huge pile of old junk in the psyche that needs clearing out. This is so much harder than if we had decided on the right response in the first place and it is a great incentive to try to do so. But whether the challenges are old or new, the principles of forgiveness are the same.

Misunderstandings alone can start a dispute, which then feeds on itself as Satan gets underway. At the first sign of offence we need to back-up and make sure we have understood the situation as well as we can. Often a person is upset about something else, or is sick, or stressed, and "lets off steam" in our direction. Then it is not about us at all, we just simply happened to have been there. It is like slapstick comedy, someone throws a pie or a punch and it lands on an unsuspecting bystander. It might be funny to watch but not funny for the person who gets in the way, but we have to realize we are not so precious that an occasional pie in the face will do us much harm.

THE PRINCIPLES OF OUR RESPONSE OF FORGIVENESS

Only Love Brings Success

In disputes there is a long chain reaction: hurt; injured pride; anger; judgment; unforgiveness; thirst for revenge; escalation. A place to start to break this chain is to try to understand how the other person feels in a dispute whether they have been the prime aggressor or not. They are often going through the same pain we are, and success in helping to bring about a resolution depends on our realizing this.

The two main emotional effects in a dispute are hurt and anger. The feeling of hurt in the other person can be huge, and totally out of proportion to what we may have predicted, or feel is appropriate. We tend to blame the person for overreacting and get impatient when they don't respond to our conciliatory advances. We might even tell them off for being obstinate. The only way to progress is to remember we love them, not only in our own fickle way, but in the strength of the Holy Spirit with the love of God.

Love is relevant to everything we do and God's love in us is the platform on which we stand in order to even want to forgive, let alone to achieve it. Paul urges us not only to forgive a wrongdoer, but as part of the process to comfort him, and tell him we love him. Isn't that what God does for us? He says in this way we defeat the schemes of Satan. The sentiments expressed in the prayer of St Francis of Assisi say it so well, "Where there is hatred let me sow love; where there is injury, pardon."

Love is the best way to defuse both hurt and anger. There is no one way to do this but the more we practice love on a daily basis the more likely we are to get it right in a dispute. Love may have to be expressed through apology, which is a subject in itself. We have to stop thinking of the other person as our enemy. If, as often happens in the heat of the feud, we can't honestly dredge up any love spontaneously, then we need to remember we owe God a debt of love in Jesus. Peter described how vital love is to our ability to forgive, "Above all, love each other deeply, because love covers over a multitude of sins." (1 Pet. 4:8). When we are involved with someone for whom we don't naturally harbor any personal love, we should always strive to express the love of God. Whatever their previous standing in our affections, while ever we think of them as our enemy we will be unable to forgive them.

Disputes are a form of suffering and during all suffering we need to take time out to be thankful to God because he knows we have a problem, he will comfort us, and he will resolve it in his time. Also if we stop to look, we can often see very positive effects flowing from the presence of the other person in our lives. They may have been actively and purposefully contributing to our well being, or their behavior even if negative may have brought us great spiritual progress. The principle is that a thankful attitude is the best way of overcoming a blaming one.

Judge the Act not the Person

The path to unforgiveness is always through judgment. We are warned we will be judged with the same love and mercy, or lack of, that we extend to others. The first mistake we make is to decide the person is horrible, and then unforgiveness follows. Refraining from judging others in the first place can avoid going into unforgiveness at all.

Here is where confusion often takes over. We are meant to be discerning, we are meant to have a clear understanding of right and wrong. Judging is not wrong in itself, we are meant to judge an act as right or wrong. The whole Bible is teaching us the right and wrong of everything according to God. He is truth and he is immutable, and therefore his truth is also absolute and unchanging. It follows an act is not right today and wrong tomorrow; it is not right if a Christian does it and wrong if an atheist does it; it is not right if our second best friend does it and wrong if a stranger does it. We are not being pedantic wowsers if we speak up against wrong practices.

Wisdom is defined as knowledge of God and we are told to get this wisdom. We need a clear and unshakeable discernment of right and wrong as seen through God's eyes.

This is of paramount importance and God helps us to gain his understanding in every situation, including one requiring forgiveness, "If any of you lacks wisdom, he should ask God, who gives generously to all without finding fault, and it will be given to him." (Jas.1:5). Note that God doesn't "find fault," though given every reason by us to do so. Similarly all our interactions with others should be on the same basis, so that while we should judge an act as right or wrong, we should stop short of finding fault with the person themselves and thereby denigrating them. Restated: we judge the act as we are meant to do, but not the person who did it.

The Importance of Prayer

A hypothetical example where forgiveness is a major issue would be the following: if someone deliberately steps with great force on our toe, when suitably clad in hobnail boots, we will sustain an injury. We will have a sore, bleeding, maybe even a broken toe. How should we react? This act is wrong and we rightly judge it to be so. We don't say, "It doesn't matter," because a wrong act always matters, so that would be untrue. The more popular option is to turn to the person and try very hard to crush a toe or three of his, or hers, in retaliation.

Rather than either of these possible alternatives there is another and very good option, which is to turn to God instead. At the first inkling of trouble our first move needs to be prayer—we tell him how painful the injury is and how hurt we are because it was a friend who did it and how our faith is wobbling because the perpetrator was a Christian. We ask him to intervene to heal everyone involved and to tell both parties what to do. Every time we turn to God with any kind of burden or sorrow he answers us, heals us, and helps us to grow. In addition, we will find it easier next time to deal with a similar situation and most importantly we will gain insight, so that we will be less likely to do the same thing to someone else. Last but not least, he rewards us with his peace because once we give him the burden of it, all negative preoccupation and our plotting and scheming for revenge is gone.

Feet on Earth, Head in Heaven

Where does this leave our attitude to the perpetrator? We need to know the answer to this question. Now that we have God leading us, instead of hoping our attacker has fallen down a mineshaft, we find we don't hate him anymore. Our love for him as a person whom God loves and cares for comes to the fore. After a while we find the emphasis of our prayers changes so that we start praying wholeheartedly to God not just for ourselves, but for our adversary, because we feel he may be in a worse position than we are. God has said, "It is mine to avenge; I will repay. In due time their foot will slip; their day of disaster is near and their doom rushes upon them." (Deut. 32:35). Turning to God changes our attitude and we realize we don't want this to happen to the perpetrator anymore than we want it to happen to us; rather we want God to heal us both. The offender is fully accountable for his actions, but it is to God he is accountable, not to us, and exactly how this is sorted out is none of our business. The psalmist sums it up in his prayer, "Against you, you only, have I sinned and done what is evil in your sight," (Ps. 51:4). It is our perfect God who suffers and is offended by sin, while we ourselves stand among the sinners. If the offender is a Christian then sooner or later the Holy Spirit will convict him. He then has the choice of going to God in repentance or not. If he does, then God will forgive him and also reward him with spiritual growth.

Prayer is such an uncomplicated way of responding to a perceived wrong. It stops the harm from escalating and leaves the matter in God's hands, which is the best way good can come from such an unpromising situation. And the resulting good will be for both perpetrator and victim. This approach is not just good in theory, it actually works. There is also a safety net in it for us. If over time the Holy Spirit reminds us we first kicked the other person in the shins before they trod on our toe, then the unthinkable happens, and we see we are in fact more the perpetrator than the victim. Because we have followed a policy involving damage control, our recovery is much more straightforward. Awareness of our own error does take time because it is hard for us to believe we are in any way at fault. It is a matter of how much egg we want on our face, how far we want to move away from God before we move back to rectify the harm we have done. Our early "oversight" followed by realization and redress is great training in overcoming pride and it is likely to be so painful we would welcome general anesthesia.

Protect the Offender

When someone affronts us we want to tell the world how horrible they were to us, but God does not allow it. It is so hard not to do this, but the harm any gossip and particularly malicious gossip can do is huge. As well, once we start, we find trying to turn ourselves away from it towards forgiveness becomes even harder. Often as bystanders we pass on information that is sixth hand or more with the same assurance with which we give our name and date of birth. The more destructive it is to someone's reputation the more the temptation to tell the world. Even when we think, probably mistakenly, we are absolutely sure of our facts we need to remember the story of Noah. One day he drank wine to excess and became drunk and undignified. One son did nothing to save Noah's reputation but went off and spread the word of his father's condition to two other brothers. These two brothers, while still treating Noah with respect, took steps to prevent others from knowing about his disgrace.

Why did these two brothers react like this? They took the action they did because they loved Noah. It should always be our first priority to protect and restore the wrongdoer. It is love in action. When he found out what had happened Noah cursed the disloyal son. What we are not told is who told Noah about what the disloyal son had done—more gossip, more harm, shame on them. Hopefully it wasn't one of the two sons who had behaved so well. Should Noah have cursed his gossiping son or forgiven him? Was it okay for Noah to get drunk in the first place? Satan always tries to get maximum mileage out of every situation once he gets started. With gossip, the ripple effect of the harm it does goes on and on.

Discuss the Problem with a Trustworthy Person

For our own mental health we usually need to discuss serious problems with someone. To avoid gossip it is vital we pick someone who can resist the temptation to pass on the information. Also they need to be capable of giving us caring support while still having the courage to tell us helpful relevant things we don't necessarily want to hear. Such people are very hard to find and run the risk of incurring a backlash and being rejected.

If we are approached by someone wanting help, we should do a lot more listening than talking. People can mostly work it out for themselves that way. It is very important for us to acknowledge their distress because this is encouraging to them. If we love them, it is possible to do this whether we think they are right or wrong. This platform of love and encouragement is what they need from us to start moving forward into reconciliation and forgiveness, and all that entails. All of us have at some time missed this point and have left the person feeling they have been mauled all over again. Another thing to remember is how easily we can get carried away and ask for too many details, and thus step over the line of the other person's privacy. Then deliberate or not, it is a form of betrayal that can permanently damage a relationship. Being the listener is very tricky and more than once I have regretted it. Professional counseling is often the best option.

Mind Our Own Business

Interference and "taking sides" comes naturally to us when we are informed of a dispute between others. We make a judgment and rush in like avenging angels when we don't even know the facts. Sometimes we congratulate ourselves for our fairness because we first ask for both sides of the story. But unless we were there to hear every word, note the whole scene including tone of voice and body language, we still don't have a clue. Even if we were actually there, if we were not directly involved, we still don't know what preceded the event, or what other factors were in play. We are hopelessly biased and will always choose to believe our relatives or friends (usually in that order), or the people we like, or those with the overall better reputation. We confuse loyalty and fair mindedness, which need not be in conflict at all if we don't interfere in the first place. Our role is always to contribute positively to the situation, which usually means being supportive to all while remaining uninvolved. God may well be trying to teach both parties and doesn't want us in the way swinging wild punches and confusing the issue.

A Truce is Not Forgiveness

Sometimes we avoid forgiveness by introducing a truce—it is convenient, much easier, and we can still hang on to our pride. We tell ourselves we have forgiven the other person, but keep them at arms-length in some way such as by excluding them from some formerly shared part of our life. In this way we can keep them in a state of permanent punishment so they will never forget what they did to us. This is vindictive, cold, calculated, and deliberate unforgiveness. We go through the motions of forgiveness so the world thinks all is well and only the "guilty" party knows the difference and suffers. We congratulate ourselves for the condescension of the partial favors we have extended and bask self-righteously in our hypocrisy. Needless to say our spiritual state is worse than when we struggle with open unforgiveness. A relationship that stutters on as a pale imitation of the past is a tragedy of unforgiveness, instead of an opportunity for spiritual growth, and an increased quality of the relationship. We make sanctimonious statements to our co-conspirators such as, "I will overlook the offense but I will never trust him/her again; the relationship will never be the same"—you would hope not; all that pain and no gain doesn't sound like God. If forgiveness has run its full course in both parties, then both will have grown spiritually. Hence the relationship will have grown too and be better than before. If we go through the motions of forgiving someone, but don't accept them back in the fullness of our affections, then we deny ourselves and the other person the marvelous ending. It also means we have pulled up short of the finish line that denotes full forgiveness, and we have forgotten the psalmist's words, "If you, O Lord, kept a record of sins, O Lord, who could stand?" (Ps. 130:3).

There Are No Valid Excuses

There are a lot of questions about forgiveness that we like to ask hoping somehow to avoid it or make it easier. Here is one – "How many times are we expected to forgive?" The answer is: "a limitless number of times." Our excuse, "But they keep doing it!" is not relevant. Peter hopefully asked Jesus if forgiving someone seven times was enough. Summed up in everyday language, Jesus's answered, "Don't bother to count just keep doing it."

"What do we have to forgive?" The answer is: "Everything." "But what he did is unforgivable"—no such thing, wrong again. Not even killing Christ was unforgivable and we all did that.

"Who do we have to forgive?" The answer is: "Everyone." Now we find this frankly alarming, "Surely not him!—he's absolutely awful and I'm not the only one who thinks so!" "What about Nero?" There is still only one answer.

Our final plea often takes the form of this question: "Do you mean I should forgive him and let him get away with it?" The answer is that God assures us he will take action against all injustice because it is against his will. In the colorful language of the Old Testament God says, "when I sharpen my flashing sword and my hand grasps it in judgment, I will take vengeance on my adversaries and repay those who hate me." (Deut. 32:41).

Accept Responsibility for Problems

How often do we see elderly adults still blaming their now dead parents for their own poor choices in life? Whether the offences are real or imagined, they hold their parents in a permanent and pervasive state of unforgiveness. We all do the same thing to some extent with the world in general and the people around us. All we need is a little honesty to realize if we have not offended others as much or more than they have offended us, then it is far more likely to be because of lack of opportunity than because of our own all-encompassing holiness. By blaming someone else for everything from a failed relationship to our flat feet we can avoid all accountability and responsibility—it is a total "cop out." This causes a progressive downhill spiral into misery. The only way to arrest our fall is by being forgiving, and then God will be there to catch and restore us.

Defensiveness Has to Go

Defensiveness is just not relevant when we remember what it cost God to secure our own forgiveness when Jesus died for us. The degree of our hurt should not affect our response. Jesus was in agony on the cross when he forgave the thief, who along with the rest of us had put him there. He gave the man no lectures, no "ifs" or "buts", rather he simply said: "I tell you the truth, today you will be with me in paradise." (Luke 23:43). While the jeering crowd was gathered around him casting lots for his clothing, he asked God to forgive them. Similarly we can learn from the dying prayer of Stephen. As he sank to his knees he asked God to forgive the crowd who were stoning him. Not much we are asked to forgive seems too hard after we consider these examples.

Forgiveness is Harder for Some than Others

There may well be many, many extenuating circumstances, past and present, obvious and hidden, in the life of the other person pertinent to their behavior. Jesus tells us in the story of the talents it is not an even playing field, we have not all been given equal resources. The other person may not have the psychological or intellectual makeup to be a world-beater in dispute resolution and forgiveness. They might have only been given one talent in this area but have turned it into two; we might have turned our five talents into six; theirs is the better effort. They may simply be early on their spiritual journey and may be a spiritual giant in the making. In that case we don't want to miss our opportunity in God's plan to help them get past their milestone and speed them on their way.

Forgiveness Must Be Unconditional

We naturally drift into a conditional approach. This is the latest lesson I have learned. We make it clear we will forgive *if* the other person complies with our wishes in some way. We want to take the relationship to a place where we will be comfortable. It might even be quite a reasonable request, but we may be asking the impossible because the other person may be incapable of going there. Also, just because God took us there it doesn't mean it is the right place for everyone. Conditions are out, we have to accept someone as they are, and pray for God's help in coping with difficulties. This obviously doesn't mean we have to put ourselves in physical or emotional danger. It is vital we behave impeccably throughout. This is easier if we are realistic about how fragile our own virtue is.

APOLOGY

Dealing with someone else's anger is even harder than dealing with our own, because we have no direct control over it. We can do one of two things. We can wait for their anger to subside. If it does so in a reasonable amount of time then it is vital to communicate. It is usually best to communicate in person rather than by telephone or in writing. This ideal approach is not always possible, for example, where the other person is not approachable or agreeable, or where there has been physical violence. If it is possible, meet in familiar surroundings in a relaxed atmosphere. If the other person stays angry then an apology on our part may be the next step, because no matter how we read it, we are almost never without some fault in some way. If, despite the lapse that caused the problem, goodwill is present in a relationship, an apology will often defuse the conflict immediately; if there hasn't been much goodwill then it may start off a move in the right direction. First we go in prayer to God to seek his forgiveness and then the way is cleared for us to approach the other person. A genuine apology is a love token whereby we forfeit our pride in order to give dignity to the other person and it is a hard heart indeed that doesn't melt when offered such a gift. It can change thinking for the better in both people. The subject of apology is huge. In order to start to do it we have to scrutinize our actions to see where we contributed to precipitating the problem. Next we have to look at our response. Things commonly happen unexpectedly and get out of control quickly. Anger itself demands an apology even if the response was otherwise appropriate. Even when we exercise restraint and then give the matter great thought before responding, we might in hindsight still get it wrong—the plank in our eye is very hard to see past.

Most of us give and attract few apologies during our lifetime. The relatively powerless such as the aged, the severely disabled, and those on the lower rungs of society are rarely on the receiving end because there are less earthly secondary gains available to the apologizer.

The benefits of an apology start with the obvious one of reconciliation. Also, even if this doesn't happen, an appropriate apology necessarily follows great consideration of the other person, and so a greater understanding of them follows. This process, together with the benefit of prayer, results in a greater love for them. We also understand ourselves better and this helps us to rectify our faults. The third and most important benefit for us as the apologizer is that we benefit enormously spiritually because we have to get over our own pride. This is why apologies are so hard, but it is also why we should do it. The person who never apologizes is likely to have a big problem with pride. The opposite is probably true also, those who lack confidence in themselves feel too threatened and vulnerable if they apologize—the cure for this is to find our security in God.

If we decide to do ourselves and everyone else a favor by apologizing, it is *how* we apologize that is all important. We don't give up on our pride easily, so if we are not very careful an apology does more harm than good. The commonest mistake is to deliver a "Clayton's" apology. Up to date in my ignorance I have always done this. I am not looking forward to the next opportunity, which is certain to arise sooner or later, of correcting this error.

The characteristics of a "Clayton's" apology are that by our wording, oral or written, we manage to still apportion blame to the other person, and at the same time excuse ourselves. This is why apologizing has such a bad reputation. People say "I don't believe in apologizing." This may be at least partly because they themselves have been subject to too many of the wrong sort of apologies. In our wording we need to be aware of using "but" or "however". If we think again of the person who deliberately trod on our toe, our apology could take this form: "I'm sorry I got angry and told you off when you trod on my toe. I was really over the top, I'm sorry." So far so good until we continue: first the blame—"but you started it"; "but you have trouble controlling yourself". Next comes the excuse—"but I didn't feel well that day"; "but you trod on my bunion." Even when we did the treading, our apology often still contains the same flaws of managing to imply our victim was the cause of it all, while at the same time implying our innocence and reinstating ourselves as really being quite lovely. When we get it wrong and issue a "Clayton's" apology we put ourselves in a position from which it is hard to recover. The other person often becomes even more indignant as they sense the hypocrisy of it, so that it may add fuel to the fire.

We also need to be aware there is a great danger to us in apologizing whether we get it right or wrong. If we have managed to swallow our pride and have then stuck to the rules, we realize we have done something pretty terrific. This is true, but unless we turn to God with heartfelt thanks for empowering us to do what we had no hope of doing in our own strength, we have set ourselves up for another extremely painful milestone—that of self-righteousness. It is a minefield out there, what would we do without our Counselor the Holy Spirit? The only safe place is to shelter with God continually.

GOD COMFORTS US WHEN SOMEONE REFUSES TO FORGIVE US

We need to ask God to heal us when we forgive someone who nevertheless fails to forgive us. The grief of a broken relationship when a loved one permanently turns away from us can be extreme, and only God can comfort us. Reconciliation requires forgiveness by both parties. If we behave correctly this helps the other person, but the responsibility of their response is nevertheless theirs.

Also, sometimes it is against God's will. Maybe a restored relationship will stunt the spiritual growth of either or both parties. In this respect sometimes the cause of a delay in reconciliation is because the other person is working through some personal issue holding them back spiritually, and not simply because they have not been forgiving. Whatever the reason, if we have forgiven them, the spiritual rewards that spring from forgiveness are still there for us.

SUMMARY

Forgiveness is like love in that God made the first move—he first loved us and he first forgave us. Proceeding from the death of Christ, the whole of the gospel stands on the principles of love and forgiveness. The cross has set the standard of mercy and forgiveness to which we should aspire.

God tells us we must forgive because it is a condition of his forgiving us—to relegate someone to the category of an enemy is to make ourselves enemies of God. Judgment is God's province alone, "There is only one Lawgiver and Judge, the one who is able to save and destroy. But you—who are you to judge your neighbor?" (Jas 4:12). As professing Christians, when we are unforgiving we mock God. The hypocrisy of it causes untold damage to Christian witness and empties the pews in churches.

Forgiveness is second only to love in being the hardest thing we are called upon to do, and it is only by using the power of the love of God that we have any hope of succeeding. Our obligation is to concentrate on God, and on his love for all of us, and from there we can start on the hard path of forgiveness. God is changing us into the image of Jesus; he is moving us towards his standards. If we could love someone as God loves us, forgiveness would not be a problem at all, so we need to pray we will be filled with the pure love of God for everyone. We also need to pray for wisdom when faced with a situation that could easily escalate into unforgiveness.

We may pay dearly in declining to defend ourselves, ignoring negative gossip, and bearing our wounded pride, but whatever this costs us it will be far less than what it cost God to forgive us through the death of Jesus. The acid test for us is whether we manage to ask God to forgive, restore, and bless the other person.[1] If this is too hard we can start by praying this way in obedience while we strive with all our might to comply and wait in God's time for our heart to catch up.

The reward after we have made this literally superhuman effort is that it gets easier each time we succeed and we grow in love and peace. With the following promise Jesus lifts us from the angst of forgiveness to the heart of God: "Blessed are the peacemakers, for they will be called sons of God." (Matt. 5:9).

---

1. Kendall, *Total Forgiveness*, 169.

7

Love, Punishment, and Blessings

HERE ARE SOME FACTS about God: The word "love" outnumbers every other significant word in the Bible—it appears over five hundred times and exceeds "hate" in a ratio of five to one and punishment three to one; "mercy" and "justice" appear about one hundred and fifty times and "freedom" appears over one hundred times.[1] Such emphasis stands as a testimony to a God of love; he is love, and all his involvement with us, and all he demands of us are on this basis of divine love. The word "righteous" is the only word of major significance to appear in the Bible nearly as often as "love." Such emphasis on righteousness was a marvelous surprise to me because it helps me to understand the awe-inspiring character and quality of divine love. Such love and righteousness meet, and are reconciled on the cross of Jesus.

The Christian belief in punishment is based on the teachings in the Bible. The concept of hell is one of the reasons most often used by atheists to discredit Christianity, and it is one of the hardest things for Christians themselves to accept. In fact many Christians just simply reject the whole idea of the serious consequences of wrongdoing or keep it very much at the back of their thinking. It is much more comfortable to dwell on God's love than on his righteousness. However, I don't see how a belief in love can be sustained without a belief in justice, from which is derived the necessity for punishment.

As an illustration we can take the example of Cain and Abel. God loved Abel and God loved Cain, but Cain killed Abel. If God was to take no action, he would in effect be saying it doesn't matter. He would be

1. Synonyms have been included.

Love, Punishment and Blessings

saying if the object of his love, Abel, is hurt that it doesn't matter and also that evil in general doesn't matter. It is not possible for God to do this because we know he is perfect in both love and righteousness. From righteousness springs justice and justice is validated by a negative consequence, which we call punishment. So for God to take no action against Cain is untenable because God cannot move outside his own nature by denying justice to Abel. The only way he can satisfy his perfect love of Abel and his own perfect righteousness is by punishing Cain and he did this by banishing him. We wouldn't have any difficulty doing that but God's love is not only perfect but also unconditional; in the Bible he tells us he loves us whether we do right or wrong. If banishing Cain is his final word on the matter he has moved outside his love for Cain. God couldn't rest there because it leaves his righteousness and love expressed on behalf of Abel in conflict with his perfect love of Cain. Instead, he went further and satisfied both—empowered by his love he satisfied his righteousness when he paid Cain's penalty himself through the sacrificial death of Jesus. Thus, in this expression of love for Cain he restored Cain's freedom to choose whether or not to inherit the kingdom of God, and if so to re-enter his presence.

GOD'S MERCY

The cross is the way God has chosen to reconcile his intrinsic nature of love and righteousness with the evil we do. God said of Jesus, "I will put my Spirit on him, and he will proclaim justice to the nations." (Matt. 12:18). Jesus's sacrifice justifies those who repent and will bring them justice when they are injured by evil. If any of us repent, including Cain, then our sin that is causing separation from God is removed through Jesus, and we will be restored to his presence.

God not only shows mercy in redeeming us from the penalty of this final death but he also acts to mitigate the immediate negative consequences of our folly, "he does not treat us as our sins deserve or repay us according to our iniquities." (Ps. 103:10). In Cain's case he put a mark on his forehead to protect him. Similarly, when he banished Adam and Eve, he showed he still cared for them by making clothing out of skin. He reassured Moses and the Israelites on this point. After the Israelites bowed down to the golden calf, God outlined in awful detail the penalties for breaking the laws he had given them. Nevertheless, he reassured Moses he would still be their God—he would not destroy them completely, and after they turned back to him in obedience he would receive them with mercy and not reject them.

Unlike us, God is perfect in faithfulness and always honors his promise to Abraham to bless him for his faith. Part of the blessing is the inheritance Abraham's Christian descendants enjoy through Jesus. In Isaiah, God declared he would blot out the sins of his people in order to be true to his covenant with Israel. They could choose to profit by God's promise, and so can we. Alternatively we can worship all the other idols we set up in our lives and so number with those who made the golden calf and like them be erased from God's book of life.

PUNISHMENT

In understanding God's love in the context of punishment there are two main things to consider. First, divine love is like diamond in both quality and toughness. It demands righteousness at any cost and God met this cost in Jesus. There are countless references in the Scriptures to God's love for Jesus. There is no doubt that in sending him to the cross under the weight of our sin that the suffering of God must have been extreme. It tells us how much he loves humankind.

The second part of the equation is that while God's love for us is unconditional, our pardon is in fact conditional on our accepting Jesus, the Great Redeemer, as the sacrifice for our sins, "he was delivered over to death for our sins and was raised to life for our justification." (Rom. 4:25). We cannot claim the benefit of our cancelled sin—our righteousness Jesus died for, unless we ask him for it. If we don't ask, we don't have any righteousness and pay the penalty for our sin ourselves. God has given us free choice so that if we choose to spend eternity away from him, which is hell, then he allows us to do so. In that sense we choose our punishment, he doesn't impose it on us. It is incredible that given the choice between enjoying divine love with God, or punishment with the forces of evil, the majority of people choose the latter.

Reading about Cain's punishment doesn't disturb us too much, because we are comfortable believing he was rotten to the core. On the contrary, because we have no problem believing we are really "underneath it all a good person", near perfect in fact, we see ourselves in a totally different category and get confused. Here's the bad news, "There is no

Love, Punishment and Blessings

one righteous, not even one;" (Rom. 3:10). We find it impossible to really grasp the purity and holiness of God or to see the enormity of our offence against him. And so knowing God loves us, we baulk at believing he could punish us, even to the extent of hell. Whatever our own particular concept of hell happens to be, it is in essence spiritual death. As we all fail the standard of God's perfection, without Jesus it is a sure thing for all of us.

All through the Old Testament we see the history of Israel marked and determined by choices. The people were always warned through the prophets in time to avert disaster but we are told they would not listen to God and so brought calamity on themselves. The Northern Kingdom was destroyed forever by the Assyrians because of their failure to listen to Jeremiah. Similarly God spoke in horrifying detail of the forthcoming conquest of Judah by the Babylonians whom the Israelites hated and despised. Those horrors came to pass and like them we can't say we haven't been warned. God always made it clear to the Israelites what choice they should make but often they still chose wrongly and paid the penalty. In the same way he has made our position clear to us and still people are getting it wrong.

At times the words are phrased so that God seems to actively punish evil, "I will punish the world for its evil, the wicked for their sins. I will put an end to the arrogance of the haughty and will humble the pride of the ruthless." (Isa. 13:11). At other times the phrasing seems to show punishment has occurred as natural cause and effect, "Your wickedness will punish you; your backsliding will rebuke you." (Jer. 2:19).

By doing what we want we move outside God's nurturing and protection and throw ourselves on the mercy of the forces of evil, specifically Satan, and he won't be slow in coming alongside. Whether God initiates our punishment or stands aside and lets us take the consequences it amounts to the same thing. In either case we have the freedom to choose to rebel or to be obedient. With all those examples nobody should be surprised at our fate when we turn away from God, but amazingly most of us are. We keep trying it on, we keep testing God who has never changed his mind, but tells us over and over again what the rules are. First, we repeatedly rebel against him then we refuse to accept a pardon for doing so. This could be described as "dumb and dumber".

Punishment can be thought of in terms of deprivation, something pleasant withheld, or alternatively as something unpleasant imposed. The ultimate example of punishment is hell. Some of us think of hell purely in terms of deprivation, in being cast out of the presence of God and therefore away from the benefits of perfect love and goodness. Others believe hell to be a place of active evil. Jesus described hell as a place where, "the fire never goes out," and "their worm does not die and the fire is not quenched," (Mark 9:8). In Revelations John described hell as a "fiery lake of burning sulfa," a place where punishment went on forever. There is a third belief that hell is purely symbolic and not to be taken too seriously, or it is an empty threat—even a bit of a laugh. After reading the Bible this latter view is the only one that leaves me mystified. There is a lot of symbolism in the Bible and it is not always clear to me whether I am reading a passage that is symbolic, or literal, or a mixture. The important thing is to understand the message God intends us to receive. Maybe those who think the references to hell in the Bible are purely symbolic are right, but even then the symbolism is telling us hell is the last place we want to be and it goes on forever. This view is certainly in line with Jesus's description. No concept of hell is comforting; if we take our warm and fuzzy glasses off it is terrifying.

C. S. Lewis expressed the interesting view that not only does God not want to be with sinners, but it is mutual—those who have chosen to spend their earthly lives without him wouldn't enjoy eternity with him. Well then, they really do have a problem, because what is certain is that they will like the alternative even less, a lot less.

Some of us certainly live to regret our earthly choice; the rich man who was in hell because he had repeatedly refused to help the beggar Lazarus was obviously one of these. We read the story about these two men who had led starkly contrasting lives and as a consequence their death and afterlife was just as big a contrast. On earth, the beggar Lazarus was laid at the gate of the rich man, presumably too weak and sick to even sit upright, covered with sores causing constant pain and discomfort, always hungry and longing to eat the household scraps. By contrast the rich man was dressed in purple and fine linen (meaning he was wealthy), and as he was well aware of the beggar's presence, it is implied he was leading an active life, passing Lazarus frequently as he went about his business and pleasure.

At the moment of Lazarus's death it all changed—we are told the angels carried him to Abraham's side. Such a simple sentence, but who wouldn't put their hand up for that! By contrast all the Scripture says about the rich man is that he died and was also buried—not a lot of comfort there; it holds all the interest and appeal of disposing of the household trash. After death we see a total reversal of what happened in life. Lazarus was by Abraham's side, surrounded forever by perfect love and comfort, while the rich man in hell describes himself as in agony as he calls out for Lazarus to put water on his tongue. He begs Lazarus for help but it is not possible. He is unable to escape from torment in his after-life in the same way as the beggar was unable to escape from torment in his earthly life. The rich man is without hope; his fate is sealed for eternity. He hears the voice of doom when Abraham tells him the chasm between heaven and hell cannot be crossed.

Even in hell the rich man seemed to have no remorse for the way he treated Lazarus. The words he spoke to Abraham were designed to relieve his own suffering and that of his family, rather than to repent and get himself back to God. He begged Abraham to send a message to his brothers to warn them to change their ways so they wouldn't incur the same fate. Abraham assured him that in the same way they were stubbornly ignoring the messages of the prophets, they would remain just as unconvinced even by someone rising from the dead. When he told the story Jesus knew he would indeed rise from the dead and these prophetic words of his would be fulfilled endlessly over the coming centuries.

Everyone chooses to be blind, or to look to God to help them to see, and in so doing bears the responsibility of their choice. Because only God knows who are fixed in their opposition to him and who are not, it is our responsibility to strive in God's love to help everyone to see, and so make the only sensible choice.

In the story of the rich man and Lazarus we are given a clear idea of the impact of hell on those who go there, while the mention of Lazarus is quietly reassuring. At the Transfiguration we see another picture of those who are with God. On this occasion Moses and Elijah "appeared in glorious splendor, talking with Jesus." (Luke 9:31). The Oxford Dictionary defines splendor in these terms: "brilliant light or luster," "magnificence," "eminence."[2] Add the word "glorious" to splendor and we see these men had become part of the "glorious splendor" of God. Encompassed in this impressive description of their existence is honor, because they had come from God as messengers to Jesus. At this personal level the contrast between heaven and hell is such as to leave only a fool trying to decide which is preferable.

---

2. Little, *The Shorter Oxford English Dictionary*.

As an aside, there is much controversy among Christians, and even worry, about what happens to us in the interval after we die and before Christ comes again. In the Bible dying is described as "falling asleep" and being dead as "being asleep in Christ". When we look at a dead body the closest description we could give is that the person looks like they are asleep; certainly children often think this is the case. So it is easy to see why this description was used. In modern English we say the person has "passed away." It seems to me both expressions are simply saying the person is no longer alive, but have no meaning as to their state after death. Paul says in the same way Adam brought death to humankind so Christ brought life, "Christ, the first fruits; then, when he comes, those who belong to him." (1 Cor. 15: 23). After the resurrection, Christ appeared walking and talking normally to living people. The phrase, "will be made alive," may mean when Christ comes again we will be restored to a physical body, living and interacting with those who have never died a physical death, but that's no more than a guess. In the meantime the "dead" Christian has a full active, thinking life with God, but cut off from normal communication with those on earth. This is mere supposition, but it explains the contradiction between the "sleeping" theory and the appearance of Moses and Elijah at the Transfiguration when they were certainly wide awake. It is also compatible with the story of the beggar Lazarus. Very importantly, it fits in with Jesus's own words when speaking of the afterlife, "But about the resurrection of the dead—have you not read what God said to you, 'I am the God of Abraham, the God of Isaac, and the God of Jacob'? He is not the God of the dead but of the living." (Matt. 22:31–32). The word "living" here implies more than just being asleep. He also told the thief on the cross they would be together in paradise "tonight."

JOY, HAPPINESS AND UNHAPPINESS

Since the days of Socrates and Plato in four hundred BC there has been a lot of debate about what happiness actually is and how to get it. Back then, the emphasis seems to have been on the purpose of life and issues related to justice. Recently the psychologists have been at the forefront with ideas on positive thinking and optimism. A holistic approach has added the goals of physical health, caring, and the recognition that man has spiritual needs. This is what the theorists have proposed and

Love, Punishment and Blessings

it is constantly changing with time. In practice in our age, the happiness many people seek is marked by self-interest and self-promotion resulting in the acquisition of material things, and on instant pleasure no matter what the cost.

Joy describes how salvation and being with God makes us feel, while happiness is dependent on our internal and external circumstances. Joy is permanent; it far surpasses happiness and permeates all our thinking and emotions. As a Christian, joy is guaranteed while continual happiness is not. Joy may generate happiness, but not the other way around. Even a Christian with a depressive illness struggles far more to feel happiness than to retain a conscious awareness of their joy in Christ. Only God gives us joy, it is spiritual, but happiness has earthly connotations and can come from God or Satan.

Fewer people seek joy than happiness. This is a paradox because the failure rate of joy is zero, no matter what life brings, while commonly we hardly have happiness in our grasp before it's gone. This is a reflection of where each state leads us. The pursuit of happiness is the pursuit of self-gratification, whereas the pursuit of joy is the pursuit of God. Joy is the result of the human spirit acting in concert with God.

An appreciation of the distinction between happiness and joy is very important. If we understand the difference, we know to seek the joy God gives us that is eternal, and not the happiness of the world, which at best ends at the grave; we are able to see our goal clearly, and to endure, and rise above the suffering and the unhappiness of adverse circumstances. Also, when we see others unhappy we won't equate it with God's disapproval of them but hopefully will be compassionate. Joy wells up from deep inside us and because it is of God, it satisfies and uplifts us. By comparison, happiness is like surface froth soon gone and forgotten. In understanding this difference, bitter comparisons on the basis of wealth, beauty, power, status, and a host of other things are swept away.

Jesus, Paul, and the other disciples were not immune to their circumstances and all knew unhappiness. Like them we can live without much happiness, but life is empty without joy. For the Christian the pursuit of happiness is somewhat pointless because all the upside of happiness—that part that comes from God, is encompassed in joy and much more. Happiness makes us feel good; joy makes us feel even better, and it lasts. Interestingly the word "happiness" only appears six times in the NIV translation, while "joy" appears two hundred and ten times. This is not surprising given that the Bible is a message of spiritual hope and the frequency of these two words is a reflection of this.

Five times "happiness" is used alone and once with the word "joy"; that there is a difference is shown by the use of both words together. Through Esther, God moved on behalf of the Jews, so that King Xerxes vindicated Mordecai and executed Haman, "For the Jews it was a time of happiness and joy, gladness and honor." (Esth. 8:16). They celebrated and this was a happy occasion, but there was joy because God had remembered his people. In the same way, we could say our children bring us happiness, but their salvation brings us joy. Not that there isn't an extra dimension to our feelings when a baby is born and children grow. Perhaps this is because in them we see the Creator.

The difference is described by Paul when he told the Corinthians about all the hardships he was facing; he said he was "sorrowful, yet always rejoicing;" (2 Cor. 6:10). Paul said it was because of the overflowing joy of God in the Macedonian churches that they were able to be generous to others, though living in severe poverty themselves, and therefore in unhappy circumstances. Happiness is dependent on circumstances and also personality, whereas joy is dependent on the state of one's spirit. Happiness doesn't always bring benefit but joy always does.

Before Jesus was born Isaiah described what Jesus's life would be like, "he was despised and rejected by men, a man of sorrows, and familiar with suffering." (Isa. 53:3). Jesus is never described as smiling or laughing. He is twice described as weeping, once at the death of Lazarus and once when thinking of the future destruction of Jerusalem. He also said that after his death there would be an appropriate time for the women to weep because of the effect the fall of Jerusalem would have on the population. When given news of the execution of John the Baptist we are told he went off on his own. In Gethsemane he told the disciples, "My soul is overwhelmed with sorrow to the point of death. Stay here and keep watch with me." (Matt. 26:38). He wanted the disciples to support him in his sorrow, but like "fair weather" Christians today they found that too hard and fell asleep.

Unhappiness at the time of God's choosing is appropriate, "The heart of the wise is in the house of mourning, but the heart of fools is in the house of pleasure." (Eccl. 7: 4). Jesus says how he views inappropriate laughter when we fail to see suffering around us, or when we put personal happiness ahead of the state of our own soul and that of others, "Woe to you who are well fed now, for you will go hungry. Woe to you who laugh now, for you will mourn and weep." (Luke 6:25).

Paul was no stranger to sorrow. He describes his state of mind when Epaphroditus was sick and Paul feared he might die, "But God had mercy on him, and not on him only but also on me, to spare me sorrow upon sorrow." (Phil. 2:27). Yet this same Paul, who was probably in jail at the time and anything but happy, was bursting with joy when he spoke these words, "Rejoice in the Lord always. I will say it again: Rejoice!" (Phil 4:4). In other words we can have little in the way of earthly blessings, so that we are unhappy and in a state of great anguish and sorrow, and yet still have joy because of the blessing of salvation and God's presence. Paul puts his sorrow and joy together in this verse, "But even if I am being poured out like a drink offering on the sacrifice and service coming from your faith, I am glad and rejoice with all of you." (Phil. 2:17).

John tells us he wept uncontrollably during his vision of heaven because it seemed no one was available to open God's scroll, which would save the world. Then he was reassured that Christ had triumphed and had opened it. One thing we don't have to weep over any more is losing contact with God. Jesus has fixed that forever.

Human psychology is such that we can't live without some happiness, which comes from earthly things. God made us, and knows us, and meets this need, but for Christians, happiness is more like an extra for which we should give thanks. Relative lack of happiness that earthly blessings bring is not something we should get bitter and discontented over if we think we are getting less than someone else. No matter how we look at it, our response to all blessings from God should be gratitude, we should enjoy them and we should remember them.

In the Bible, when referring to God directly, the word "joy" is used, "Splendor and majesty are before him; strength and joy in his dwelling place." (1 Chr. 16:27). In the New Testament the word "joy" is always used when referring directly, or indirectly, to our reconciliation with God. As an example we read of the joy of Paul's jailer after he and his whole family were converted.

There was joy surrounding the birth of John the Baptist because his ministry was to herald the Messiah. During her pregnancy, Elizabeth was told many people would rejoice because of his birth. She said at the moment when Mary told her she was pregnant with Jesus she felt her baby leap for joy in her womb. When John the Baptist recognized Jesus as the Messiah and that his own work was done, he said he was full of complete joy. It is comforting to remember he knew this joy because it puts a totally different emphasis on his death. His defeat by beheading at the hands of an evil woman and an arrogant corrupt ruler, such a popular story, is for a moment in time, while his joy is forever.

Jesus is described as anointed with joy; his birth heralded salvation and so brought joy to the world. When he was on earth he brought joy to those alive at that time. There was joy in his followers when they saw him after the resurrection, "So the women hurried away from the tomb, afraid yet filled with joy, and ran to tell his disciples." (Matt. 28:8). Note that we are unhappy when we are afraid, so this verse shows we can be both unhappy and joyful at the same time.

I have been with dying Christians and have known the great sorrow of human suffering and grief, but at the same time been aware of the joy of their salvation and mine. Before his crucifixion when the disciples were overcome by grief, Jesus foreshadowed his resurrection and the joy this would bring them. For them it was not only the joy of being reunited with Christ, but also of knowing he had defeated death and opened the way for us all to spend eternity with God.

Jesus felt it was important for the disciples to understand the true nature of joy. After they returned joyfully from a mission trip where they had exorcised demons, he told them not to confuse the thrill of power, which made them happy, with the joy that comes from the knowledge of their salvation. Jesus explained the reason for his own joy was because he always remained in the love of the Father. He told the disciples they could have this same joy if they were obedient to his commands, and so remained in his love, "I have told you this so that my joy may be in you and that your joy may be complete." (John 15:11). He promises not just joy, but complete joy.

Joy is not passive; it is vibrant and active. The motivation to satisfy the human spirit by exploring, striving, and growing is there in joy. At the same time it brings peace and contentment in the present, and hope for the future, whether in "happy" circumstances or sad. We all receive the gift of joy through the Holy Spirit immediately we accept the gospel of salvation. Unfortunately, happiness usually takes our focus off God, and it is easy to forget he gave it to us, whereas the spiritual blessings of love, rest, peace, and joy by their very nature are part of him, and so immediately bring our focus back to him. It takes a committed person to remember God as clearly in the happy times as in the unhappy. We might forget the Giver of good things, but we immediately lay our suffering at God's door and demand to know why he has done this to us. We are all different and Christians derive happiness from different things. Some Christians are happy mud wrestling, some like doing embroidery, but the reason for our joy is always the same—it is everything we have in God, and everything we are in him.

BLESSINGS

Of course we want God to bless us in this life. This means we want him to provide not only the necessities of life and to help in hard times, but also to give us happy things like holidays, sunny days and celebrations, family, friends, pets, gardens, and for some of us heavy metal music and car rallies. God wants us to be happy as we see by the good wishes the disciples send in their letters to the churches.

James tells us we miss out on what we want because we don't put our requests before God in prayer. However, in the same passage he also goes on to say if we are in rebellion against God when we ask, we won't get what we want anyway. This would be partly because without Jesus leading us we are likely to want something that is in nobody's best spiritual interests—either ours, or those around us. Once we are focused on God and intent on doing his will, the following verse seems to say it is almost more a matter of courtesy rather than of necessity to make specific requests, "But seek first his kingdom and his righteousness and all these things will be given to you as well." (Matt. 6:33). Asking for things that will bring us happiness is part of one of the greatest blessings of all that we have been given. It is a way we can enjoy the amazing privilege of being not only allowed, but encouraged, to communicate with God. Perhaps this communication is really the main point of asking for blessings.

As in everything, God is always way ahead of us—he not only knows what we want, but is always actively working on giving us everything within the constraints of our spiritual well being. We can ask for anything, nothing is too big or too small, and nothing is off limits if we are living in God's will. If we ask for a shiny red sports car, will we get it? Maybe. If we ask for spiritual growth will we get it? Yes, absolutely!

Two of the most relevant verses in our understanding of when God may say "No" to a request and when he may say "Yes," are the following:

> "And we know that in all things God works for the good of those
> who love him, who have been called according to his purpose.

For those God foreknew he also predestined to be conformed to the likeness of his Son, that he might be the firstborn among many brothers" (Romans 8:28–29).

The first of these two verses is one of the best known verses in the Bible. Unfortunately, the second is much less commonly quoted so that we don't realize that it is *spiritual* blessings we are promised here. If owning the shiny red sports car would have negative spiritual consequences—for example, if we were to spend time and money on it that should be spent elsewhere, or if we let it boost our ego, which should be satisfied in Jesus, then God won't do us the disservice of giving it to us. To insist on having it against God's will is to forfeit the spiritual advantage of not having it, and may even set us back on our journey. Even so, along with spiritual blessings, he certainly does also give us earthly blessings. We only have to consider the splendor of Solomon to recognize this.

God emphasizes repeatedly that his blessings, like our pardon, are conditional. He uses many illustrations to say the same thing. If we walk in obedience and not in rebellion then in every way we will be blessed. There are two verses in particular which give us some slight idea of the amazing expanse of God's generosity to us when we are obedient to him. The first is: "'Bring the whole tithe into the storehouse, that there may be food in my house. Test me in this,' says the Lord Almighty, 'and see if I will not throw open the floodgates of heaven and pour out so much blessing that you will not have room enough for it.'" (Mal. 3:10). If this was in the business world we would say "What's the catch"? In everyday life it has the ring of a third-world telephone scam. With God there is no catch. Even so, this is against our natural inclination, which is to take for ourselves first, after which we struggle to give anything back at all. Paraphrased, God is saying, "If you first give everything to me, then you will be amazed at my response."

In this next verse he is saying if we are generous to others then he will return this generosity to us, "Give, and it will be given to you. A good measure, pressed down, shaken together and running over, will be poured into your lap. For with the measure you use, it will be measured to you." (Luke 6:38). The last sentence focuses the mind—how many times has the average Christian used the measure that gives to someone like this?

In both these verses the promised blessings have conditions attached. The condition in the first is that we acknowledge all we have belongs to

Love, Punishment and Blessings

God and should be returned to him to distribute back to us. In the second verse the condition is that we should honor our responsibility to give generously to others as he has given to us. Often we get it backwards and demand God first gives us what we want and promise our allegiance if he does. First, it doesn't work that way—God sets the rules not us. Second, we are fickle, faithless, and unpredictable, and our promises mean little.

I am certain every Christian has seen and felt God's blessings countless times in their lives. He does bless us. I think all Christians would agree this is beyond dispute. Personally, I am constantly "undone" as God shows me he understands my needs and meets those needs. Recently I bought an appliance I needed for health reasons and it was quite expensive. But it was faulty. So I prayed that God would sort it all out and the vendors would get it working without too much of a hassle. Even with their best effort I thought this would take time and I wasn't certain a best effort would be forthcoming. In the third communication of what I anticipated would be many, I was offered a top of the range substitute valued 50 percent dearer for the same price. I had considered getting that item in the first place but decided it was too expensive. The offer came without asking. I had put no pressure on the vendors but was plodding along politely talking with them, but praying hard. This is typical of God; his plans are bigger and better than ours. We just need to get out of his way in all but prayer. Even when my faith is firm that he will act for me, I am constantly surprised, not that he does act, but how he does, and the scale of the result.

Unlike the two words "happiness" and "joy", there are not two words to distinguish the type of blessing that brings us one or the other. It is an earthly blessing that brings happiness and a spiritual blessing that brings joy. The only thing these two types of blessing have in common is that they are both undeserved gifts from a loving God, but in their importance and effect on us they couldn't be more different. We are all given the chance to receive the indescribable blessing of salvation and if we accept it, it outranks all the other blessings put together. Of these truly spiritually blessed people, some of them seem to get very little in the way of earthly blessings and happiness. We need only to think of Mother Teresa, or marvelous Christians who are chronically ill or handicapped in some way, the hungry, homeless, lonely or abused, and there are many such people in first-world countries let alone third-world.

We don't like it if we are *not* blessed, but should we worry if we *are* "blessed"? No prize for the answer, which is: only if we are not totally committed to God through Jesus. Christians have been entrusted with blessings to use them to the glory of God. It can be charm, money, status, family, or skills. What an honor and opportunity that is! The alternative is for us to refuse to cooperate with God's improvement plans for us by using our resources selfishly to serve ourselves and not him. When we consistently misuse and abuse God's blessings he may leave us in relative comfort; there wouldn't be much point in continuing to send homework that is never done.

The other thing to remember is that God has always given man a long rope. Because we are happy doesn't mean we are approved of by God. He says, "All day long I have held out my hands to an obstinate people, who walk in ways not good, pursuing their own imaginations," (Isa. 65:2). This passage goes on to say his patience will be exhausted. Sodom and Gomorrah went along happily for some time. The Assyrians prospered for hundreds of years and it wasn't because God approved of them, they weren't pleasing God, they weren't being rewarded. Rather, God used them to bring Israel back to himself spiritually.

I have heard Christians say non-Christian countries are devastated by natural disasters because they are not Christian. It is true God protects his own, but we can't feel secure in our fortunate state given how far most first-world countries fall short in obedience to God. Unlike most other democratic countries in the world, Australia doesn't have a Charter of Human Rights and huge sectors of our population are disadvantaged, for example, the Indigenous, the aged, the disabled, and the mentally ill. Thousands of years ago in the days of Isaiah, we were warned God would act against those people who support unfair legislation that promotes greed and results in oppression of the defenseless in society. We know better yet we turn a blind eye—are we exhausting God's patience? Rather than name punishment as the reason why non-Christian countries suffer monumental natural disasters, and blessing as the reason why Christian countries suffer much less, we need to be thankful, give all the aid we can, and clean up our own backyard. That was the message Jesus gave when he described two events where people died. Some Galileans had been massacred and a tower fell on others. He said those killed were no guiltier than the rest and warned his audience unless they repented they would also perish.

Without God supervising, the dangers of earthly blessings are huge, they very easily become curses and very much to be feared. When we read the popular magazines we see all too clearly those who haven't put

God first, their lives are disastrous because of the earthly blessings that have weighed them down and destroyed them. When we err, but God sees nevertheless we have potential, because we really do want to progress spiritually, he calls us to account by placing a milestone on our journey. This gives us the option of learning a hard but very profitable lesson. If we persist in our blindness we will get stuck there and waste a lot of time. Often spiritual progress can easily be traced to some huge reversal of fortune at a milestone.

Jim Bakker was a celebrated prosperity preacher on television in the USA until God took almost everything he had from him—his status in Christian circles, his fame, his money, his marriage, and his freedom. His story is the closest to a modern Job I have heard of in terms of what he lost, though the cause was nothing like that of Job. Since then by his own witness this man has renounced prosperity preaching, repented, and declared the glory of God. God stripped him of all his earthly blessings in order to reinstate him spiritually. The story of Jim Bakker shows how sometimes our spiritual growth depends on having our blessings withdrawn, in being punished. Similarly, a real blessing may also lie in not being "blessed" in the first place because such deprivation is a form of suffering, and we know how that brings us to God. Far from implying spiritual inferiority, it is often the sign of someone who has a faith that is growing. After writing a letter admonishing the Corinthians Paul said, "yet now I am happy, not because you were made sorry, but because your sorrow led you to repentance." (2 Cor. 7:9). Here the Corinthians temporarily lost their happiness but moved forward in their faith.

We may ponder over a person who we think is living with little in the way of blessings in their life and may wonder what they are doing wrong spiritually. They may in fact be striding through their journey with Jesus, and so can be trusted by God as Paul was to keep their faith without the blessings we take for granted that prop us up. Then they are used by God to be a powerful witness to the spiritually weaker. Many people have heard of Joni Eareckson Tada who became a severe paraplegic following a diving accident as a teenager. She has certainly had a positive effect on my faith. Recently after forty three years in a wheelchair she was diagnosed with breast cancer, yet she has kept her faith and continues to give God glory. Her words and her whole attitude imply that despite her considerable suffering, she considers herself hugely blessed in the true spiritual sense. The suffering of a Christian is often a sign of the true disciple.

Feet on Earth, Head in Heaven

There are very clear-cut examples in the Bible of God punishing evil men while protecting those people who were his. Noah was spared in the flood; Lot was spared in the destruction of Sodom and Gomorrah. Then like the writer of Ecclesiastes we also see the paradoxes in God's response, "I have seen both of these: a righteous man perishing in his righteousness, and a wicked man living long in his wickedness." (Eccl. 7:15).

Job, whose earthly blessings were all taken away, agonized over God's seeming unfairness in doing this. He wanted to know why the wicked often prospered and died in peace, even though they lived in conscious opposition to God. As soon as he said this Job then admitted the opposite is also true and the wicked often perished. At the end of Job's story just the sight of God fulfilled his every desire and all these considerations couldn't have been further from his mind. Job maintained his faith in God throughout his ordeal. It was no accident when he was bereft of all earthly blessings, he was given the central thing he longed for, the greatest spiritual blessing recorded in the Bible—he saw God. Through Job's experience it is clear whatever God's reasons for why he gives blessings as he does, we have to constantly remind ourselves that compared to being with him, the blessings of this earth just don't matter.

To get balance in our thinking about the distribution of earthly blessings we need to look at the following two verses, which at first glance seem conflicting: "Tell the righteous it will be well with them, for they will enjoy the fruit of their deeds." (Isa. 3:10); "He causes his sun to rise on the evil and the good, and sends rain on the righteous and the unrighteous." (Matt. 5:45).

We need to consider them one at a time and then put them both together. Of these two verses not surprisingly the first is the more popular. God is telling us in the first verse he will bless us for our righteousness. As our only righteousness is the righteousness we have through the death of Jesus, he is saying we will be blessed in every way for accepting Jesus as Lord. First, God gives us the gift of Jesus, and if we accept and place him in a supreme position of honor in our lives, then God gives us a second never-ending raft of gifts—spiritual and earthly. Our "deeds" mentioned here are of course the things he empowers us to do in his name.

We also have to understand, he is not saying we *deserve* to be blessed for the "good" deeds we do, because without Jesus our efforts are puny and often misdirected. Jesus came to our rescue purely out of the love and mercy of God after we had done nothing to deserve life and everything to deserve death. We are not blessed because we deserve it, it is not a reward, rather it is a consequence of walking with Jesus and thus expressing a living faith in everything we do. He won all our blessings for us on the cross. Unfortunately we misunderstand this verse and leap to the conclusion that when we are blessed it is because we deserve it, and someone else is not blessed because they don't deserve it, or in other words we are holier or more loved by God than those less fortunate. The truth is we are saved by grace and we are blessed by grace.

The other apparently opposing verse says: "He causes his sun to rise on the evil and the good, and sends rain on the righteous and the unrighteous." (Matt. 5:45). Here he is saying he not only blesses Christians—"the good" people, who are only good because they are covered by the goodness of Christ, but also "the evil" people, those who are not in Christ and so not covered by his goodness. He also says he sends unhappiness to both. We don't know exactly why at times there seems to be this impartiality, but we can be sure it is not random; rather it is to do with furthering the Kingdom of Heaven.

Where we are concerned, being undeserving is like righteousness, it is absolute. Whatever God gives us is because of his love and mercy. If we grasp this well and truly then we will have only one appropriate response when we are blessed in any way and that is to be thankful. When we see God's gifts as a reward it leads us into wearing these gifts like badges of holiness and approval, forgetting God loves sinners. Because the reward mentality denotes self-righteousness, it inevitably leads us to judging less fortunate people as spiritually deficient, and to see their suffering as just punishment. Then there is the very real danger we will react by being less compassionate to them and by having less of the servant heart. The disciples got this wrong too when they assumed a man was blind because he was being punished for his own or his parent's sin.

As a general rule it takes ruthlessness, selfishness, and greed to get to the top of the tree and stay there; or it takes the power of God—but he usually doesn't work that way, so there are few exceptions. As a group, those people who put God first will certainly be worse off materially than those who don't. It is easy to forget this when we read the verses about God's generosity to us. To reconcile them with what we see happening, they have to mean a great part of the promised blessings are spiritual, not material. One would hope so; we would all rather die with Jesus than with our shiny red sports car. When faithful Christians are older they can't help but see inequalities in the distribution of life's luxuries and the obvious gap between their material wealth and that of the ungodly. It is sometimes a struggle not to become bitter and discontented. This inequality is inevitable; it is also bearable if we really believe God's love for us is worth far more than money and the easier lifestyle it brings. How many houses can we live in, how many rooms can we live in, how many holidays can we have and really enjoy them, how much rich food can we eat, how beautiful can we look in expensive clothes? The "poor little rich girl" phrase came about for good reason. When we are relatively underdone on life's trivia, the things of value are seen all the more starkly and appreciated all the more. The lonely old lady in a nursing home can live for a week on a few kind words, the social butterfly searches restlessly for more and more gratification. The blessings God promises and gives us satisfy us; the material things even at best never quite satisfy.

Jesus tells us God is always aware of our needs like food and clothing, and can be trusted to meet these needs. He doesn't stop there with the bare minimum but adds moments of pure joy reminiscent of the splendor of his creation when he touches us in some extra way over and above supplying basic necessities of life. We only know this joy in the midst of the happiness a material blessing brings if we look behind the gift and see the Giver.

We should never make comparisons where the bestowal of blessings is concerned. We can't even get our own spiritual journey right, and certainly not that of anyone else. Peter wanted to make comparisons between himself and John, but Jesus promptly told him it was not his concern and to look to himself. It is very much a matter of minding our own business.

PROSPERITY PREACHING, WEALTHY CHRISTIANS, WEALTHY CHURCHES

The idea of seeking God's approval and his blessings has been grossly distorted by the modern day "prosperity" preachers. The idea is, if we give materially to God then he will give materially to us, but as he is far more generous than we are, we will make a handsome profit on the transaction. This is a half truth. God is infinitely more generous than we are, but in this approach there are two catches.

First, God looks at our heart and our motives and there is a stench in this "prosperity" thinking; it is all about us and what we can do for ourselves. Where is the self-sacrificing love of God? Second, although cold hard cash and material wealth are not excluded from God's gifts to

Christians, unless it is a path to spiritual benefit for us or for someone else, then it won't happen. In that case God won't give it to us and we should be glad—and neither do we want a gift from Satan complete with fuse and timer.

Chasing after money is living about as dangerously as it gets. Any assets we do hold belong to God to serve his purpose. Christ tells us bluntly it is not possible to serve both God and money. Even where "prosperity preaching" is not taught officially in churches, the accumulation of wealth by churches can outstrip the distribution of it. Corrupt church leaders have used emotional blackmail and the threat of hell to wring money from people over and above what they can afford. Paul wanted to avoid doing this and so advised the Corinthians that as long as they had a heart willing to give, then a gift within their means would be acceptable.

Unfortunately because of bad practices in some churches, people inside and outside the church often point the finger inappropriately with comments like, "the church is only interested in money." Instead of putting their hand on their wallet as they should, some members of the congregation put a "widow's mite" in the plate for God's work, as well as expecting their leaders to live far below their own standard of living. Paul also told the Corinthians giving is a way of saying thank you to Jesus. It is up to Christians to show the world by their attitude and actions, that both personal and church wealth is safe in their hands and is being used appropriately.

SATAN BRIBES US

The source of a blessing is so important. The happiness of a Christian has been freely given to him by God, "To the man who pleases him, God gives wisdom, knowledge and happiness, but to the sinner he gives the task of gathering and storing up wealth to hand it over to the one who pleases God." (Eccl. 2:26). The happiness paid for with wages earned from Satan will be lost whether on this side of the grave or the other. Herod the Great, a grotesquely evil man, was a good example of this. In twenty BC he started the building of a magnificent temple in Jerusalem, which was finally completed by his successors in sixty four AD; it lasted six years before being completely destroyed.

Jesus called Satan the prince of this earth. It is where we have to live for a while—it is the devil's playground. In the same way Satan told

Jesus he would give him great pomp and power if he bowed down to him, he will buy our loyalty too. We don't have to be quick to spot the catch. Christians know better, but we like the idea of a foot in two camps. We think we can live with God in charge but invite Satan over for frequent visits. Then we find out he is one of those guests who doesn't know when to go home. Soon he is running the household and organizing a move to a location that suits him better—hell to be specific. Satan can be so attractive, so deceptive, so reassuring, so infiltrative, and so final.

There is no such thing as being a little bit disloyal to God; it is like being a little bit pregnant. If we live with mixed loyalties then one day, like the rich man in the life of the beggar Lazarus, we will look back to God too late and see the drawbridge across the divide between heaven and hell pulled up behind us. We should not underestimate the power of Satan; he is not to be toyed with. We have called him names and derided him in cartoons, but we are warned to be careful not to overreach ourselves. Jude tells us even the archangel Michael did not dare to accost Satan in his own power, but called on God to rebuke him. The only safe place to be, when we defy Satan, is to be looking over Jesus's shoulder with a firm grip on him.

Satan doesn't just send presents to the ungodly, he sends them to Christians also, or maybe especially. But the Holy Spirit will tell us, if we listen, whether the gift brings spiritual danger and then we should "return to sender." It might be a small thing like an invitation to go with a group of friends to a movie Jesus wouldn't watch, so that we would have to go without him. It might be a large thing such as a promotion at work, which might mean spending time carousing with superiors rather than fulfilling other commitments. God gives us freely, Satan always charges. Within the glossy packaging of his gifts Satan always inserts a price tag, and these presents always come at top of the range prices and rock bottom value. He may demand payment in this life or in the next.

Often, on casual observation the cost of indulging ourselves outside God's will doesn't seem too high. A little lie, a little flirtation, a little callousness, a little coldness, a little lack of compassion, a little cruelty, a little unforgiveness, a little revenge—surely everyone does that? We certainly do, and we see the result. We see Jesus hanging on a cross in the middle of a shattered creation. Is anything worth that? Is a better job, an illicit "love" affair, more money, two or three TV sets worth that?

JESUS PROMISES A YOKE, A BURDEN, REST, AND PEACE

We could describe Jesus's promises to us as good news and bad news. Probably the key verses are the following ones: "Take my yoke upon you and learn from me, for I am gentle and humble in heart, and you will find rest for your souls. For my yoke is easy and my burden is light." (Matt. 11:29-30). Here Jesus tells us he is giving us his "yoke" and his "burden." A yoke implies restriction while a burden, as distinct from a load, implies struggle. When we think of what he was called upon to bear, the use of the word "my" doesn't have a lot of appeal either. And yet paradoxically he describes his yoke as easy and his burden as light. What is meant is that even if we are joined to Jesus and therefore his suffering, he will help us to bear the burden of the distress it causes us. This is not the same as promising we will float through an easy life; rather he tells us that with him we can withstand the storms that will come.

Throughout the Scriptures, Jesus tells us to come to him with the trials of life that weigh us down, and when we do, we will find rest in him. We gain this rest because of the peace he promises us when we are with him, "Peace I leave with you; my peace I give you. I do not give to you as the world gives. Do not let your hearts be troubled and do not be afraid." (John 14:27). It is through this peace that Jesus makes our burden light.

Anybody who has lost their peace, and tossed and turned all night because of a problem without an obvious solution values this peace as much as any of the gifts God has given us. We know by the community rate of mental breakdown and suicide what can happen to us without Jesus and his peace. Praying Christians don't need it to be explained, but probably we all need to be reminded at times. How often has a problem seemed overwhelming and all absorbing until prayer restores the tranquility of our mind, even though the problem remains? A Christian friend told me she had had a problem that had greatly distressed her for many years and for which she could see no solution. One time while praying in anguish, she felt the physical sensation of someone lifting a heavy load off her body. The problem is still there, but the reassurance of this revelation continues to bring great comfort, and peace, and has helped her to move forward in her faith.

Feet on Earth, Head in Heaven

JESUS PROMISES PERSECUTION, VICTORY, AND JOY

Jesus promised trouble ahead for his disciples more than once when he told them that because of their faith in him they would be hated, arrested, and persecuted. Jesus left the church in Smyrna in no doubt as to how hard it would get for them, but at the same time he assured them if they persevered he would give them eternal life. First there was suffering, during which he would sustain them with his rest and peace, and then they would have victory and honor.

Significantly he didn't say he would deliver the disciples from this persecution, but he promised to support them during such times. He would give them words of wisdom to speak, which would stand against the protestations of their adversaries. This was true, so that even when his disciples were killed, as many were, the rulers who killed them did in fact recognize the truth of their message—because it was Jesus speaking through them. Paul was called before the Sanhedrin and testified to them. It was a rowdy meeting because some Pharisees argued strongly that Paul was innocent. Felix was another one discomfited by the truth, but unrepentant when Paul appeared before him. In fear, he broke into Paul's conversation about righteousness and judgment, and dismissed him. Herod initially protected John the Baptist from Herodias by jailing him rather than executing him because he knew John was righteous and holy. Later, he was tricked and pressured into executing him. Afterwards when Herod heard of Jesus's ministry his guilty conscience made him afraid and he blurted out to his attendants that Jesus must be John the Baptist risen from the dead.

Jesus's words in Luke 21:15 were restated by Tolstoy who said, "Truth cannot be told so as to be understood and not believed." Truth may be dismissed but it lingers forever in the mind of the hearer whose conscience then convicts him. None of these persecutors acted in ignorance and so their day of judgment will be an awful one.

The joy that changes us as Christians was promised to us by Jesus. The writer of the book of Hebrews agrees we don't have to wait until eternity to get it, but have only to fix our eyes on Christ now. Paul survived that way, and we can too, because joy energizes us to persevere. We will not avoid suffering in this world, but Jesus shoulders the burden of it if we ask, and our joy grows. It is a joy that finds its completion and cancels out all unhappiness when we know we will spend eternity with God. Jesus doesn't tell us not to weep when in dire circumstances, or to "pull ourselves together", but because he promises relief and victory he does say we should "leap for joy, because great is your reward in heaven." (Luke 6:23).

Often we suffer for his sake when we serve others, and this takes us to the foot of the cross because he suffers with us. How we react to help others tells us how we would have looked upon Jesus at the crucifixion. Would we have stood with John, Mary, and the others who loved him, or would we have stood with the crowd of onlookers who at best were idly curious and unmoved, or at worst enjoyed the spectacle? Jesus tells us how he will judge us if we fail to help those people who are hungry, thirsty, naked, sick, imprisoned, or rejected—we will go to hell.

For it all to come right for us, for us to be permanently appropriately happy, we will have to wait to see Jesus in person; whereas right now we have his spiritual promises of rest, peace, joy, and final victory.

SUMMARY

We must choose to serve God or to serve our own interests. This choice determines the blessings and punishments we experience in this life as well as our fate after death.

Sometimes as Christians we think we are being punished when we are not—when we are being tested, or trained. At other times, we are suffering like Jesus, to further the Kingdom of God. Then it is a great honor bestowed on the spiritually elite, those closest to the image of Christ. Even when we fail to do God's will, our punishment is an expression of God's love and mercy to bring us spiritual benefit. When he punishes us God never withdraws his love from us. He said when David sinned he would punish him severely but would never stop loving him.

On the contrary, for those who live outside the righteousness of Jesus, punishment may be an expression of his wrath. Death, the final punishment, is God's last resort in the defeat of evil, "I take no pleasure in the death of the wicked, but rather that they turn from their ways and live. Turn! Turn from your evil ways! Why will you die, O house of Israel?'" (Ezek. 33:11).

Earthly blessings from God are meant to be asked for, anticipated, and enjoyed with Jesus. There is however, an inequality in the distribution of earthly blessings to Christians and non-Christians alike that we need to acknowledge and accept; only God knows his plans and why this is so. In addition, unless we recognize the difference between earthly happiness and spiritual joy, then very little about the distribution of material things and suffering makes sense. When God gives us earthly blessings they bring us happiness, but when we look behind the blessing and see God, then they bring us joy.

For the Christian, even when happiness is in short supply, joy never is. Not knowing the reason behind a particular adverse situation affecting us should not detract from our joy and our gratitude, because in all circumstances our merciful loving God is with us. Knowing this, we can keep our faith and reflect his glory. If only we could always be like Job, who at the height of his misery said: "'Naked I came from my mother's womb, and naked I will depart. The Lord gave and the Lord has taken away; may the name of the Lord be praised.' In all this, Job did not sin by charging God with wrongdoing." (Job 1:21–22).

The whole subject of blessing and punishment is complex and even somewhat pointless for those who love God. This is because if we work on ourselves with God, then all blessings or the lack of them, as well as punishment, have the common end point of spiritual joy as we are changed into the likeness of Jesus. When we love Jesus we are filled with a joy that is hard to express. Peter explains why this is so, "for you are receiving the goal of your faith, the salvation of your souls." (1 Pet. 1:9).

8

How to Love and Delight God

It is by our obedience we show our love for God and delight him. Obedience is strongly emphasized throughout the Bible and summarized here, "Fear God and keep his commandments, for this is the whole duty of man." (Eccl. 12:13). Therein lies the problem for us because we know we can't do it. Paul said even though he delighted in God's law, yet as if by some inner compulsion, he repeatedly broke it.

Obedience is one of the major battlefields where war is waged for our soul. We can succumb as Hosea points out, "They delight the king with their wickedness, the princes with their lies." (Hos. 7:3). Most of us won't be delighting kings and princes, but some members of our family, friends, and workmates. In either case it is the same, the greatest delight is Satan's. By our disobedient behavior we don't cause God to love us less, but rather than being a delight to him we are an offence. Through Jesus we have perfection and we are a delight, but we only stand with him in his perfection if he has our heart, and for this to be so we must show we are genuine in our efforts to obey God's laws. We serve a God who has great plans for us, "They will be called oaks of righteousness, a planting of the Lord for the display of his splendor." (Isa. 61:3). This is because he already sees us as having the perfect righteousness of Jesus. It is in his power we will see the dawning of an obedient life and though our progress will be slow and incomplete, every little victory in obedience will bring us closer to the likeness of Jesus, and the joy of a closer walk with him into the presence of God.

Feet on Earth, Head in Heaven

EXACTLY WHAT ARE WE COMMANDED TO DO?

There are the official "Commandments" we all know. First, there are the timeless Ten Commandments that tell us God's standards for us. The manner in which they were given to the ancient Israelites leaves no doubt God meant what he said. The people were first washed and consecrated and there was the death penalty for those who went past designated limits around Mt Sinai; there was fire on the mountain, which belched smoke and shook violently; there was thunder, lightning, and trumpet blasts and the people themselves trembled with the fear of God. Then Moses was given the commandments inscribed on stone by God. It wasn't the casual giving of a few instructions to go on with—these commandments in Exodus 20:2–17 are for all time. The following list is a summary of them:

1. God is to be our only God.
2. God alone is to be worshipped.
3. Blasphemy is forbidden.
4. The Sabbath is to be kept holy.
5. Our parents are to be honored.
6. Murder is forbidden.
7. Adultery is forbidden.
8. Stealing is forbidden.
9. Telling lies against others is forbidden.
10. Coveting the property of others is forbidden.

Three and a half thousand years after they were written the last six commandments relating to the fair treatment of others are still accepted by non-believer and believer alike as the basis of civilized society. Added to these Ten, there are the Two Commandments given by Jesus. He said all the Law and the prophets hang on these two commandments. Matthew 22:37–40:

1. We are to love God with our whole being. This is the greatest commandment.
2. We are to love our neighbor as ourself.

The first four of the Ten Commandments relating directly to God are summarized in the first of Jesus's commandments and the last six of the Ten Commandments relating to others are summarized in his second commandment. These two additional commandments encompass the same messages of the law but are written in the language of love. They balance the emphasis between God, the righteous implacable upholder of the law, and God the lover of man's soul. Jesus certainly doesn't change the laws of the Ten Commandments or detract in any way from them. He says, "I have not come to abolish them but to fulfill them. I tell you the truth, until heaven and earth disappear, not the smallest letter, not the least stroke of a pen, will by any means disappear from the Law until everything is accomplished." (Matt. 5:17–18). Those people who think God is soft, and because of his love for us will turn a blind eye to our willfully shoddy behavior, need to focus on those verses. Jesus also said our attitude to the law would determine our standing in heaven.

We have to personalize the commandments by obeying them and by our actions and words be seen to be obeying them. In his beautiful life and ministry Jesus practiced what he preached—he was loving, forgiving, prayerful, obedient, and moral. His presence moves man from the darkness and foreboding of certain penalty under the law of the Ten Commandments into the light of their teaching. He said, "I am the light of the world. Whoever follows me will never walk in darkness, but will have the light of life." (John 8:12). There is no downside to anything God has given us or asks of us if he has our allegiance in Jesus.

The Twelve Commandments represent the law, the perfect standard to which we should aspire but are unable to achieve. The consequence of breaking any law is punishment and it is a capital offence to break God's law. That leaves us floundering because even with our best efforts, we have all broken these laws many times. It wouldn't matter how many chances God gave us, we would keep using them up, because we simply can't overcome our innately flawed character. As a result we deserve to stand condemned by a Holy God, banished from his life-giving presence for all eternity. Yet the prophets knew God would not abandon us in this condemned state, "Who is a God like you, who pardons sin and forgives the transgression of the remnant of his inheritance? You do not stay angry forever but delight to show mercy." (Mic. 7:18). And so our Holy God, the same loving God, rescued us through Jesus who died to pay the penalty for us. Through repentance we can claim this amnesty. In doing so, the second set of commandments from Jesus becomes relevant, because we can only live in God's presence under the cloak of his righteousness. There we live in his redeeming love, which is a love that never stops flowing, is never confined, knows no limits, has no conditions, and never comes to an end. In his commandments Jesus tells us it is on this love that all our relationships, attitudes, and obedience should be based. Inspired by it our goal should be excellence because we serve an excellent God, who is perfect in every way, including in his holiness.

There is the parable of the servant who owed money and who had the debt cancelled by his master but then refused to cancel a lesser debt owed to him by someone else. When his master found out he threw him in jail to be tortured until he paid back all he owed. At the end of the story Jesus said we will suffer the same sort of fate if we behave in a similar callous and unforgiving way. Those are the rules—after we fail the standards of the law God has given, but then choose to be exonerated by the law of love, we must in turn extend that same law of love to others when they fail. The consequences if we don't will be that we will forfeit our own pardon we claimed through love. Then we find ourselves under the merciless law of the Ten Commandments without the protection of God's love and mercy in Jesus and we will incur the full penalty. We live by love or we don't live at all. "Be imitators of God, therefore, as dearly loved children and live a life of love, just as Christ loved us and gave himself up for us as a fragrant offering and sacrifice to God." (Eph. 5:1–2).

PROBLEMS OF THE WOULD-BE OBEDIENT

We Will Fail

Non-believers look at themselves, their relatives, and friends and with biased eye decide they are all good decent people. Christians don't have this luxury. Rather than comparing ourselves to our fellow Christians who are also underperforming, we are obliged to look up to God to see his perfection. The danger then is that a realistic acceptance of our woeful state can lead to a tendency to rely on faith and God's forgiveness and forget performance. Why try to be obedient when we know we are incapable of it? Because it is in trying as much as succeeding that we grow spiritually. When we ask for anything, including the gift of growing in obedience, believing in faith that God will enable us to do so, then he will reward us with success. Jesus told the woman who asked for her daughter to be healed that he would grant her request because of her faith.

How to Love and Delight God

Like the rich young ruler we are into window dressing, so we try to pick and choose which commands we will make some attempt to follow, when it is convenient, and put the ones we find harder to one side and hope for the best. This man asked Jesus what good thing he had to do to have eternal life. Jesus very plainly told him to obey the commandments. The issue was open and shut but the young man hopefully pressed the point and asked which ones Jesus meant. You can almost hear him thinking "surely not all of them." Jesus began listing them and concluded by telling him to give his possessions to the poor. On hearing this, the young man went away downcast. He knew by not using his wealth to express love for his neighbor that he had chosen money over God. In doing so he had broken the first and second of the Ten Commandments and both of Jesus's commandments about love. He found the price of obedience too high.

For those who are serious about complying, the first hurdle is to cope with failure. It can get very depressing when we try to do something but don't succeed. We see the frustration of little children in their behavior when they try to do something beyond their capabilities. Adults cover up their feelings, but failure affects us the same. The closer we get to God the more upset we feel with ourselves when we continually miss the mark. It is interesting one of the definitions of "to sin" is "to miss the mark." "They do not turn to the Most high; they are like a faulty bow." (Hos. 7:16). This emphasizes the fact that to be considered sinless and therefore acceptable to God in our own right, we have to hit the bull's eye 100 percent of the time. Even though we are progressing we may feel defeated. Conscientious Christians can become ridden with guilt. But we don't have to go there, because God knows better than we do how far we are from his perfection and has already turned all our struggles into profit through Jesus. He has freed us from the penalty of the law, "the law of the Spirit of life set me free from the law of sin and death." (Rom. 8:2). In this way he has already given us a perfect score and we have only just started. The only way out of the dilemma of our inability to obey God is for the Christian to follow Paul's example. After describing himself as a helpless prisoner of sin, he took refuge in the righteousness he knew he had through Jesus. When he looked at himself he was filled with despair, when he looked at his salvation he was victorious. Jesus has done his part, ours is to persevere in God's power in trying to overcome our entrenched disobedience until the day we die.

Hypocrisy

The second problem that may be encountered in this striving for obedience is the feeling of hypocrisy. I became acutely aware of it when I prayed for God to forgive and bless my enemies. Such a prayer should be built on my own forgiveness of the person but there are people in my past and present whom I have so far been unable to forgive. Mine was therefore a prayer of pure hypocrisy. The poet, Robert Burns, described a character with this problem in his poem, "Holy Willie's Prayer". In this prayer Holy Willie says of himself: "I'm here a pillar of thy Temple, strong as a rock, a guide, a buckler, and example to all Thy flock!" The prayer for one's enemy goes like this: "Lord, in Thy day of vengeance try him! Lord, visit him who did employ him! And pass not in Thy mercy by them, Nor hear their prayer, But for Thy people's sake destroy them, An dinna spare! But, Lord remember me and mine with mercies temporal and divine," and so it goes on. It is so blatant it is humorous, but it is also a stark and sobering exposé of oneself—like looking in the mirror under a good light. So now I admit to God my failure to forgive my enemies and pray in obedience he will forgive and bless them, but also that he will change my heart, so that one day I will be able to forgive them too. I have faith God rewards whole-hearted effort, however any prayer asking for spiritual progress should not be made lightly because we only seem to change through suffering, "The sacrifices of God are a broken spirit; a broken and contrite heart, O God, you will not despise." (Ps. 51:17). The path to a broken and contrite heart is about as painful as it gets.

Hypocrisy is both on a private scale between ourselves and God, and on a public scale when we interact with others. Christian hypocrisy is what the secular world sees and tragically may consist of most of what it perceives about the gospel. In a nominally Christian country everyone knows what the broad standards of Christian behavior are supposed to be, but when we fail to deliver, the teachings are seen to be sanctimonious talk without substance. Then Jesus is portrayed as an ineffectual leader of a godless church. Jesus showed us God hates hypocrisy and many of his attacks on the Pharisees concerned their hypocrisy. It seems it is second only to blasphemy against the Holy Spirit in terms of seriousness in offending God.

Self-righteousness

There is a third problem we encounter when we try to be obedient. Jesus says: "Blessed are those who hunger and thirst for righteousness, for they will be filled. Blessed are the merciful, for they will be shown mercy. Blessed are the pure in heart, for they will see God." (Matt. 5:6–8). It is interesting how the teaching on mercy comes between that on righteousness and a pure heart. It seems like a timely warning because in placing a high priority on our own obedience as we should, we can become avenging "angels" where others are concerned. When Jesus defended the disciples against accusations that they had broken the law of the Sabbath, he told the Pharisees that God values mercy not meaningless sacrifice caused by blind adherence to rules. Rather than rush in and judge others when we think they have erred, we should be merciful, because Jesus has said that is what he wants, and also just as he is the Lord of the Sabbath, he is the Lord of Judgment.

OBEDIENCE HAS ITS OWN REWARDS

Our Obedience Delights God

Jesus tells us it is by obedience we show our love for him, "Whoever has my commands and obeys them, he is the one who loves me." (John 14:21). Obedience is the vehicle of our love and this is what happens when it reaches him: "He who loves me will be loved by my Father, and I too will love him and show myself to him." (John 14:21). He does this by giving us the Holy Spirit as Counselor. Jesus made it clear his ministry was based on obedience as we see in this statement of his, "Here I am—it is written about me in the scroll—I have come to do your will, O God." (Heb. 10:7).

One of the many rewards for attempted obedience we enjoy is that we delight God, and it will be a shared delight. Moses told the Israelites if they renewed their obedience to God, "The Lord will again delight in you and make you prosperous, just as he delighted in your fathers," (Deut. 30:8–9). To this the psalmist answered: "his delight is in the law of the Lord, and on his law he meditates day and night." (Ps. 1:2). Any amount of dedication and struggle is worth this amazing and almost incomprehensible privilege of delighting God.

Feet on Earth, Head in Heaven

Brothers and Sisters of Christ

Jesus confirms it is through our obedience to God that he will own us as brothers and sisters. What an incredible relationship we have as Christians with God. We agree to obedience, we fail miserably to deliver on our word, but by returning repeatedly to God in the repentance that is validated by genuinely persevering in trying to be obedient, we become part of Christ's family. It is Jesus who saves us with his righteousness and guides us through ever-improving obedience on the path of God's love.

Obedience Harnesses God's Wisdom

Not only does obedience bring spiritual rewards, but most of the time it makes our daily lives easier and they run more smoothly, because we are constantly benefiting from God's wisdom, "Your statutes are my delight; they are my counselors." (Ps. 119:24). Habitual liars live very stressfully trying to remember what they said to whom, and like a juggler with too many balls in the air, it is only a matter of time before their world tumbles around them. God's commands don't drag us down; rather they build us up and are to be welcomed, "Let me live that I may praise you, and may your laws sustain me." (Ps. 119:175). The psalmist was very clear on both the importance and benefit of God's laws and he was prepared to put great effort into understanding them, "Direct me in the path of your commands, for there I find delight." (Ps. 119:35). It is our spiritual rebirth, which gives us a new nature, which in turn instills in us the desire to be obedient.

SUFFERING THROUGH OBEDIENCE

There are times of course when the comfort and order of our lives is interrupted by some more important plan of God. Obedience can then cost us dearly as the apostles found out. But the price we pay for obedience is in earthly coin and transient, while the reward is spiritual and eternal. When we obey God's laws in minor things we are often thought by others to be idiots. Anyone who doesn't cheat in small ways on their income tax or gives back excess change in a shop is mocked as a fool. This denies the fact obedience should be absolute. Whether the issue is small or large is

How to Love and Delight God

irrelevant, as Jesus tells us in the parable about the nobleman who rewarded his trustworthy servant with greater responsibility.

SUMMARY

We have been given two major sets of commandments by which we should live, not some of the time, but all of the time. The first set is the Ten Commandments, which represent the impossible statutes of the law to which we should strenuously aspire. The second set from Jesus is the equally impossible laws of love, which show us how we should interpret and live to the standards of the first set. The twelve commandments together give us the perfect guide to putting God's will into practice.

God has given us a clear choice. He tells us if we obey him, "I will walk among you and be your God, and you will be my people." (Lev. 26:12); but if we disobey him, "I will break down your stubborn pride and make the sky above you like iron and the ground beneath you like bronze." (Lev. 26:19). It is clear the standard of behavior demanded by our Holy God is perfection and turning a blind eye to his commandments is not an option. He will not tolerate willful disobedience and the penalty for breaking these laws is spiritual death. This dilemma of our best performance falling far short of God's standard of perfection is addressed by his saving grace in Jesus, because through him we are seen to have his perfect righteousness. But we can't claim this amnesty unless we love Jesus and he tells us he will only accept our love as genuine if it is expressed through obedience. Our obligation is to persevere in this goal of perfection, so that when we are whole-hearted in our effort our repented failures are forgiven, leaving no place for guilt and negative recriminations.

The demands God places on us are always accompanied by over-the-top rewards. John tells us everlasting life is both Jesus himself and knowing God. Even here on earth where we get only a glimpse, it dwarfs our expectations. Added to this, in obedience we also enjoy blessings in this life as well, because we are doing life God's way, the smart way. The best way to show our gratitude is to try to conform to his standards of excellence. What can we possibly do for God? Incredibly, through obedience we can delight him. Surely delighting God is the best reward of all.

Because Jesus has taken away the penalty of the law we are left only with the blessing of it. He said, "Blessed rather are those who hear the word of God and obey it." (Luke 11:28). Our response should be to "Praise the Lord. Blessed is the man who fears the Lord, who finds great delight in his commands." (Ps. 112:1).

9

Off the Starting Blocks and into the Race

WE ARE NOT ABLE to drift back to God on the tide of some fantasy where we see him in the role of an indulgent benefactor, someone who will fix up the mess in our life for us while we look on. On the contrary, we need to be galvanized into action. Paul often described the Christian life as a race. In this race when we first choose to turn back to God we put our feet on the starting blocks. Then when we accept his forgiveness and enter his program of maturing into the likeness of Christ, we surge forward into the race of our life with Jesus. Only then do we have salvation, which means we have the guarantee of life with God for ever. When the ancient Israelites travelled they took the Ark of the Covenant with them. It symbolized God's presence among them; it was where they met God and they guarded it as though it were God himself. Now in Jesus, God has come amongst us, and has taken the place of the Ark in the spiritual journey of the believer. In the same way the Israelites physically guarded the Ark, so the modern Christian must guard the gospel of Jesus Christ by being seen to be progressing towards his image.

JESUS THE REDEEMER

Across the spectrum of religious beliefs, humankind from the beginning of existence has had an awareness of the titanic struggle between good and evil. Here on earth we are enmeshed in a web of evil and unable to extricate ourselves. Our helplessness makes sense because the war between these two supernatural forces is on a cosmic scale.

Feet on Earth, Head in Heaven

If we look at the time frame, we can assume eliminating evil is not easy even for God. We don't know the origin of evil. We do know that the gift of free will God gave us is the channel evil exploits to hold sway over the world. Presumably this is at least part of the problem in the heavenly realms also because Satan along with some of the angels was willing and able to rebel against him. As a result, God cast him and his co-conspirators out of his presence forever; for them there is no way back—and it was no dignified departure. Although banished from heaven, on earth Satan still has enormous power, second only to God.

Fortunately for us we broke God's heart when we rebelled against him. He responded with his love, mercy, and grace and gave us a second chance by offering us a lifeline in Jesus Christ. Who is he? John answers this question very clearly in his gospel, which begins with this description of Jesus: "In the beginning was the Word, and the Word was with God, and the Word was God. He was with God in the beginning." (John 1:1–2). "The Word" means God himself in action—we see the reasoning character, law, purpose, and power of God. Those are Jesus's credentials. He is divine, as a rescuer would need to be, because human power is to Satan what pop guns are to nuclear warheads. We have no choice but to throw ourselves on the mercy of God. Without divine intervention, we have no hope of overcoming evil.

God is life and everything good. Suffering and death were never meant to be part of our world and spring directly from Satan and the forces of evil he commands. When he raised Jesus Christ back to life God proved he has the power to overcome evil and its ultimate expression, which is death. No doubt Satan threw everything he could at Jesus on the cross and during the time he was away from the presence of God. Left alone in Satan's camp their previous confrontation in the desert would have been trifling by comparison; the suffering in Jesus's soul would have been far greater than the physical suffering he endured. This is what spiritual death is—being away from God and at the mercy of the powers of evil.

What is the point though, why would Jesus voluntarily leave God's kingdom of light and life and step into Satan's stronghold of darkness and death? In the following verse, Jesus himself clearly told us his purpose: "The Christ will suffer and rise from the dead on the third day, and repentance and forgiveness of sins will be preached in his name to all nations," (Luke 24:46–47). We can't undo the evil we have done in order to achieve God's perfect standards. We have forfeited our soul and the only way to get it back is for Christ, who was innocent, to give his life for it. Jesus never once rebelled against God and this obedience carried through into his death. Because of this perfect submission he was able to redeem us and in so doing we see the radiance of God's glory. When the divine—the perfect—suffered and died, the full penalty of the law was met for all the accumulated evil in the world for all time. The result is everyone stands forgiven—if they are willing to stand with Jesus by repenting of their rebellion and its sinful consequences. As Jesus himself told us many times, it is only by using his name, which covers us with his perfect righteousness, that we can be rescued and with him raised to spiritual life to be with our perfectly Holy God after physical death. We either go back to God with Jesus or we don't go at all. He paid the full price of our sin for us, so that unlike him we need never know the horror of separation from our Creator and Lord. Jesus said, "I am the way and the truth and the life. No one comes to the Father except through me." (John 14:6). It is through Jesus we know God both on earth and in heaven, "no one knows the Father except the Son and those to whom the Son chooses to reveal him." (Matt. 11:27).

God will forgive *any one* of us who is willing to admit guilt, repent of it, and accept Jesus's sacrificial death as the means of redemption. Does this mean he would forgive Hitler? Absolutely! Under Jesus's cloak of righteousness and his healing power we can get back home to God where we belong. That is all it takes from us for the barrier to come down—a *heartfelt, genuine* plea to God for forgiveness. Empowered by divine love, Jesus has done all the heavy lifting for us on the cross. We can pray along these lines, "Dear Lord, I come to you with a heart full of sorrow because I have ignored you, failed to return your love, and done many things against your laws. Now I know Jesus is Lord and I ask you to forgive me in his name. I pray that through your Spirit you will lead me into your truth." When the full impact of the love of God first hits us, when we realize what our Redeemer did for us, it can be so overwhelming we are left without words at all, but that is no problem because at such times the Holy Spirit prays for us. The thief on the cross didn't say any formal words. An apparent non-believer by requesting a prayer or a hymn at his funeral may be expressing the same sentiments of repentance from his heart, only God knows, because only God can read our heart. There are no man-made rules when we die, it is God's domain.

Feet on Earth, Head in Heaven

THE MEANING OF CONVERSION

When we accept God's offer in Jesus we say we have been converted. It is a very apt word and encapsulates the full effect this decision has on us. In the Oxford Dictionary the word "convert" is defined as: "to reverse the course of," and "to turn into something different; to transform; to change in character and function."[1] This definition makes it clear a relationship with Jesus, and through him with God, is a two-step process. The first step occurs when we realize the full enormity of our offence against God and reverse course and turn around to face him, and the second step begins when we accept a full pardon through Jesus's sacrifice. Acceptance is only the beginning of this second step, because if genuine, the Holy Spirit immediately begins transforming us into the likeness of Christ. We are those people Jesus sent Paul to rescue when he gave him his mission on the road to Damascus, "to open their eyes and turn them from darkness to light, and from the power of Satan to God, so that they may receive forgiveness of sins and a place among those who are sanctified by faith in me." (Acts 26:17–18). Here Jesus is quoted as saying that our conversion begins with an awareness of our lost spiritual state, a turning to God. If we choose to go on, the benefits that follow are twofold— "forgiveness of sins *and* a place among those who are sanctified by faith in me [Jesus]." Forgiveness and sanctification, (the process of becoming more like Christ), go together; both are integral parts of the gift Jesus has given us.

When we start over like this we say we are born again. Jesus explained to Nicodemus that to be eligible to enter the Kingdom of Heaven everyone has to be born again. He didn't just mean this to be understood as the acceptance of his atoning death with a few mumbled words. He said to our physical birth we must add spiritual birth. He meant we needed to actually start over again spiritually and to become so deeply part of God that the Holy Spirit is in us as an inseparable part of us. When we show our sincerity by obeying and loving Jesus, then we are given the Holy Spirit who enables this spiritual rebirth, and he will remain as our Counselor forever. Jesus says receiving the Holy Spirit is *only* dependent on both loving and obeying him; he doesn't say in addition we need to be circumcised, or baptized in a human ceremony, or speak in tongues, or belong to a particular denomination. That is not to say church baptism is not a huge privilege, or speaking in tongues is not a wonderful spiritual gift, and we know different people are more comfortable in different

1. Little, *The Shorter Oxford English Dictionary*.

denominations. Marvelous as these things are, there is only one gift we cannot do without—our baptism by Jesus when he pours the Holy Spirit over us and fills up our soul. It is this new birth that gives us the desire to become Christ-like.

Acceptance and spiritual maturity have two things in common. Both are only possible through the love, mercy, grace, and power of God in Christ, and we only acquire either of them through a definite choice; neither just lands in our lap. They are distinct though. Acceptance may take seconds whereas to become more like Christ takes a lifetime and is never complete. Salvation, meaning acceptance plus striving with the Holy Spirit for this change, like the opposite state of spiritual death, is all or nothing—we can't be a little bit saved and we can't be a little bit dead.

However, that part of salvation that is spiritual maturity is on a sliding scale according to how much progress we make, how well we run our race, and this is what will be up for discussion on Judgment Day: "For God will bring every deed into judgment, including every hidden thing, whether it is good or evil." (Eccl. 12:14); "For we will all stand before God's judgment seat. It is written: 'As surely as I live', says the Lord, 'every knee will bow before me; every tongue will confess to God'. So then, each of us will give an account of himself to God." (Rom. 14:10–12).

LIVING BY THE SPIRIT

Salvation doesn't involve a glance over the shoulder or a half turn or a quick pirouette. Rather, we have to turn right around and look full face to God, and then we should never look back. Lot's wife looked back to Sodom and became a pillar of salt. The same symbolism applies to us if we look wistfully back to the world and its evil—we stay fixed far away from God with as much life as a pile of salt. More than simply not looking back, salvation entails moving forward—and observers shouldn't have to line us up with the gatepost to discern any movement. Paul says, "*continue* [my emphasis] to work out your salvation with fear and trembling, for it is God who works in you to will and to act according to his good purpose." (Phil. 2:12–13). The NIV Study Bible explains this verse as follows: "Salvation is not merely a gift received once for all; it expresses itself in an ongoing process [of spiritual growth and development] in which the believer is strenuously involved".

After acceptance we are in the same type of situation as the prodigal son when he first decided to go home to his father. Like him we find even the decision to turn around, to agree to be rescued, such a hard thing that few do it. And yet this wasn't enough. The prodigal son would have died in his misery in an alien land if he had not taken the next step of putting his decision into action by setting out on the long journey back home. To do this he had to change everything about himself, his character, and his actions. His journey back represents the process of recapturing the image of God, which occurs over the whole life of a Christian. There is one vital difference—the prodigal son made it home unaccompanied—but only just; we won't. Bad as his situation was, ours is utterly hopeless without our live-in travelling companion, Jesus. As we run our race with him we learn from him, in mutual love he nourishes our soul, and in his power we change to become more like him. We draw on him for all our strength, we are utterly dependent on him, "I am the vine; you are the branches. If a man remains in me and I in him, he will bear much fruit; apart from me you can do nothing." (John 15:5). This is what it means to be sanctified; it means to live by the Spirit with Jesus.

We can resist evil only by living that way. If we only look briefly to God on Sundays to still our conscience, but never start on the journey home, we will continue to live outside God's will in opposition to the Holy Spirit. This means we will be involved in many negative patterns of thought and behavior. Fifteen things we humans commonly do that are abhorrent to God are listed in Galatians chapter 5. Willfully continuing in our former ways would be like the prodigal son reconciling with his father by letter but choosing to stay in the pig pens of foreign countries. It is worse for us because Paul said, "I warn you, as I did before, that those who live like this will not inherit the kingdom of God." (Gal. 5:21).

EXPRESSING CHRIST IN US IS A TEST OF SALVATION

It is Jesus who both saves us and changes us. People give their lives for others for a variety of reasons, mostly very praiseworthy. Jesus gave his life only because of his love for God and his intense personal love for each of us; like the one hundredth lost sheep we all matter to him. When we first meet him it is the quality of his divine love that makes him such an irresistible savior, and it is this love that launches and sustains our relationship with him. Unfortunately a lot of us stop after the first meeting, never getting really close. He remains an acquaintance for whom we have respect and gratitude, but tragically we fail to grasp how intensely personal God is through our relationship with Jesus. We can see this irresistible Jesus throughout the gospels every time he spoke with people and every time he healed them. The effect on us when we continue on with him is that we can't get enough of him; we want to be closer and closer to him and to be as like him as possible. He is the greatest inspiration there is—it is just not possible to be in his company and not to change for the better. If we don't start progressing towards the goal of his perfection, it means we are not saved, we are just talking about it; it means we are not with Jesus, we are just talking about him.

God tests us, Satan tempts us, and complying with either has consequences—tests successfully passed bring reward, whereas giving in to temptations brings destruction. We saw how God tested the obedience of the Israelites in the desert after the Exodus from Egypt. Just before that Pharaoh showed how fickle a man can be. Several times immediately after one of the plagues he seemed genuinely remorseful and willing to acknowledge his sin and the power of the God of Israel. He even asked Moses to pray for him. He sounded as though he meant it, but either he didn't or his remorse didn't last, because every time as soon as the crisis was over he reverted to his old self. His mouth was right but his heart wasn't. Similarly the Israelites praised God after the crossing of the Red Sea but very soon after they made the golden calf to worship. We can't be taken at our word anymore than they could.

Some Christians baulk at the importance of trying to live a Christ-like life. This is because such emphasis is misunderstood as advocating salvation by good works rather than by faith alone in the redemptive power of Jesus. But this is not the case at all. It distinguishes the lip service of those who agree to salvation from the heartfelt decision of the true believer who strives to stick like glue to Jesus and to go right back home with him to God. Many of us find it very difficult to see this and so Christians often fall into one of two groups. One group says good works far exceed the importance of faith and alone will get us to heaven. The other group says faith in Christ without works will get us there. Neither is right. Good works without Christ mean nothing. Faith in Christ without works means nothing. Even Satan had faith that Christ was who he said he was; he knew Christ was the son of God as his conversation during their meeting in the desert revealed. The only thing that guarantees everlasting life with God is the faith that reveals the indwelling of the Holy

Spirit and it will result in Christ-likeness. Jesus spent his entire ministry doing the good works that God had planned for him to do and the same principle applies to us. As an aside, I think the confusion about faith and good works may have occurred after the Reformation, which saw the birth of the doctrine of "justification by faith alone." Opinion became polarized into two camps—the good works camp and the faith camp. It was not realized that they are part of the one whole because saving faith will result in good works. It is by our striving to live like Christ that God tests the soil of our faith. Jesus said, "But the seed on good soil stands for those with a noble and good heart, who hear the word, retain it, and by persevering produce a crop." (Luke 8:15). Paul said that God not only intends us to do good works but planned ahead what these should be. James explained how faith and works go together to result in salvation. He said Abraham was considered righteous because he put his faith in the goodness of God to the test by taking Isaac up the mountain to a place of sacrifice. James gives the clearest explanation about the relationship between faith and works: "You see that his [Abraham's] faith and his actions were working together, and his faith was made complete by what he did." (Jas 2:22); "You see that a person is justified by what he does and not by faith alone." (James 2:24). "As the body without the spirit is dead, so faith without deeds is dead." (Jas 2:26).

At the moment we accept Jesus we are handed the empty plate of spiritual maturity and led to a table loaded with the fruits of the Spirit. For this food we should be ravenous, we should hold out our plate to God until it is piled high. The changes we ask the Holy Spirit to make in us and what we strive for, what he sees on our plate at the end of our life, qualifies our faith as either lip service or genuine. He sees either dead faith or true faith and on this hangs our salvation. We need to aspire to arrive with Jesus on Judgment Day, carrying our plate piled high with the fruits of the Spirit, which are love, joy, peace, patience, kindness, goodness, faithfulness, gentleness, and self control. Those who come alone without Jesus, hopefully displaying earthly certificates of achievement, titles of church office, impressive financial statements, and awards for good works, hold a plate filled by Satan the deceiver, who will be master of ceremonies at the welcoming party.

Satan hates all this talk of faith in action and the trap he sets to bring us undone is baited with our pride, his favorite weapon. He makes it easy for us to take personal pride in our progress, to become "holier than thou", and if we do so it means we have made a "U" turn on our

Off the Starting Blocks and into the Race

journey away from God and back to Satan. We must understand when we live to be like Christ that as in every good thing we enjoy, it is another of God's gifts to us through the power of the Holy Spirit working in us. The gift is ours to keep; the glory is God's.

So do we all rapidly become paragons of virtue? Silly question and don't ask a non-believer to answer it for us! But if God holds our heart, we certainly improve and this improvement will eventually be obvious to others. It is the best witness we can be to the good news of the gospel. We need to be seen as an illustration of what we are talking about; our presence has to be good news for those around us.

Our dedication to becoming sanctified is a test of the state of our heart. If faith is genuine, if God can see we are sincerely trying to follow Jesus's lead, he is merciful and in his love for us he accepts us with all our flaws. No one is too rotten to be given a chance to conform to the image of Christ. God allows us to try and fail, but not to fail to try. And if we have faith we won't fail too badly for too long because it is our faith that enables God's power to effect the changes in us he seeks. We have to remember though, as the psalmist tells us, we count in days whereas God counts in thousand of years. We can't hurry God to conform to our schedule, as I used to wish I could do. It seems as though we all get frustrated with our progress and have to be put on ice at times—Moses spent forty years in Midian before the Exodus, which began his forty years on active service in the desert. I tried to hurry God, and eagerly rushed forward to grasp all his promises. I underestimated the changes that are needed, and the preparation time involved before God can really use us according to his plan for our life, and then we move not in our power but in his. Not surprisingly Jesus was young during his ministry, whereas many of us are most suited to his work when we are past the prime of our life and know it. As we age we are more aware of our dependency on God, and also we see the messes we have made, and so hopefully we are less proud and hence less obstructive to his will.

David seemed to be compelled from within himself to progress through Satan's entire handbook of evil deeds, including murder and adultery. Yet every time David went back to God in genuine repentance. As far as I know he didn't revisit the same major sin twice. David's road on the way to holiness was a very bumpy one with huge milestones, some directly of his own making, which delayed him spiritually for a while and caused him and others great pain. He had to bear the death of his first son to Bathsheba and the treason and death of another son, Absalom, to name just two great sorrows. Because of his insatiable hunger for God's presence and the love and blessings he knew there, David was untiring in his efforts to obey God and come back from his failures time and again. It was the lack of this quality in Saul and the foreknowledge of it in David, that accounted for Samuel telling Saul his kingdom would end and David would replace him. Samuel said God considered David to be a man after his own heart because he tried with all his might to keep God's commandments. I can't imagine anything I would rather hear from God than to be called a person after his own heart. The details that make up our lives may seem trivial to us by comparison with David's, but we have the identical opportunity to share the same love and blessings he knew, the same opportunity to be called a man or woman after God's own heart. The decision to obey and keep coming back to God after failure is basic to our progress in living in the Spirit, and like agreeing to be saved it is our choice.

BEING CHRIST-LIKE IS ESSENTIAL FOR POSITIVE CHRISTIAN WITNESS

We should not trade on the forgiveness and patience of a loving God but endeavor to delight him in everything we do. We are fairly clear on our responsibility to make a definite acceptance of Jesus's sacrifice to gain salvation but we seem to be very hazy on our responsibility to keep progressing toward the image of Christ. Failure in this meant Jesus in the gospels, and Paul and others in the letters, have had to continually exhort Christians to behave better. This would not have been necessary if God intended to do this unilaterally for us. It is hard, because we not only have to turn away from all the things of the world that are outside God's will, but as well we have to give to others a love that reflects the generosity and abundance of God's love to us. If the impossible and unthinkable had happened and Jesus had lapsed in his love for humankind, and at times failed in his excellence, then his gospel would have died with him. It can have exactly the same effect when we claim to represent him to others but behave badly.

The words of real wisdom we impart to others will be relatively few but our life and our behavior are always on display. We should be constantly growing spiritually and this should be obvious to everyone by our improving character and actions. Others should be able to see this

Off the Starting Blocks and into the Race

change and be thinking things like, "I never thought he/she would do this, say that . . . ." Positive words should be coming out of our mouths that others thought they would never hear and we should be doing positive deeds they thought they would never see. And it should all come from our heart. This is the best witness we can be to others, they should like what they see and want to know more of the God who is the powerful force behind our change for the better. Even though we have this great responsibility of Christian witness we need not beat ourselves up when we fail, but keep our eyes on the cross and come back stronger as Peter and countless others have done. John tells us to put aside self-condemnation because God is greater than this.

Many Christians sit back comfortable in their salvation, basking in the love of God for them while giving back only token love, token gratitude, token obedience—and their behavior reflects this. That is when the cry "hypocrite" rings out long and loud from a broken world. Most of the time we are no worse than non-believers, and sometimes even better, but while we tell of a gospel founded on the high ground of Jesus we ourselves fail to live up to anything like the expectations we create. Then our listeners recoil in disappointment and disgust, and decide that like us, Jesus is a sham, and God—if there is one, is untrustworthy. We want to make as much progress as possible in this second step of spiritual maturity. Even if we are saved, unless we become increasingly like Jesus, nobody except us and God will know it. Then we are of little use to him and are often a positive hindrance to furthering the Kingdom of God. Satan must love having God's people do his work for him. We can deprive him of this pleasure by knowing what God wants and then doing it. Paul says we will succeed in this if we give up worldly thinking and allow our mind to be changed into a heavenly perspective.

Non-believers look sideways at each other and feel reassured that they are no worse than anyone else, but the Christian must look up to God to imitate his perfection, and by our behavior we should be seen to be striving for that goal. It is not an even playing field. When Christians err non-believers respond by throwing out Christianity; if only these same critics would throw out atheism and all the other false religions when those adherents err. It is as though deep within themselves all people really do understand the perfection of the One True God and that he is the gold standard. They see him immeasurably above all the rest, to be cut down—the tall poppy over the earthly setting of the lesser gods. Rather than meeting his standards in Jesus, they take the easy way out by proffering the failings of Christians as an inadequate excuse for their unbelief.

Our failures particularly impact spiritually in a negative way on the many well-motivated non-believers out there in the world trying to change it for the better. They share our vital concerns of justice and compassion, but they use the power of their own human love not realizing it just can't be done without God. At times they are an embarrassment to the church because they are often more dedicated to loving and helping others than we are! Some put in a really valiant effort and at a human level deserve their Nobel Peace Prizes and community awards. But they all fail in their purpose of perfecting themselves and the world around them, and because they have no redemption through Christ, Satan claims them in the end. Tragically they are "separate from Christ, excluded from citizenship in Israel and foreigners to the covenants of the promise, without hope and without God in the world." (Eph. 2:12). Satan doesn't tell them this when they receive the reassurance of man's transient praise for their efforts. We owe it to them to show by our behavior that Jesus is not only a better way, but the only way. This would be a far more fitting, far greater reward for them, because it lasts not just for a lifetime but for eternity. When we sing the song of our great God and Redeemer it is not our voice but that of Jesus they need to hear.

It is often the most dedicated Christians who do the most harm. In our enthusiasm we seem to so easily get out of balance in our pursuit of God and the practical application of Christian doctrine. God shows us he is a God of balance and weighs everything—he balances justice with mercy, punishment with love. We need to pray and think hard before we express a dogmatic opinion or address a problem by charging off, albeit with good intentions, in a one-eyed over-controlling way wreaking havoc for our fellow Christians and non-believers alike. When God inevitably brings us to a screeching halt—often after a perfect three-point landing on nose and knees, we need to go back to first principles. These are to stop trying in our own human strength, to pray, to rest in God, and to wait patiently for the solution, which will surely come from him. We need to use our recovery time remembering the many times God showed his faithfulness to us in the past, and then we can rest in the present and maintain our hope in the future. He will pick us up and get us going again, hopefully looking a bit more like Christ.

SPIRITUAL MATURITY, A BIG TICKET ITEM

The death of Jesus opened up the way for us to be forgiven, and this is a free gift, but we pay for acquiring a progressive likeness to Christ, and it is both costly and painful. The cost is in earthly coin, and although God faithfully returns our investment in his far more valuable spiritual currency, as well as in a multitude of earthly blessings, every time we initiate another transaction it hurts. We give up some coveted bauble with which Satan has lured us. Then we go through a difficult waiting period because it takes time for God to replace our pining after it with an appreciation of something far better from him. We have to travel with Jesus to many milestones in order to be increasingly conformed to his holiness and we suffer there. We can tell ourselves it is too hard and opt out of God's plan for us, or we can find the strength to keep going by actively harnessing the power of the Holy Spirit. We don't give up a lot to accept Christ's sacrifice and call ourselves Christian when we are born into a Christian family in a Christian country, but if we take it seriously then it gets hard. None of us progress easily; it is not a passive process; it doesn't just happen. Even though it requires a long and very hard struggle on our part, this is really of little consequence when compared to the rewards God continually showers upon us. The further we go the more impatient we are to go on. This is despite the fact that often—in my experience usually—it means our struggles get harder as God takes us higher and closer to him. We see him more and more clearly and pursue him more and more vigorously. As we do this, our life should become a truer picture of God's love. By our behavior all those we meet should see this change as we mature spiritually and become a truer channel for this love of God. Some of us run a very long race with Jesus, some like the thief on the cross a very short one. Even so, his defense of Jesus on the cross, and the humility and faith he showed stands as an example to us for all time.

WE HAVE A DUTY TO HELP THE OTHER RUNNERS

Once we have recognized the pattern of progress on our journey, it is much easier to allow for lapses in others and to help them to recover their forward progress. When we believe others to be in error, prayer should be our first move. Paul told the Thessalonians his team was praying for them constantly so that they would succeed in acts of faith. We all serve the one true God under the one blood-stained banner of Jesus, "Therefore encourage one another and build each other up," (1 Thess. 5:11).

We must accept the fact that Christians, even though flawed, are still Christian. It is not a case of one or two or any number of strikes and you're out. The people who make the most or the worst mistakes may be the people making the most progress. Their spiritual standing turns only on true repentance and the change in them their repentance brings about. After witnessing some particularly distasteful act by a practicing Christian, the plank in my eye would cause a problem and I used to say "he/she can't be a Christian or he/she wouldn't have done that." Oh yes, they are Christian! And, Oh yes, they would do it! Like humanity in general there is nothing so horrendous that we Christians would not involve ourselves in it. The issue that distinguishes us as Christians from the non-believer is whether we repent, learn by our failure, and resolve to do better next time. When we are running our race with Jesus, the lover of our soul, it is easier to train ourselves to see God at work in others as we know he is in us. We need to copy Jesus and drop the judgment and the condemnation and become a loving peacemaker. Tested love should be stronger for the testing. Who benefits? No prizes, we all do.

SUMMARY

God said, "be holy, because I am holy." (Lev. 11:45). We acquire this holiness through progressively changing into the likeness of Christ. The Scriptures tell us this is by God's grace. His love is unconditional, but the part of salvation that embodies this change is conditional on our accepting responsibility for doing so—hence in Philippians we are told to work out our salvation. While the will to comply comes from us, the power to do so comes from God and his power is love. We need to get on with living the holy life God planned for us. The image of God in which we were made should become clearer and clearer to others.

If we accept God's saving grace in Christ, it is a total acceptance. It means we run our race back to God with Jesus and along the way become increasingly conformed to his likeness, while benefiting more and more from his love, peace, and joy. The alternative is to reject Jesus outright, or refuse to run with him. It amounts to the same thing; it amounts to hell, because acceptance and Christ-likeness together make up the gift that is salvation.

Off the Starting Blocks and into the Race

In Jesus is a beauty we see nowhere else because he is the full revelation of God to us. Running the race of our life with him is about as exhilarating as it gets, "let us throw off everything that hinders and the sin that so easily entangles, and let us run with perseverance the race marked out for us. Let us fix our eyes on Jesus, the author and perfecter of our faith, who for the joy set before him endured the cross, scorning its shame, and sat down at the right hand of the throne of God." (Heb. 12:1–2). What a race we can choose to run and what a prize we can choose to claim!

10

Has the Church Forsaken Its First Love?

As we move through life there is a constant struggle within each of us to choose between our unbridled humanity and the sovereignty of our Creator. Put us all together in the church and it easily becomes all about us and not about God. Then the challenge to present the gospel to the world as a message of the love of God in Christ is not met.

All countries, and human institutions rise and fall, and yet the Jewish-Christian church is traceable back about four thousand five hundred years.[1] Guilty as it is of the most terrible mistakes and yet empowered as it is by the Spirit of God, its survival is to me a testimony to God's power second only to the resurrection of Jesus. The Old Testament is a record of the church repeatedly losing its way and being brought back on track by God as he kept his Covenant with humankind. It was obvious to the prophets how bad things were but not to the priests and people as a whole. In Jesus's day the church had distorted their side of the bargain in the Old Covenant to the point that the God of the Scriptures was almost unrecognizable as part of church practice. The church hierarchy was self-serving and entrenched in self righteousness, and the people went along with it. That sounds familiar! Rather than embrace Jesus as the Messiah and follow his teachings, they killed him.

God holds the congregation as a whole accountable as well as the individual. Jesus's description of the church at Ephesus sounds pretty impressive judging by the standards of many churches in the Western world today. But still he goes on to warn them, "Yet I hold this against you: You have forsaken your first love. Remember the height from which

---

1. The NIV Study Bible, Map Old Testament Chronology.

you have fallen! Repent and do the things you did at first" (Rev. 2:4–5). He said if they did not do so he would judge the church and no longer be part of it. We must try to do better. Here, he says the love of the congregation for him—their "first love", must be greater than all other loves. Jesus *is* the church so that it is his love that founded and sustains the church; he says our love for him must be both paramount and expressed in our behavior—"do the things you did at first." Jesus's criticism applies to many churches today. Is our failure to put our love for Christ above that of the organized church the reason for the decline of the church in first-world countries?

Paul took up the baton and his letters to the churches are full of exhortations to the people to avoid polluting the church with wrong thinking and wrong behavior. He tries continually to bring them back from error and finds it extremely frustrating in the process. It is sobering that it was the founding church in Jerusalem that tried to enforce the Jewish tradition of circumcision and this threatened to split the church in its infancy. Had Paul not convinced them of their error they would have perpetuated the Old Covenant and undermined the core of the New Covenant—that of justification only by saving faith in Jesus and not by obeying church rules. To the modern-day Christian this mistake of the pro-circumcision group seems not only hopelessly wrong but even childish. But don't look around because in our own way we are making mistakes that should be just as obvious. No doubt there are many modern churches Jesus doesn't even visit.

From the beginning to the present, God has raised up men who will remain true to him, who will speak up against wrong practices. Like Jesus, many have been executed by the church. In our times, dissenters are usually simply marginalized or ostracized and this is also an effective way of delaying reform. The authorities don't seem to have learnt if it is something God wants it can't be stopped.

Jesus himself was accused of being mad. No doubt the prophets were often dismissed as being too strange to be taken seriously. Everyday on television news programs we see this same ploy of vested interests countering rational argument by discrediting the speaker. Similarly the common response of the organized church always has been and still is marked by control, denial, cover up, and the discrediting and persecution of dissenters or whistleblowers. That approach only works for a time, God says enough is enough and the church loses momentum or God abandons it. No wonder he has such a long program in order to position the world for the second coming of Jesus.

Whether we are leaders or members of the congregation, we justify ourselves and the wrong position we have taken by pleading our own holiness and superiority because we profess to Christianity. The rules apply to everyone except us and we are confident we are the exception when a red flag goes up in our conscience. This is particularly easy to do if we have the status of having been a Christian for many years, of being a leader, or of being new and ignorant—that just about covers everyone. Eventually a forest of red flags goes unnoticed and our conscience may cease to register at all. We are smug in our assurance that God sanctions our actions when we are far from him and trotting along with Satan. We don't fool even fellow Christians forever. Non-believers, who are at least honest enough to admit they are going it alone without God, are unencumbered by our sanctimonious protestations and so often see very clearly the full dismal picture of a church existing in disobedience to God. What an awful witness that is. Thankfully, if we go so far we can't get back on track, even though we want to, God will bring us back, but there is usually pain for us and we may have done great damage to others. It is not that Christians are necessarily worse than non-Christians but expectations are much higher, so failure is all the more stark and clothed in a sickening hypocrisy. Often there is nothing about our behavior that would lead anyone to recognize our claim that we have been made in the image of God, or that we follow Jesus, who is the loftiest example of self-sacrificing love the world has known.

God says, "If I tell the righteous man he will surely live, but then he trusts in his righteousness and does evil, none of the righteous things he has done will be remembered; he will die for the evil he has done." (Ezek. 33:13). Individually our salvation is at stake. This came as a rude shock to me. I thought once I said "yes" to Jesus that my salvation was assured forever. It seems not. The crucial point in this verse is that there is a deliberate decision to put God second to an evil desire and then to trust in the righteousness of self and not in the righteousness of Jesus, which saves us. Either God rules our life and Jesus saves us, or we rule it and die. After we choose to enter his kingdom God never locks the door behind us; it is always open; we are free to leave at any time. Our free will is something we have from birth to death. Our choice for salvation must be ongoing because we can choose to slip out of the kingdom of heaven whenever we like. Often nobody notices—we fool everyone but God. We think we

Has the Church Forsaken Its First Love?

can go absent without leave and then sneak back. We might get back through the door of a church but we won't get back through the heavenly door. We will find it has been locked against us and we can't go back. "It is impossible for those who have once been enlightened, who have tasted the heavenly gift, who have shared in the Holy Spirit, who have tasted the goodness of the word of God and the powers of the coming age, if they fall away, to be brought back to repentance, because to their loss they are crucifying the Son of God all over again and subjecting him to public disgrace." (Heb. 6: 4-6). This leaves no room for complacency.

There is much criticism of the church and Christians in this chapter and this is because I think it is vital for us to be aware of our failings so we can do better. I don't apologize for this approach, but it is with great regret and sorrow that I feel it is necessary to do so, especially as many of the mistakes I describe are self-portraits. We have been commissioned by Jesus to teach others, and we can't do this unless we look squarely at ourselves, and then aspire to the standards of our Holy God.

NOTABLE VICTORIES OF SATAN IN HISTORY

The historical record of the church since the death of Christ at times reads more like the script of a horror movie than of the greatest love story ever told. Two obvious events that stand out are the Crusades and the Inquisition. The Crusades occurred from 1095 to 1270 AD and were characterized by barbarity and atrocities. It is recorded in history books that during battle the streets of Jerusalem ran with blood up to the horses' girth. The Medieval Inquisitions started in the 1200s AD and were instituted by the church; a papal bull was issued by Pope Innocent IV to authorize torture. The later Spanish Inquisition, from 1478 to 1834, was established by the Spanish monarchy but run by the church and note that it went for three hundred and fifty years! Torture and execution were daily occurrences but the church showed "mercy" in that if the condemned repented, they were garroted before burning; if not, they were burned alive. Interestingly the victims were handed over to the secular authorities for the actual execution because the church recognized it could not kill—how reminiscent of Jesus's trial. Then there were of course all the martyrs of the Reformation from both sides. Galileo was another victim of the blind arrogance that has permeated the organized church throughout its history. He supported the scientific discovery that the sun is the centre of the universe, which was in opposition to the church astronomers who clung to the outdated and wrong view that the earth is at the centre of the universe. The church retaliated by excommunicating him and confining him to house arrest for the last ten years of his life. Galileo was described as the Father of Modern Science and his treatment by the church may well have marked the start of the feud between science and religion that we see so prevalent today. It is no wonder people want to see the church humbled by Darwin's Theory of Evolution. It doesn't stop with Galileo in the 1600s, another well-known modern example of the church bowing to evil and abandoning God occurred in Nazi Germany, as illustrated by the events surrounding the ministry and death of the modern theologian and martyr, Dietrich Bonhoeffer.

We can't deny or duck the issue of the horrendous and ongoing failings of the Christian church. We can't undo these evils but we can acknowledge them, repent, and try to learn by the mistakes made—something we haven't done so far. With this in view, consideration of the life of Bonhoeffer is very helpful because he lived in modern times, and so it is easier for us to relate to the human failings that caused such tragedy. His story is a most graphic and disturbing illustration of the failure of Christians, particularly leaders, to fulfill their obligations to God and man alike. Bonhoeffer was born in Germany in 1906. His family was well educated, held high office in that country, and was among the socially elite. He was ordained as a Lutheran Pastor and held a teaching post at the University of Berlin. In the 1930s he realized the dangers of the Third Reich both to civilization and to the church, which it infiltrated. In an effort to firmly realign the German churches with God and not Hitler, he co-wrote the Bethel Confession, which reaffirmed the allegiance of the church to Christ and the covenant between God and the Jewish race. He sent this paper to more than twenty eminent theologians of the day but all but one refused to support him. In the end it was so watered down that he himself refused to sign it. He formed the breakaway Confessing Church, which was the major source of Christian opposition to the government. The mainstream church put Hitler first before Christ by acquiescing to its Nazification and in 1933 the national church synod approved the Aryan paragraph, which prohibited non-Aryans, including Jews, from taking parish posts. In 1936, The German Evangelical Church denounced Bonhoeffer as a pacifist and enemy of the state, after which he was dismissed from his theological teaching post at the University of Berlin (note the title of the church—an example of Satan's sense of humor), and he was

Has the Church Forsaken Its First Love?

eventually goaled for two years. As the war progressed Bonhoeffer decided that in choosing Christ over Hitler, the church over the state, he would have to work for the defeat of Germany and he became actively involved in plots to kill Hitler. It was for this he was executed. A month before the end of the war, on a cold morning, he was taken from his prison cell in Flossenburg Concentration Camp and hung naked by the neck with piano wire.

Bonhoeffer's writings make it clear that he saw the mainstream church in Germany and its leaders as complete failures in their duty to put Christ first and oppose evil. He believed the two elements of faith in the true Christ-centric church were the implementation of justice and the acceptance by Christians that they had to share in divine suffering. This meant Christians should not retreat from the world but act within it; he said there was no place for "cheap" grace, but that it was costly, and the Christian when necessary should be willing to suffer with God—and he did. He was a leader of a stature we rarely see with faith that dwarfs that of most of us.

The vast majority of his fellow clergy forsook Bonhoeffer and in doing so they not only turned away from God themselves, but even worse, they took their congregations of misguided Christians with them. Why did these men fail to fulfill their sacred duty as leaders? No doubt there were a number of reasons including fear, loss of status, money, and power. Given the circumstances at the time many of us would have done the same. The core of the problem was they forgot the church belongs to Christ.

In World War Two six million Jews and fifty million people in total perished. We can only guess at how different the outcome of this period in world history might have been if these Christian leaders had behaved differently and kept Jesus as their first love. In our community in peacetime, when we choose between church and state we don't risk death, but there are still huge conflicts between our faith and the pressures to compromise with the secular world and secular thinking. Similarly, but less dramatically than in the major events in history, we continually see the body of Christ assaulted when Christians put their own agendas and interests ahead of Christ.

Like Bonhoeffer we must be alert to the first sign of Satan on the move and be uncompromising in our opposition. What starts as a ripple can end as a tsunami. The record of the evil in the history of the organized church goes on and on and to list even major things would entail writing a book far longer than the Bible and "War and Peace" put together. In fact there is only one place that can and does hold this record in minute detail, and that is with our righteous and just God, who will surely call everyone to account.

UNIQUE RESPONSIBILITY OF LEADERS

We see destructive influences at play in all organizations including the church. Self interest, power, nepotism, status, money, sex—these all weaken or destroy individual Christians, but when church leaders succumb then whole congregations are shaken and corrupted. This poses a huge dilemma for members of the congregation. On the one hand we are told to respect our leaders, while on the other hand we follow Christ who was one of the greatest whistleblowers of all time. Like the Pharisees, some leaders today trade on the holiness of their church office. We need to have safeguards in place, to be aware of the dangers and be prepared to move quickly and decisively when necessary. And it will be necessary. Nobody who has ever attended a church could claim to have not seen the destructive effect of some of these problems close at hand. I have had the very definite impression the church is at least as vulnerable as the average secular organization. It may be more vulnerable because there are fewer checks and balances in place such as unions, media access to decision making etc. So there is less public accountability in either the preventive sense or the corrective sense. There has to be a scandal involving subjects the public finds titillating like embezzlement or pedophilia for the public spotlight to be shone on the failings of church leaders. Even adultery on the part of leaders usually remains in house and failing to obey God's teachings or work in his love doesn't even raise a public yawn. Although airing problems outside the church is so bad in terms of witnessing to the gospel, yet there is a very powerful incentive to do the right thing when we fear we will be found out. It is ironic Christians sometimes duck their responsibility to correct errors and so allow considerations of immediate worldly accountability to outweigh the hopefully distant final judgment of God.

When the leadership is in error it is in conflict with the teachings from the pulpit every Sunday. Then a lot of the time there is an atmosphere of uneasy denial until there is a huge upheaval. The church may split, or there is a steady leak of people away to another church where the cycle is likely to be well underway as well. Some people are so disillusioned they stop going to church at all.

As individuals we constantly find we struggle with trying to integrate our Christian life with our necessary involvement with the world around us. Our leaders have a threefold responsibility. They not only have the same personal challenges as everyone else, but they have a responsibility to every member of their congregation, and they also have to place the church as seamlessly as possible in the surrounding community. To be responsible for the nurturing of another person's soul is very sobering and it is not surprising that as James tells us, God demands higher standards from teachers. In other words the buck stops there. You would think we would all think twice before opening our mouth with advice. But we don't hesitate to do so any more than the parishioners Paul describes to Timothy. He accused an arrogant faction of wanting to teach others despite being ignorant and talking rubbish. We are meant to be channels through which God works, but we need to constantly endeavor to dwell in his presence or it won't be his words coming out of our mouth but our own, with very negative results.

Job and his friends had a lot to say on spiritual matters, but finally, when in God's presence, Job admitted he had spoken about things beyond his understanding. It is hard for us to face the fact we are so ignorant. We need to pray constantly that whatever we say or write—uh, oh! in the way of spiritual advice is not only correct but appropriate. Unless it is the Holy Spirit in charge we should worry. This is because wrong teaching, by word or example, can have such dire effects.

TRAPS FOR LEADERS

Power, Control

The power a church leader wields in the world at large may be small but within the church it is huge. This is because there he is seen to be God's special representative and as such he deserves great respect. If he is acting for God, his power will be the love of God, but if not, he will be harnessing the power of the world. Then with God not part of leadership, the congregation finds it is easy to fall into the trap of hearkening to the singer and not the song. The leader becomes the people's priority and not

Jesus and his gospel. Some of the people start to believe if they are popular with their leader then they are popular with God. They may go even further and see their approval by the leader as ensuring their salvation; they see him as the gatekeeper to heaven standing between them and God; they think he can forgive sins. Where is Jesus? His role has clearly been usurped. The book of Hebrews tells us that in his perfection he has superseded all human priests who are themselves sinful. They are in the same need of the pardon Jesus won on the cross once and for all for everyone. When Christ's position is usurped we find extreme practices set up where salvation is up for sale and money changes hands. The cost of noncompliance may be the threat of consignment to hell, which is used as the ultimate weapon of emotional and spiritual blackmail. Today it is usually more subtle than this and many congregations suffer from an over focus on the leader at the expense of the gospel.

We all know power corrupts. The safeguard against this is for the leader to constantly acknowledge to God, to himself or herself, and to everyone else that it is God who is the source of all his or her wisdom, power, eloquence, and success. As humans this is so hard to do. Attitudes can be seen in comments such as references to "my" church—what is to be done in "my" church, who is welcome to attend "my" church. This can result in the leader becoming over-controlling, so edicts are issued, and suggestions from members of the congregation while tolerated, are never acted upon. No person, no matter how holy, owns any church—only Jesus can make this claim.

Favoritism

In any organization there is usually an "in group" and churches are no exception. Obviously, everyone whether "in" or "out", should have equal access to leaders, especially in times of trouble to put their viewpoints. Jesus said Christian leaders should not behave with the arrogance we often see in the secular world, but should be servants of all.

Stonewalling and delay is a common strategy we are all likely to use at sometime to avoid doing our duty. Some people in the hierarchy in the church seem to have developed this into an art form and some seem more like politicians than God's elect, not that the two roles are necessarily mutually exclusive. A group of Christians, who were appealing against an unpopular decision to move their leader away, formed a delegation and went to the ruling body for discussion. They were promptly called to prayer. In itself one would hope this would be the way to start and finish the meeting. The problem was there was nothing meaningful in between. It was "horizontal prayer" meant to silence those present, it was never meant to ascend to God to make him a party to discussions. It is not the only time I have known "prayer" used in this blasphemous way as a weapon against an adversary.

There can be a culture of different standards for different people. We see that those who are approved of by their leader or church elders can have a false sense of their spiritual health and be overly reassured, while those not popular may feel a challenge to their belief that God loves them. Some people by reason of age, low socio-economic standing, quiet, or shy personalities can be inadvertently overlooked. If they have strong faith it will probably become even stronger as a result, but to the weak it can be too disheartening to persevere in the church. We need to remember "God does not show favoritism." (Rom. 2:11), and neither should we.

Denial and Cover Up

All of us groan in despair and put our head in our hands when we think of the public humiliation of Christ that has occurred over the centuries, and no less in our time, when scandals in the church have been highlighted in the media. As an example, the whole of Australia is well aware of the pervasive occurrence of pedophilia in churches around the world and here in this country. Every effort should be made to keep this horrifying evil out of churches, but to eradicate it completely is not possible any more than it is possible to eradicate any other form of evil. To deny it and cover it up is simply devastatingly unacceptable. Our Governor General fell from office on these grounds. Where was his support base? Who else in high church office gave him the bad advice he acted upon? It is a lesson we must all learn because we have all erred many times in our lives in some way that has had negative effects on others and we have seen others err. Then instead of doing something about fixing the problem, we have covered it up, or by our silence have colluded in covering it up. This results not only in harm and denial of justice to others but also we are harmed. Our actions are not only self-serving, but are self-destructive as well. It takes great courage to come out in the open when someone has been damaged. But God will see to it that the usually high price we pay for doing so will be far outweighed by the alternative. The point is God is omniscient and it is to him we have to answer, now and always. He tells us, "If a person sins because he does not speak up when he hears a public charge to testify regarding something he has seen or learned about, he will be held responsible." (Lev. 5:1).

In practice this means our evidence must be truthful and unbiased by our personal loyalties, and agendas, and any negative consequences to us and our loved ones. It is an extremely hard thing to do but God requires that we do it. Cover up in the church is so distasteful because it contravenes the very principles it espouses, so that considerations of personal and church power triumph over love of others. Regardless of earthly status, everyone has a right before God and man to equality, for truth to be acknowledged, to receive protection, and to see justice done. In cover up love has gone out the door and so has Jesus.

Where there is an ever-present threat like pedophilia, denial means it will flourish. The clergy involved must be removed from office. It is blatantly obvious it is not right to try to protect the reputation of the church and its officers at the expense of a lifetime of emotional damage to children. To do so is to move out of the presence of God.

Similarly, in the role of aged care advocate I met a high profile Christian in authority with the power to change things for the better in church-run homes. But he chose to protect his own position and presumably that of the organized church rather than to bring about necessary reform. Other high profile Christians to whom I appealed supported the abusers of the elderly in aged care by refusing to take any action and by covering up. These people still represent one of my own personal challenges in forgiveness. Incredibly they preferred to protect their own reputation, status, and job, (which at the worst would have taken only a very minor hit), and that of friends, rather than take steps to redress a wrong and prevent ongoing major abuse. It was the polished performance, the bland smile, the earnest but false promises that made it so disturbing—Satan at his "best". Isaiah described such people and the judgment of God, which will surely fall on them, "Woe to those who call evil good and good evil, who put darkness for light and light for darkness, who put bitter for sweet and sweet for bitter." (Isa. 5:20).

Direct abuse of the very powerless is an extreme example of which most of us are not guilty, hopefully not just because of lack of opportunity. That we are similarly vulnerable to putting our interests first in major issues seems obvious when we examine our own record in minor matters. That is where we have to start so that when something major comes unexpectedly, we will get it right and work with Jesus not against him.

In one case of elder abuse a very nervous carer, who badly needed to keep her job, gave evidence in a tribunal because she wished to protect the elderly where she worked. As a result she was sacked, despite the fact the head man in the organization was a high profile Christian whom I had personally acquainted with the facts. Jesus won't forget what happened and all those involved will have to give an account. The nurse is significantly younger than I am, so I am likely to be in the audience when she sees Jesus face to face—what a reception she will get! I can't wait to hear exactly what he will say to her, but I guess it will be along the lines that whatever we do for or against another falls with full force on him, "The King will reply, 'I tell you the truth, whatever you did for one of the least of these brothers of mine, you did for me.'" (Matt. 25:40).

We should see all our actions in this light: if we hurt anyone in any way we hurt Jesus, and if we act in mercy we delight him. Realizing this full implication of our behavior and always being aware of the big picture makes it much easier for us to lift our game, because even if our love for another is under strain our love for Jesus is not. We can then act wholeheartedly for him if not for the other person, and having done so, love for the other person is nurtured and blossoms.

It is said we are judged by works and saved by faith, but this is only true if we have *saving* faith. Only the faith that results in good works is saving faith; so it is not just that expressing our love for Jesus by right behavior to others is necessary for his sake, but it is critical for our own salvation. This is not because we earn our way to heaven by good works but because rejecting others is the same as rejecting him—which is to let go of our lifeline. To say we forfeit salvation by bad behavior is not to say we earn salvation by good behavior. We can't lose what we don't have and without Jesus we don't have salvation; good works are only relevant after that. After we have been saved by Jesus and demonstrated this saving faith by good works, we then face judgment on the basis of what we have done, both good and bad. In the same way we go to extraordinary lengths for those people we love, why not for Jesus?

Corrupting the Message of Scripture with Prevailing Culture and Tradition

In the recent past, excommunication was pretty popular with the ruling body of the church and that often meant banishment from the community as well. To the person concerned this meant abandoning all hope in this life with the promise of hell after death. It seems to have been as easy to qualify in the church for excommunication two hundred years ago as it was to qualify in the courts for a trip from the old country to permanent residence in the colonies. Justice seems to have been as misrepresented in one as the other. It was more about defending the ruling power whether church or secular than about reform and rehabilitation. Fortunately for us this approach has waned in popularity and we are more clearly hearing Jesus calling and encouraging sinners to turn to him and be restored.

It is so easy to see the flaws of history and these flaws seem so grossly obvious we wonder how they happened. The problem is we do the same; we are just more subtle. We may be less obvious than in the past but unfortunately future generations are likely to regard us in the same light. I remember losing a certain amount of confidence in my doctor when I read a medical textbook my grandmother left me. Born in 1871, she had been a midwife but the book was a handbook of general medicine and described the understanding and treatment of diseases in her time. After reading it, I wondered what my doctor would do to me just as confidently and just as wrongly. At one time the discovery of the application of leeches was a great breakthrough in medical science. Whoever thought of that was greatly praised. Recently it was maggots for wound care. Now it is chemotherapy. In another one hundred years all these treatments will have been relegated to the same category of the quaint, the extraordinary, and the horrifying. The misguided medical practices of the past demonstrate how sure and persuasive the current experts in any field always are in their ideas, but how wrong history often proves them to be. If the result is that someone dies in the company of a leech who would otherwise have died anyway, then not a lot is lost. But in the spiritual realm if it means someone is hindered in finding God, then everything of value is lost.

The Scriptures were written against the background of the prevailing politics and culture of ancient Israel. Jesus's ability to show the alignment of the eternal scriptural messages with the culture of his day, as well as that of Abraham's day, and with modern times has had a huge ongoing impact on our understanding. He made it clear the Old Testament is as much a part of the story of God's Covenant with us as the New Testament, although some Christians miss this point. Since Jesus, we have had to rely on the Holy Spirit to enlighten us about God's truth and to interpret previously unknown scenarios we meet today. The more we do so, the more we will move with the times and the fewer mistakes we will make—the less we will apply the spiritual equivalent of leeches to a sick soul.

Emotional Isolation

One of the costs of leadership and responsibility in any profession is isolation because it is the nature of leadership that some distance has to be maintained from those who are being led. The result is there are fewer people around the leader with common problems. This strain is high in any arena but particularly so in the church. Satan ensures that leadership outside the church has compensations like money with the comfort and power it brings. The world is impressed and offers a somewhat reluctant respect to these people. Not so church leaders. In the entertainment media they are often portrayed as ineffectual, confused, or even ridiculous. Maybe this is because our leaders bring a message of hope from someone who was by worldly standards a loser and who died two thousand years ago, "we preach Christ crucified: a stumbling block to Jews and foolishness to Gentiles," (1 Cor. 1:23). Jesus is foolishness to those who only see his death and not the power of God in his resurrection.

As a member of a congregation, I have been upset by the lack of support for stressed leaders given by their fellow clergy or their superiors in the hierarchy of the church when significant problems have arisen. I suspect this is often the case. Leaders can feel outnumbered and under siege and develop a defensive sense of "me against the world", as they struggle unaided. This may not be paranoia but reality. Paul suffered in this way. At one of his trials all his support fell away as everyone left him. In one letter he said everyone in the Provence of Asia had deserted him. That really could be described as a mass exodus! To make his sense of abandonment complete it evidently included those he trusted the most.

On one occasion I saw members of a minority power group oppose their leader like a lynch mob. This was a leader who had served God faithfully preaching the gospel for over thirty years. A considerable part of that time he and his family were in physical danger and as well he had spent many years in the midst of his attackers serving them. The events were reminiscent of the death of Caesar in the secular world, because the coup leader held a position of trust— "et tu Brute?", but occurring within the church as it did, it was a replay of Judas's betrayal of Christ, whom this man represented.

We are so arrogant. Many of us have a record of service to God that is pathetic in comparison to our leaders whom we tear down. People who lead a coup and unseat the leader should think soberly of what they are doing. It has the same effect as it had on the disciples on the night of Jesus's arrest. He told them, "It is written: 'I will strike the shepherd, and the sheep of the flock will be scattered.'" (Matt. 26:31). It is the same in the church today when we attack the leader, members of the congregation may be set back spiritually or lost altogether and this is whether they are the ones who stood with the leader or against him, whether they were on the "winning" side or the "losing" side. We can't do much worse than this. God says, "all you who light fires and provide yourselves with flaming torches, go, walk in the light of your fires and of the torches you have set ablaze. This is what you shall receive from my hand: You will lie down in torment." (Isa. 50:11).

When a member of the church has behaved so divisively that he has caused a split in the church, surely he has thereby disqualified himself from holding a position of authority in that church. To have succeeded he has obviously wielded power and by its very effect it is unlikely to have been God's power. The next leader may feel it is too hard to take away this man's authority. It may be far easier to close his mind and bow to him, and thus become a puppet on a string. How then does the leader do God's will at the same time? Higher authorities in the church should clear the way for the new leader by banning trouble-makers from holding office.

Short of organizing a coup, there are always those members of the congregation who have an attitude of criticism or want to compete with the leader in holiness or defining church priorities. Probably just as hard to handle, some relate with sycophantic adulation, "Whoever flatters his neighbor is spreading a net for his feet." (Prov. 29:5). We are called upon to praise God for our leaders and to love, respect, and support them but this other human flattery is destructive to everything that should be the aim of the church. A mix of criticism and flattery is all pretty confusing feedback and potentially equally damaging. Paul sets us the example to follow when speaking of Epaphroditus, "Welcome him in the Lord with great joy, and honor men like him." (Phil. 2:29).

High Standards, Flawed People

We require our leaders to be "all things to all men." There is an expectation they should be perfect in both their behavior and their ability. We require our leader to be a good teacher, hold our hand at a moment's notice any hour of the day or night if we are in trouble, live on a pittance, never get annoyed or frustrated, always hold the right opinion, (ours), and always make the right decision. All we want is perfection. Not only should the leader be perfect himself, but so should his wife, children, grandchildren, and second cousin twice removed. We don't allow for youth and worldly inexperience, or for age and battle fatigue, or for the fact the leader like us is also on a spiritual journey and has to start somewhere, and will have trouble with some of his milestones along the way. We can quote Scripture to justify our unloving attitude—after all God told Abraham to be blameless. Unfortunately there has only been one Abraham and he is not in our local church. Paul told Titus before he went to minister at Crete that an overseer must be blameless. This refers to the leaders so that is all fair enough, we can accept that, until we find one of many verses describing the standards God has set for the rest of us because we are also told to be blameless. This is a bit disconcerting, we know we are altogether delightful and lovely, but "blameless"? Not quite. Where does this leave us? It leaves us at the foot of the cross, all of us together there—our leaders and us.

Christ leads us towards this ever present goal of holiness, but unlike God who is perfect in his excellence, we will never achieve it in our own right. To think we can succeed is Old Covenant thinking. If we could do it there would be no need for Jesus. As it is, we are only blameless when covered by his cloak of righteousness. If we do not strive ourselves to move towards this blameless state then we are not travelling with Christ because that is the travel plan he has designed for us, "Be perfect, therefore, as your heavenly Father is perfect." (Matt. 5:48). We will know many failures. Not only do we have to forgive ourselves and pick ourselves up, but we have to do the same for our fellow travelers including our leaders when they fail. Paul told the Galatians to restore a sinner gently and to carry each other's burdens, while all the time being aware we are also vulnerable to temptation. Right behavior brings praise to God.

Peter's story is an inspiring example of someone who started out like many of us, confident in his faith and his ability and then put in a very patchy performance. He was the first to identify Jesus as the Messiah, yet on the night of his betrayal he denied knowing him, withdrew his support, and abandoned him. He left Jesus alone but for his enemies surrounding him and this action heaped sorrow upon Jesus and himself. What if we had been there in Peter's time and because of this awful lapse banished him from the company of the apostles? Jesus foresaw Peter's failures, but he also foresaw that Peter would eventually spread the gospel, the rock of the Christian faith. Peter preached the first sermon at Pentecost after Jesus's death and three thousand people were redeemed to God.

In the name of Christ we should always pick each other up, because the person failing badly spiritually today might come back to succeed tomorrow as Peter did. It is by God's grace through Jesus and his power in us through the Holy Spirit that we can rise again and again after failure. Is it worth the effort, this continual cycle of trying, and failing, and trying again? Through his bitter tears Peter showed he knew his faults, but he also knew the love of God and could give us this message from God: "But you are a chosen people, a royal priesthood, a Holy nation, a people belonging to God, that you may declare the praises of him who called you out of darkness into his wonderful light." (1 Pet. 2:9). When compared to the fact of our flawed performance, this marvelous verse taken seriously should be enough to make us humble.

Pressure to Perform to Earthly Values

Leaders are not immune to objective measurements of their performance like numbers of regular church attenders or amount of money collected. This translates into pressure to give the congregation the warm fuzzy stuff, the spiritual milk off a spoon and to stay away from or water down the confrontational topics such as standards of behavior or hell. If a real life example of bad behavior is recounted in the sermon the congregation is often first soothed by being told it happened elsewhere. It is usually about something so gross that even in our worst moments we are unlikely to do it. The only likely effect is to make us more self righteous. Better challenges might be to ask, "how many strangers did you talk to at morning tea last week, how many people did you inconvenience yourself to help during the last week, to how many people did you turn the other cheek in the last week, for whom did you pray beside you and yours?" It takes guts to challenge the congregation and shift us out of our comfort zone. This dilemma was foreseen, "For the time will come when men will not put up with sound doctrine. Instead, to suit their own desires, they will gather around them a great number of teachers to say what their itching ears want to hear." (2 Tim. 4:3). It comes back to you and me and giving our continuing support to the leader whether he is telling us something that makes us feel comfortable or uncomfortable.

Obligation to Rebuke Wrongdoers

Any organization has the right to set the rules for membership and the Christian church has this right. Similarly if an individual doesn't like Christian doctrine then that person can choose not to belong to a Christian church. Christ spoke against the Jewish church and was accused of blasphemy, but the difference is that Christ upheld the doctrine of the Old Testament and his "blasphemy" was to show the church of his day was not doing this. This is not what many anti-establishment people do, they destroy but they do not build up.

There is the option of taking the ultimate step with someone who is seen to have erred by removing them from the church. Less draconian action is to ban them from teaching their views from a position of authority. This decision has to turn on whether basic doctrine is in danger rather than that controversial issues are under discussion. If we ban a perceived offender from attending church at all, we may exclude someone who with a little more love and patience would have eventually come to an understanding of the truth. No doubt God raises up people when action is necessary, some will be godly like the prophets of old, some will be ungodly as the Assyrian nation was. For the godly it must be one of the greatest responsibilities we could be given, and for all but a few, a no-go zone. Most Christians have more than enough difficulty in deciding on the correct opinion and attitude in such a situation, let alone on what should be done about it. Frankly, I hope I never have to make a decision to exclude someone from the congregation, and for obvious reasons I feel confident God has no intention of asking me.

Paul told Titus to be prepared to rebuke anyone causing problems in the church. It is the unhappy duty of leaders to do this rebuking of other Christians and no one wins a popularity poll this way. So it is usually not done effectively other than in extreme circumstances. Within the congregation sometimes the conscientious majority lose heart because someone who is continually disruptive to the smooth running of the church is not being restrained by the leader.

When he saw a problem Paul didn't pussyfoot around, even with other leaders. It seems Peter let himself be pressured into confusion against his better judgment by people from the church in Jerusalem who were preaching that dietary rules and circumcision were necessary for salvation. Paul spoke up openly against him because this false doctrine was leading people astray including Barnabas. If someone is misrepresenting the gospel by their talk or behavior then other people may follow in this error, not only the unfaithful, but also the confused faithful.

When we are the one rebuked, we often react by blaming the leader rather than ourselves, and with a toss of our curls we not only leave the church, but try to take as many people as possible with us. Not all have a listening ear, "Like an earring of gold or an ornament of fine gold is a wise man's rebuke to a listening ear." (Prov. 25:12). Not only members of the congregation but the leader himself must be prepared to be rebuked and respond appropriately. It is disappointing when a mistake is seen to have been made but a lesson has not been learned.

I heard a member of the congregation level charges against the leader in such a way that it was obvious there was deep hurt following events that had occurred. I had no knowledge of these events but what was described certainly happens in churches; whether it happened in this case, I don't know. But I do know the person concerned was extremely distraught. This alone should make it very important to the leader, but I did not find his response impressive. Private conversations were leaked, loose judgmental discussion occurred amongst others not in a position of authority, and the person's reliability as a witness was questioned. It seemed people confused loyalty to their leader and the implied criticism of themselves, with a genuine desire to see a fair and loving resolution. Some weeks later the same leader gave a sermon on responsibilities of the congregation to their leader, without reference to the responsibilities of leaders to the congregation. He saw the need to teach others, but may have missed the opportunity to grow himself. The manner of handling the situation seemed to me to be secular not spiritual. Those with a judgmental attitude would have been hardened; those without would have been disheartened by a perceived abuse of power on the part of the leadership that resulted in lack of justice—which was the right to be heard in a fair, confidential, and unbiased way.

Unbalanced Teaching, Half Truths, Pushing Own Agenda

Sermons can be used to push the leader's own opinions. The teaching of basic indisputable doctrine on a scriptural basis can give way to the preaching of opinion on controversial topics not discussed in the Bible. Many such topics were not an issue in Christ's time, e.g., abortion, female clergy. Of course the leader has every right to have an opinion on these things and to express it. Given that he has been chosen as a teacher by God we would hope he would make his ideas known to us. But the pulpit may not be the place to do so because it can detract from the importance of God's word, especially if verses are interpreted in an unbalanced way. Maybe more informal meetings would be better suited to deal with these issues. The gospel is the leader's forte but sometimes people with a wider experience of living in the world outside the church have valuable insights to offer into these modern issues.

The media love to publicize a strongly held view by a church leader and present it in a biased and bigoted way. This is especially easy to do if the leader *is* biased and bigoted. It can be so hard to stand firm in the faith but not err by inappropriate intransigence. It is only in the delivery of one message that all Christians should demonstrate an immovable attitude whether in private or public, and that message is the love of God in Christ.

Pride

Knowledge infused with the wisdom of God is something we should all seek and it will make us humble. Without this wisdom, the accumulation of knowledge will enable our pride to flourish. Paul illustrated the fact with this comment to the Corinthians about eating food that had been sacrificed to idols: "We know that we all possess knowledge. Knowledge puffs up, but love builds up." (1 Cor. 8:1). In decision making about dietary restrictions on spiritual grounds the elders were relying on the knowledge they carried in their own heads, which was misleading as it often is, rather than God's wisdom, which is always interpreted through love. The relevance to us is there is a real danger that the more familiar we are with the Scriptures, and church organization, and activities the more proud we become. Then instead of becoming less proud overall, we just swap our pride in earthly achievements for pride in our religious achievements. So we listen to our own ego more and more, and to the Holy Spirit less and less. The essence of pride is that we praise ourselves not God. The more learned we are and the more earthly power we wield, the more vulnerable we are to this problem. This leaves the leaders in the greatest danger and amongst them it is the hierarchy at the top who must have the biggest battle. We have all seen some leaders exuding smugness, self importance, or false humility. Subjecting them to our own wobbly values doesn't help them. Our focus should be to love God so that we might be of some real support to them.

Keeping the Congregation in the Loop

There has to be a chain of command in every organization and Paul made this very clear. However, I think when difficulties or dissent occur in the church involving leaders or the members of the congregation, the latter should be informed and given the opportunity to comment. A leader was once asked to call the congregation to prayer to address a major upheaval that was occurring. That idea didn't get off the ground. I don't know why, prayer should be our first priority. I suspect it was because the leaders wanted to deal with the situation in their own way, and so the less the congregation knew the easier this would be. Many people who had been faithfully serving the church for many years said they had no idea of any of the issues. The matter escalated and people left the church. I wonder if any permanently turned away from God; we may never know—but that some are permanently scarred is something I can personally confirm. Informing the congregation doesn't mean it has to be a "free for all". It seems better to have open orderly involvement than gossip, half truths, and lies.

Delegating

There should be recognition by the leader and the congregation that no leader can be strong in every aspect of church activities. We all relate better to one age group than another; some of us feel comfortable being with children, some with the aged. Some are skilled teachers, some skilled in pastoral care, some in evangelism. There is a congregation full of talent because God has seen to it that there is. The leader needs to encourage people outside his field of interest at least as much as those inside it. He can do this by distributing responsibility to the congregation appropriately while remaining actively supportive of all. Otherwise it will be an unbalanced weakened church not fulfilling its potential and the leader will come under criticism.

The End Doesn't Justify the Means

If we feel very strongly about achieving something, it is easy to decide the end justifies the means. This is dangerous because sooner or later we risk compromising those principles of behavior that honor God. We are not meant to have tunnel vision and forge ahead recklessly in the pursuit of our God-given vision or some goal regardless of whom we run over in the process. How unlike Jesus that thinking is! If a goal is pursued in such a way that people are offended and leave the church, then this negative feedback should be used to modify the approach. It is not good enough to consider, for example, that new people should be brought into the church at the cost of others leaving. If the method is right there will be a place for everyone. It is not that a vision should be abandoned, but it should be pursued in the right way.

RESPONSIBILITIES OF THE CONGREGATION

Only the Power of God Changes Us

Getting our own spiritual journey on track will result in the best support we can give to our leaders. There are many passages in the Bible teaching us the behavior God wants from us. We know these goals but not how to reach them. We hear a sermon from Titus and go home full of resolve. By lunch time the whole idea seems a bit daunting. By Monday we are too busy to think about it and by Tuesday we have altogether given up on the impossible. That is because in human strength it is impossible. We simply can't live up to God's standards on our own, and even with him it takes a lifetime to really progress. Besides, we comfort ourselves with the desperate hope that only religious fanatics worry enough about all that holiness to actually try to do it. But once we accept we want to please God, and we can't do it alone without his power, then we have already made a great start. Maybe the people who give up little for salvation have a greater struggle in pursuing their path to spiritual maturity. If the rich man seeking eternal life in Jesus's parable had given up his wealth then everything after that might have seemed relatively easy. The Muslim converting to Christianity in the Middle East puts his life on the line. It is usually the converse in Australia; we don't give up a lot to call ourselves Christian. When we live in a Christian country and are born into a Christian family, if we become Christian ourselves, we are in agreement with those around us, and so gain in popularity, and our life actually becomes easier. Even so, there is still the outside world to live in, and if our decision is all encompassing from the heart, after that it gets hard.

It is the same old formula for success, which means focusing fully on God and endeavoring to dwell in his presence. Then the Holy Spirit will be our Counselor. If we leave ourselves open to him, then when the time is right he will make us aware of some terrible character flaw or pattern of bad behavior we never knew we had. I have found it is often something I have for years accused someone else of doing. It takes a while for me to believe it. At first I think I must be mistaken. It is not the sort of revelation one hopes for, but eventually the truth has to be faced and a long hard journey to change begins. It is a great buzz the first time an opportunity to err is successfully resisted. I imagine it is very like the feeling one would get after bungee jumping for the first time—a comparison I never intend to verify. This striving for perfection never ends. It is so hard because it means constantly putting God's agenda ahead of our own, and where our behavior is concerned that means putting the interests of others ahead of our own. It means when someone hurts us in some way we should not tell the world how rotten they are but react with love and forgiveness. In symbolic language Jesus has told us what to do if someone takes something from us, whether it is their love, their support, our reputation, our money, or anything else. In effect, he said we are to freely give double what is being taken from us.

Aspiring to the perfect standards of Jesus's behavior should be reflected in our whole interaction with the world. We should be taking the initiative ever aware that we are God's representatives and what we do affects his reputation. If our motive is truly to serve God and not ourselves then our service will have the effect God wants it to have, and that means doing it his way. If God is in our heart then he will be seen to be in everything we do because it will be in his power we are doing it. It is sobering to read this warning from John the Baptist: "The ax is already at the root of the trees, and every tree that does not produce good fruit will be cut down and thrown into the fire." (Luke 3:9). It is only the amazing patience of God that Jesus describes in the following parable that enables us to dither around for so long. In this story the owner of a vineyard gave instructions for a fig tree to be cut down because it had failed to bear fruit over a three-year period. The man who cared for the vineyard asked if he could first give the tree extra care, and then if it still bore no fruit in another year, he would cut it down. We need to heed the warning; "a year" goes by very quickly.

Honoring Leaders

Paul tells us not only to accept the leader's authority, but to do so willingly in a supportive way to lighten the leader's task of responsibility. This helps to establish an atmosphere of mutual cooperation and everyone benefits. Paul speaks as one with authority, but immediately after exhorting the congregation to obey their leader and still in the middle of urging good behavior, he asks them almost as an aside to pray for him and his companions. This shows Paul's amazing humility and his recognition of the fact that leaders and those they lead are all involved in a joint effort serving God. Shouldn't we jump at the chance of having the tax collector in Jesus's parable pray for us? Imagine if he had prayed for the Pharisee present at the time. That may be what is on offer. New Christians don't feel holy enough to pray for others in church gatherings and prefer the perceived church elite to do so. Paul had no such concerns.

The Impartiality of God's Law

In the Old Testament the law applied equally to the Israelite and the alien. Jesus also confirmed God does not show favoritism when he told the Pharisees that tracing their genes back to Abraham would not excuse their sin. Certainly when something questionable has been done, Christians seem to have a scale of holiness in their mind relevant to the offender, against which they rate the offence. On that they base their response. The result is atheists are seen to be unquestionably wrong, fellow Christians are seen to have meant well, clergy must have some special insight, and those at the top in the hierarchy are simply always right. In other words we see wrong as right. This doesn't serve justice. God is impartial. His truth is absolute.

Similarly within the congregation, it is as though we have an artificial distinction in our minds to explain the discord we are forced to admit exists in the church. We distinguish two groups, the good people and the sinners. The first group is very godly, and much loved by God and their few mistakes are always entirely defensible. This group consists of us, and our friends, and the people who like us. The second group is all the other people, the sinners, who are forever doing and saying the wrong thing and we feel sorry for God who must be struggling to love them. We wonder what they are doing in the church at all and when God's patience will wear out and all those dire warnings in the Bible will fall on their unworthy heads. This concept works very well for us and enables us to feel warm and fuzzy in our comfort zone until we are reminded, "There is no difference, for all have sinned and fall short of the glory of God," (Rom. 3:22– 23). No difference—surely not? That sounds like there are no good and bad people but we are all one motley throng. That means us, our friends, our leaders, the people who don't like us—the whole congregation are all sinners, are all flawed. It is hard to believe and many of us can only recognize we are the exception. If we do come to terms with our own standing, which in our natural state is up to our neck in evil, Jesus will be able to do something of value with us. For our part, the first thing we have to lay down is our pride, and this won't happen unless we realize the full enormity of our own shortcomings and the love of God with which we were ransomed. The only righteousness we have is the righteousness we have in Jesus.

When it comes to taking action against someone in the church who in our opinion has transgressed, we typically give them "the cold shoulder". We first need to remember who and what we are ourselves, then to remember the love and mercy God shows us continually, to walk as closely to Jesus as we can, and to pray ceaselessly for guidance from the Holy Spirit. The easiest place for God to touch any of us should be in church. So it would seem to follow that this is the best place for sinners—all of us, to be. If we pressure all those we consider wrongdoers, to the extent they leave the church, if we are realistic and fair, there would be no one left.

Has the Church Forsaken Its First Love?

Our Role in Opposing Evil in the Church: To Act or Not to Act

Human nature is such that many times thinking Christians will be in disagreement with a member of the congregation or the leader. At times this will not be just a matter of opinion on some trivial matter, but concern transgression of Christian doctrine, or the behavior expected of Christians as written in the Bible. When and how to speak up, and when to be silent, is perhaps the greatest challenge we face. The hardest aspect of this topic is that mostly, particularly in relation to the leaders, we are not talking about a perceived wrong action on the part of the ungodly, but of the godly. This should be deeply concerning to us. The principles are on the one hand, the church as a whole as well as individuals have to be protected against pollution, but on the other hand, we are not to be critical, judgmental, and self-righteous in how we go about achieving this.

There are numerous Bible verses to choose from to support both the silent and the vocal approach. In the context of our behavior as a member of a church, there are those verses that warn about the destructive effects of false doctrine, the ease with which people are led astray, how quickly we fall into sin and blasphemy, and our duty to act decisively to prevent and address these problems. There is no shortage of verses directing us to take draconian action. In Proverbs we find this: "Blows and wounds cleanse away evil, and beatings purge the inmost being." (Prov. 20:30)—we could have a baseball bat beside the pulpit! We know many church institutions like schools and orphanages have followed such verses enthusiastically.

Paul says when talking about trouble-makers in the Thessalonian church: "Do not associate with him, in order that he may feel ashamed." (2 Thess. 3:14–15). To make us all the more confused he concludes the instructions to the Thessalonians by saying, "Yet do not regard him as an enemy, but warn him as a friend." Here there is ambiguity because we are told to take it upon ourselves to punish the other person by causing him to feel shame, and to do so by exclusion, which is a very cruel and cowardly action to take. How you would do this while continuing to regard him as a friend and not an enemy is hard to believe, because to paraphrase Paul's words he says: "think of the person as a friend but treat him like an enemy." Just before those verses Paul was exhorting the church to stay strong in their faith and saw a group of people amongst them as a real threat in this regard. In Titus he says, "Warn a divisive person once, and then warn him a second time. After that, have nothing to do with him. You may be sure that such a man is warped and sinful; he is self-condemned," (Titus 3:10–11).

Jesus was divisive, and judging by the way the church leaders treated him, they could have written those verses. Jesus said his gospel would even turn members of a family against each other. And so we crucified this divisive man, our Lord of glory. Of course he was God and we are not, but his life is an example for us to copy. Similarly the purpose of the prophets before Jesus was mostly to condemn Israel for its rebellious ways. And they often died for it. It is the tiny minority of whistleblowers who eventually hear applause ringing in their ears in this earthly life. If this is your unhappy duty one day, then be prepared. We see people of integrity in the spotlight in the media trying to clean up a mess or frank corruption in the community. They usually lose their job and become the victims of character assassination as well as failing to change the status quo. That doesn't mean they have failed to do God's will. It would be a world without hope if Jesus had not spoken up. Jesus brought a message of God's love and even his words in anger were motivated by love. When we sort out problems among us in the church, anger is dangerous territory; it is like a two-year-old playing with a loaded gun. Speaking genuinely in peace from our heart should be our aim.

Paul takes a different approach with the Galatian church when he says if someone transgresses, "you who are spiritual should restore him gently. But watch yourself, or you also may be tempted." (Gal. 6:1). For reasons known only to Paul, the right advice for each church was totally different. All these verses taken together show we cannot take any one set as a stand-alone instruction, not those in Proverbs, not those directed to the Galatian church and not those directed to the Thessalonian church. If we consider all the wrong decisions we see all the time, it obviously takes the wisdom of God to know what course of action we should take when faced with a particular circumstance.

It gets even harder for us to sort out—in a letter to the Corinthians Paul made a distinction between how we should react to fellow Christians and how we should react to non-Christians when they are in error. He says judging those outside the church is none of his business. The disciples were sometimes as confused as we are as to how they should react when they saw error in non-believers. In Gethsemane, when men came to arrest Jesus, Peter stepped forward and cut off the ear of one of them, an action Jesus promptly reversed. When the Samaritan village refused hospitality to Jesus, James and John asked if Jesus wanted them to pray for the village to be consumed by fire, but he rebuked them. In the first case it was understandable that because of the direct and urgent threat of the circumstances Peter didn't refer to Jesus—he just acted reflexly, whereas James and John didn't act unilaterally, rather they asked Jesus. That is the crux of the matter, because we can't know the mind of God. In order to know his will in anything we have to specifically ask him. The disciples also showed great faith in believing that with Jesus's approval they had the power to set the town on fire. These events should be a warning to us to ask him first and act later rather than the other way around.

The dangers of condoning evil are all too true but the measures we take to confront it must be tempered by all the other pertinent instructions about love and forgiveness. In the gospels Jesus repeatedly tells us not to judge anyone and if we do we will incur judgment. There is a critical point on which Paul's instructions and those of Jesus are reconciled: where the role of judge is forced upon us by circumstances, there is no place for unilateral decision making without God, (and even then we should judge the act and not the person). Jesus says if he judges then he does so according to what pleases God. He always acted in God's will; often we don't, especially if we are in conflict with someone. On the infrequent occasions where we feel it is our duty to intervene in a situation, we need to do so from our knees not from a lofty height. Mostly what God wants us to do is to mind our own business so we can do what we are supposed to be doing, which is cleaning ourselves up, "You hypocrite, first take the plank out of your own eye, and then you will see clearly to remove the speck from your brother's eye." (Matt. 7:5). We are supposed to be looking to Jesus not at each other. When we compare ourselves to him we will eventually see the plank.

Some people favor never speaking up, especially against leaders; they have a lot of material to which they can refer and this material includes the scriptural principles of submitting to leaders, not judging others, and being peace loving. On the other hand in Ezekiel, God says he will hold us equally guilty with the perpetrator of evil if we don't speak up. The difficulty arises because no situation or circumstance we meet is ever the same. So at times we should do one thing while at other times the opposite. If we always reach for the same verse for advice to cover the same type of situation we may as well flip a coin.

The measuring rod we instinctively use is always our own interest and not the love and laws of God. When we are unhappy about the leader, or any one else our first action should be to pray. We need to know what Bible verses to act on, those encouraging us to speak up or those discouraging us from doing so. To the mind of man there is ambiguity everywhere in the Scriptures. There is no way we can work out what we should do; sometimes we should and sometimes we shouldn't. We don't know God's plans in the matter and we can't see the immediate chain of events let alone events down the track. We need to familiarize ourselves with the full spectrum of wisdom on every topic in the Bible, but we have to rely totally on the Holy Spirit to direct us to the relevant instructions in any particular circumstance. Jesus's example of constant prayer should be our goal. We may have to pray many times before we know what we should do, if anything. God doesn't take us into his confidence in everything. Even when the situation remains unresolved, if that is what God wants, then through our prayer he will give us peace about it and take the burden of it from us.

Pressures of Congregation on Clergy

Wherever humans are found grouped together there will be power struggles to establish a pecking order. The church is no exception. The really ambitious may eventually totally undermine the leader. Most of us recognize that we are blessed with the love of God and try in his power to express this love, but at the same time we constantly struggle against our basic instinct to promote ourselves in some way. We take on some role in the church, and then our natural inclination often leads us to become quite ferocious in guarding what we now perceive as our very own territory. Woe betides anyone who thinks they have a good suggestion about a better way of going about something relevant to our patch. It is so bad because it is inefficient and alienates others, especially new-comers who feel more at home if they are allowed relaxed participation. We excuse ourselves by fostering the idea in our own mind, and the minds of a few other very gullible people whom we gather around us, that we are being very Holy serving God while fortunately at the same time being blessed with incredible talent. If we have to face morning tea with scones badly arranged on a plate we will probably all be able to cope. We forget God doesn't need our talent, he likes to work with the weak and the foolish—something for which I am personally very grateful.

There is always another aspect of course and that is we all make better armchair critics than workers. The cure for this is to take on some chore slightly out of our comfort zone. It is great training in humility—if we can stay the course. If only we could all be like the people who have a record of cleaning the church for years. It is an unpleasant job without status. They are never in the public eye receiving accolades and usually only get a mention, and then not by name, when there is a plaintive cry from the pulpit for more manpower. How they must delight God! We would all much rather run a Bible study group or arrange a social function—not that these activities are easy. Whatever it is God puts on our heart to do, we have to constantly remind ourselves Jesus expects us to have the servant heart.

War in the Heavenly Realms

It is easy to forget every struggle we are involved in here on earth is also part of a cosmic war that is raging unseen around us, "For our struggle is not against flesh and blood, but against the rulers, against the authorities, against the powers of this dark world and against the spiritual forces of evil in the heavenly realms." (Eph. 6:12). The earth is enemy territory and here we are involved in this other greater war whether it is an inner struggle to overcome some flaw in ourselves like unforgiveness, or whether we are struggling against another person whom we consider to be not acting in God's will. Any action we take, or fail to take, could have effects far exceeding our realization. It is like fighting at an outpost where we can't see the main action. Whether deliberately or in ignorance, we don't want to be engaging in "friendly fire" on our own troops, thereby compromising this unseen spiritual battle of which we are a part. There is no place for ad hoc decisions or knee jerk reactions; we are always out of our depth. We have to continually defer in prayer to God in everything because what we do within ourselves, in our church, and here on earth impacts on the entire Kingdom of God.

God Moves without Our Help

Any behavior that dishonors God from the apparently trivial to the apparently major is blasphemy, so where do we draw the line, how much wrongdoing in the church should we tolerate before taking action? We know an evil can start small but spread like a cancer through the congregation. Equally we have to realize faith is God-given and will be tested, strengthened, and protected by him. Much of the time we are not directly responsible for the actions of others and probably just get in his way. Sapphira and Ananias withheld money from God and lied about it to the congregation. When confronted, both Ananias and his wife Sapphira immediately dropped down dead and yet in both cases no human lifted a finger. In the same way God can move without human aid against sin, he also moves to protect his own, "he holds victory in store for the upright, he is a shield to those whose walk is blameless, for he guards the course of the just and protects the way of his faithful ones." (Prov. 2:7–8). In deciding to rush to God's defense it is easy to forget he has it all under control without us. He often chooses to work in concert with us and through us, but he is omnipotent and certainly doesn't have to involve us at all. Often it is in spite of our strenuous but misguided efforts on his behalf that he executes his will. The best way for us to defend God is to remove everything within ourselves that offends him.

Choosing the Company We Keep

Old Covenant wisdom has to be enriched by the New Covenant law of love so that the combined effect is God's will in action. An example of taking the law in isolation could be this general advice, "Do not set foot on the path of the wicked or walk in the way of evil men. Avoid it, do not travel on it; turn from it and go on your way." (Prov. 4:14-15). To some extent the importance of these words is self evident to thinking Christians. We know we risk starting on a downhill slide when we are in bad company and our standards drop. However, maybe it doesn't always mean so much that we should remove ourselves physically from the presence of evil people, but rather we should remove ourselves spiritually from their influence. Jesus never removed himself physically from the company of sinners, but he certainly was never influenced by their evil ways. When the Pharisees queried Jesus about his choice of dinner companions, he answered, "It is not the healthy who need a doctor, but the sick. But go and learn what this means: 'I desire mercy, not sacrifice.' For I have not come to call the righteous, but sinners." (Matt. 9:12–13). Thankfully, if there is one thing Jesus can't do, it is to turn away from sinners. If he had removed himself physically from us we would never have been saved. Yet it is true that we don't harness the fullness of his strength. We are so weak that at times we would lose our way if we didn't turn our back when we see sin in action. Jude strikes a balance here, "Be merciful to those who doubt; snatch others from the fire and save them; to others show mercy, mixed with fear—hating even the clothing stained by corrupted flesh." (Jude 1:22–23). The point to grasp is that we should position ourselves spiritually so we always go where Jesus is leading us, whether it is amongst "the wicked" for the sake of the gospel, or away from them for our own protection.

KEEPING ON TRACK

Please God not Man

God doesn't want most of our allegiance, he wants it all and this is for good reason. It is how he protects us from evil and nourishes us with his love and blessings. It is from this platform we interact with others. Our unswerving aim throughout our life should be to please him, not the world around us. The only praise it is safe to seek is the praise of God.

Self praise from our own ego or praise from men is usually derived from the image we work so hard to project to the world and usually has little relevance to the state of our soul. Such praise can either weaken us if we believe it, or strengthen us if we treat it as of no consequence, "The crucible for silver and the furnace for gold, but man is tested by the praise he receives." (Prov. 27:21). To receive man's praise we have to please him. Sometimes this will lead us into positive territory but sooner or later, if we let ourselves be influenced by it, we will find ourselves compromising godly principles. We can avoid the problem by consciously making sure our activities from the mundane to the spectacular are to the glory of God. To bring glory to God is a huge incentive for us to do our best for him. Added to this we should thank and praise him continually for sustaining us and empowering us in everything we do. The result will be far above our expectations and we will see the glory flowing to God.

Rejoice in the Differences Between People

I presume it is embedded in human psychology to be suspicious of any difference in anyone we meet. Perhaps it is to do with Stone Age man recognizing an enemy and thereby protecting himself. We scrutinize all physical characteristics, general demeanor, style of dress, listen to speech, assess level of education, and rate social standing. Once we have assessed a person we want to categorize them, put them in a labeled box, and then do our best to mould and change them to be just like us or rather what we think we are.

At times we get a revelation about the physical image we ourselves project; anyone who has ever had a passport photo or driver's license photo taken may have come close to needing sedation. Mostly to the impartial observer we are projecting an overall image that bears little resemblance to the one we think we project. Thankfully God rates us spiritually according to our heart, not our outward appearance, and always on the basis of his love. The humble would get a pleasant surprise and most teenagers certainly would. Most of the latter agonize over something others don't see, while failing to see the God-given beauty that radiates from them. The main item in our rating system might be physical appearance. Anybody who looks dowdy, can't color co-ordinate, or features a multicolored Mohawk cut, or has grey hair gets relegated to the bottom of our list. I have to lie down before I fall down when confronted with body piercing and tattoos. Whatever our particular priority happens to be, our broad general aim is to change those around us into our own personal clones. If only we could see how utterly boring that would be. Our God is a God of diversity. Look at nature, we are still discovering species. If we watch a nature film on a most unpromising creature like the lizard, the complexity, variation, and appeal is hard to comprehend. We wouldn't want all lizards to look alike, or all birds to make the same nests, or to have just one breed of dog. The French say "vive la difference." I think they are exuberant about God making male and female and most of us have agreed with them at least at some time in our life. Accepting differences in people is a challenge to our own coping strategies. It means we can't just have one simple approach to everyone who speaks beautifully or has bad table manners or is pigeon-toed. It means we have to see people as individuals and recognize that God has made us all different on purpose. It is a marvelous thing to be surrounded by people who are different from us; it is interesting and stimulating. When it comes down to the practicalities of doing God's will it is essential for us to have different skills and dovetail in together. We need to go even further and accept that people fulfilling the same role will all approach and execute their task differently from each other—they are meant to. Jesus spoke about the validity of different methods of serving. He said people considered that John the Baptist was demon possessed, because he didn't sit down to meals, and eat and drink. At the same time they called Jesus a glutton, and a drunkard, and a friend of sinners because he did. Paul gives us the right perspective when he points out that regardless of who does what it is God who makes our efforts prosper. Clichés may be somewhat stale but they have value in being succinct; here are two: "Different doesn't mean wrong"; "One size doesn't fit all." It is this appreciation of variability that is necessary in order for any organization including the church to run smoothly.

We have all seen people have the life crushed out of them by majority rule because they have been different in some way. Some obvious difference has excluded them and sometimes a valuable contribution has been forfeited. Women are particularly affected by this attitude. The role of women is undergoing great change in society in general but the church is lagging behind. It is hard for them to break the mould of housewife, mother, and general handmaiden in order to express their other God-given gifts. I look at the wives of the pastors and wonder how they survive, many with great difficulty I suspect. We would all benefit if we gave up stereotypes.

If someone is struggling at a milestone that makes them hard to get along with in some way, (all of us some of the time), it doesn't mean they are unable to serve. How personable does someone have to be to hand out a meal to a homeless person or read out a passage of the Scriptures? Just because someone has an obvious difficulty functioning in some area of daily living doesn't mean their opinion on spiritual matters should be dismissed out of hand. Those people who don't run with the pack, lack the social niceties, have a mental illness like depression, or emotional problems, are at an awful disadvantage even though they may have great faith, and therefore great spiritual insights. It is very liberating for all of us if we can sweep our prejudices aside. Our world opens up if we can recognize that each of us is a component part of the one body of Christ and each part has an obligation to the rest.

Secret Ballots

Why don't we introduce some of the principles of democracy into the running of the church? A lone voice in any organization will usually be ignored, excluded, or diminished in some way. The modern church is the same and people are too fearful to put a point of view that may conflict with that of the leader or another powerful person in the church. Often it is some minor change someone wants introduced and may be an idea that reflects the suffering silent majority. Lack of communication is often the reason given by people for their decision to stop attending church services. There is usually no formal reliable way for valuable feedback to get back to the leader, considered, and acted upon.

A very clear-cut but ever present example of a point of contention is the format of the Sunday services. There are those people who prefer very formal services with an atmosphere of serenity, use of the prayer book, organ accompanied hymns hundreds of years old and the children present, (preferably not), being seen and not heard. At the other end of the spectrum are those who like modern songs with guitars and bongo drums, hand waving, running about, and calling out with words of encouragement. There is every preference in between. Effort is made to cater for the tastes of all by having several different types of services at different times. With falling numbers of people attending churches regularly and especially with the youth dropping out, the leaders feel great pressure to make the format of the services more attractive. Often in an effort to avoid an atmosphere of a memorial service to the death of everything, other services are more like a three-ring circus. Sometimes it is as though we have to hide God and then ease him in unnoticed. The church can't compete successfully either as a lawn cemetery or a disco; it has to be seen quite clearly to be a house of God. That will only happen when he is the focus and the aim is to please him by rendering genuine worship to him. If services are tailored with the priority being to please the people attending, then it won't work. As in everything, there needs to be a balance, so that if those present are too distracted by some aspect of the service to be able to worship, then that won't work either.

Suggestion boxes are mandated in many organizations. Why not in all churches? In aged care homes these suggestions are mostly filed under "lost" and the box is there simply to fulfill government regulations. To be effective in the church, the box would need to be emptied before meetings of the Board, all suggestions documented, and regular meetings called for the congregation to vote in a secret ballot. A Cooperative has the potential to work better than a Dictatorship. The rumblings of discontent would be channeled into something positive and the crazy ideas quickly abandoned. Members of the congregation would be happier and more confident in their own particular role. Hopefully they don't consist of an unruly godless rabble but are sincere Christians who are walking with Christ and dwelling in the presence of God. To exclude them from decision making seems not only wrong, but a huge waste of talent.

Forums

Modern controversial topics not mentioned in the Bible need to be part of a general discussion with the congregation, rather than disregarded or dismissed by trite edicts from the pulpit. Abortion is an example. Most churches take an official anti-abortion stance and the sermons usually reflect this. I think most Christians would not need convincing of the sanctity of life, although the obvious does have to be stated. If only it was as simple as that, but life as it is lived is complex. The closest I have heard to addressing the difficult area of medical abortion was an informal comment where reference was made to hastening the death of a fetus that had no hope of survival to the end of the pregnancy anyway. Medical technology can now diagnose many problems in the baby before birth, even when it consists of a few cells. Some of these problems can be fixed or very successfully treated, but not always, and many times the baby would be born with a problem that would allow survival, but significantly impair the quality of life. When a Christian family suddenly finds itself in this situation and has to decide whether to abort or not to abort, it usually turns to secular advice. Those concerned go through great anguish because the church has never acknowledged the depth of the problem and the superficial view they know is not a helpful one on which to base a decision. It is a decision that has to be made very quickly under great emotional pressure, so it is not surprising people may take a course of action they regret for the rest of their life.

If controversial issues such as submission on the grounds of gender, women as clergy, euthanasia, Darwin's theory of evolution, abortion, homosexuality, and capital punishment were thrown open to everyone as in a workshop setting, every aspect of the topic would come to the surface. Hopefully this would be achieved without the acrimony of similar secular gatherings. Then when the issue arises in our own lives, we would have a practical basis on which to make a decision. Also, most people would be likely to be more tolerant of views opposite to their own because they would have a deeper understanding. People leave the church because they have only ever heard superficial rote advice, but then because of circumstances that develop in their lives they find their need is much greater. Christian parents of much-loved homosexual children often go through great torment because of the judgmental attitude of a non-compassionate church, and some leave and struggle with their faith alone.

How many of us truly have a day of rest on the Sabbath? Should we go to the supermarket on Sunday? Maybe we lost the Sabbath because we shut our eyes and washed away on the secular tide. If the church doesn't define its path then it will be dragged along by secular thinking. Open discussion would help the church to move appropriately with the times instead of being seen to be less and less relevant.

It is also vital we listen to our fellow Christians who have had to face a difficulty we have not experienced. If we have been born without physical impairment shouldn't we listen to those who have some impairment and find out if they would have preferred to have been aborted, and if not why not? Shouldn't we listen to the homosexual's experience of Christianity? Those without personal experience should have the least to say on these difficult issues. There are plenty of public forums on these topics but the secular perspective dominates. We need informed discussions based on real life experiences, biblical principles, Jesus, and the Holy Spirit.

SUMMARY

Over the centuries the Christian Church has been guilty of everything in the Bible that God finds abhorrent and has repeatedly warned us against. At times it has orchestrated or been part of the most horrendous crimes against humanity. To counter this recurring problem the organization of the church needs to be far more transparent and accountable within itself and to the secular world. Improved democratic processes are needed to allow better communication and increased accessibility of the hierarchy and individual leaders to both members of the congregation and the wider community. Everything of God is in the light for all to see and everything in the dark and hidden is of Satan. In the past, short-term cover up has predominated over long-term solutions. What could be less like God? Why are we surprised it hasn't worked and atrocities have occurred?

What we ask and expect of our leaders and each other should be no more than we ask of ourselves. Any denomination of the Christian church, and any individual church, can only dwell in the presence of God if its people do; every one of us has a responsibility to continually and strenuously aspire to this goal. It is the only way to minimize trouble and address it appropriately when it arises.

Satan will never give up battering and weakening the church from within. It can only withstand these attacks and function to further God's will by being upheld and propelled by the power of God. Individually and corporately we need to get rid of the "them and us mentality", by identifying with the sinner, while aspiring to be the saint. Each of us must admit that of ourselves we are no better than our fellow Christian or the person we see as the worst sinner in the community. It is only by fully recognizing our privileged and undeserved standing in the righteousness and love of Jesus that we can be effective in spreading the gospel, in guarding the pearl of great price. Have we forgotten the church is the body of Christ? Unless we Christians work together in his holiness and love, then we fail the secular world by promoting Satan in the name of Jesus, and thus we commit the worst kind of blasphemy possible.

The psalmist describes the quality of life we can enjoy when we truly represent Christ in our churches, "how good and pleasant it is when brothers live together in unity! It is like precious oil poured on the head, running down on the beard, running down on Aaron's beard, down upon the collar of his robes. It is as if the dew of Hermon were falling on Mount Zion. For there the Lord bestows his blessing, even life forevermore." (Ps. 133:1).

11

The Bible and Tradition

THE ACCURACY OF THE BIBLE

THERE IS MUCH DEBATE about the accuracy of the Bible. Many fundamentalist Christians believe literally in every word as written in their favorite translation. Other schools of thought admire the principles espoused but don't regard the Bible as the inspired word of God. Some consider it to be an ancient document written by people who may have been sincere, or deluded, or both, but in any case were writing about ancient times for ancient people with little relevance to today. Variations on these beliefs are held by the Christian and non-Christian alike.

I hope and believe the majority Christian view of the Bible is that it is God's written Word and as such should be held in the highest esteem. In the same way God is truth, omniscient and unchanging, so is his Word. It follows that the Bible is 100 percent accurate. Our concern is how to preserve this accuracy in our understanding and preaching.

One thing that is obvious even to an impartial reader is the quality and continuity in the train of thought in the Bible. It far surpasses that of any other religion. This is all the more amazing when we consider that it was written over a period of about fifteen hundred years, in different countries, by more than forty authors of diverse backgrounds—kings, tax collectors, fishermen, and scholars.

The Bible and Tradition

THE TRUTH

There is a huge emphasis on truth in the Bible; the word "truth" appears two hundred and fourteen times. The Jews took great pains to record the Scriptures with minute accuracy. Those people given the responsibility for preserving the Scriptures over the centuries went to amazing lengths to do so in every detail of word, phrase and punctuation. It is something for which we need to be very grateful. The following verses summarize the spectrum of truth in the Bible:

- God is the "God of truth." (Isa 65:16).
- In Jesus, the world saw truth. "For the law was given through Moses; grace and truth came through Jesus Christ." (John 1:17).
- Jesus prefaced almost all his teachings with the words: "I tell you the truth"—if we accept Jesus, we accept his truth.
- The Bible is truth, "the word of truth, the gospel of your salvation." (Eph. 1:13).
- "Jerusalem will be called the City of Truth," (Zech. 8:3).
- We are told truth is pivotal to worship, "God is spirit, and his worshipers must worship in spirit and in truth." (John 4:24).
- Jesus tells us if we absorb the truth in the Bible we will become more like the people we are meant to be. He said: "Sanctify them by the truth; your word is truth." (John 17:17).
- He told us the result of embracing the truth: "the truth will set you free." (John 8:32).

It is on this basis of truth that we can serve in God's love. Jesus informs us of the alternative to living in the truth—we belong to Satan, whom he calls the father of lies.

The above snapshot tells us about the truth recorded in the Bible. It is referring directly to the gospel message. But it is interesting even the historical facts are proving to be accurate as archaeological discoveries are made. So the pre-eminent place of truth in the Bible is all-encompassing. Jesus never got himself out of a tight situation by telling a lie and at his trial his truthfulness condemned him. We should remember this priority on truth when we consider telling a lie—large or small, black or white.

Not so long ago in secular society the emphasis on truth in the Bible was recognized, so if someone wanted to emphasize that what they were saying on any subject was absolutely true, they would use this common phrase, "and that is the gospel truth." Swearing on the Bible in court before giving evidence and also before taking public office was routine, but not any longer as we saw in our recent change of government. I think this is regrettable, but with or without this symbolism, God calls us to account for our actions just as surely.

However we view this truth there are dangers. Some people believe truth is absolute, as I do. It is easy though from this position, on the occasions when one gets it wrong by misinterpretation or misapplication, to easily fall into bigotry and narrow entrenched views. Such thinking has always been prevalent in Christianity and may have had its origins in the necessarily very dogmatic views of Paul. He had an enormous task of planting a new religion in diverse countries among very different people speaking different languages. He achieved all this in a hostile environment. He was jailed, flogged, stoned, shipwrecked, betrayed by friend and enemy, and as far as we know finally executed. With all these pressures on him, one would assume he had to be very forthright to ensure the gospel he preached at the beginning of his ministry was exactly the same as at the end.

This view that truth is absolute has changed in our society and may not represent the majority view any more even in the church; the modern view seems to be that truth is relative. I think this latter "relative" view holds much greater danger than the "absolute" view. It suits the slackers who find it easy to go with the flow as they bend and manipulate the truth to suit themselves. They don't have to make hard decisions and can blithely choose personal gratification over the defense of an absolute truth—because they don't believe there is one. Hence such expressions have arisen as, "if it feels good, do it." Tibetan Buddhism teaches truth is not absolute but is relative and changes with circumstances.[1] This belief is one of the major differences between Christian and Buddhist teaching. Slack behavior is certainly not advocated in Buddhism, yet it is easy to see why belief in relative truth makes it attractive to the thinking of today.

Those who accept the truth of the Bible have produced ever more translations trying to get perfection in the meaning. They are rightly concerned to ensure God's word is not adulterated in any way and want to get the words and phrases exactly right, as well as correcting for shifts in language with time. Perhaps others feel the search for new and "better"

---

1. His Holiness the Dalai Lama, *The Good Heart*, 82.

translations addresses the dissent as to meaning that has led not only to many denominations, but continually to divisions within individual churches. One imagines however, considering all the research by all the scholars to date to improve accuracy in translation that we must be getting to the point of diminishing returns, and may be in danger of going beyond the best point. In any case it seems to be the minor part of the problem of gaining an accurate understanding.

The pivotal question when we pursue God's truth seems to me not to be "how accurate is the Bible?" or "how accurate are we in our translation of the Bible?" but rather this question: "how can we accurately *use* the Bible" so that we avoid the pitfalls and hear and speak its truth? This question leads to four major considerations. First, we have to recognize the difficulty of going from the general to the particular. Second, we need to always enlist the help of Jesus and the Holy Spirit. Third, we need to avoid corrupting our interpretation of Scripture with culture and tradition, which happens when we confuse the Word of God with the word of man. Fourth, we need to distinguish the symbolic from the literal.

MOVING FROM THE GENERAL TO THE PARTICULAR

Any area of life involving the necessity for having ethical standards of behavior has to have a general set of rules defining what the standards are. In practice, there is always a problem here, because the evaluation of a particular circumstance has to be deduced from the general rule, and judgment is unavoidable in making this leap. It is very relevant in the health field and especially in end-of-life decisions, such as when to stop active treatment when faced with a patient who is not recovering. In human affairs it is left to individuals to make deductions and if it is thought an error has been made then tribunals or courts may be consulted.

When we use the Bible to guide us in all our thinking and actions this difficulty of moving from the general to the particular is very relevant. As we read in the newspapers every day, human judgment alone will let us down; we have to use the spiritual resources we have been given.

THE POWER OF THE WRITTEN WORD, JESUS, AND THE HOLY SPIRIT

When using the Scriptures people often revert to the Old Covenant because they use the Bible like a book of rules. It is an easy formula approach to every question. It is used to validate preconceived ideas. You don't even need to give much of your time to God to be able to do this. Using the Bible in this way there is bound to be disagreement, because each person is familiar with, picks out, and interprets the verses that suit his or her own views, agendas, and prejudices. Only the New Covenant approach with Jesus and the Holy Spirit has any chance of overriding our ego and winding up with the verses relevant to the will of God in any given situation. Then we will be led to the right verses, at the right time, and given the right understanding of what we read.

We need to remember Jesus is the living Word of God and the Holy Spirit interprets Scripture for us. The Bible doesn't stand alone; rather these three revelations of God are complementary. When we go to the Bible for advice we need this balance. We know the dangers of verses out of context but the problem of using the Bible without Jesus and the Holy Spirit is far less recognized and therefore the ramifications far more subtle and damaging. Unaided in this way, the moment we reach for our favorite translation we are in danger of error. It is easy to see how this has come about, because only the Bible is tangible and we can support our own view by saying, "look there it is in black and white." The opposite problem arises when someone says, "God said to me," whereupon someone else will reply, "strange—he said the opposite to me." Then we can get into a state of awful acrimony and confusion, and end up trying to resolve the situation by throwing out the whole concept of using anything but the written word in isolation.

To minimize the chances of this dilemma arising we all need to ensure we are in the right place spiritually—we should be unceasing in worship and prayer with constant reference to Jesus and his love, which always underpinned his teachings. Then if disagreement still arises we need to be alert to the fact that in our imperfection we may be wrong, or there may be a nuance of meaning that both parties in disagreement have missed. We need to try to think outside the square because God is often found out there and may be trying to tell us something we didn't know, something important and therefore exciting. I personally wouldn't want to miss out on that.

The Bible and Tradition

The written word of God is so powerful that used correctly it is one of our greatest defenses against evil. The temptation of Christ in the desert by Satan is an example of just this. Satan threw down three temptations to Christ who rebuffed them all by quoting Scripture. But it is easy to overlook the fact Satan himself also quoted scripture. Yet Jesus triumphed over him. If we reflect on the whole scene, we see Jesus had just been baptized and the Spirit was seen to descend on him. He was then led into the desert by the Holy Spirit. So on one side in this battle for the soul of Jesus, we have: Jesus himself—the perfect Son of God, the Living Word; the Holy Spirit—the Counselor; thirdly, in his head at least, Jesus carried the Bible—the written Word of God. Satan quoted Scripture as a stand-alone attack.

Without the Living Word, and the Counselor, the power of the written Word can be used by Satan to cause confusion and dissent, and he does this at every opportunity. Gate crashing is his forte—he went to the desert with Jesus uninvited and he always turns up hopefully at every gathering of believers. But as happened then, he won't hang around if he sees us consulting the Bible not in our own strength, but standing with Jesus and relying on the wisdom of the counsel of the Holy Spirit.

A very clear-cut example of the danger of using the Bible in isolation is the question of whether killing another human being is ever justified. If the Bible is used as a book of rules we find both answers, "No" and "Yes." We have the sixth commandment where we are told unequivocally not to murder. Yet we also find David being empowered by God to kill Goliath. Straight away we could digress and bring in the idea of "lawful killing", but there are no rules in the Bible about that. We could get involved in "what is the correct translation" approach, but inevitably this fails because all the references in the Bible no matter how they are translated can ever all be reconciled into a "Yes," or a "No," on the subject of killing. Current controversies among Christians about killing include the topics of therapeutic abortion, embryonic stem cell medicine, and defensive pre-emptive strikes against other countries, to name just a few. It is stretching a long bow indeed to be sure any verse in the Bible taken alone is specifically describing at least the first two of these situations because they were unknown at the time the Bible was written.

Surely the conflicting answers of "Yes" and "No" on countless topics in the Bible has been given to us, not to cause controversy and confusion, but to provide flexibility for the Holy Spirit to tailor the advice for the particular facets of any situation in any period of history. The only way for the body of the church to come out with a correct unified policy on important issues is for each of us as individual Christians to be meticulous about the conduct of our own journey and how we approach Scripture. The responsibility is ours to put ourselves in the right spiritual position, so that when we go to the Bible for an answer, the Holy Spirit will lead us to the correct one.

THE BIBLE: THE RECORD OF ETERNAL SPIRITUAL TRUTH ON THE BACKGROUND OF HISTORY

We can divide our biblical knowledge of God into two parts. First, there are the eternal truths that never change; second, there is advice in the Scriptures springing from these truths and consistent with them but only relevant to the period in history in which they were written. The written culture and traditions of the Bible are fixed in time; its spiritual wisdom is not.

The eternal truths are all the following: God's nature—which includes his love, holiness, mercy, goodness, wisdom, righteousness, and justice; the reality of sin resulting in man's alienation from God; Jesus's combined humanity and divinity, and his role as Redeemer, teacher, and intercessor, and a belief that he will return to judge and to restore God's perfect creation; our need to repent, to accept and follow Jesus, to be obedient to God and to serve him all our lives. All these indisputable, unchangeable facts make up the Christian religion. Paul tells us the basis for these beliefs, "that Christ died for our sins according to the Scriptures, that he was buried, that he was raised on the third day according to the Scriptures." (1 Cor. 15:3-4).

The stories in the Bible show these truths being seamlessly applied to the times during which the Old and New Testaments were written. We need to be very careful in our interpretation of what we read. It is absolutely critical to distinguish eternal spiritual truth from the backdrop—passing cultures and traditions in which these truths were set. We also need to be aware that our own understanding is biased by the culture and tradition of our times. If we do not allow for these influences we will fail to discern God's wisdom.

Culture is defined as "the training and refinement of mind, tastes, and manners ... the intellectual side of civilization". It is constantly changing and interacting with the environment of the day, and from this interaction tradition is born. With tradition comes the transmission of rules and customs and once they become long established and generally accepted, these traditions, even if not actually written into law, may acquire the force of law. It is against this moving background of culture and tradition that civilization progresses, and in concert with this, God's unchanging purpose of salvation continually unfolds towards completion. So history is written.

God is eternal and his teachings in the Bible are timeless, his word "stands forever." (Isa. 40:8). As he takes us forward in history into a more sophisticated world, our interpretation and understanding of the Scriptures should mature and adapt so that we still see their relevance to the times we live in, whenever that happens to be. Counterproductive to this is the irrelevant and misleading accumulation of tradition that has become built into the teaching of the Scriptures, and holds us back on our spiritual journey.

The Jews experienced a quantum leap forward in the application of God's eternal truths to their daily lives when Jesus arrived on the scene and infused the love of God into the letter of the law. In doing so he cut away much of the accumulated tradition that was corrupting Jewish worship. We keep forgetting this. We revert to the thinking of the Old Covenant and adopt a legalistic approach to sin in both our attitude and actions instead of overcoming it with the love of God. This is futile, even God only used the law as a preliminary step until the time was right for Jesus to build on it and show us a better way. Jesus plainly told the people of his day that if they were to remain in God's will they would have to change their attitude by using the law with love. Most of them couldn't handle either the concept of change or the erosion of their power base were they to embrace his teachings, and so they stuck to their old ideas. Only a small minority made the transition successfully, the rest hung onto the outdated traditions that had become built into the organized church. Since then Jesus has left us with the Holy Spirit who guides us through the centuries by showing us the relevance of God's wisdom to the wide sweep of any period in history, to any culture, and to the intricate details of the life of any individual—we no longer have to let culture and tradition impact negatively on our spiritual understanding and practice.

Neither the meaning of the intriguing parables of Jesus nor the counseling of the Holy Spirit to individuals can be boiled down to isolated Bible texts or simple rules. If that had been the case then Jesus would simply have made a few more insightful comments or added a few more new rules. This approach doesn't work because life is not simple and it is not stationary, and to have a text that covers every situation in every period of time would be too enormous for even a computer chip to store. God's wisdom really does dwarf our intellect. The psalmists were in awe of their Creator when they studied their limited view of the sky with its stars, planets, sun, and moon. Through our telescopes and space exploration we see so much more—just enough to realize we are getting a mere glimpse of what is there. There is not a Bible text that word for word covers God's thoughts on every situation but there is a text that gives the principles that covers every situation, and the Holy Spirit can find it, interpret it, and apply it for us.

It is not that God's word changes, either his written Word, or Jesus, his Living Word. God himself is unchangeable and his purpose of salvation is unchangeable. As he moves civilization forward he is always relevant within the changing cultures and traditions of history. We struggle to keep pace and understand this relevance and then we misrepresent him as an irrelevant God of the past. To keep up with God's agenda as time passes we have to rely on being as informed as possible. This comes through intensive study of the Bible and on this marvelous knowledge base we ask him in prayer to build the answer for us. Then we hear the counseling of the Holy Spirit. Otherwise we default in our service to him through failure to interpret and apply spiritual truths correctly to the changing demands, over time, of God's unchanging purpose.

1. Cultural and traditional influence of ancient Israel on the Old Testament

Life was very black and white in Old Testament times and this was reflected in very black and white thinking in the population. The life of an individual was often short, terminated prematurely by violence, disease, and war. There were the highlights of birth, marriage, and death, but life progressed with great uncertainty in between. The main interest had to be physical survival, your own and that of your descendants. So life was brutal and all was fair in the pursuit of this pressing need for survival. If you had power you used it openly to promote your own interests, wealth, and security. Whether wielding this power in the priesthood, or the power of men over women, or the power of a rich man over a slave, it was all considered legitimate. In warfare, total annihilation of an enemy was the only course of action contemplated—it was kill or be killed. But the Jews are God's elect, and this God of love whom they worshipped countered the barbarity of the culture and traditions of those days with a multitude of rules. Particularly in Leviticus, there were rules and detailed instructions on almost every aspect of life. It was a temporary and incomplete solution for uncivilized times.

David lived in one thousand BC, but was a man appropriate to all time because he was driven by a desire to be with God. His deeply spiritual life was all about his hunger for God's presence; he hung on it, he knew he couldn't live outside it, and he didn't want to. For this reason no doubt had he been on earth in thirty AD he would have embraced Jesus as the Messiah. But he would have used the thinking of thirty AD to arrive at the correct conclusion, not that of one thousand BC. Similarly had he been born in the twenty-first century, although he would have been quite different, he would have fitted into God's will just as surely. His closeness to God would have ensured that he could have lived in any period of history and been just as relevant then as he was to the ancient Israelites, and just as true to God's purpose. God spoke to him through the culture of his day and he heard accurately. Similarly, if like David, we strive to dwell in God's presence the Holy Spirit will enable us to adapt and interpret God's message on the background of the culture and traditions of our day. It has to be an adaptive process to be effective; David could not have been effective if he had lived today but hung onto his cultural beliefs of one thousand BC. Because David and the prophets knew the wisdom of God, even though they lived and died before Jesus, they recognized the love of God underpinning the law and nourishing their spirit, but the people as a whole just didn't get it. They didn't get it then and many don't get it now.

2. Cultural and traditional influence of ancient Israel on the New Testament

Jesus changed the world and the course of history because he was God and came with the power of God. His aim was to cause a spiritual revolution with his gospel of salvation. Even so, in delivering his message effectively he had to do it within the cultural context of the first century. He would have detracted from this focus had he caused social upheaval by preaching that slavery should be abolished or that women should leave abusive husbands. He would have caused political upheaval if he had spoken against Roman rule, and this was the great fear of the ruling parties both Jewish and Roman. As an occupying foreign power we wouldn't expect the Romans to see Jesus's mass popularity any other way, but in fact Pilate did realize at Jesus's trial that he was innocent. We might have expected the Jews to see the truth because they had had access to God and the Scriptures for thousands of years. Not so, they got it horribly wrong. On reflection we can see why. While they had had all that time to absorb spiritual truth, they had allowed their understanding of it to become distorted by the accumulation of tradition. The Romans had come fresh to the scene and their thinking was undistorted by such influence. Spiritual challenges arise for every generation of Christians to face, and most people make the same sort of mistake. It is easy to stay entrenched in yesterday's thinking, and allow ourselves to be hamstrung by outdated culture and traditions, and lag behind in God's plans.

When we look at Jesus's ministry we can see how he taught spiritual truth in order to undercut the corrupting effect of centuries of accumulated tradition in the church. At the time, basic human rights were appallingly deficient, and there seemed to be scant realization of the fact. Jesus did very little directly about this, rather he taught us to love one another and from that came desirable social change. The Pharisees often set traps for him by designing questions they thought he would have to answer in such a way that he would be accused of treason or blasphemy. His answers made it clear that his intention to be divisive related only to spiritual issues. When the woman was about to be stoned for adultery his words left a spiritual legacy, "he straightened up and said to them, 'If any one of you is without sin, let him be the first to throw a stone at her.'" (John 8:7). He didn't take up a petition to change the law to abolish the penalty of stoning for adultery or speak on the equality of men and women. His failure to do so doesn't mean he condoned these things; rather it was not God's will for him to do so. But it doesn't make sense to assume because of the way Jesus performed his mission in thirty AD that from then on we should never protest against any political regime or never try to make any direct change to the social structure. It is obvious to us today that the stoning of a woman for adultery by a lynch mob is wrong, and it is a view God would expect us to uphold strenuously. As an aside, note that before Jesus took his stand and spoke out, we are told "he straightened up"; we have to do that when we take our stand for God. It implies deliberate action after forethought, and a readiness, and courage to defend the position.

3. The individual and the interpretation of Scripture

Before Jesus intervened, the lynch mob in the story described above almost certainly considered they were right in their actions because they were blindly following their tradition. How many times do we in our own small way do the same? We keep regurgitating to everyone who is unfortunate enough to have to listen, some potted wisdom or some catchy phrase that was used in our family when we were kids. It may have been exactly right for then but not for ever. Even worse, we pick up unbalanced or wrong ideas and refuse to let them go, just because we think wrongly that time has a hallowing effect. We do it into old age and the audience groans when we open our mouth knowing we are about to play the same old record yet again. Many of us cling to the religious beliefs of our parents, even though they were obviously struggling and not able to find their way. We quote their confused half truths and negative views and use that as an excuse not to think for ourselves. We rationalize if it was good enough for dear old Dad to quote a few philosophers and insightful intellectuals who were fashionable in his day, that we can do the same, and like him avoid our responsibility to put in an effort of our own to find God.

There is another similar big trap here in how we use the Bible and one that we all fall into at some time. It relates to our journey. We keep going back to old milestones instead of approaching each one in a new light with a new lesson. We come to a situation like one we met before. It may be a minor or a major one. We remember all about the previous milestone and the mistakes we made and others made, and what our thinking should have been, and what we should have done. At the time we read our Bible, prayed and finally struggled past the milestone, and acquired a bit more of the likeness of Jesus. As a result we form an opinion on how to handle a situation like this next time. "Okay," we say to ourselves, "here it is again; I know what to do about this; I remember there were these helpful verses I read at the time." So we find the verses and confident in our opinion we treat the current situation as we should have treated the previous one. Unfortunately, this new situation is not exactly the same, so that the verses that were helpful in dealing with the previous instance may actually be counterproductive in this next one. Each new situation has to be looked at afresh. This is not to say we shouldn't learn by past experience; God specifically tells us to remember. No two set of circumstances are ever exactly the same. There is great danger of becoming rigid, inflexible, and stale. How often do we hear the same Bible verse quoted with only a superficial relevance to the problem?

As Christians we want to know God and so we study the Bible. In the process we learn the principles we should live by, how we should act in our daily living as the events large and small unfold in our lives. When we confuse traditional beliefs with eternal truths, then without being fully aware of what we are doing, we practice a very subtle and corrosive form of blindness. We demonstrate patterns of thinking and behavior that haven't progressed past the Old and/or New Testament and so we diminish the gospel. Then like the ancient Israelites, our Christian views and practices are all law and no love, all rules, regulations, and dogmatic views influenced by the culture, politics, traditions, and fashions of yesterday and today. Spiritually some of us ride on camels rather than in T-model Fords. Yes, folks, that is about as good as it gets, not many of us progress to dusting off our Toyotas. It is a failing we all have to some extent in some areas of our Christian thinking. Our misplaced zeal for the traditional correctness of two thousand years ago and today brings a result that is the opposite to what we anticipated—far from upholding the law, the effect is that the Ten Commandments are overlooked while things like dress code aren't. How many people in the western world would not appear in church without shoes, but would commit adultery?

Jesus knew the danger and showed us how to fulfill the law without changing it; he consolidated and clarified the Scriptures by teaching us that we need to interpret the letter of the law on the basis of the spirit of the law. He spoke out very strongly about this and his words imply we do have a choice in whether we get it right or not. When the Pharisees and teachers of the church law challenged him over lack of hand washing before eating he replied, "And why do you break the command of God for the sake of your tradition?" (Matt. 15:3). Note that he didn't say we should not wash our hands before eating; it is a wonder that hasn't become church tradition! He is talking about putting a greater emphasis on tradition than on God's will. He illustrated what he meant by accusing them of giving to the church instead of needy parents. He said they were guilty of false piety and breaking the commandment to honor their parents. His conclusion was unequivocal: "you nullify the word of God for the sake of your tradition. You hypocrites! Isaiah was right when he prophesied about you: 'These people honor me with their lips, but their hearts are far from me. They worship me in vain; their teachings are but rules taught by men.'" (Matt. 15:7–9).

The Bible and Tradition

How did the Pharisees make their mistake? Many times in the past they had read the Bible texts indicating we should give back to God some of the wealth he has given to us. No doubt they were also familiar with texts about honoring parents but decided the former overruled the latter. Then it became accepted church tradition to make a great public display of their offering when they attended the temple. Probably it was an easy error to make because it would bring them more of the praise of men than the less obvious giving of financial help to their parents. Whatever their reason Jesus was completely affronted. Others of course make the opposite mistake and give in excess to kin and forget God. The point is one text doesn't over-ride another; we have to ask God in order to know which of them is relevant to a particular occasion.

Jesus was telling the Pharisees we are not to change the spirit of God's word into rules or customs and then emphasize one thing over another as it suits us. Rather we are to interpret everything in the light of the meaning of the underlying principles which the Holy Spirit will give us. Then the customs and rules of men don't assume the status of the word of God, corrupt it, and infiltrate our worship. Similarly we can see what traditional hangovers we have inherited and get rid of them.

We have to see the need to do better, to do what Jesus taught us, so that we think beyond culture and tradition, both old and new. Then without compromising God's truth we can fit ourselves into both modern society and into God's plan. That is not easy and we need all the help from God we can get. The Israelites tried to do the opposite and fit God into their culture and their plans and it didn't work, it led them to crucifying Jesus. Similarly with us it is impossible to get it right by applying our cultural and traditional beliefs to our knowledge of God and then hope we get the right answer. Rather we have to do it the other way around. We have to apply God to the world around us. God doesn't change, but we must and the world must.

The cultural blindness of previous generations sticks to us like glue and causes conflict among believers. Five hundred years after the crisis of the Reformation in Europe, Protestants and Catholics in this country have only just stopped hating each other and progressed to an uncertain trust. It started off as a difference in doctrinal beliefs important to Christianity, for which people on both sides of the argument died. When the Reformation started, people knew what it was about, but in the last hundred or so years the animosity became traditional, so that the ordinary people on both sides forgot the real issues and only remembered to hate each other. Catholics in this country have told me of their belief that the Protestant faith arose because Henry VIII wanted to commit adultery legally—they had no knowledge of the prior spiritual movement in Europe that gave Henry his bright idea. Some of today's Protestants are just as critical of Catholics whom they think lack spiritual freedom—it is just unfortunate that often these same Protestants don't have any interest in thinking about spiritual issues at all. God knows his children are all different; we can leave it to him to sort out. For our part, we have to disentangle ourselves from tradition.

4. Cultural and traditional influences corrupt the working of the organized church

Taking the gospel message, and the benefits of civilization in England, to uncivilized countries hundreds of years ago was in line with Christian principles, but the slavery and many other things that happened on the way were not. Through the unrelenting effort of William Wilberforce over decades, slavery was finally outlawed in England in eighteen hundred and thirty three. It was a Christian country, why did it take Wilberforce so long? Presumably the church was back in the time of the Old and New Testament and like the Pharisees of those days refused to budge in their thinking. The Christians in England blindly accepted the ideas handed down to them over the entire preceding period of civilization. Presumably they read Paul's instructions that slaves were to obey their masters, as meaning slavery was okay. Slavery was not something Paul had the power to change in his day, but that didn't make it right in God's eyes. We don't know exactly what was in Paul's mind when he wrote this. But had he not done so, the result might well have been the Christian message of the equality of all people would have caused slaves to rebel against their masters. In those days the slaves would have been slaughtered or cast out to starve. Paul's words were obviously appropriate advice for then, not for all time, but it suited greedy heartless men to continue the practice long after they should have known it was temporary traditional advice meant only for that period in history. It took eighteen hundred years of Christianity before the spirit of love Jesus taught was correctly applied to Paul's words.

With the help of the "retrospectoscope" we look with horror at the history of the church and hang our heads in shame. How could the

The Bible and Tradition

church sanction the barbaric Crusades? How could the church orchestrate the horrendous tortures of the Spanish Inquisition? How could Christian countries, like the allies and Germany, be engaged in a war that cost fifty million lives? How could the church sanction pedophilia? No doubt many Bible verses were wrapped neatly in acceptable culture and tradition and so misused to support the flawed policies. And no doubt we are guilty of the same thing with present challenges, of which pedophilia is currently at the forefront. These disasters have come about because we have repeatedly allowed politics, tradition, and culture to overrule God. It is amazing that despite the often abysmal performance of the organized church and its members, the body of Christ lives on and God's will for man's salvation moves ever closer to completion. It is not only a cause for humility but also for gratitude that it is God's will and not man's that prevails.

5. Church leaders, responsibility and blasphemy

Church leaders have the responsibility of incorporating the doctrine of the Bible into the principles of the working of their churches in such a way that the surrounding secular culture can be accepting. This is a huge unenviable responsibility and they don't always get it right. On the one hand loss of relevance of the Christian church has been a constant threat for two thousand years and no less today when the pace of change in the world has accelerated in an exponential way. On the other hand there has also been huge corruption with many sects and cults abounding whose only claim to Christianity is in the names they give themselves. Only the godly, those who dwell in God's presence, have any hope of guiding the church whether they be leaders or members of the congregation.

It would not have been all self-promotion and hypocrisy that caused the Pharisees and Sadducees to err in Jesus's day, or resulted in the errors of church leaders since then. There was the personal terror of incurring God's wrath. The Pharisees believed if they did not obey the inordinate number of rules in the Old Testament that disaster would befall them. When God gave the Ten Commandments to the Israelites he emphasized their importance with the frightening accompaniments of thunder, lightning, fire, smoke, and trumpet blasts while the ground shook violently. Predictably this got everyone's attention so that they obeyed when God told Moses to tell the people they would die if they went beyond certain limits. The ancient Israelites had seen and felt God's wrath repeatedly throughout their history—they saw it after the flight from Egypt, at the time of the Assyrian and Babylonian invasions, and when individuals disobeyed him. As they were currently suffering under Roman rule the Jews of Jesus's day would have been very familiar at a personal level with this wrath of God. Like the ancient Pharisees, our leaders since then have had a real fear they will similarly transgress by allowing the meaning of the Scriptures to become corrupted by the heretics and blasphemers of the day—and there has never been any shortage of such people.

I can really relate to this fear of the blasphemy of false teaching and have prayed continuously that the Holy Spirit will guard this book against it. Preserving God's truth is the greatest responsibility of all Christians. It is very dangerous ground deciding some things in the Bible are no longer relevant. It is easy to see there is the real possibility after each person erroneously throws out anything he or she finds awkward or disagrees with that there wouldn't be anything of value left. The downside of this valid concern is that it can easily lead unintentionally into the same trap the Pharisees fell into—that of defending outdated traditional interpretations of the Bible.

It is also easy for unscrupulous powerbrokers to use tradition as a means of launching a false accusation of blasphemy, so that they can manipulate others, as they did at Jesus's trial. The irony was that those confused people, whom the Pharisees managed to convince would be guilty of blasphemy if they supported Jesus, became accessories to the greatest blasphemy of all time—they killed God on earth in the person of Jesus. The deliberate manipulation of a congregation through imposition of outdated traditional values still occurs in most modern churches to some extent. More subtle than deliberate evil is that we rationalize by telling ourselves and everyone else we are defending God against blasphemy, while we are actually defending our own egos and the selfish interests that make up our own precious world. We have to step away from ourselves and the arrogance with which we close our minds to the consideration of a new understanding. It has to be a full-on genuine effort to determine God's will in the matter and to follow his lead, even when it takes us out of our comfort zone.

Whether modern corruptions are preached or whether outdated tradition is preached, it is all blasphemy. In the Old Testament, blasphemy has the root meaning of "an act of effrontery in which the honor of God is insulted by man."[2] Jesus was certainly affronted when he accused the Pharisees of elevating their tradition—"their rules taught by men", above the true meaning of God's word. When we do the same, we are similarly guilty of blasphemy and find ourselves back in the desert lined up with Satan against Jesus. People blame the church for the decline of Christianity because they say the church is refusing to modernize. It is essential to modernize by casting off old outdated tradition and it is equally essential to preserve spiritual truth in all its purity.

6. Dysfunctional solutions

We might wonder why God allowed these cultural and traditional things, which cause people to stumble, to be included in the Bible. The answer is there is nothing in the Bible that doesn't teach us something valuable. In "the slaves obey your masters" advice we no longer agree with slavery, but there is also a great principle here on the appropriate attitude we should have when we are in a position of trust and service—we should serve wholeheartedly because ultimately it is God whom we are serving. The literal message is obsolete, but Paul's underlying spiritual message is as relevant today as it ever was and we can find it by removing the culture and tradition in which he wrapped it. Then we can apply it directly to determine our motivation and attitude in our work as we earn our living.

If we try to apply all Paul's cultural advice on many practical issues of his time literally word for word to our time, then sooner or later we will find ourselves in a circumstance where it simply doesn't work. Then we find ourselves trying a lot of dysfunctional approaches. We might stick our head in the sand and pretend a real problem doesn't exist—this is the pressure cooker approach because everything builds up inside us until we explode emotionally with the strain of trying to do the impossible. We may go on a guilt trip by blaming ourselves for our inability to cope, so that the conscientious Christian can even become mentally ill. We become angry and blame others for our lack of success in trying to cope with a situation we should abandon. We decide God is demanding the impossible and turn a deaf ear to his advice. We become expert at finding loopholes and get-out clauses. We drop out of Scripture altogether. Usually we do all these things at some time to some degree, and then resort to hypocrisy. While publicly paying lip service to the idea the meaning of

---

2. Douglas, *The New Bible Dictionary*, 2nd Edition.

something is literal, in private we know differently and finish up with so many exceptions to suit us that we finish up with a belief system even we couldn't define. We really are very tricky.

We don't let others off so lightly. We often make it very clear by our sanctimonious statements and lofty advice that our fellow Christians should find solutions within the narrow confines of first century traditional values; we imply to do otherwise is to be offside with God, and even worse, with ourselves as well. This is very easy to do when we don't have the problem, which allows us to take the high ground and stay in our comfort zone. If we do have the problem, and have attempted to solve it in a dysfunctional way, then our ill-founded piety is reinforced. At times we get flashes of brilliant insight, so for example we might say it is okay for a woman to leave a husband who is physically abusive, but it is not okay to leave one who is psychologically abusive. Rather than try and patch up a belief in female subservience, isn't it better to recognize the concept for what it is—not spiritual truth but outdated tradition? Then the dust settles and we can look at the eternal principles that we should love one another as Christ loves us; that we should submit to God in everything, and in submitting to him, then at times he will want us to submit to someone else and at times he won't. We don't have to make it hard by getting all tangled up trying to fit modern living into old traditions. We need to constantly look for the principle behind a text, which is always relevant, and not just at the ancient example that has been given.

Unfortunately, dispute over what advice is to be taken for all time and what is to be discarded as out of date, has and still does cause great conflict among believers. This is not good, for as Jesus pointed out division brings failure. We have to stop squabbling amongst ourselves about individual issues that reflect outdated tradition and agree instead on the eternal truths and apply them. If we don't do this we lose our focus on God and plough on in our own strength, and we are soon in trouble. In Revelations, Jesus described us as being ignorant of our wretched state of spiritual poverty and blindness. Like the Pharisees of old, one of the things that blinds us is tradition. The result is we can nod enthusiastically at the concept of loving our neighbor, while acting daily towards others with at best indifference, and at worst aggression. Instead, it is crucial we meet all issues unsullied by tradition by removing that tradition, and then looking afresh in the light of the love of God.

Our spiritual blindness is spoken about a lot in church sermons; we know about "the plank" that obscures vision but we hear the warning

The Bible and Tradition

as "the plank in *your* eye" and relate it to the person sitting beside us. Even so we know we suffer from personal blindness. The Holy Spirit does cause us to have uncomfortable moments of clarity on this point; there is a well-trodden path to this milestone and round and round it. Unfortunately when it comes to the evils of outdated tradition we have very little insight. Because the organized church sometimes condones or promotes this form of blindness, it is a milestone where we can comfortably camp out—and we do.

SYMBOLISM

Another difficulty in practicing the gospel is distinguishing between symbolism and literal meaning. At times the distinction would be clear to all as in this verse, "if your eye causes you to sin, pluck it out." (Mark 9:47)—we would all agree we are not being advised to self-mutilate.

Another area that is not as obvious and has split the church into various denominations is that of baptism, and this serves as a good example of the difficulties that can arise. There is controversy over whether the word "baptism" is meant to be understood symbolically as spiritual washing by the Holy Spirit, or literally as a human ceremony using water in some way. There is much symbolism linking the Holy Spirit and water, "Whoever believes in me, as the Scripture has said, streams of living water will flow from within him." (John 7:38). After Jesus's baptism John the Baptist said of him, "he will baptize you with the Holy Spirit and with fire." Matt. 3:11). Such symbolic use of the word "fire" would then match a symbolic interpretation of being filled with the "living water" of the Holy Spirit.

Jesus said, "Therefore go and make disciples of all nations, baptizing them in the name of the Father and of the Son and of the Holy Spirit," (Matt. 28:19). This verse gives a clear spiritual message, which is that we must spread the gospel to other people so that they become disciples of Jesus and so will bear the name of the Father and the Son and the Holy Spirit. The practicalities are not stated. You could say, "Why look for symbolism, it simply means the obvious—we are being directed to do both the preaching and the baptizing and therefore should use a ceremony like Jesus's baptism"; after all he is our role model. Or you could feel strongly that it is another example of the symbolism in the Scriptures that has characterized discussion of the Holy Spirit, so that by successfully preaching the gospel the new believer's baptism is automatic according to Jesus's promises. Going to the root Latin or Greek won't help in that respect because we know what the word means, but not whether in Matthew 28:19 it is being used literally or symbolically.

It seems to me we have to allow that either the literal or the symbolic view could be correct. That has several implications—our priority must lie in understanding and instituting the spiritual message, which is that we must tell others about the gospel of salvation. Also the last thing Jesus would want is for Christians to split into acrimonious camps and argue about what he means, so we need to be tolerant of a God-fearing point of view that is different from our own.

A particular danger is that we should never put controversial human interpretation of the Scriptures as a condition of salvation. This was in line with Paul's views when he said Abraham's circumcision was merely a sign pointing to the faith and righteousness he already had. The thief on the cross was saved without baptism or the laying on of hands, Jesus simply read his heart.

When Cornelius and his family believed, they received the Holy Spirit. Peter said, "Can anyone keep these people from being baptized with water? They have received the Holy Spirit just as we have." (Acts 10:47). Peter's baptism ceremony was simply symbolic of the baptism of the Holy Spirit that they had already been given immediately after they accepted Christ. Even so Peter obviously felt very sure about the value of adding this symbolism.

God gives different Christians different blessings, the human ceremony of baptism may be an instance of the individuality with which he relates to us—maybe it is a blessing he gives to some of us but not to all of us. Equally, if God lays anything on our heart for us to do, and we do it, then he will richly bless us and this includes baptism, immersion or otherwise. Similarly when we take communion, though not essential to salvation, many find a spiritual dimension opens up that gives an increased awareness of the love in which we stand.

THE MODERN VOICE OF DISSENT

People love a rebel and they like to see tall poppies cut down. There has always been something romantically heroic about the lone figure who will take on the establishment in any field of human activity. There are

The Bible and Tradition

many areas in the Christian doctrine that even with God's help are difficult to understand and some beyond our understanding. Anyone who is personable, articulate, and confidant can look good simply by capitalizing on people's confusion and their pack instinct to tear down the establishment. Those in the hierarchy of the church often provide an opening by appearing distant and arrogant, preferring to take the high ground rather than participate in discussions with their parishioners. Also, speaking to the media is very difficult because traps are set and sections of interviews can be cut out causing opinions to be misrepresented.

John Spong is a well-known example of someone trying to change orthodox Christian teaching from within the framework of the church. He does so by overturning the authority of the Bible. In this way he is able to deny the truth of core Christian doctrine, which is that Christ died for our sins and was raised back to life. There is evidence Paul consistently preached this foundational belief of Christianity within twenty years of the crucifixion. This means if you do not believe Christ died for sin, you can argue you are right but you cannot claim to be Christian. Spong's unorthodox views include the following: he does not believe Christ was God on earth; he does not believe Jesus is the only way to God; he does not believe in miracles; prayer cannot be used as a request to God to act in a particular way; there is no standard in Scripture that will govern our ethical behavior. Just to give a balanced view, he does believe the following: God is real and can be met through the person of Jesus; God's love is available to us all; he regards the Bible as a treasure; our journey into God is also a journey into our selfhood.

To me, his views taken together are not logical. He talks of love and holiness and views Christ's life as an example for us to follow. There are no detailed accounts of Christ's ministry on earth other than in the Bible. But if the Bible is without authority then surely it is not valid to refer to it at all. He says parts of it are wrong—which parts? Who says? Why would Spong be able to discern truth where presumably many brilliant godly people over the centuries have failed? The purpose of the Bible is to witness to Christ as the divine savior. John says this is why he wrote about the miracles Christ performed: "that you may believe that Jesus is the Christ, the Son of God, and that by believing you may have life in his name." (John 20:31). Spong says he understands the Bible better than most scholars and recognizes the importance of love. One wonders how he could read John's gospel, sometimes alluded to as the "gospel of love," but fail to see the purpose for which it was written. He claims scientific discoveries of Newton and Keppler have debunked many biblical conclusions. It is interesting that both these men were Christians, so they obviously felt their discoveries were compatible with the Scriptures. In interviews Spong talks of the importance to him of the life of Jesus almost apologetically, as though it is an accident of his own birth place.

Mixed in with explanations of his views are liberal doses of valid descriptions of the failings of the Christian church. People see the truth of that in his teachings and in this way the flaws in the rest of his ideas are obscured. A proportion of those who follow Spong and others like him consist of people who are disaffected church-goers. They are disillusioned by mainstream religion. They see people of high standing in the church acting in opposition to the love of God and from there make the same basic error I believe Spong is making. They blame the doctrine and not the people who abuse it. So they try to make up something better. People who listen hopefully to the Spongs of the world are not so much attracted to their ideas as driven there by the failings of the mainstream church. We have confused the symbolic and the literal, confused tradition and God's truth, and drawn wrong conclusions when moving from a general statement in the Bible to a particular example in life. All this is frighteningly easy to do when we leave God's love out of our thinking. So we see minority groups abused and cut off from his love. Spong and his followers are right—at times we are not teaching the truth about God. The tragedy for them is they don't realize the flaw is in the singer not the song.

SUMMARY

By his word God created and governs every known and unknown universe. It is a power too great for us in any way to match or even fully comprehend. The Bible, as God's written word, expresses his power as it tells the progressing story of the wisdom, love, and mercy of God in his interaction with humankind. It is a record of the love story between God and man and we should use it as a message of love to the world and not take God's heart out of it so that all that is left is a lifeless book of rules. Maybe every Bible should come with a cautionary label, "WARNING: Powerful. Use with great care, reverence, love, and gratitude. Only to be opened in the company of Jesus and under the instruction of the Holy Spirit".

When we read the Bible we have to put our own preconceived ideas behind us and look with a fresh mind. When it comes to interpretation, we are told to "Test everything. Hold on to the good." (1 Thess. 5:21). Forming a point of view that is aggressive or oppressive rather than loving won't be correct—God has never forced himself on us; he has simply informed us of the consequences of our choices.

Traditional dross gets built into both our community culture and into our interpretation of the Scriptures. Its removal is what characterizes the refinement of modern society and it is also the way to promote truth and clarity in spiritual values. It is not a one off thing but an ongoing process. Each time we open the Bible in search of an answer, we need to keep up with God's unfolding purpose by recognizing the difference between advice tailored to cultural circumstances before one hundred and ten AD, when the Bible was completed, and the spiritual truths that stand forever. While he is truth, absolute and unchanging, the manner of expression of this truth does change even as its essence does not.

Our leaders have to walk the tightrope between the blasphemy of preaching outdated tradition as God's truth and the blasphemy of giving the modern cultural ideas of today equal or greater value than the eternal Word of God. It is an unenviable task.

At the "coalface" how do we know what verse to apply and how to interpret it in any circumstance? This is how—when studied with Jesus and the Holy Spirit we recognize that God's wisdom has a character all of its own: "the wisdom that comes from heaven is first of all pure; then peace-loving, considerate, submissive, full of mercy and good fruit, impartial and sincere." (Jas. 3:17).

12

Submission

SUBMISSION IS DEFINED IN the Oxford Dictionary as, "agreement to abide by a decision or to obey an authority; reference to the decision or judgment of a (third) party." It is also defined as occasionally meaning "humiliation or abasement".[1] As Christians we should line these definitions up with the relationship we have with God because he is the authority in every area of our lives and he is the "third party" to all our relationships with other people. Because our obligation to submit to him stands absolutely, then we should submit or not to others according to his will; he may want us to submit or he may not. Either way there will never be the consequence to us of spiritual "humiliation and abasement" because this runs contrary to his character. We should submit to others if it is in the course of submitting to God—if he requires us to do so. But it won't be his will if it runs contrary to our spiritual well being.

When we read about David, we see he asked God to be with him in every thought and action. If we do the same, then during every second of our lives we should be in conscious total submission to God. Once we choose to dwell in this closeness to him, the rule on submission can be summarized very easily: submit to everything that is God's will and to nothing that isn't. In every instance, legitimate submission to others is derived from submission to God and not independent of it. God's will and man's will are so often in conflict it is not possible to have a blanket rule that dictates submission to both at the same time. When it comes down to the practicalities, there is a lot of confused thinking. Some sincere Christians believe it is God's will that certain areas of daily living

---

1. Little, *The Shorter Oxford English Dictionary.*

require total blind unequivocal submission of one person to another, while at the same time they overlook the relevance of submission to God in every area of life.

A leading politician known to be a practicing Christian was asked whether a particular political matter should be laid before God. The answer was, "that is not something that should be taken to God; that is something that should be taken to the people." The question was reminiscent of the word games the Pharisees used to play with Jesus when they were trying to trap him. If this politician had answered that like everything else it should be laid before God then before long the headline might have been, "Church Rules Parliament," or something implying that. So the politically correct answer was given. The politician in question was under great pressure surrounded by a forest of microphones thrust aggressively close. That scene would be enough to intimidate most of us but of course it was the wrong answer. Such Christian leaders need to be in constant communication with God, recognize everything they are involved in should be taken to him, and then rely on the Holy Spirit to promote God through them appropriately at every opportunity.

In another instance of a Christian politician and a media question the politician said his first loyalty was to his family. Again a vote-catching political answer and another lost opportunity for God. This answer worked very well politically for a while, but only for a while. Admittedly, another New South Wales politician, who has been very forthright in his views, some of which are very controversial, including in Christian circles, has often been made a figure of public ridicule. It is a risky business deferring to God in the public arena, but Jesus did it and so should his followers today. It needs to be recognized that only the Holy Spirit can supply the finesse to frame the correct answer to the questions that are meant to trap.

There are many instructions in the Bible exhorting us to submit. It is easy to get lost in the particulars and fail to recognize the underlying principle of submitting directly only to God and then to him in everything. This will often lead on to appropriate submission to another. We are given broad examples in the Bible and our own situation will have things in common and things that are different. No one example given as a guide is intended in its literal interpretation to cover every possible variation in the life of every Christian who ever lives.

The reverse of our submitting to others occurs when others submit to us. In a way, considering this clears the confusion because God never wants us to diminish anyone; rather by our interaction with them we are to build them up. When we are in a position of power over someone else we should never forget this principle. We should model ourselves on Jesus who was gentle and humble of heart. Similarly, if we are in a situation where our submission to another involves "humiliation and abasement" of us, then it is not likely to be God's will for us to continue in submission.

CREATION

Imposing submission wrongfully doesn't just stop with other people. Consider the almost universal belief that God's creatures should always submit to humans. God said to man at creation, "fill the earth and subdue it. Rule over the fish of the sea and the birds of the air and over every living creature that moves on the ground... And to all the beasts of the earth and all the birds of the air and all the creatures that move on the ground—everything that has the breath of life in it—I give every green plant for food." (Gen. 1:28–30). In these verses God made provision for all Creation, not just man, but for the other creatures as well. He gave man responsibility for them, but he didn't intend that humans in their greed and callousness should have the right to disregard the negative effects of their own wants on these other creatures. In Exodus he gave detailed instructions to rest the land, the vineyards, and the olive groves every seventh year so the poor and the wild animals could eat. Part of the purpose of the Sabbath was to refresh not only the people but also the working animals.

Surely no Christian could agree with habitats being destroyed to the extent that species have become extinct. Methods of pig farming in Australia must be an offence to God. No wonder Paul said, "We know that the whole creation has been groaning as in the pains of childbirth right up to the present time." (Rom. 8:22). God cares for every creature and they share the promise in the Kingdom of God that is to come: "creation itself will be liberated from its bondage to decay and brought into the glorious freedom of the children of God." (Rom. 8:21). Unfortunately Christians have fixated on the words "subdue" and "rule over" in Genesis 1:28 and dismissed everything else relevant. We know we are told we are made in the image of God, but that is not to say the rest of creation is not. Obviously the image of God is not a physical image, it is a spiritual image. As Christians we are not nearly as disturbed as we ought to be that the caring responsibility allotted to man for creation has been ignored or abused. The submission we have imposed on creation has brought "humiliation and abasement" to it. It is selective obedience, resulting in our submission to God going wrong.

It was God's business to make the earth, he did it without out help, and yet we feel obliged to get ourselves into unnecessary and fruitless arguments over exactly how he did it. We should attend to our own business, which is to care for all he made, but we have neglected to fully understand or have willfully misunderstood his instructions, and so failed to follow them.

GOVERNING BODIES

Jesus was so adept at applying spiritual principles while recognizing the uniqueness of each situation. He was able to show clearly it was possible to obey the law of the land and God's law when he spoke about taxes. Indirectly he said it was God's will for the Jews to submit to Caesar by paying him taxes. Mindful of God's purpose for him and the background of the political scene at the time, his answer was both brilliant and very careful. At times in history evil regimes have ruled and to pay taxes to them may well not have been God's will. The bad news for us living in first-world countries today and filling in tax returns is probably that we fall exactly under the advice Jesus gave the Pharisees, so to cheat on our taxes is to cheat God.

It is also clear the Israelites who had submitted to the rule of Pharaoh for four hundred years were fulfilling God's will during their time in Egypt and were equally moving in his will when they rebelled against the Pharaoh at the time of the Exodus. So which is right for us, which should we copy? Should we always submit to the state or should we always be lawless? Obviously neither answer is always correct and neither answer is always incorrect. We have to ask God to answer the question for us whenever we find ourselves in a complex situation with many relevant but apparently conflicting Bible verses. Joseph was sure he should submit to Egyptian rule; Moses was sure he shouldn't. Both were godly men. Moses talked with God continuously during the plagues and the flight from Egypt, and although he doubted his own ability, he was never in doubt Israel's time for submission to Pharaoh was over. Not so the Israelites, who in their worship were often far from God and changed their minds frequently. Far from being appreciative of the effort Moses was making on their behalf they accused him of misleading them. The Israelites didn't have a clue whether they should be submitting to Moses or submitting to Pharaoh, because like us they were often not listening to God.

SLAVERY

Paul said quite a lot on slavery. It is interesting to note he seemed to have discarded the out-dated cultural advice in Exodus about the treatment of slaves. Then it was Okay to beat a slave so long as he was able to recover enough from his injuries to be mobile again after a day or two. Moses gave the people this rule, and it was probably as caring as he could make it, and still be acceptable to the culture of fifteen hundred BC. I wonder if there were people living in Paul's time who still held that view, in the same way there are people today holding to other now out-dated cultural ideas of Paul. It was necessary for him to comment on slavery because many new converts were slaves. It is obvious from the emphasis on freedom and equality in the Bible that it has always been God's ultimate purpose that nobody should be a slave. It was Jesus's purpose to bring this about indirectly by spreading the gospel of spiritual freedom and not directly by insurrection. Paul told Christians who were slaves to obey their masters, "just as you would obey Christ." (Eph. 6:5). His words emphasized that the submission involved has to be to God and from there correct actions follow—in this case obedience to earthly masters. His advice was obviously given to allow them to understand the teachings of equality in the gospel while not causing political and social upheaval. The institution of slavery was so strong at the time that if Christian slaves had rebelled, there would have been a bloodbath, and it would have achieved nothing other than to obstruct the spread of the gospel. God often calls for the spilling of Christian blood, but in this instance, in hindsight, we can now see his immediate purpose then was to spread the gospel and not to abolish slavery.

Does this mean nearly two thousand years later in the USA the African American slaves were meant to follow Paul's advice and submit to their white masters? Did Martin Luther King's role in the political unrest that led to the recognition of African American equality cast him in the role of villain or martyr? The obvious explanation is that God's unchanging purpose for man is always moving towards completion and everything concerning us has to be interpreted in this light. Advice tailored for a particular time in history may be quite the opposite for another time. The culture and traditions of the first century AD are not relevant to today in their particulars but only as an illustration of underlying spiritual principle. Culture and tradition change; God's relationship with us and his purpose of salvation never change.

SUBMISSION ON THE BASIS OF GENDER

A key verse in the Scriptures is: "So God created man in his own image, in the image of God he created him; male and female he created them." (Gen. 1:27). There is no inequality, no concept of submission of one person to the other in this simple clear statement.

This verse was quoted by Jesus himself in Matthew 19:4 when he was teaching on divorce. It first appeared in the Scriptures when things were still rosy in the Garden of Eden. The Fall of Man changed all that and God outlined to Adam and Eve the negative consequences of their disobedience. "To the woman he said, 'I will greatly increase your pains in childbearing; with pain you will give birth to children. Your desire will be for your husband, and he will rule over you.'" (Gen. 3:16). All in the one speech God included the words "pain" and "rule". He didn't say, "this is the way I want it to be," but rather God made it clear to us that "rule" like "pain" is a mark of Satan's triumph and certainly not what he first gave us or wants for us. Neither childbirth nor the relationship between men and women was meant to be like this. God's words of punishment were a result of Adam and Eve's disobedience. They came under the Old Covenant of the law, but Paul tells us God has moved on from there, "through Christ Jesus the law of the Spirit of life set me free from the law of sin and death." (Rom. 8:2). Man has been forgiven, the penalty has been lifted. The argument that God ever intended that women should submit to men is not valid. Satan in retreat is still deceiving us and would have us believe Christ came for nothing. He wants to keep us forever enmeshed in the consequences of sin but we have been set free by the power of the resurrected Jesus. We feel free to relieve the pain of childbirth, but not to declare the equality of the sexes. Neither of these two things was ever what God wanted for us; they were as temporary as the power of the law was to condemn us. It all ended with the cross. Where is the sense in sitting in prison with the doors wide open?

Feet on Earth, Head in Heaven

In the Creation story we are told man was created first. Most of the account is about the man, his need for a helper and his naming of the other creatures. The woman is presented as an afterthought, after the creation of the man and after the naming of the animals. Even if we were to accept the literal interpretation of the origin of the female that woman came from the rib of man, this flesh would have been nothing more than a piece of decaying meat if God had not breathed life into it. In this vital sense there was no difference in the creation of the two sexes. As an aside, perhaps the account of the rib origin of woman was only intended to symbolize the close physical, and spiritual unity, and unity of purpose God wants between the sexes. The order of creation in time has nothing to do with God's order of supremacy or Adam would have been created before plants and animals. This means his arrival before Eve is irrelevant as an argument that woman should submit to man.

Overall the account of creation in the Old Testament poses a bit of a dilemma. We have to see it as a story full of symbolism. There are bits missing vital to a literal understanding. For example, when were the females of other species created—after their males and before or after the human female? And were they also taken from the rib of the male, which is impossible in species without ribs? Whatever the actual meaning of the Creation story it has not helped the cause of equality for women. Perhaps this is because it is only about creation and not about equality. If so, the Ancient Israelites missed the point as have many Christians since. Perhaps out of all the symbolism we are meant only to understand that God is the Creator of all things.

In this chapter I have tried to explain why I believe it is time to recognize that submission of the female to the male on the grounds of gender is no longer tenable. As most of the teachings supporting submission come from Paul's writings it may seem at first glance that there is gross unfair criticism of Paul himself. This is the last thing I would wish to do. In criticizing their stance on gender inequality I by no means wish to criticize any of the disciples personally or cast a shadow on their high spiritual standing. So it is crucial, in order to avoid such misunderstanding, to realize the now outdated teaching in the Bible based on culture and tradition is no mistake. I'm sure God meant the disciples to write as they did. There is no way the men of Paul's time would have listened to him if he had preached on the equality of men and women. This would have meant his extensive successful planting of the new churches would never have happened. Like all Christians, I feel so indebted to all the disciples for the lives they led, their inspirational faith, and the sacrifices they made to share the gospel with all people. This doesn't alter the fact that having served its purpose, their first century traditional teaching is no longer relevant to today and should now be abandoned. Not to do so diminishes God's word. With that said, I will move on to a full discussion of the subject.

Paul gives his view of events in the Fall of Man when he said it was the woman who sinned and she is almost seen to provide an excuse for Adam's sin, "Adam was not the one deceived; it was the woman who was deceived and became a sinner." (1Tim. 2:14). Paul also seemed to think Adam had greater status than Eve because he was created first. This faulty logic would mean all other creatures, who were created before Adam, would have a higher status ascribed to them than Adam.

Also Paul says, unlike men, justification by faith *alone* is not enough for women to be saved but as well they have to earn their way by works and by behaving themselves: "But women will be saved through childbearing—*if* [my emphasis] they continue in faith, love and holiness with propriety." (1Tim. 2:15). Bad luck for Mother Teresa who was childless. Contrast that statement with this one that he also made: "There is neither Jew nor Greek, slave nor free, male nor female, for you are all one in Christ Jesus. If you belong to Christ, then you are Abraham's seed, and heirs according to the promise." (Gal. 3:28–29). The conflict between these two statements shows that while Paul was very clear on doctrine as illustrated in this quote from Galatians, yet he got lost once he departed from spiritual principles to sexist conjecture based on culture, as in the Timothy quote. This was because like all men of his time he really believed women were inferior to men. Paul had been trained in Jewish tradition so couldn't put the two things together—he couldn't see that spiritual equality in Christ translates into earthly equality of the sexes.

It doesn't make sense God would make one rule on earth and the opposite in heaven. Ironically in the above verse from Galatians, Paul was himself arguing against an outdated tradition—that of circumcision. The time was right for the church to recognize this; it was time for thousands of years of appropriate church teaching on the value of circumcision to be abandoned and something better to take its place. Had the pro-circumcision lobby been successful they would have destroyed the doctrine of the New Covenant of justification by faith alone. The current Pauline traditional sexists are doing exactly the same and destroying the values of love and equality today. Just as Paul spoke out against outdated circumcision, we should speak out against outdated ideas of submission on grounds of gender.

Based on Paul's whole attitude to women as expressed in some of the things he said, he would in all honesty have to be labeled today as a male chauvinist. This is an unfair comment only because he lived in the first century AD, thought like everyone else did then, and knew no better. This was because it was God's will for him to think and teach on that subject within the culture of that time in history. Peter agreed with him, "Wives, in the same way be submissive to your husbands" (1 Pet. 3:1); and Peter was approving of Sarah because she obeyed Abraham and called him "Master." Both disciples were appropriate to their times and shouldn't themselves be judged by today's standards, but the cultural opinions they expressed, which are wrong for us today, should be judged, and should be condemned.

When Paul said, "Submit to one another out of reverence for Christ," (Eph. 5:21), presumably he was directing his comment solely to the males in the audience. Either that or the words, "submit to one another," has to mean the husband should submit to his wife in the same way his wife should submit to him. Some denominations in the church obviously don't think so and Paul's words that follow on in this next verse don't support that idea, "Wives, submit to your husbands as to the Lord." (Eph. 5:22). So that in Ephesians 5:21 when he said "submit to one another," he was almost certainly not including women at all. He gave instructions that women should be in full silent submission in church and if they spoke he called it a disgrace. Any queries they had were to wait until they could ask their husbands at home. He probably wrote everything in the expectation only men would hear it or read it and women would get all instruction second hand from their husbands. This is probably usually what happened. In the synagogues women were in a separate section to the men where they couldn't hear clearly anyway. It is not hard to see that parts of the writings of the disciples represent their human voice speaking through the tradition and culture of the first century AD. Our problem arises largely because of their habit of packaging transient traditional customs with timeless spiritual truths while seemingly giving them equal importance and thereby causing great confusion to modern believers.

Paul seems to indicate some awareness of the difficulty by the defensive tone underlying this statement about women praying with uncovered heads, "If anyone wants to be contentious about this, we have no other practice—nor do the churches of God." (1 Cor. 11:16). He was speaking in his times, but now we do have another practice, women worship with bare heads and are just as godly for it. Within the last two thousand years the church has mostly accepted worship by women without head covering, but not the overall concept of female equality.

Blatant bias against women as a way of life had been part of Jewish culture for millennia as we see in this statement from the Old Testament, "I found one upright man among a thousand, but not one upright woman among them all." (Eccl. 7:28). In Leviticus higher monetary value was placed on men than women. Of course this may be related to ability to work and fight, but it doesn't sound good on the background of all the other practices of those days.

In ancient days this thinking caused problems for men as well as for women. Abimelech had a nasty moment when he thought he was facing a fate worse than death itself. When besieging Thebez he approached a tower in the city wall in order to set it on fire because many of the inhabitants had fled there. Unfortunately for him a woman dropped a millstone from above onto his head, mortally wounding him. He immediately summoned his armor-bearer and said, "Draw your sword and kill me, so that they can't say, 'A woman killed him.'" (Jdg. 9:54), and his servant immediately obliged him. Strange priorities by our thinking, but based on the cultural belief in the inferiority of women, very logical to him.

In far ancient times because of sin in the head male of the family, whole families and their animals were executed, not just women but subservient men also. A typical example occurred about fourteen hundred BC when Achan sinned—every relative and even all his animals were stoned and then burned. The whole family, including the males, was in full submission to Achan, the head male. They had the impossible task of submitting to God and submitting to the head of the family, even when he moved outside God's will, and they unfairly bore his punishment. Time has lifted this unjust submission imposed upon men but not from women.

Four hundred years after that, in about one thousand BC, David had some insight into the unfairness of punishing people for the sin of those to whom they had to submit. He had counted the number of men in his army to assess his military strength and by so doing did not acknowledge God could defeat the enemy whether by few or by many. When David saw the effect on the people of the plague sent as punishment, he pleaded with God to punish him alone, because the decision had been his and the people were innocent.

Another one thousand years later, in the first century AD, we are told about the interesting case of Sapphira. By now it seems society had moved on from the customs in the days of Achan and David where it was considered just to punish family members and innocent strangers for wrong-doing. Nevertheless a wife was still in full submission to her husband and this was Paul's teaching. Saphira's husband, Ananias cheated the church and lied about it. In obedience Sapphira submitted to her husband, which in this instance meant agreeing to lie, so technically she became an accessory to his crime. Ananias was caught out and Peter then asked Sapphira if she would confirm her husband's lie. She did and Peter told her she would drop down dead as her husband had just done. Regardless of whether she was a willing accomplice or not, she would have had to submit to Ananias in his will to cheat and in supporting his lie. Hence the expression, "between a rock and a hard place"; she couldn't win. She was doomed by the conflicting rules of the church that demanded submission both to God and to her husband, whose will was in opposition to God's will.

If we fail to understand the difference between spiritual teachings and traditional teachings then The Old and New Testament alike will be seen to be giving very mixed messages. Insisting everything written represents God's will for us today results in women struggling with the same conflict of interest of former days arising between God's will and man's will. At times there will be the same unjust outcomes. Men have extricated themselves from the yoke of submission that tradition imposed on them in Achan's day, while women still labor unjustly under it thousands of years later.

Why did God allow Paul to write very dogmatic instructions that are no longer relevant to today? We believe the Bible is the inspired word of God so Paul was meant to write as he did. As we have seen, an obvious explanation is that God's purpose for Paul was to spread the gospel, and not to change the order of society. He was trying to show the new Christians the practicalities of putting these truths into the context of their daily lives. So he had to get into details and these details had to fit seamlessly into the lives of those living in the first century AD. That was as difficult a task then as we find it today. Living a Christian life in a secular world is a massive challenge. His words about women, although less insightful than those about slaves, did have the effect of the male population listening to his words on salvation. The women in Paul's day weren't put off, they were used to it. But the women of today are put off, and rightly so, because as

Submission

God moves forward in his purpose for man's salvation he is also refining our society. In contrast, the church is clinging to the fixed views of two thousand years ago. It took the Christian world eighteen hundred years to catch up to God and abolish slavery, but similar outdated ideas on the submission of the female to the male remain today.

Women's Rights

"Women's Rights" is an unfortunate term because through modern usage it has acquired overtones of belligerence and aggression as well as being an uncomfortable challenge to the status quo in our society. Those opposed to change rest their case after pointing to the suffragettes, to the modern bra-burners and other "in your face" campaigners like Germaine Greer. Some of these people are a bit frightening to behold and while admiring their courage, we would all rather fall into the hands of Florence Nightingale. I don't think she ever made her views known on the place of women in society, which is a pity, but obviously her main focus was on other things. We should be thankful for the well-meaning extremists in our society, because it takes the extreme views and actions to wake up the apathetic majority to injustice, and to bring about change. There are so many vested interests in injustice and so many power bases dependent on it that change is protracted and hard fought by those first to take up the challenge; the front line is not a place for the timorous. Later those women with a more balanced view have the opening to follow on and the latitude to be relatively sweet and lovely while they do it.

In my childhood, my sister and I would often make a grab for equality with the slogan, "Up with the women and down with the men!" It sounded less than sweet and lovely but we were on the front line. The "threatened" males in the family tolerated the outburst with an amused yawn, which of course we found not to our liking. They probably would have patted Germaine Greer on the head; that would have been interesting. Like her we wanted "to bring it on", although unlike her our horizons were rather more restricted—to things like the allotment of the coins in our grandmother's Christmas pudding regardless of the sex of the recipient. If that meant cutting a sixpence in half with bolt cutters then so be it! Obviously we hadn't heard of the precedent set by Solomon's judgment on which claimant should be given the baby. The fact we were allowed to repeatedly voice our refrain probably meant we didn't have a lot to complain about.

My parents gave me equal opportunity in everything including in education. In my work I was fairly well insulated from sex discrimination, but it is still rife. In this country much progress has been made but we are not there yet. Many women still have to submit to male bosses who are less qualified and capable than they are simply because of the sex difference. Of the high executive positions in Australia only 8 percent are held by women. Equal pay for equal work is obviously another right principle and one I enjoyed all my working life.

It is not just men in the church and outside it who try to keep women down. Many women find their security in a submissive role and feel threatened by those who have the confidence to move outside this security. I have been the object of at least as much sex discrimination in my life from women as from men. Conversely, some women hopefully banging their heads against the glass ceiling in the business world denigrate those who find fulfillment in the home. Neither role is right, neither is wrong, rather each person has to find out what God wants them to do and then do it. It comes down to letting God mind our business and everyone else's.

Submission has to do with power and we never get that right. The Bible was set in a time when power was derived from brute force. It was the basis of all human relationships, those between countries, in communities, and within families. Women were physically weaker and further disadvantaged by child bearing, and so they were subservient to men in everything. They had no political voice, no right of property ownership, and no right to determine family decisions. Today, in general the source of power and therefore dominance has shifted from the physical to the intellectual. In this, women are equal and they know they are. Not surprisingly they feel the old order of things should change. They now have incomes of their own, property of their own, and the ability to have goals and realize them outside the confines of marriage. There is no longer any survival value in submission. Many Christians individually are able to arrive at the logic of equality for women in all things, but the church doesn't seem to be able to do so.

Church teaching is often set and promoted by those people in the organized church who feel their power base is dependent on male dominance. This is not the official reason of course; Bible verses are presented as evidence only of spiritual truth and not of outdated traditions. I find the worry many leaders have about erosion of their power base to be quite extraordinary—do they really believe female equality could out-muscle God and unseat those he has put in place? Either they know their own motives are not pure, or they lack faith in God and confidence in themselves so derived, or they are genuinely confused.

Once the Bible is wrongly applied and distorted to support a power base, it becomes a powerful tool with which to emotionally blackmail the believer. That is how religious sects gain support and allegiance. Cults are often on such a grand scale and the effects so blatantly destructive to the human mind, or even to human life, that they come to public notice—an example is the siege at Wako in 1993, where more than seventy people died. The mainstream church has always been guilty of the same thing, but here the human suffering has usually been more subtle because evil has been gradually woven into the tradition of the church. The secular world sees it and turns away from all of us. Jesus described those religious teachers who deliberately do this, as having a thin veneer of apparent righteousness covering up a heart full of hypocrisy and evil.

Both inside and outside the church verbal tactics are commonly used to undermine the status of women and the opinions they express when they are considered to be encroaching on the male domain. These attacks are so lacking in subtlety it is surprising they are still effective, but they are. Derisive comments abound such as suggestions the woman speaking out is bitter and twisted because of an unhappy love affair, or she is a closet lesbian, or she is premenstrual or menopausal. This is a great foil to logical argument, and allows the threatened male to look like a bit of a comedian and very insightful, and under this cover he can retreat to his patch and guard it. It is the old under-the-belt tactic where character assassination is substituted for sensible comments. The humiliated female doesn't want her hormonal or emotional state put under public scrutiny so usually she tries to salvage as much dignity as she can by letting the subject drop. A woman is likely to come under this type of attack when commenting on a topic pertaining to equality with men. This includes the validity of female preachers in the church, or a broader topic like female submission to the male, or if she makes suggestions to counter sexual crimes and pornography in the church based on the overwhelming and undisputed evidence this is predominantly a male problem. To be successful, remedial approaches need to be based on this fact. Needless to say the mockers may not only be the people with the most power to lose, but also those members of both sexes who are the most insecure in their own sexual identity and role. Unfair sexist comments have nothing to do with the validity of the opinion expressed and are so cowardly. Do these people who oppose female equality with their King Canute mentality really suppose in fifty years it won't have happened in first-world countries? It will, but in the meantime there is suffering and the spread of the gospel is held back. This topic should have been resolved in the church centuries ago.

The majority of Christian leaders are not "white washed tombs", but rather they are greatly concerned for our sake and theirs to teach the truth and not corrupt God's teaching in any way. This principle is something for us to be profoundly thankful for, but it can result in many leaders "playing it safe" in areas of controversy by teaching the majority church view. This is a stance God has turned down; there is no safety in numbers, "For wide is the gate and broad is the road that leads to destruction, and many enter through it." (Matt. 7:13). The punishment outlined in this verse may or may not be relevant to erring in the topic under discussion, but the principle of not finding spiritual safety by running with the herd is the same. Similarly the hope a crime of omission is rated less seriously than one of commission is a vain one.

So in the submission argument motives are as usual mixed. The negative area of finger pointing and name calling is not a place to linger. I went there because that is how the secular world sees it. Denial and lack of honesty on our part means God's requirement for us to submit to him, and only through him to others, will not be obeyed.

Marriage

I have left the really hard area of submission to late in the discussion. Hugely controversial in Christian circles is the submission of women to men in marriage. It is an area where many Christian women struggle to know what they should do. Many go on guilt trips and many force guilt trips on others. The secular world has no such worries. There, both sexes are equal and neither is required to submit to the other. This is partly because in the secular world submission is a dirty word running counter to human pride. Of great concern to us is that the very narrow view held by some of us has the effect of making all of Christianity look wrong, outdated, and irrelevant.

Interestingly, even the strict view today in favor of submission in marriage would probably have been considered to be radically undisciplined by the Ancient Israelites. They believed women should be totally subservient to their husbands while men could divorce their wives on a whim by announcing the fact three times. Jesus showed he wasn't happy about this, but constrained by his main purpose to redeem our souls, chose to do little directly about it. Those Christians who believe women should submit to men in marriage are horrified at the extreme teachings of some other world religions in this regard, but can't see their own beliefs are similarly grounded in nothing more than outdated tradition—just less blatant.

Submission in marriage is offensive to the majority of modern women who believe in complete equality of the sexes. When trying to justify submission, Christians use apologetic terms such as, "men and women are equal but different," and even if it doesn't convince others it helps us to rationalize our own doubts and difficulties. Hearing platitudes like this has the same effect on me as the dentist drilling a nerve in my tooth. It is not an answer at all, instead, although maybe unintentional, it is a trite and untrue dismissal of the topic without addressing the issue. We have realized men and women are different since we were toddlers, while inequality is intrinsic to the meaning of the word submission. In the particular circumstance where one person submits to another in a relationship then it is an unequal one. When applied to marriage it means the whole marriage relationship is built on inequality.

Paul seemed to have a very uneasy relationship with women and somewhat confused thoughts on whether Christians should live married lives or not. He also seems to have been confused by the hierarchical order. In Genesis 1:27 we read, "So God created man in his own image, in the image of God he created him; male and female he created them." Paul seems to me to deny this verse when he says, "A man ought not to cover his head, since he is the image and glory of God; but the woman is the glory of man". (1 Cor. 11:7). His concept here of our glory seems to contradict everything else in the Scriptures on the subject.

Unfortunately for modern believers, though not for believers alive in the first century, Paul expanded his cultural beliefs in Ephesians with this advice: "Wives, submit to your husbands as to the Lord. For the husband is the head of the wife as Christ is the head of the church, his body, of which he is the Savior. Now as the church submits to Christ, so also wives should submit to their husbands in everything. Husbands, love your wives, just as Christ loved the church and gave himself up for her" (Eph. 5:22–25). The last sentence is often quoted by those who believe God meant wives to be in submission to their husbands in a marriage based solely on love. They focus on the word "love" and overlook the word "submit" in the preceding sentence and conclude the whole relationship is based on love. This is not the case because the men are told to love while the women are told to submit. Paul orders total submission by the wives to their husbands—even equal to their submission to God!—in return for perfect love from the husbands. The reality for women actually was, and for some women still is, total submission to their husband in return for imperfect love. His advice to husbands would have been very welcome to women of his day because the women were in total submission anyway—they had nothing to lose, whereas the men didn't put a great emphasis on their part of the bargain as outlined by Paul. His views on the subject are very understandable, because all his life he had been steeped in Jewish tradition.

His teaching on submission of women to men based on gender as an overarching principle is for us outdated ancient Jewish tradition, and supports Satan's dislocation of the perfect world God created. Once we identify and remove this ancient history from the writings of the disciples we see the same clear spiritual messages Jesus taught. The Bible is God's word. It is a true historical record and it is true spiritually, but we have to learn to distinguish between the two. As an historical record it tells us the way things were after The Fall; as spiritual truth it tells us the way things should be. We have to be sure we can see the difference and know when we submit it is in love to God's will, and not in superstitious fear because of some outdated belief based only on tradition.

There are two crucial interwoven points to remember. The first is that the issue is not primarily about either party submitting to the other, but about both submitting to God. The second point is that in a marriage where you have love and goodwill on both sides acting within the framework of submission to God, then submission to each other becomes an act of love and not a power struggle. Where one party is in default of this mutual responsibility then in practice it means it is God's will for some unhappy marriages to continue and for some to end.

Jesus Related to Women without Regard to the Sexist Culture of Ancient Israel

Now we get to the easy part and the good part. We only ever have to look to Jesus to feel his peace, and this is the case when we take a close look at his attitude to women during his ministry. In everything he was always so concerned with teaching spiritual truths unencumbered by the tradition of the day. He was never asked direct questions on the topic of female submission, probably because it was taken for granted. Also, probably as a reflection of their inequality, women never approached Jesus with a question of doctrine and this particular topic certainly wasn't one any of the men would want to raise. Neither was it necessary to do so. Everything Jesus said and did made it clear his love for humankind was all inclusive and quite unrelated to gender. He certainly took the angst and controversy out of ideas and statements about female submission that were written in the Scriptures after his death. If we take his lead we can clearly distinguish tradition from timeless truth. It is part of his beauty that in his humanity he was very comfortable in the company of women and his interactions with them so loving and harmonious. His attitude contrasts with Paul who often gave the impression women were the enemy and had to be kept at bay. When Jesus interacted with women he seemed always to lead with his heart, whereas Paul led with the cold hard facts of traditional religious law as he saw it from the perspective of the first century AD. This difference in attitude and teaching concerning women reflects the difference between the humanity of Paul and the divinity of Jesus. Christ saw the big picture, Paul was meant only to see the part he had to play in initiating the spread of the gospel.

The twelve apostles were all male, but there were a number of women in Jesus's life who were often with him and played important parts in his ministry. Outstanding among them were Mary Magdalene and Mary and Martha of Bethany. Mary Magdalene and other women were present at the cross trying to comfort Jesus and went to his tomb to prepare his body for burial. Jesus often went to the home of Mary and Martha at Bethany where he taught them and they nurtured him. There is no record of any female deserting or betraying Jesus in any way, unlike Peter, Judas, and the Pharisees. Even Pontius Pilate's wife said Jesus was innocent and tried to influence Pilate to free him, not that her motives were necessarily quite pure. The women who were friends of Jesus had a marvelous apparently unblemished record, a loyalty based on mutual love.

Jesus publicly bestowed honor and public recognition on women. And how he did it! It was no token gesture: he was born of woman; it was a woman who anointed him to prepare him for burial and he gave her permanent recognition in the Scriptures; the first person he appeared to after the crucifixion was a woman; it was a woman who first delivered the gospel news of his resurrection.

On Mary Magdalene he bestowed a double honor. She was the first to see him after he rose from the dead. Then he commissioned her to relay the gospel news to the disciples that he was risen, that he had conquered death—he gave her the tremendous honor and joy of placing that central piece into the final picture of the salvation of humankind. His resurrection was the seal of victory, not only on Jesus's own death, but on the death of all of us. Thus the first preacher of the gospel was appointed by Christ and was a woman—those clergy banning women preachers should take note! And what was the disciples' response to the best news the world had ever been given?—they did not believe it! Every preacher could relate to that!

Contrast Jesus's instructions to Mary Magdalene with Paul's words: "A woman should learn in quietness and full submission. I do not permit a woman to teach or to have authority over a man; she must be silent." (1Tim. 2:11-12). As a timeless principle this instruction just doesn't ring true when compared with the events at the tomb. Nor does it ring true to this verse, "And afterward, I will pour out my Spirit on all people. Your sons and daughters will prophesy," (Joel 2:28); it was quoted again in Acts 2:17-18.

Jesus had a natural empathy for women. We see this when he raised from the dead the son of the widow from Nain. She hadn't asked for help—the funeral procession was simply passing nearby. When he saw her, we are told his heart went out to her, he approached and told her not to cry. It is clear he felt the pain of the mother's grief as well as her sense of desolation and he no doubt also recognized a family without a male member was in a very precarious position. Jesus's respect for the widow who gave to the temple everything she had was very obvious when he spoke to the disciples about it. He was so gallant and loving in his attitude to women and at times let them interrupt him without becoming irritated. He responded to a need for help with the deepest love and compassion. He never told women to wait in line behind men for healing, they had the same right of approach as men had, and there are numerous examples of this, such as the woman with the hemorrhage and Jairus's daughter.

Speaking on divorce he said: "at the beginning the Creator made them male and female," (Matt. 19:4), which is the statement in Genesis 1:27 containing the assumption of equality. Then he took up the cause of women, which would have been a most surprising thing to do in those days—probably unheard of, when he said divorce was not according to God's will in the beginning, but Moses had permitted it because the people's hearts were hard. The ministry of Jesus really was always full of surprises and the Pharisees must have been in fear and trembling wondering what he would say next, while those with a heart for God must have followed him with such joyful expectancy.

Elsewhere on the subject of adultery, Jesus brought the male to account spiritually to a degree not recognized previously when he equated lust with adultery. Contrast the Old Testament where men were told not to have sexual intercourse with their daughters-in-law because it would dishonor them; not a word about the woman's feelings or rights. When the woman caught in adultery was surrounded by a lynch mob Jesus defended her by subtly and skillfully accusing the men present, some of whom may well have slept with her. His dismissal of her was gentle in the extreme.

Jesus confirmed that faith had the same central role in his relationship with women as with men when he healed the woman with the hemorrhage and said, "your faith has healed you." (Matt. 9:22). Unlike Paul, he didn't tell her that her faith would only be effective in her healing if she also promised not to talk in church and always wear a hat. He also extended equal kinship to the women as to the men who do God's will.

Jesus just simply does not entertain any of the first century human ideas on status, inequality, and submission. Where submission is concerned some people today are still as wrong in these areas as the disciples were. Every interaction Jesus had with women was on the basis of their equality, both on earth and spiritually before God. The depth of his compassion for everyone, and the beauty and purity of his love for us is so well illustrated by his attitude to the women he encountered in his life. If we could all drink this in then all the confusion and wrong thinking about gender inequality would surely melt away.

CONTRACEPTION

We read where God said to Adam and Eve, "Be fruitful and increase in number; fill the earth." (Gen. 1:28). Presumably it is based on this instruction that even as the human population rises to plague proportions, some church authorities label contraception as a sin and force their congregation to submit to this ruling. We have outstripped our ability to cater for every person's needs—not that we even want to. Global population is expected to grow from 6.7 billion to 9 billion by 2042. Ban Ki-moon, the UN Secretary General, said world farm production will need to rise by 50 percent by 2030 to meet growing demand. There are of course other factors at play than population growth, and these include the increasing use of crops for fuel rather than food; the Westernization of diets in the Far East; a diminishing bank of farming land due to urbanization; climate change and human greed, which results in some of us being overfed while others starve, and that won't change until the second coming. Given all these factors it is true we have not only filled the earth, we have over-filled it. Obviously where contraception is concerned vested interests in the organized church "tie up heavy loads and put them on men's shoulders, but they themselves are not willing to lift a finger to move them." (Matt. 23:4).

Interestingly the pressure of an ever-expanding human population has already resulted in the extinction of many species of God's creatures and this runs counter to his Word. When God first made the other creatures he "blessed them and said, 'Be fruitful and increase in number and fill the water in the seas, and let the birds increase on the earth.'" (Gen. 1:22). Immediately after Creation the sea was described as teeming with life, now only man is "teeming", and because of this, other species are disappearing.

THE BASIS OF SUBMISSION: LOVE, NOT POWER

God is love; the whole gospel is a message of love; Jesus is our living word of love. Love is the key to the submission God requires of us. Submitting to the law of God without the love of God is no fun, as the Israelites found out—they hated it and they failed. Conversely, when we really love someone with the divine unconditional love of God that sits in our heart with Jesus, there are simply no negative issues with submission; we want to do it and even when it is hard we can do it. In extending this love to others our submission to them comes automatically. Any decision not to submit to them should be a definite choice based only on the belief it would be in conflict with God's will. As an example, I don't submit to the principle of women submitting to men in anything when the decision to do so is based purely on gender, and this opinion is based on my belief this is not what God intended. I do wholeheartedly believe, unless in a specific situation it is against God's will, that in marriage each partner should submit to the other, in friendship each friend should submit to the other, and in the workplace each worker should submit to the other. Why? Because we do so out of the love of God in us, a love we return to him and to one another. Paul's good advice to the Christians subject to human slavery is pertinent to us, because in the same way they were slaves of Christ, so are we. Our attitude in submission should reflect our dedication to Jesus and our love for him. When Jesus swept aside his earthly and heavenly status and washed the feet of the disciples he showed us an example of loving submission that we are meant to follow. Such love should underpin everything we do, including every act of submission.

SUFFERING IN SUBMISSION

There is a difference between earthly and spiritual humiliation and abasement. It is not always God's will for us to "cut and run" just because we are being treated unfairly. Sometimes he wants us to persevere, not because he wants us to suffer, but because there is a higher spiritual purpose for us or for others. Often while we are being most abused in the earthly sense we are reaching greater spiritual heights.

Jesus spent his whole life in submission to God even though it meant he was constantly under attack from the vested interests of the day. Most of the time in his ministry his will was instinctively and peacefully in concert with that of God. It was different in Gethsemane, where in great distress he prostrated himself before God and begged to be spared from crucifixion. Even so, in his final words he submitted his wishes to the will of God. We couldn't get a more perfect example of submission than this. Jesus's whole approach turned on prayer. He didn't move away from God with an attitude of rebellion and mumble to himself that it just wasn't fair, as we are so apt to do. Rather he remained with God throughout and in constant communication with him. In prayer he asked, he pleaded, but he never demanded. Because of his love for God he never for an instant departed from his desire and will to submit to him. He was facing the ultimate horror of separation from God on the cross and because he submitted to this fate for our sake, we need never lose contact with God. We can get through the hardship that is sometimes involved in submission. When we are suffering in any way our God of all comfort closes in on us, because we are the people won for him by Christ. Only God knows the whole picture and where it fits into his will.

If we are the one suffering, knowing whether to continue in submission or not, will come from dwelling as closely to him as we can. If we see others suffering like this we should support the sufferer as much as possible, but should usually refrain from giving an opinion about what they should or should not do. The only way we will get our part right in helping them is the same way they will—stick with Jesus, he never got it wrong. The difference between submission in the Kingdom of God and the secular world is that in the former it flows from love, whereas in Satan's world it is dictated by power.

SUMMARY

Some denominations of the organized church are floundering in their teachings on submission and as a result Christians are totally confused and non-believers derisive. The core Christian teaching of obedience by full submission to God in everything is not well followed, while first-century cultural beliefs of submission on such grounds as gender are promoted. The traditions of two thousand years ago in the writings of Paul are being wrongly taught as eternal spiritual truth. In matters of submission the church has to decide whom it is going to follow—Jesus through his personal example and timeless teachings or the disciples with their outdated traditions. The church has been having an each way bet trying to teach both and this is not credible. We can embrace Jesus totally, everything he did and everything he said, but with Paul we have to sift out the tradition to find the abundance of spiritual gems God gave us through his writings. Jesus's own words about divorce apply equally to the whole subject of submission of women to men when he said the imperfect was permitted, "because your hearts were hard. But it was not this way from the beginning," (Matt. 19:8).

The Bible has to be seen to be a historical record of what happened and not necessarily a recommendation of this history, much of which reflects the evil consequences of the Fall of Man. How can non-believers trust us to tell them the truth about God and the submission due to him, when they can't trust us to see the difference between spiritual truth and historical record? We will never convince them of the truth of the gospel and the rightness and benefits of submission to God in all things, unless we do it ourselves appropriately in the power of his love, untainted by outdated wrong human values.

We need to remember two things. First, we submit unreservedly in everything only to God. In this we follow Jesus's example, "For I have come down from heaven not to do my will but to do the will of him who sent me," (John 6:38). Second, love is absolutely indispensable in motivating us and empowering us to submit.

The submission God demands is enormously difficult for us to do. This is because we stumble over our pride and considerations of power blind us. Satan plays us like a fiddle when we succumb to these two great weaknesses. He has been making music in both the world and the organized church for far too long, but not in the kingdom of God where love rules. If we can only get over ourselves, we can submit to God in all things and find a marvelous spiritual place of peace with him. If we can't do this then we stay back in Satan's world of pain and discord. It is never God, never love, where there is enforced inequality, repression of the human spirit, or hardness of heart. Let us live according to this eternal truth in Paul's writings: "You, my brothers, were called to be free. But do not use your freedom to indulge the sinful nature; rather, serve one another in love." (Gal. 5:13).

13

Sexuality and the Church

Sex is a hot topic in the Bible with many teachings and warnings. This is for good reason, we are obsessed with it and just don't seem to be able to get it into perspective or control it in our lives. For centuries up until the last fifty years or so, Church policy seems to have been to frown upon all sexual practice as evil. It was only grudgingly tolerated as a means of survival of the species, but under no circumstances was it to be enjoyed. This was in keeping with the general thinking that where there was enjoyment there was evil. In my childhood, anyone caught smiling about anything came under suspicion—most people born before the baby boomer generation knew smiling was a risky thing to do unless there was a very ready and wholesome explanation.

In the twentieth century the pendulum in the secular world in Western countries swung even further the other way so the theme became, "If it feels good, do it." Now depravity is openly accepted as a valid option. Possibly this change was influenced by the increased freedom of women in many areas that came as a result of their wider roles in the war effort, particularly in World War Two, when many boundaries between the sexes were removed. After that, reliable contraception in the seventies meant women no longer needed to fear the negative consequence of unwanted pregnancy. Today women who don't want to be involved in indiscriminate sex can be more easily pressured into complying, because they are no longer seen by their peers to have a valid excuse not to do so. Many modern young unmarried women have been hoodwinked by the plethora of media messages that advocate random sex as an instant path to the glamorous life, while reducing the importance of it to an after-dinner drink. Its greater role as an integral part of a permanent, loving, and committed relationship is denied, resulting in great cost to the psyche and emotional well being of both women and men.

The church is on the back foot with an official policy of sex only within marriage and very little is said at all in sermons on the issues of sex outside marriage. When repression was the order of the day and the church held a central position in society, hellfire and damnation for every reason was frequently presented to a quivering congregation. Now the church is marginalized, and only treated with respect by many people at funerals and some sentimentalists at weddings, not much that is confrontational is said from the pulpit. This is partly because if all the adulterers, and fornicators, and those wistfully lusting were to take offence and leave, then it might be difficult to find even a quorum left in the congregation.

We need to get the message across that every aspect of all our relationships is precious and to be valued within the context of God's great love for us. If we put him first, look to him for guidance and build our ego on him, then all the difficult issues we face become so much easier. God never wants to take back or restrict any of the gifts he has given us. He wants us to enjoy them all to the full, but this will only happen when we do it his way. Jesus tells us, "The thief comes only to steal and kill and destroy; I have come that they may have life, and have it to the full." (John 10:10). Too often we welcome and play host to the thief.

THE SPECTRUM OF HUMAN SEXUALITY

Heterosexuality, homosexuality, pedophilia, addiction to pornography etc. are being seen increasingly as variations in sexuality with which people are born rather than a matter of choice. Medical advances such as functional brain scanning may well uphold this view in the future. Research has found hormonal influences at various times in the development of the brain of the fetus can affect sexual behavior. The more boys there are in a family, the more likely a younger one will be homosexual. This doesn't necessarily mean that anything with a medical, genetic or neuroanatomical basis is either desirable or according to God's will, e.g., differences are showing up in the brain of the psychopath; maturity-onset diabetes has a genetic predisposition but it is a harmful thing to have and can be avoided or controlled by personal effort. This knowledge of causality does help us to take a lot of the blame (which we shouldn't have anyway), out of the whole subject of sexual preference and practices within that preference. The church needs to be consistent in attitude—diabetes is an evil, but the person suffering from it is a victim of it and no more evil than anyone else. This thinking needs to be extended to the sexual sphere. Logically, heterosexuality with its potential for a full family life seems to be the ideal in terms of human happiness and the Bible clearly upholds this view.

If fulfilling one's desire, whatever it is, brings harm to anyone, then it should be forfeited. The harm done might be emotional or spiritual. An act is also wrong if it brings harm on oneself, because we are told our bodies belong to Christ and are a temple of the Holy Spirit. Jesus said in the context of adultery that we should remove it from our lives in the same way we would amputate an injured or diseased limb that is a threat to life. Whenever we degrade ourselves by putting one of our gods before God, whether it is sex or anything else, we dishonor him, our Creator, and he will not tolerate it. When referring to the Israelites's unfaithfulness in worship including child sacrifice, he said these acts had been done against him and the perpetrators would be punished. This applies to all areas of activity as much as to idolatry and sexual conduct, and it means we should guard our health, avoid such things as smoking, excess alcohol intake, and be responsible in the way we drive.

Random sex with multiple partners, predatory or lewd behavior, and festivals modeled on Sodom and Gomorrah are fairly obviously not of God and cause no confusion in the mind of a Christian. Apart from the enormous self-harm and harm to others such behavior causes, how could we cause such offence to our loving God who died for us? Nothing is worth that.

HETEROSEXUALITY

Although accepted as the valid norm in both the secular and the Christian world, heterosexuality is not without its problems. Because it is the way most people live it has been at the centre of more heartache and strife than any of the alternatives put together. The ideal lifestyle is to have one partner for life and around this relationship to build a solid, loving, family structure. This doesn't commonly happen because like every other gift God has given us we have trashed it—in this context by substituting normal libido founded on a loving relationship with one partner, for casual lust and depravity. Many people who pay lip service to God in other relationships struggle in this area. The result is dysfunctional families, single parent families, children in distress, and sexually transmitted diseases. We should remember all this heartache when we are tempted into sexual promiscuity. Unfortunately we do go there and shrug it off, or treat it with a nod and a wink, or enjoy it vicariously through crude comments and jokes. The culture today outside the church and unofficially inside it is to be very liberal, so that we make excuses for ourselves and our friends when standards are lowered. Within congregations adultery is ignored and fornication is covertly accepted by both the congregation and the clergy.

As an aside it should be noted the word "fornication" does not appear in the NIV Study Bible. The word "adultery" on the other hand is prolific and this is probably a reflection of the assumption in ancient Israel that all sexual activity should be confined to marriage. Presumably, what we call "fornication" was encompassed by the words "adultery" or "sexual immorality". In considering what God's will is, where sex between two consenting but unmarried adults is concerned, we have to look at all the advice in the Scriptures about morality, lust, and holiness in order to draw conclusions. This is not as straightforward as it seems because the conclusion will depend on how we define these other things—so that the argument easily becomes circular. Some people feel so long as pregnancy and infection are avoided that there are no untoward effects and restraint simply reflects now outdated cultural taboos. In our times it is a very important subject because of pressures on young people and the increased number of single older adults. Many people today are in situations where it is very relevant to their spiritual growth to resolve the dilemma. Since being born again, my belief is sex should be confined to marriage. Jesus equated lust with adultery, which seems to make it clear that this is an area where God demands the strictest of standards. As usual it is for our own good. If we stand back and look at our society today it is decadent and desperately unhappy. We have swung from the repression and hypocrisy of Victorian times to the moral anarchy of today. As Christians our aim is to live a holy life that honors our Holy God. It seems to me to be a matter of faith. He knows our needs better than we do and if we wait on him we can trust him to always work in our best interests. There is nothing on earth to compare with his presence in our life.

Sex outside marriage is not just a trap for the morally depraved; we are all vulnerable because it is the strongest of the basic instincts. When we are tempted, we are likely to see the object of our desire as the personification of love in all its splendor, whereas of course he or she has simply been gift-wrapped by Satan. A married person is probably less of a challenge to bring undone because the spouse is there every day, always surrounded by life's tedious and tiring demands—such things as work, bills, and head colds, and often displaying the irritating habits we all have, while looking anything but glamorous with eyeballs dragging in the breakfast cereal. For the married person, time with the lover has to be snatched rather than forced predictably upon them. There is the lure of the forbidden and the excitement of romantic clandestine meetings in places insulated from the tedium of daily routine. In other words adultery and fornication are forms of escapism. Far better to escape to God; his solutions bring us and those around us everything that is good and nothing that is destructive to us or to others.

Lust is such a dangerous area and the only safe way is to stop it right there and remove it from our mind, because the situation rapidly escalates beyond control. When we are tempted we also need to realize we cannot build our own happiness on the unhappiness of others; it just doesn't work. The pain of turning away from the giddy heights of our desire can be excruciating, but we can do it if we turn to God and bring his strength to bear, and his blessings will be there waiting for us.

The biblical teaching is that we are meant to be monogamous for life. If we accept this, then it would seem it is going to take an enormous effort by both parties to make such a relationship work. A survey by the National Opinion Research Centre (University of Chicago), found that 25 percent of men and seventeen percent of women admitted to having been unfaithful.[1] The same website states that a 1988 survey of nearly one thousand Protestant clergy by *Leadership* magazine found 12 percent admitted to sexual intercourse outside of marriage. The Kinsey Institute[2] gave figures for adultery in non-clergy and these were similar to the National Opinion Research Centre figures.

Although it can be a very difficult area for people to control it is in fact the same as any other idol we can't tear ourselves away from. Putting anything including sexual satisfaction as a priority in our lives ahead of God is wrong. David was a prize example of this, even resorting to murder in order to sleep with Bathsheba, another man's wife. It must have

---

1. Anderson, http://www.leaderu.com/orgs/probe/docs/adultery.html.

2. The Kinsey Institute, http://www.kinseyinstitute.org/resources/FAQ.html#amato.

been even more difficult in those days when the king could do almost anything, when women had few rights, and concubines were a way of life. Despite his inability to control his sex drive David was a godly man and always turned back to God in repentance. Anything wrong in our lives requires God's intervention but like David we need to be willing to cooperate.

To compound the dilemma when problems arise, we don't see the basic issue, which is wrong priorities, rather we go off at tangent and find someone to blame other than ourselves. If we are the guilty party we are never without excuses that seem more than adequate to us. Similarly, we let our friends and the people we like off the hook. Conversely, if we are the innocent party or our allegiance lies there, we plunge easily into a lifetime of bitterness and unforgiveness. The ramifications of uncontrolled lust are huge, and like all sin it gathers in strength and oozes into every aspect of our lives and thinking. It causes us to be sexist, to bring sorrow to ourselves and to others, to tell lies, to gossip, to judge, and condemn.

Whether we are the transgressor or a bystander, we often blame the uninvolved wife either by seizing on some minor personality fault, or lack of outward beauty as an excuse for the husband's adultery, or by blaming her for some assumed sexual underperformance that is spewed up from the sewer of our own mind. I heard a person excuse a leader, who was a serial adulterer in his own congregation, on these grounds. This reinforcement of sexism seems to be one of the many negative effects of condoning philandering. The "blokey" culture amongst sporting stars is accepted by their adoring public, while the women involved are forever regarded as immoral. Sometimes it seems not a lot has changed since the story of the woman caught in adultery, doubtless some of the crowd who had gathered to stone her had behaved just as badly. Culture has changed somewhat. Now there is some tolerance for adultery in women, but overall they are still judged harshly compared to men because our perverted society aligns sexual conquest with masculinity in men and foul play in women.

Triggered by secular pressure, after centuries of repression, the church has changed its stance by acknowledging sex is something to be enjoyed within marriage. Formerly, women particularly, were expected to participate as unenthusiastically as possible and when necessary to think of England. In recent years the pendulum has swung the other way and sex has been put on something of a pedestal. Now we seem to wax lyrical on the subject. Sometimes I think we could handle it better if we were to trivialize it more. Food is to be enjoyed, sunshine and friendship are to be enjoyed, but like all of God's blessings we have to keep our perspective. We know it is not in our best interests to eat our head off, to burn ourselves to a crisp in the sun, or drink coffee with friends to the exclusion of everything else. Sex also has its place but is no more of an amazing thing than the other blessings God has given us; even species of worms do it. With that in mind it is puzzling to consider why sexual performance has become so much part of our ego, and this is so now for both men and women. The Christian can get sex in perspective by instead building his or her ego on the love God has individually and especially for each of us—he has written our names on the palms of his hands and counted the hairs on our heads.

DIVORCE

If there has been divorce on grounds other than adultery, is remarriage considered to be adultery in the eyes of God? Church teaching has always been that it is. Jesus said divorce was only allowed in his time because of hardness of heart. Our hearts are no softer today. If divorce was inevitable and acceptable in ancient days for this reason then it may be correct to say it is today also. Jesus seems to be saying both that lifelong marriage is the perfect way to go and that we are incapable of this perfection. This is no surprise, there is sin in the world and perfection in anything eludes us.

The considerable physical, psychological, and emotional suffering that is so common within marriage is simply not addressed in the Scriptures. Surely Jesus in his compassion would not expect someone to stay in a marriage for life if caught in an intolerable example of those circumstances. Similarly, the option of staying celibate after a marriage breakup for someone young, especially if they haven't had children, also doesn't seem to be what he would want for the majority of people so affected. Nevertheless it is obvious divorce is not a trivial thing. That we should turn to God with all our might to help us to resolve marriage difficulties is as relevant as with all our problems. The divorce rate in Australia is about forty percent and sadly Christian marriages do no better than non-Christian ones. This has to be partly a reflection of the low priority we Christians place on asking God to run our lives. Counseling may be of benefit. However it takes two people of goodwill to succeed and this is often not the case.

As usual those with all the head knowledge and little heart knowledge and those who are blessed with an easier marriage, judge those people harshly who have failed. Rather than give loving support they imply a failed marriage means spiritual failure. We hear a lot about "submission", mostly out of context and with little understanding of what God wants. Perhaps those who stand in judgment and lack compassion are in a state of greater sin; perhaps they are in a lot more spiritual trouble than the divorced person.

CELIBACY

This topic is only discussed here because I feel the unmarried need a word of encouragement and the married need to have a better understanding of the unmarried state. It takes intestinal fortitude to go through life without a partner. In Genesis God said it wasn't good for us to be alone. A happy marriage seems to be the best option. However since God made that statement, we have had to live in a fallen world and the best option in anything is often not available—in this case not the "happy" part of marriage, or for some any marriage at all.

It is okay to be unmarried; Jesus was unmarried. It is a state that does not make the person inferior. Jesus commented, "others have renounced marriage because of the kingdom of heaven. The one who can accept this should accept it." (Matt. 19:12). This statement is not just referring to celibate clergy but also to anyone for whom marriage is not God's will, in which case their unmarried state will further the kingdom of heaven within and around them. The problem is most people cannot accept being unmarried, and are either very unhappy or sublimate in undesirable ways. Like everything else in our life, we have to follow Jesus's instruction in the above verse and decide to marry or not on the grounds of whether or not it is God's will for us to do so. If it is his will for us to be single, then we should be peacefully accepting of it, because being aligned with his will is the best state for us to be in.

Those who are unmarried are often diminished or derided by society, either subtly by exclusion or in the jokes that abound. They are in good company; as a result of Jesus's unmarried state he has been labeled an adulterer with Mary Magdalene and a homosexual with John. Not a lot has changed in our thinking, we still see the unmarried as inferior at best and perverted at worst. It is all part of mob majority mentality.

For their part the unmarried need to understand a successful marriage is mostly hard slog and has problems they are fortunate enough never to have to face. Even so, the single people are more likely to understand the problems of married life better than the married people understand the problems of the single life. This is because most of us spent our childhood in a family. Also most of the supportive talks and discussions held by the church are for the married and not for the single members of the congregation, and this oversight includes the never married, the divorced, and the widowed.

Fortunately as the empowerment of women is increasing, the negative attitude to the unmarried state is changing, so that we are starting to see it as a valid option. As usual in the church, change is slower and I see many couple and family social events organized and very few tailored to the single Christian, who is usually lonelier and more in need of companionship. It is the minority of Christians who will host a dinner party with uneven numbers of men and women at their table, something the recently widowed or divorced find more hurtful than the never married, who have grown used to it and learned to cope. This demonstrates our earthly priorities, as Jesus said marriage won't be part of life in heaven.

Probably the main issue single people battle with is loneliness and its ramifications—such as not having the assurance of being anyone's priority and not having the security and support of close family. The upside to this is it is easier for the single person to depend on God for these things—which is as it should be.

Another irritation for the single person to overcome is usually they are seen to have nothing much to do and so their service is often less appreciated, whereas a committed Christian whether single or married won't be idle. Again there is a spiritual upside, the single person relies less on the praise of man and more on the praise of God.

There is much more accountability in the lives of single people; how can you scapegoat someone else for your problems if there is no one there? (Overcoming this problem by blaming the single state or long dead parents is not to be recommended). This ready accountability opens up the way for rapid spiritual growth.

A great blessing God has given the single person is an abundance of freedom in every area of life that a married person doesn't have. There is the potential for greater freedom of thought, of action, and most importantly of worship. This is a huge gift and makes it easier to put God in first place, to talk with him, to be aware of his presence, and to gain the only true security that we find in him. For the single person there may be fewer earthly blessings, but for those who love God there is far easier access to his priceless spiritual blessings.

Perhaps we should give more attention to Paul who said the unmarried should stay that way unless they found celibacy too hard. Maybe with this advice to be single he was getting ready for the second coming a bit early. If everyone had complied, the Christian would have become extinct—do we hear a roar of approval from the secular world? His words do lend an interesting perspective to the subject and hopefully help to abolish the false pride, prejudice, envy, and lack of love that abounds.

HOMOSEXUALITY

For the Christian, the subject of homosexuality is difficult. Most of the references in the Scriptures condemning it, but not all, are in the context of orgies, pedophilia, and child sacrifice. So it is not as straightforward to sort out the teaching specifically on homosexuality as is often implied. What is clear is that whatever a person's sexual preference and however that stands with God, it is wrong in God's eyes if it brings harm on anyone.

A minority view is gaining in strength among Christians that homosexual church leaders should be allowed and some have been appointed, with a resulting huge schism in some churches. Both sides are made up of godly people, both sides claim their view is supported by the Bible, and both sides have adopted a very strong stance in defense of God's word as they understand it. They can't both be right. I am relieved I don't have to make any practical decisions. I think those people who are against allowing homosexual leaders are also unduly worried homosexuality will take over and result in many people in our church congregations and many leaders becoming homosexual. This is not logical and is an unfounded fear. Homosexuality is seen in the animal kingdom, but it has always been a minor part of sexual behavior and has never been a challenge to heterosexuality.

I saw an interview in a religious program on the television where a homosexual man was interviewed. He was a Christian who believed homosexuality was wrong and he wanted to overcome it and was putting in a maximum effort to do so. To that point in time he hadn't succeeded. But God doesn't demand the attainment of perfection in anything because Jesus makes our effort perfect for us. God does demand that we be willing to do his will, as Jesus's appeal to Jerusalem makes clear—he longed for the people to accept him, and so avert the sacking of their city, but they were not willing to do so; instead, they killed him as they had done to the prophets before him, who had also tried to warn them. The television interview was a great lesson in humility because the heterosexual Christian interviewer showed such a commitment to understand the problem and to extend compassion and support to the other man. Both men were inspiring. The homosexual man himself must have tremendous faith in God to be trying publicly to resolve his suffering within the context of the Christian faith that has a record of being so unsympathetic, so unrealistic, and so cruel on this subject.

As an aside, clergy sometimes think they can solve the problem of homosexuality in the congregation in which they work by saying a homosexual person can attend the church if he or she abstains from sex. This doesn't work because the homosexual finds it no easier to abstain from sex than the heterosexual. A good reply to this proposal would be, "I will, if you will." Acceptance conditional upon abstinence is not only unrealistic because it demands the impossible, but it also represents the hypocrisy of double standards.

Because sexuality is a basic instinct, changing sexual orientation must be one of the hardest things to do. Christians who think homosexuality is evil should be encouraging such people to join the rest of the congregation who are in the grip of fornication, adultery, and lustful thoughts. The church of God is the best place for us all to be—it is our only hope.

Those people who wish to change their sexual preference should remember that difficult though this is to do, it won't be harder than a camel going through the eye of a needle. Jesus used that interesting phenomenon to illustrate how difficult it is to give up wealth and said the camel trick was easier. He cheered the disciples up by adding that although humanly impossible, all things are possible to God. That is just as well for the Christians in first-world countries today, most of whom are wealthy compared to many other populations. There is nothing we can't do in the power of God if we are willing. As in everything it is a matter of whether we decide to cling to our idols or cling to God.

PORNOGRAPHY

Pornography to some extent represents a failure to mature. It is a normal phase of childhood development, probably springing from curiosity and testing the boundaries.

We never quite give it up, the entertainment we choose proves that. But when it becomes an obsession over which we have no control, the negative effects are proportionally much greater. It wastes time better spent on other things; it takes the mind into depravity and degrades us, and so we move away from God and his holiness. A three-year, federal government-funded study, Understanding Pornography in Australia, found 82 percent of people who view pornography are male.[3] Clergy who are mostly male need not be defensive about this male predominance because it is not grounds for diminishing men, it is simply a problem they have, for reasons unknown, to a much greater degree than women. But remedial programs need to take this male majority into account. An association between pornography and increased incidence of sex offences is unproven despite considerable research.

PEDOPHILIA

Pedophilia is one of the most abhorrent of the sexual deviations. Although practiced and accepted in ancient times it was always officially condemned in the Jewish church (Leviticus chapter 18), and the Christian church after that. It inflicts immense physical and emotional degradation and injury on children. As such it is abhorrent and totally outside the teachings of Christianity. It must be self-evident to most people that it is not an option. But there are those who by their actions think otherwise, even church leaders. "For certain men whose condemnation was written about long ago have secretly slipped in among you. They are godless men, who change the grace of our God into a license for immorality and deny Jesus Christ our only Sovereign and Lord." (Jude 1:4). Despite scriptural condemnation, for many centuries there has been an accepted tradition within the clergy of at worst practicing it, and at best condoning it and covering it up. This is changing, but shamefully the change has been due to external pressure, not internal enlightenment. Even so some dinosaurs in the organized church are still hanging on in the defense of evil.

---

3. Lunn, *The Australian Newspaper*, Feb 22nd 2008.

Corrupted by power, wealth, and status they can successfully shut their eyes and their hearts to their duty to God to protect and nurture children. The majority of Christians can only puzzle over what kind of faith these people have that they could take such a stance. The easy explanation is that they don't have any faith and are not Christians. Alas, I fear some do have faith and are Christians! We have to own them and the church has to own the problem. Until we do, it will be a recurring problem that destroys young lives, destroys the church, and brings Christians and non-Christians alike to despair.

Pedophiles in the church must be removed from church office and proximity to children if the gospel is to retain any credibility at all. The organized church is still failing to do this and is thereby an accessory and as guilty as the perpetrators, "Woe to the world because of the things that cause people to sin! Such things must come, but woe to the man through whom they come!" (Matt. 18:7). Every church official with the power to remove evil of any kind from the church and fails to do so will bear the full weight of guilt. Pedophilia is a great evil, and as such is an offence against God. Like Belshazzar all people who knowingly set themselves up against the will of God, will also hear these same words of doom, "You have been weighed on the scales and found wanting." (Dan. 5:27).

FIXING THE PROBLEM

Whatever the difficulty we are experiencing, whether it is uncontrolled lust, or unhappiness due to sexual orientation, or addiction to pornography, or anything else, it is not outside God's ability to change or heal. Isaiah said this of Christ, "He has sent me to bind up the brokenhearted, to proclaim freedom for the captives and release from darkness for the prisoners." (Isa. 61:1). Christ came to set us free from all the chains with which Satan has bound us and to lead us from all the dark places where Satan has imprisoned us.

We need to put God first and thank him for the power in Jesus to overcome all problems and with him we should get on with making changes. We must take responsibility for our actions and for our choices. Paul warns us that when we willingly follow evil God will abandon us to our depravity. If we insist on self-gratification when we know it to be wrong we will get worse not better.

SUMMARY

The only way for us to avoid going wrong with sex, or getting back on track if we have a problem, is to dwell in the presence of God. All sin is anathema to God. We can count on him to understand, to forgive, and to heal. Whatever the sin is that has us in its grip, we will have to battle mightily and will only succeed in God's power. There is no place for guilt, only effort and trust in God. If we do not try to change then the sin along with the guilt it causes will destroy us. We need Jesus to guard our heart for us.

Where others are concerned, as usual we are not to judge the person, only the behavior itself and its relationship to God's will. Where there is sexual sin it is like any other sin and the perpetrators should not be routinely excluded from the church. I personally believe though that they should be removed from any church office because an essential role of leadership is to set a good example. Where relevant, the defenseless or the weak in the congregation need to be protected, but there should be people who are strong enough in their faith to come alongside the person with the problem. Those people not able to help need to stay well clear and pray. It should rarely be necessary to exclude anyone from the church; we should be able to embrace them in the love of God and help them to turn to him.

The pervading attitude of not owning any sexual problem in the church has the effect of rotting it on the inside, and of driving many people away from God. If the church can become less defensive it will see the issues and the remedies more clearly. As it is we usually draw ourselves up with our great reserves of self-righteousness and distance ourselves. This is usually not because we have battled the problem and overcome it, but because we never had that particular problem at all—anyway not yet. In that case it is cause for gratitude, thanks, humility, and service.

14

Terminal Illness

People both outside and inside the medical field may have great difficulty knowing how to talk to a person who is dying. By worrying we will say the wrong thing we say nothing at all and may avoid contact. So the dying person feels isolated, abandoned, and unloved. High on the priority list is the need for everybody to maintain normal though more supportive relationships with the sufferer. The overall aim is to help the sick person to continue their preferred lifestyle for as long as possible. It is a time to rally around in a "hands on" way to give support in all the practical details of living—such things as transport, shopping, cleaning, personal care, and respite for close relatives. If asked, God will gather around the dying Christian all those people he wants to be there. Each of those he calls will have an area of competence with complementary talents so that together they form a whole caring team. If we go in our own name we may be very helpful, but when we come in the power of Jesus's name the results will be above and beyond what we envisage.

Of paramount importance is supporting the sufferer in their faith. This is no great production. It simply results from showing our faith in action by being there with them, and when appropriate, by declaring our hope based on the many times in our lives we have experienced the fulfillment of God's promises to us. Overall the main thing is our attitude; we need to give loving support with a happy and positive approach. The ability to do this is a reflection of the strength of our faith and how strongly we believe Jesus has conquered death. The irony is that the reverse often applies and the faith of the dying person is itself like a beacon to those gathered around them.

Conversation doesn't need to be deep and meaningful. Just talking about the mundane events of the day, or subjects of mutual interest, or humorous stories from the past can lift everyone's spirits. Starting off talking about ordinary things helps everyone to relax and makes it easy to begin. Such an atmosphere allows the sick person to choose to talk about anything, whether it is their fears about their illness or their death, their funeral, their regrets, their unresolved problems, or what their dog did that morning. It is a great honor when people bare themselves frankly and sincerely, they bestow a precious gift on the listener. We need to remember if we impart any information of a private nature to others we betray the trust Jesus placed in us when he sent us to them.

Sympathy over symptoms and help to relieve discomfort is appropriate. It is important to show acknowledgement of the seriousness of the situation and that we care. We do this by sincere inquiry and frank discussion and go as far into this as the sick person wants; they set the limits. They don't want glib reassurances, they don't want to be told what someone thinks they want to hear, they want truth at all times. Truth gives dignity, promotes trust, and builds confidence. It has to be presented in the manner the person wants—some people want to avoid dwelling on negative details and only require they not be told lies; others may want total disclosure as to what is going on in their bodies, what is causing their symptoms, what they can expect in deterioration, and when and how they are likely to die. It is a good rule if they ask a question then they want an answer. The person who answers must be enough in touch with the situation and the sufferer's feelings that while answering truthfully, they reply in such a way the person can handle it. If the sick person has reason to believe they have ten years to live, then obviously we wouldn't tell them they should expect more like ten days. But we can be truthful in telling them their situation has become very serious, and they need to do anything they feel is important as their time may be much less than formerly thought. We should never guess; if we don't know the answer to a question then we need to say so and if possible find someone who does know.

Breaking down in front of a dying person often can't be avoided and I have found most people handle it very well. This is probably because in our tears is recognition of their suffering, and that we will miss them, and so is an expression of our love for them. However if we pray constantly for God to help us to be appropriate to the person's needs then losing control is far less of a problem.

Feet on Earth, Head in Heaven

PREPARATION

Aged Christians, or "battered" Christians who have run a good race, often yearn for death. We become old and tired, and struggle with disabilities. It can then become more of a challenge to live than to die. Elderly Christians often pray for death. Maybe they just have the wisdom to know the difference between earth and heaven, and want the good things God has promised them in heaven, and have the faith to claim those promises. For them, wanting to die is understandable, but it reminds me of John Milton's poem, "On his Blindness", which reads:

> "God doth not need
> Either man's work or his own gifts. Who best
> Bear his mild yoke, they serve him best. His state
> Is kingly: thousands at his bidding speed,
> And post o'er land and ocean without rest;
> They also serve who only stand and wait."

Add Christian witness and a prayerful life to "standing and waiting," and it is no wonder that God leaves Christians here who consider that through age or ill health they are well past their use-by date.

God gives us a sense of winding down as we age, or as a serious illness becomes terminal and this prepares us to meet the challenge of dying. Even the moment of death as observed from this side of the grave is a great anticlimax. We don't need to fear being with a loved one when they die, or seeing and touching them after death. The body without the spirit is the same body we have loved in life, what is there to fear?

In another group are those who think the final stages of their life will be a huge hurdle and worry about things that will never happen, and so they are pleasantly surprised when they get there. Also, even if it is tough it is always worse for loved ones. Surveys on people who have survived a horror run in an Intensive Care Unit consistently show they have a general amnesia for their pain and suffering, whereas it remains stark in the minds of relatives. When the patient does not survive, a burden of the memory of their suffering may remain with their loved ones forever. It is vital for the carers to realize that their own mental anguish as a helpless observer is the main issue, because their loved one was unaware of much of what was going on around them at the time; in particular the sick person's amnesia for suffering was insulating them to a significant degree. Most importantly, when it is over for the sufferer, the last thing they would want is that anyone should continue to suffer on their behalf.

Some burden will always remain and it is vital for it to be given to God or it can become unbearable.

There is very little human comfort when a child suffers and dies, or a person is killed in an accident, or a loved one is murdered, or medical care has fallen badly short. These sorts of circumstances are much harder to go through, but the principles are the same and prayer is at the core of our response. Only God can heal and he can only do so if we agree. This cycle of wounding and healing is not what God wants, but it occurs as he navigates our path to salvation through the sin in the world. In Jesus he binds us up and heals us both emotionally and spiritually.

FEAR

When we are confronted by death there is a natural fear of the unknown, but the whole of our life is like that. We simply do what we've done before in all the events large and small we have had to deal with in our lives—we depend on God. When we die we won't go alone, "God has said, 'Never will I leave you; never will I forsake you.'" (Heb. 13:5). Jesus has conquered death. We are safe on our journey on earth with him and safe when he takes us through death. "My Father, who has given them to me, is greater than all; no one can snatch them out of my Father's hand." (John 10:29). For the Christian it should not be an anxiety-ridden last minute disorganized scramble like many earthly trips we organize for ourselves. Jesus wants to prepare us all our life for this final journey, "You anoint my head with oil; my cup overflows. Surely goodness and love will follow me all the days of my life, and I will dwell in the house of the Lord forever." (Ps. 23:5–6).

GRIEF

Of course there is grief because it is a time of great change and loss and both these things scare us as well as sadden us. We look back to the earthly life that is lost, the good times and the pleasures we knew and the loved ones from whom we will be separated for a period of indeterminate length. This grief is legitimate. It occurs in the dying person as much as in the carers. Jesus spoke of it a number of times to the disciples in relation to his own death. He never suggests we shouldn't grieve; rather he speaks of it as a natural consequence of death, but assures us of a final joy that no one can take away.

As Christians we are not grieving over the finality of death because for us there is no death, merely a transition from the physical to the spiritual. It can be hard to wrap our minds around the reality of such a radical change, but believing a chrysalis in a cocoon regularly becomes a moth is easy for our mind to cope with and the changes are huge. Similarly, two single cells at conception become a human being—something we take for granted. We should not find the concept itself difficult, rather the difficulty lies in not being able to see examples. Although anecdotal accounts of people being seen after death abound, most of us have not had that experience. This is where we rely on scriptural accounts such as the Transfiguration, when Moses and Elijah were seen more than a thousand years after their deaths, and of course it was recorded that Jesus himself was seen many times after his death. In this way he contradicted the modern catchy phrase, "when you are dead, you are dead." Also he said: "But about the resurrection of the dead—have you not read what God said to you, 'I am the God of Abraham, the God of Isaac, and the God of Jacob?' He is not the God of the dead but of the living." (Matt. 22:31–32).

Jesus wept when Lazarus died. I have always found this puzzling. Did he weep because his friend Lazarus was dead, even though he knew he was about to raise him back to life? Did he weep because of the grief of the relatives? Did he weep because of the sin in the world that caused this endless cycle of suffering and death? Perhaps he wept both in his humanity and in his divinity so wept for all these reasons and more. Whatever the reason, amidst the distress of all those present, there was a crucial point he wanted everyone to understand. It was that in him lay the solution not just to this instance of the death of Lazarus, but for the death of everyone. He said to Mary, the sister of Lazarus, "I am the resurrection and the life. He who believes in me will live, even though he dies and whoever lives and believes in me will never die." He didn't leave it as a bald statement, he wanted to make quite sure he had been understood and added, "Do you believe this?" (John 11:25–26). Exactly why we as Christians weep is complex too, but it is valid and necessary psychologically and it won't be like this forever, physical death itself is in its final moments, "There will be no more death or mourning or crying or pain, for the old order of things has passed away." (Rev. 21:4).

GUILT

Guilt in the carers and loved ones is an expression of normal human psychology and part of the grieving process. Understanding this helps to alleviate the natural psychological tendency of the carers to feel they should have done better. Of course sometimes this is so and then it is vital to learn by the mistake.

Death may be spiritually tidy for the dying Christian, but organizationally it is never as tidy as the carers would like and there is disarray around the dying person to some extent. Gathered together is a disparate group of people comprising relatives, friends, medical, and nursing staff. This means there will be hiccoughs. I always seem to look back and want to dot every "i" and cross every "t". At the same time I am aware that the few things I would have liked to have seen done differently have not impacted greatly on the dying person.

PEACE AND JOY

Dying is crunch time for everyone. Our own death is something we are forced to think actively about from time to time during our lifetime. It particularly comes to mind if we have a serious illness or accident, attend someone else's funeral, or watch the devastation of some natural disaster on television. We even make some sort of provision for it by making wills, taking out insurance policies on our lives, and pre-paying our funeral. Most of the time though, in fear we push it to the back of our mind, but it is always there hovering like some persistent stranger determined to be heard. Human psychology relies heavily on denial to cope with overwhelming problems. Where our mortality is concerned it works well for most of our life, so that we never fully grasp and face the reality of our own death until ill health or old age overtakes us, or our doctors tell us the end is near. Even then we have a few pet fancies we dig out of the cupboard. One of them is the great emphasis most cultures place on having children, especially sons, to carry on the family line in the mistaken belief that somehow this will ensure some meaningful existence of the forebears after death. Conversely those without offspring worry they will soon be forgotten—well they will, but only by the world and not where it counts when eternity is spent with God.

When we view life from the perspective of death and we look back at the ups and downs of our life it is easy to wonder what it was all about.

Feet on Earth, Head in Heaven

The entire time spent alive can seem pointless, especially for those who have spent their time pursuing earthly treasures and not fulfilling their spiritual purpose; it is only the wisdom of God that gives anything real meaning. The psychologists have studied our state of mind in detail when death is centre stage and this human understanding is helpful to most people. It is normal to progress through a range of emotions including denial, fear, acceptance, resignation, and grief. Christians in their humanity are no different, but unlike the non-believer, God is there to guide us through. He shows us that terror is only relevant to those without Jesus, appropriate denial is the denial of spiritual death, grief is temporary, acceptance is a positive decision, and resignation is replaced by eager anticipation.

At this time, as much or more than at any other, God fulfills his promise to give us his peace, "Peace I leave with you; my peace I give you. I do not give to you as the world gives. Do not let your hearts be troubled and do not be afraid." (John 14:27). It is a peace based on peace with God, won for us by Jesus, and can only be experienced and not described. The non-believer just can't understand it. To me as a believer it is synonymous with the awareness of God's presence. Before I turned back to God it meant nothing, and I vaguely thought about it as just part of the airy-fairy stuff that the "pie-in-the-sky-when-you-die" people waffled on about. I have found out that it is perhaps the greatest gift God has given us to shield and protect us from the fears of life, many imagined and some real, which erode our coping mechanisms and either detract from the quality of our life, or destroy us psychologically. Unlike the peace of the non-believer it is not logical in that though present in good times it is even greater when things have spun out of human control.

How do we get this peace of God? Simply ask for it, "Do not be anxious about anything, but in everything, by prayer and petition, with thanksgiving, present your requests to God. And the peace of God, which transcends all understanding, will guard your hearts and your minds in Christ Jesus." (Phil. 4:6–7).

Jesus wants us to have the type of faith that would enable us to walk on water and change the landscape. We know we don't have this degree of faith and can only aspire to it, and Jesus knows this too. Peter obeyed Jesus's call to walk over the water to him. He stepped down out of the boat, and started to walk. At this crucial time as he began moving toward Jesus his faith failed and he was soon hit with the full impact of panic and began to sink until Jesus grabbed him. This story of Peter's failure is

Terminal Illness

a great comfort to us. When his faith deserted him he didn't sink down into the depths of the ocean because Jesus immediately reached out and caught him. Similarly when we face death, if our faith falters, he will reach out to us.

Jesus never promised we would not have to endure the same troubles as everyone else, but rather he promised he would take the burden of it all and carry it for us. Many Christians fail to fully appreciate this distinction, so that when faced with illness and death they panic and ask why God let this happen. The "name it and claim it" Christians are especially vulnerable. God doesn't give us everything we want, but only what is according to his will, and that will always be the best spiritually for us. When speaking of his imminent death, Jesus explained this to the disciples, "I have told you these things, so that in me you may have peace. In this world you will have trouble. But take heart! I have overcome the world." (John 16:33). He made it very clear that with him beside us we can overcome everything Satan can throw at us, even death.

For Christians, from this platform of peace, dying is the bursting forth of joy; it is the beginning of the realization of everything we long for. Our joy during our lifetime is like watching the beauty of the first rays of dawn. Slowly the colors appear more and more above the horizon as the joy of Jesus increases with the passing of our life, then suddenly the full sunrise is there spreading across the sky and we see him face to face. If we look at the story of the prodigal son we get some idea of the reception we will get in heaven, and even if it is only the faintest idea it is more than enough for me. The Father's joy when the son returned home was almost indescribable. Although an elderly man of status he threw his dignity aside and after seeing his son a long way away he ran to meet him, embracing and kissing him. In the same way we will see first hand the joy felt in heaven when we first turned back to God and started on the long journey home. For many of us the circumstances of our death means it will be a trial, and like the prodigal son, we will arrive in heaven bruised and battered. But James tells us our perseverance in the love of God and faith in him will be rewarded. Jesus will place on our head the crown of life and we will wear his cloak of righteousness, neither of which we could ever deserve. These are powerful promises symbolizing welcome, reunion, love, and boundless joy. Once we see the big picture in perspective and anticipate this scene when we see Jesus, we know we can die not only with peace, but with eager anticipation, and we can agree with Paul that our earthly sufferings do not compare with the glory ahead.

THANKSGIVING

We recognize the relevance of thanksgiving routinely at funeral services but it is also highlighted during the time spent in the end stage of life. I have been so impressed by the thankful attitude of the dying Christian. Despite the suffering, they demonstrate a deep sincere gratitude to God for many things—the blessings received throughout their life, the love and care they are receiving in their last days, the stunning knowledge that they are one of God's elect, the anticipation of being led by Jesus into the presence of God. They know they have perfect assurance of salvation and can count on their inheritance waiting in heaven. As a carer standing there, I have shared in praise for God as I see him working in the small daily details to bring comfort to all those present. Later, when I look back on these times and see the wood and not just the trees, I am always so grateful for God's love, his meticulous planning of the important things, the people whom he sent at the right time, and the overall completeness and perfection of his care. It is a time of victory, praise, thanksgiving, and humility.

A TIME OF SPIRITUAL BLESSING

In the same way Jesus was deeply affected by the sorrow of Lazarus's death, so it is when we come alongside someone who is dying, we can't be effective without suffering ourselves. The greatest help we can be comes from giving of ourselves without measure. For carers this means it is a time of inconvenience, fatigue, strain, and sorrow. But as usual, whenever we are in God's will and put the interests of someone else before our own, we ourselves benefit on a scale we wouldn't have envisaged. All those gathered around are serving Jesus by serving one of his beloved and so it is a time of spiritual growth for everyone. Time I have spent with dying friends has been the most uplifting of my life. It is a mix of great sorrow and great joy. I have often driven home from a visit and felt my heart uplifted, like the disciples after they talked to Jesus on the road to Emmaus. It is a time of intense prayer and awareness of God, his love abounds, and we feel Jesus very close. Everyone, and particularly the sick person, seems to suddenly see life in perspective. The rubbish in our thinking and in our lives falls away and there is a realization and acceptance of the fact that in ourselves we can do nothing, and in everything we are totally dependent on God. The starkness of this insight gives great freedom. To his followers Jesus said, "you will know the truth, and the truth will set you free." (John 8:32). This freedom he gives us is not only freedom from eternal death itself, but also freedom from the torment in our minds, which flows from the fear of it.

For the Christian, whether we are the sufferer or the carer, confronting death can be the fulfillment of the faith we have struggled to achieve. It brings joy because we are facing one of the greatest challenges of our lives, and yet we know with Jesus we can not only do it, but do it magnificently. It is a state of mind that is quite different from either the fear or the brave stoicism of the atheist, who as a final act of resignation accepts death as a fact of life.

JESUS'S VICTORY IS OURS

Jesus has conquered spiritual death for all those who believe in his gospel of redemption through the forgiveness of sins. In this way the sting and defeat of physical death has been cancelled by his atoning death and resurrection, which have overcome the finality of the grave. But until Jesus comes again physical death will continue to be part of life, or as some wit said, "life is a terminal illness." Undesirable as this is, we have inflated this physical death out of all proportion in our thinking.

Our natural inclination is to rejoice over birth and despair over death, yet both are an equally valid part of the whole spectrum of the life God planned for us. We hear this sentiment expressed often at funeral services in this Scripture, "There is a time for everything, and a season for every activity under heaven: a time to be born and a time to die," (Eccl. 3:1–2). Like the atheist we easily pick up on the quiet resignation in these words as they tell us death is inevitable. But the Christian recognizes the "time" is God's time, the "season" is God's season, and the "heaven" is God's heaven. For now, death is part of his permissive will. The details of our lives are known by God before we are conceived; he is with us at our birth; he is with us throughout our life; and he is with us at our death. Throughout all these stages he is equally in control and never leaves us. Our life goes through a cycle of change but God never changes.

When things go well in life we find it easy to delude ourselves into thinking we have everything under control, but when we are dying we see the delusion, we know we have lost all semblance of control and the natural reaction is to be fearful. The sooner in life we come to realize and accept that no person is ever in control, and only God is in control, then the easier we can cope with the concept of death, "In his hand is the life of every creature and the breath of all mankind." (Job 12:10). After we make a decision to put ourselves in God's hands we see what a mess we have made and how foolish we have been to go through life making decisions without him. We can't get through life in its fullest sense without God and we can't get through death as we would wish without him. It is tragic some people never understand this during their life and it is equally tragic that even some Christians don't realize it in their death, and so they do death hard instead of easy; they do it with a spirit of defeat instead of a spirit of victory. Many times the Scriptures tell us to "take heart." To me this emphasizes the compassion of God that underlies all his care of us. Especially where suffering and healing is concerned he wants to encourage us and give us an eternal perspective; he wants us to have peace.

There is suffering in life especially for the Christian, but we nevertheless embrace life and it is just as appropriate to embrace death. It is no different, it is another trial with the same ups and downs and follows the same rules as all the other trials we have faced and conquered with Jesus. Paul reminds us, "Therefore we do not lose heart. Though outwardly we are wasting away, yet inwardly we are being renewed day by day. For our light and momentary troubles are achieving for us an eternal glory that far outweighs them all. So we fix our eyes not on what is seen, but on what is unseen. For what is seen is temporary, but what is unseen is eternal." (2 Cor. 4:16–18).

THE NON-BELIEVER

All the comfort the dying Christian knows is not available to the non-believer. It is a devastating feeling when hearing a beloved friend who is a non-believer has died. We feel especially bad if they suffered needlessly through fear by not knowing God's love and peace because they left it too late to find out, or we left it too late to tell them about Jesus, or were ineffective in our attempts. It is not a matter of judging them and it is true only God knows the spiritual standing of anyone, but it is a fact some people are cast from his presence for eternity because they failed to choose to turn to him in life. Some churches teach you can pray for the dead, some say not. I can't help myself, I pray for them and let God decide how appropriate that is. One thing is certain, if we can do anything for the dead it will be through prayer, not money. More relevant to us is to pray strenuously and ceaselessly for non-believers during their lifetime. We should also take every opportunity to do everything practical to promote the gospel to them. It is very hard to live with ourselves when we look back after someone has died and realize we did nothing to help them see the truth. This doesn't mean we should pester people and force our ideas on them, especially because this is often counterproductive, but if we are prayerful and watchful God will give us appropriate opportunities.

MIRACLE HEALING

Miracle healing is something we have all longed for at some time for loved ones or for ourselves, and not surprisingly charlatans trade on the dying. Curing disease is a major platform in the Bible. It is basic to Christian faith and was an integral part of the ministry of Jesus, foreseen by Isaiah. His prophesy came to pass and we learn that the disciples went from one town to another preaching to the people and healing them. The words "preaching" and "healing" appear frequently together in the gospels and this emphasizes that healing of the soul should always accompany healing of the body. In his ministry Jesus made a very definite connection between physical healing and forgiveness, and by inference, salvation. After a paralyzed man was lowered through the roof of the building where he was preaching, Jesus first forgave his sins, then talked about his own authority to do so, and after that he healed the man. It is interesting to note the forgiveness—the healing of the man's soul, came first and took priority over the physical healing, which came second. People who go to a healing service for a quick fix, but fail to put God in his rightful place have missed the point. It is also interesting that in the previous story the faith of the companions seemed relevant. This highlights our responsibility to dwell with God so that our faith is as strong as possible, not only for our own benefit but to help others.

Unfortunately some churches promote faith healing with such emphasis in their belief system that for them it is proof there is a God. They also see it as a test of the faith of the sick person, who will earn a pass or fail spiritual rating depending on whether or not they are healed. It is a very emotive topic and if healing is approached in the wrong way, in human strength and without acknowledging the sovereignty of God, much heartbreak and loss of faith can occur. As well, those who claim to be healers are often given false status among Christians. When genuine, it is a gift given to them by God, no different in significance to any spiritual gift. People find it difficult to remember it is not the personal power of the healer at work, but the power of Christ at work within them. It is not that comparisons should be made by us, but Paul ranks the teaching of the gospel before the rest of the gifts including healing.

Personal Experience of Physical Healing

Physical healing is a huge subject, which I have not researched in the Bible in any depth and only include the subject here because many of us dabble in it, and others turn to it when in a desperate situation. It is a topic we should think about seriously and before a crisis occurs in our life. To date my own interpretation of the subject has been heavily influenced by two personal experiences of healing, which I will describe in detail in order to give every opportunity for readers to draw their own conclusions.

One healing occurred during a meeting held by a visiting American preacher known for his healing ministry. The meeting took place at the Homebush Olympic site. There were about fifteen thousand people gathered in the building, which on the inside was oval in shape. Those who were mobile were in the tiered seats around the perimeter and those in wheelchairs were on the floor area in the middle.

I had tendon problems in both shoulders. This caused a recurring, gradually increasing inability to raise my arms from my side to overhead. I had had about 5 injections on one side and three or four on the other over a period of about four years. At the time of the meeting my right arm was going into the deteriorating cycle again and was short of full movement by about forty degrees. I had gone more for the sermon than the healing, but thought as I was there I might as well "do" my shoulders. When I took my seat I looked down at the people gathered in the floor area. They were in wheelchairs, a few of the chairs looked more like beds and some had oxygen cylinders. As I looked down on them I not only felt compassion for them, I also felt guilty that I was self-absorbed over a minor problem and would waste God's time when he had more important healings to attend to. I thought if instead I joined in intercessory prayer for those people present who were in desperate situations that this would

Terminal Illness

help God to heal them?! So I directed my prayers to God for those on the floor area.

Yes, I cringe too—I saw God as a human who was limited in power and overwhelmed by responsibilities who might fail if I didn't help him out! I was turned half sideways to see the preacher, and along with the rest of the audience, I spent most of the time standing with my arms in the air. I remember thinking fleetingly, when I seemed to be aching everywhere, that far from having my shoulders healed, I could finish up with them being much worse, and have neck and back strain as well.

The next morning I was thinking about the meeting the night before and lifted both arms up beside my head. The left arm was moving normally as it was before the meeting; the right arm had improved from forty degrees to about ten degrees short of full movement. That was five years ago. Since then I have had no more cortisone injections. The left shoulder has remained normal and the right gradually improved to 100 percent over a few weeks following the meeting. The left shoulder also has a displaced tendon and this is apparent to me sometimes when I carry things, but the recurring cycle of inflammation has never returned in either shoulder. It is true this type of shoulder problem often gets spontaneously better over a period of time. Nevertheless, it is a fact that I was well and truly in the active phase with the right shoulder deteriorating at the time of the meeting, but within twelve hours there was a dramatic permanent change for the better. In my mind I am convinced this was a spiritual healing.

The other occasion occurred after I watched a preacher on the television. It was a regular program and I watched most episodes. Every few weeks there would be a healing prayer at the end of the talk. During the prayer I would focus on a particular close relative with a serious chronic health problem. After many months, suddenly one day just as the prayer started, I thought to myself, "that hasn't worked, [for my relative] I'll do my giddiness". Another cringe—note the "I"! I had benign positional vertigo and for ten years or so had had more than six episodes per year of dizziness, which lasted from hours to days. During a bout it wasn't bad enough to incapacitate me but it was a real nuisance. I suddenly started thinking about this problem of mine and so with the pastor's prayer, I directed my mind to God.

Since then, which was six years ago, I have had no further bouts of vertigo. I do still have a substandard balance system with a tendency to walk into people who may think I am a little too friendly.

Feet on Earth, Head in Heaven

It is interesting to think about these two episodes of healing. I have had a number of thoughts: how does our Almighty God stay patient with people like me? In retrospect my whole approach to him was so unaware of his nature and casual to the point of being disrespectful. Maybe it was because I was genuinely ignorant; maybe it was because no matter how correctly we try to approach God, we are still so tacky it is only through his grace, mercy, and love that we survive another moment in his presence. Why did God overlook my shortcomings and heal me on both occasions? Why not? He is doing that constantly, and fortunately never gives any of us who seek him the destruction we deserve, but rather he gives us a constant flow of blessings we could never deserve. There is only one answer—he loves us with a love beyond our comprehension.

There is no formula when it comes to physical healing because we can't study the mind of God and then work out a set of rules that he follows, as if he were some giant computer. Despite this, in order to learn what he means me to learn, I have thought about what may be relevant to me. On both occasions I had had compassion for others—this is love and where there is love there is God. Although on one occasion I thought of God as not being able to multi-task and on the other was inappropriately casual, I did have absolute faith that nothing is impossible for him, and if it was his will he could, and would, heal me. My faith was more in the nature of a definite feeling of assurance than a conscious major part of my belief system. Still, he took me by surprise as he so often does. I think the reason on these two occasions was because I did not have an adequate appreciation of his interest, love, and concern for the individual, and especially so because that individual was me.

Faith alone is essential to healing as Jesus told the woman with the bleeding. Like that woman, the only relevant input from any sufferer is the personal effort required to put ourselves in God's hands, and the resolve to do this comes from our faith. It is also plain in my case that any other contribution from me was totally irrelevant because my shoulders were healed after I changed my mind and decided not to ask. Also, perhaps very importantly, there were fifteen thousand people present all praying with their hearts turned to God. This would seem to be plenty given Jesus's advice that if two people pray in agreement with each other, and with God, then God will answer their request in the affirmative. Also he promised to always be present at a meeting of as few as two or three Christians, and where Jesus is, there is healing.

Terminal Illness

My healings occurred in the first two years after I was born again and hadn't gone any distance at all along the path to holiness, so glib explanations of success related to the spiritual state of the sick person just don't stand up. We do not get healed because we are spiritually strong, we get healed despite being spiritually weak; those people who are not healed are just as godly or ungodly as those who are. It is fortunately not our own holiness that is relevant but the perfect holiness of God and his power to heal.

Though of significance to me, my problems were minor compared to many other people at the meeting, and yet I didn't see any of those other people stand up from their wheelchairs or discard their oxygen masks. I only became aware of my shoulders being improved twelve hours later, so healing isn't necessarily instant, but even so, based on what I saw I was disappointed for these people. It means we have to accept that God chooses whom he will heal and when, and the magnitude of the problem is not relevant. There is no scale by which requests are rated as worthy or otherwise of consideration. We would expect him to be interested in our life and death illnesses, but what was less obvious to me is nothing is too small—if it is something worrying to us and we ask for help then he listens. The idea that like some harassed mother of quads there is a limit to what he can do at any one time is naïve in the extreme. God is omnipotent; he never says, "Wait your turn," "Get in the queue." I think any Christian who has health issues and doesn't ask God to be healed is a bit of a puzzle.

Interestingly, since then I have had serious health issues and for these there has been no healing bolt from the blue, but I have come to a place of peace knowing I am in God's hands. This is because I know whatever the outcome he chooses, he always does what is in the best interests of those who love him. Overall my own approach is to have faith in God's willingness and ability to heal, but added to this is an acceptance of his decision whether "Yes," or "No," and a willingness to abide peacefully in it. This is often thought to be double-minded, self-defeating, and faith-eroding because some people believe you must believe 100 percent you will be healed or God won't do it. I think there is an obvious flaw in this thinking because it implies God can't act unilaterally and also that we know better than he does what should happen in our life. Not only does the latter view seem illogical, but also I can't agree because my personal experience was different, and any valid explanation has to cover all examples. I was healed and my faith has grown. If we ask, have peace, and trust God whether he answers "Yes," or "No," this seems a surer foundation for faith.

A Christian friend died recently of cancer after much illness and treatment over a five-year period. She went to many healing services, she had things she wanted to live for, but she was full of thanks to God for the extended period of time God had given her, which was far beyond her doctor's expectations. The healing services gave her great peace, not because success was assured, but because her trust in God strengthened. Anyone who is given a diagnosis of a disease that may cause death has also been given an immediate huge spiritual advantage. Suddenly the issues are clear-cut—it becomes "me and God" in every way. If we are smart, we scramble into his presence and want to stay there. I know this personally, and now I realize it is the only way to live and wonder why I didn't do so anyway. When we dwell in the presence of God we come under the blessing announced by the angels at Jesus's birth, "Glory to God in the highest, and on earth peace to men on whom his favor rests." (Luke 2:14)

Lourdes in France has been a site people have visited for healing since the mid eighteen hundreds. There are now about five million visitors per year and one would assume people of devout faith would be well represented. In 1947 a committee was established, which is now called the Lourdes International Medical Committee. It documents and assesses claimed healings independently of the church. Some of the people on the Committee are skeptics and the need for documentation is very exhaustive. The number of cures proven in this way does not exceed the number of random unexplained cures in the general population. This is disappointing in one way, but apart from the problem of availability of acceptable documentation prejudicing the results, we have to consider the implications if there was proof beyond doubt. Almost certainly people would focus on physical healing and over-emphasize this in their life to the detriment of seeking God in his fullness, and so neglect their far more important spiritual growth.

Statistics abound to prove or disprove whether miracles of healing occur, and predictably the internet is a mine of information and misinformation, with the distinction between the two impossible to discern. It is especially confusing on this subject because data is so hard to collect according to the rules of good quality research. As an aside, anybody in the medical field is understandably cynical about research as the pendulum swings from proof to disproof, and to and fro on any subject. A medical practitioner may be sued for *not doing* something today and sued for *doing* it tomorrow when new research is published, which in its turn is likely to be debunked sometime in the future. As well there are always vested interests happy to distort the truth on both sides of the argument based on statistics. Nothing much has changed since the 1800s when this quote originated: "there are lies, damned lies, and statistics." What can be said is that anybody like me who has had an experience of healing doesn't need statistics because we have all the proof we need.

We can conclude that like everything about God, the subject of miracle healing is complex. That shouldn't come as a surprise because with our finite minds we only have a very limited understanding of God. Everyone's journey is different and this is a very relevant consideration. Some enthusiasts overlook this fact and say that because God is love then he wants to heal everyone, and if he doesn't, then the faith of the sufferer is at fault. Simply observing our fellow Christians and their experience of being healed or not healed tells us this is not so. Personally, living or dying has ceased to be an issue for me, and I see my death simply as the last milestone on my journey—and I will pass by it with Jesus.

DEMENTIA

There is a general terror in the community at the thought of cancer, but there is both terror and horror when the subject of dementia arises, and this is because of the loss of independence and dignity that characterizes it. With the aging population it is hardly ever out of the press, and as we get older the fear of it can overshadow us. For this reason I will digress briefly with this story:

I heard that a relatively young minister, whose church I had attended in the past, was very ill and had dementia secondary to another illness. I wrote a rather useless letter to his wife to try to convey my sympathy. She wrote back to me and in her letter she said although "John" was no longer aware of God's promises to him they nevertheless still stood.

I was so grateful for these words because of the comfort they conveyed to me. Until then I hadn't thought about the fact that whether we are aware or not, God never forgets his everlasting covenant with us and our descendants. The world may abandon those with dementia, but to God they are still his children with all the protection and dignity that entails, "But you are a chosen people, a royal priesthood, a Holy nation, a people belonging to God," (1 Pet. 2:9). Nothing at all can ever quench the outpouring of God's love for us. Even when we are in a state of complete physical and mental breakdown, the Christian can say, "in all these things we are more than conquerors through him who loved us." (Rom. 8:37) For years this minister had declared God's praises, and now although no longer able to do so, he was still under the shelter of God's promises. It makes sense, because when we can't think for ourselves we are at our most vulnerable, and that is when God is closest to us. This man's situation was so different to those who go through life, death, and eternity without God. For them there is no comfort, and our realization of this must keep us praying for them, and for each other for saving faith.

SUMMARY

Facing death is the ultimate test of our faith in the goodness, love, and wisdom of God. It is understandable we have moments of worry that at the end, just when we need it most, our faith will fail. At times our faith does fail, but Jesus always steps forward as he did for Peter. Sinking was not an option for Peter when he failed in his attempt to walk to Jesus on the water, and when God calls us to make the final journey home we will get there safely too. In fact, we mostly pleasantly surprise ourselves when tested in the big issues of life, because our faith does hold—we shouldn't be surprised of course, because Jesus is our intercessor in heaven. We know he prays for our faith to be strong because he said to Peter, "I have prayed for you, Simon, that your faith may not fail." (Luke 22:32)

God infuses us with his strength and so enables us to do great things for him and to withstand suffering. When a desperate Satan is going all out for a final victory to take us down to the grave, God raises us to the heights to dwell with him forever. Praise was a large part of the worship of believers in the Old Testament. As modern believers, we also need to give ceaseless praise to God that through salvation we have such a marvelous eternal future with him.

On the subject of living and dying, Paul said he was equally happy either way, because whether he was on earth or in heaven he was with Christ. The core gospel message of Jesus's triumph over death is not alluded to in an occasional vague debatable statement in the Bible—it is beyond dispute. At the last supper Jesus said: "I am the living bread that came down from heaven. If anyone eats of this bread, he will live forever."

(John 6:51). In verse after verse Paul tells us about the love of God for us and our inheritance through Christ, "For I am convinced that neither death nor life, neither angels nor demons, neither the present nor the future, nor any powers, neither height nor depth, nor anything else in all creation, will be able to separate us from the love of God that is in Christ Jesus our Lord." (Rom. 8:38–39); and again: "I have fought the good fight, I have finished the race, I have kept the faith. Now there is in store for me the crown of righteousness, which the Lord, the righteous Judge, will award to me on that day—and not only to me, but also to all who have longed for his appearing." (2 Tim. 4:7–8)

15

Non Believers

MAN'S NEED TO WORSHIP

THE ATHEIST SAYS THERE is no God and the agnostic says he can't know because God is not material. Yet seemingly unaware, they choose lesser gods whom they often worship more enthusiastically than the Christian worships God. It has been said everyone has a God-shaped hole in them that demands to be filled. Certainly those who don't pursue God, pursue something else with equal fervor. They do so with the same attitude of mind with which we see religion pursued—some laid-back, some maniacal and all degrees of dedication in between. The goal is to worship something; the manner of the pursuit seems to be related to personality, ego, and the need for a sense of purpose. These are all-powerful drives and unless God is in charge can lead to disaster.

The false gods of money, status, power, sex, other people, and politics claim the allegiance of society as a whole, despite their shortcomings being obvious to all from time immemorial. We don't seek to worship them, we just do; it comes naturally. Most people in our country at least pay lip service to the inherent dangers they present so that although these things drive our society they are unofficial gods. In fact, they are publicly disparaged by society in general and often worshipped grudgingly. We are lured by the deceit of false glamour, false promises, and ego massage. It is not at all subtle. As gods we know they are overstated, they disappoint, and they fail to satisfy this deep hunger for the true God.

Non Believers

Atheism, which is vocal in its opposition to Christianity, is on a roll in Western society. It is based both on idealism and on man's instinct to destroy. Many of those who practice it want to cleanse society by ridding it of all that is negative in religion and they want to tear down the establishment along with the tall poppies who are part of it. The cloak of respectability is afforded their cause because of the undesirable trappings that accompany everything man touches including spirituality. Instead of putting effort into trying to heal the church they would rather destroy it. In doing so they are throwing out everything of real value—redeeming love, the peace of God, and the ultimate joy to be found in life and death.

Over the centuries the organized church, steeped in hypocrisy, has misused its power, pursued the things of man not those of God, and thus has made itself an easy target. I heard a church leader express concerns over the rise of atheism in our country, but he was a man whose public image of bigotry and arrogance has done much harm to the image of the church. He and others with similar attitudes can't see they are a bigger threat to Christianity than the people they oppose.

Weakness of faith causes the Christian to go into a panic and often plain denial of the obvious when the atheist mounts a plausible attack through some subject like evolution, cloning, or the possibility of discovery of life elsewhere in the universe. We say God is in control of everything, but quickly feel threatened by modern discoveries and ideas, and may then behave irrationally. The result can be a refusal to countenance discussions on views contrary to Christianity, or refusal to see the demarcation between tradition and doctrine, or between the literal and the symbolic meaning of Scripture. Also we may fail to support the difficult aspects of our own belief, particularly the concept of suffering, and allow the atheists to claim everything has to be "happy" along the way to be acceptable—hence the rise of prosperity preaching and the "name it and claim it" lobby. The mainstream Christian goes through suffering to be with God while the atheist aims for a fun time along the path that leads away from God. We are doorkeepers of God's wisdom and in guarding it we can't deny the unpalatable parts of the Bible or the controversial issues. We should be robust and confident in our defense of the Scriptures and not apologetic. To do this successfully we need to dwell in the presence of God and bring the power of the Holy Spirit to cast light on any discussion. Then we will be wearing our spiritual armor, which equips us for the struggle and enables us to stand firm.

Feet on Earth, Head in Heaven

Many atheists are not destroyers and seekers of personal power, but like Christians they are idealists. Their idealism takes the form of a vision of society without the evils of religion. We would all like that, but their solution is to make a clean sweep and deny God. Their belief is embodied in John Lennon's hit song "Imagine". His theory is that without heaven, hell, religion, countries or possessions, that killing, greed, and hunger would cease, and peace and brotherhood would follow. The promises are fantasy and the conclusion not logical—how is life sustainable without possessions? Greed, aggression and intolerance are ingrained in the human psyche; of ourselves we are incapable of a lifestyle based on sharing and when constraints are removed there is anarchy. Christians more than others want the perfection he sings about, but it is only through Christ it will come. The popularity of the song is not hard to understand. The tune and words, like much that Satan offers, has a powerful but superficial charm and appeal, but when assessed unemotionally it is very plain the sentiments the song expresses are proven failures.

In this nominally Christian country of ours, our atheists want a society without the shackles of religion, but at the same time feel fortunate to call Australia home. They see very clearly the difference in quality of life here compared to countries run by atheistic or non-Christian regimes, and yet they fail to see why. It is the very Christianity they despise that has resulted in this country being such a privileged place in which to live. In the 1960s J.B. Phillips made the point that society in the Western world was already living off the legacy left by Christianity over the previous centuries, and if we failed to pursue God seriously then the fabric of our society would fall apart. Far from reforming as he suggested, we have slipped even further away from God. Statistics for crime and violence and the general uncaring attitude we have for one another demonstrate the awful truth of his words. Well-meaning atheists are aspiring to a better world, but can't tell us how to have an atheistic regime we would prefer to a Christian one. They do not acknowledge, probably even to themselves, this proof of the failure of their false philosophy.

Everything about God is inspiring and both the individual and the society steeped in his love have the power to rise to the heights of human endeavor and behavior. I'm sure many atheists would agree that love is the strongest power in the world and yet inexplicably they fail to see its source. Like his love, God's truth can be recognized by the quality of it, and the superficial appeal of counter views just doesn't stand up to scrutiny.

THE GOD OF SCIENTIFIC KNOWLEDGE

The god that now stands astride our society above all the rest is the god of knowledge. It is the god of the modern atheist. A Christian's first love is God and his wisdom; an atheist's first love is human knowledge, particularly if it is called science. The wisdom of God is complete; the knowledge of man is dwarfed by what there is yet to know and the search on the way leads up many blind alleys. It was not a surprise when a world famous atheist in a recent television interview was unable to define wisdom when asked by the interviewer to do so. Stated baldly, if you don't know God, you don't know what wisdom is.

The mindset of this scientific age is that if it is called science it must be right. How many times has science been proved wrong? In the therapeutic field, today's wonder drug often becomes tomorrow's poison as the next wave of research findings is published. In the field of physics, how many theories have there been explaining the origin of the universe? What is hailed in any scientific field as dizzying progress one day is likely to be debunked the next. It happens over and over again, but those who are followers are very forgiving of this god of knowledge, they keep the faith. Christians could learn from this. We give God one chance to answer a prayer within a narrow time frame and if he doesn't give us the result we want, we shrug him off. This is not to say man's knowledge base is not expanding rapidly. The flat earth theory is gone forever. But we will not be able to trust in knowledge until it is complete, and it will only be complete when God wills it so. Why start at the end and work backwards? Why not start with God because he is where the worshippers of knowledge will end up if he gives them enough time. Also there is a danger in human knowledge because unless it is infused with the wisdom of God it can lead to destruction. This destructive outcome can be deliberate, as in the development of the nuclear bomb, or as an unfortunate side effect as in global warming. When man has ultimate control of anything it is a legitimate worry.

Both the followers of God and those of "knowledge" can be just as blind and bigoted. All of us must have a clear understanding of our belief. The Bible has limitless layers of understanding and no one can plumb its depths in a lifetime, so that it takes continual time and effort to enlarge our understanding of this written Word of God. We should do so not only for our own sake, but in order to serve him better. In particular we need clarity in our thinking so that we can help those who oppose the gospel to see the truth. There is of course a trap, which is that the knowledge Christians acquire often stays in the head and doesn't get as far as the heart, "always learning but never able to acknowledge the truth." (2 Tim. 3:7) This is not only useless but dangerous, because in our heads it generates pride, which expresses itself in the self absorption of "I, me and mine." Pride is the pervasive enemy; we even take pride in our humility. It is so destructive because it is the embodiment of self-love, which is in direct opposition to the love of God. This love, which the Holy Spirit pours into us, should be flowing freely from us back to him and out to others. Pride can only be defeated by the redeeming love of Jesus in us, enabled by his place in our heart. Without God, the atheist is free to take pride in anything, and his greatest source of pride is his knowledge. Internet access allows almost all that is known, and all that is guessed at, to be available to anyone at the press of a key. Knowledge is a very positive thing, but only when tempered by the wisdom of God.

A speaker for an atheist's convention said, "Let's have a belief system based on knowledge." This is a great idea but what knowledge? In Christianity the belief system is the knowledge of God. Our God is omniscient, unchanging, and trustworthy. The god of human knowledge is incomplete, changeable, and flawed. It seems like a no contest. The non-believers are still blindly following the trail like a bloodhound with its nose to the ground, but the Christian knows where the trail ends. Science is not in opposition to Christianity or a threat to it, but is part of it. It is ironic that the Creator of science in all its forms—of the laws of physics, of mathematics, of logic, is considered by the non-believer to be irrelevant to the modern world. This irony might be the answer to the joke, "How do you make God laugh?" Johannes Keppler, the seventeenth century German mathematician and astronomer, put it succinctly when he said, "Science is thinking God's thoughts after him."

The Problem of Measurement

"Ah! But wait," say the atheists, "our knowledge is based on proof; give us your proof there is a God." Even if we overlook the incompleteness and changeability of scientific proof and request something more convincing from them, there is a problem with comparisons. It is the nature of science to progress step by step by adding two and two to get four. But how do you reduce spiritual concepts to formulas? It is like comparing oranges and cars. It would be nonsense to road-test an orange or taste-test a car. The two things cannot be evaluated the same way.

Scientific experiments often result in something tangible we can see. We can mix two chemical compounds together and see that a chemical reaction has changed the character of the contents. Proof in the spiritual realm is not something we can capture in a test tube or on a microscope slide. This is a big problem to many people. Even the apostle Thomas needed tangible proof and didn't believe Christ had risen until he put his fingers into the nail marks in Christ's hands, and his hand into the wound in Christ's side.

We can't see trust, love, faith, or hope. Neither can we see electricity or the wind. But we know all these things are real because we see their effects. The effects of electricity or wind can be measured in a laboratory. The disciples demonstrated the effect of their faith after they saw Jesus resurrected when they changed from cowards to martyrs. Paul changed from a persecutor of Christians to a defender of the faith after he met Jesus on the road to Damascus. Christians shine in adversity; they display trust in suffering; love in forgiveness; and hope in terminal illness. But there is a problem as to how these effects can be measured in a laboratory setting, which is the only proof the scientific worshippers will accept or can understand. There are things that cannot be studied in a test tube or even fully explained unless they are experienced. How do you describe the perfume of a rose to someone born without a sense of smell? How do you give them any understanding of what it is?

The core of Christianity is love, specifically the love of God. Capturing it in any measurable form is not possible, even describing it fully is not possible. Paul said the love of Christ is a, "love that surpasses knowledge," (Ephes. 3:19). The definition of love in the Oxford Dictionary gives no real idea of what love is. The closest I could pick out were the following excerpts: "to entertain a great regard for; to hold dear; to entertain a strong affection for; to be devoted to or addicted to; to be unwilling to part with."[1] Each phrase describes an aspect of love, but even after putting all the phrases together the quintessence of love is not there. How many hymns and secular songs do we have in an effort to describe the emotional content of love? It can't be done. We have all experienced love in at least one of its many forms and so we know what it is and believe it exists, but we can never really fully describe how it sits in our heart and

---

1 Little, *The Shorter Oxford English Dictionary.*

mind. We struggle to define love as it pertains to anything, and we fail even more miserably when we try to define the love of God. Paul did as well as anyone in 1 Corinthians 13, and these writings have moved the hearts of millions of people, both Christians and non-Christians alike, ever since he wrote them. In Jesus love finds its ultimate expression, "This is how we know what love is: Jesus Christ laid down his life for us. And we ought to lay down our lives for our brothers." (1 John 3:16) This love has to be experienced to be understood and this personal understanding cannot be fully described to another or measured objectively. The gospel explains God's love of man countless times in many ways, but we need to remember that unless the effects of this love are obvious in the lives of Christians it will not be understood, and even misunderstood.

In ancient times before scientific experimentation, gods were tested according to measurements of things like prosperity of the faithful, or victory in war, or number of male offspring. This testing of God is not new. But as Job found out there is no reliable test one can apply; God cannot be put into a box or made subject to rules to suit man's limited understanding. Job entered God's presence due to blind faith and in spite of the failure of the measuring system of the day. Conversely because his friends used a flawed system, they confidently believed prosperity, health, and happiness equaled favor with God. They were completely wrong and they failed the test God gave them. People with similar thinking today have gone one step further by saying if God doesn't conform to their testing procedures then he doesn't exist at all.

COMMON ASSERTIONS OF THE NON-BELIEVER

As Christians we realize we can't possibly know everything about God, in fact we know very little, but because we recognize the pivotal importance of faith we are content in this. We can know all God wants us to know and this is all we need. Unfortunately when challenged to explain unanswerable questions, such as why there is suffering in the world, we are often clean-bowled by the non-believer who concludes that our inability to answer means there is no God. It is just as valid to expect such a person to stop believing there are stars in the sky simply because he is unable to tell us exactly how many there are. As Christians we can be very relaxed about our ignorance because we rely on God to know, whereas the seeker of knowledge relies on his own knowledge and understanding, and so is

Non Believers

on very shaky ground. If anyone has cause for worry, it is he. There are some common criticisms.

1. "No one has ever seen God."

The non-believer tells us as God has never been seen no one can be expected to believe he exists. Paul says we see the proof of God in creation and Christians certainly do. In the past this was a very powerful consideration and pagans often worshipped natural phenomena like the sun or moon. The prophet Habakkuk pointed out the futility of worshipping the created rather than the Creator. That penny finally dropped for most people and the pantheists then stepped forward to fit these material objects into a concept. They believe God and the universe are identical, which denies the personality and transcendence of God. The pantheists just made the worship of created things a bit fuzzier. For some reason if we make something into a concept, especially if it is vague, then we feel more comfortable. But this idea has fallen out of favor with today's enthusiastic non-believer who would rather ascribe creation quite definitely to science. That is natural because science is the foremost of the modern gods and there has always been an underlying realization by everyone that creation is not of man but of "god".

The statement that no one has seen God is untrue. Jesus told us many times he is God, "I and the Father are one." (John 10:30); "Anyone who has seen me has seen the Father." (John 14:9). People who have done little Bible study don't realize this and mistakenly think Jesus's deity was only ascribed to him after his death by the disciples, or even Christians hundreds of years later.

Realization Jesus called himself God leads to questions about his reliability and so to three possibilities—he was Lord, lunatic, or liar. C.S. Lewis discusses this in his book "Mere Christianity".[2]

The conclusion that he was a liar is easy to dismiss because not one of Jesus's many other statements in the Scriptures were lies; anyone who is guilty of telling a big lie is also guilty of telling many little ones.

The second possibility, that he was insane, doesn't stand up either. The wisdom of Jesus, his verbal clashes with the Pharisees, his understanding of the human mind and heart, and his own very rational behavior all rule out insanity. The Pharisees set many traps for him by posing

---

2. Lewis, *Mere Christianity*.

pre-planned unexpected questions with the very real possibility of incriminating answers, but they never succeeded because Jesus answered with such brilliance that they walked away in amazement. Non-believers in general would agree he was certainly one of the great minds of all time.

This leaves us with the third possibility; he is who he said he is—he is God. We have seen Jesus; we have seen God.

2. "When you are dead, you are dead."

The person who believes this says, "You can't show me a person who was dead for a period of time and then started walking around again." This again is untrue because after three days Jesus rose from the dead and it was this event that galvanized the disciples into establishing Christianity, and for doing so they risked death without a backward glance.

Jesus was seen by many people in a convincing way between the third day after his crucifixion, when he rose from the dead, and the fortieth day after his resurrection when he ascended into heaven. It has been proven all these sightings were preached and recorded within eighty years of the death of Christ. They were described by the people who were alive at the time and not added on later second hand to embellish a good story, "This salvation, which was first announced by the Lord, was confirmed to us by those who heard him." (Heb. 2:3).

There are 11 separate appearances of Jesus recorded in those forty days:

- To Mary Magdalene alone (Mark 16:9, John 20:14)
- To the women returning from the tomb (Matt. 28:9)
- To Simon Peter alone (Luke 24:34)
- To the two disciples going to Emmaus (Luke 24:15)
- To the apostles at Jerusalem, except for Thomas who was absent (Luke 24:36)
- To the apostles at Jerusalem the second time, when Thomas was present (John 20:26)
- At the sea of Tiberius, when seven disciples were fishing (John 21:1)
- To the eleven disciples, on a mountain in Galilee (Matt. 28:16)
- To more than 500 brethren at one time (1 Cor. 15:6)

- To James on his own (1 Cor. 15:7)
- To all the apostles on Mount Oliphet at his ascension (Luke 24:50)

After the ascension, Jesus appeared to Paul on the road to Damascus and to Stephen, the first Christian martyr at his trial. The book of Revelations is a record of his appearance to John. Since then until the present day Jesus has appeared to countless numbers of people personally.

3. "If there is a God, who made him and where did he come from?"

God tells us this: "I am the Alpha and the Omega, the Beginning and the End." (Rev. 21:6). He didn't tell us how this happened and he is the only source of this information, so for us for now, the subject is closed. The answer to the counter question, "Who made science?" is easy—"God did." To expect to be able to answer every question about God seems to me to reflect sheer human arrogance rather than to be a cause for discomfort. Explaining the very beginning is something nobody can do. In both viewpoints faith underpins our belief—faith in God or faith in science. Whether we see the very beginning to be God as Christians do, or as some phenomenon of physics as the worshippers of knowledge do, nobody can explain the origin of either. It is an even playing field in this respect. We don't need to know but it is very interesting for us to consider, because God has made man more curious than the cat. The pursuit of knowledge, like Creation itself, is one of the enjoyable and potentially fruitful things of life, but it was never meant to be an end in itself, and it was certainly never meant to be worshipped.

4. Blaming God or denying his existence because of evil and suffering in the world.

Consider these accusations: "A good and loving god would not allow suffering"; "An all powerful god is responsible for everything wrong in the world"; "A loving god would not send anyone to hell."

The basic oversight in these statements is that they cut man out of the equation. God doesn't have to work with and through man, but because his purpose is to save our souls he has chosen to do so. He has given man the choice of partnership with him in this divine purpose, but most turn away.

The Australian Bureau of Statistics (ABS) in 2001 found 74 percent of Australians aged 18 years and over reported affiliating with a religion. However, in the ABS 2002 General Social Survey only 23 percent Australian adults participated in church or religious activities during the three months prior to interview.

One has to conclude that the majority of Australians spend only a tiny part of their time, if any, seeking God's company and presumably his wisdom. We see the reality is that of the 100 percent, about 26 percent spend virtually *all* of their time ignoring him, and of the remaining 74 percent all but 23 percent are exercising their free will to live *most* of their time regardless of God's will. Of those outside the 23 percent, some knowingly do evil, while many of the rest make decisions based on self-interest regardless of the effect on others. Even the few of us who strain to serve him are on a steep spiritual learning curve and make many wrong decisions. It is amazing and miraculous that despite this lack of cooperation and deliberate opposition, our country and others like it, are far better places to live in than countries that are not even nominally Christian. If it weren't for God's promises to his elect, there would not only be suffering in the world but total chaos. If the overwhelming majority of people insist on exercising their free will by trying to run the world without God, then the fault for the resulting suffering lies with them. Their foolish and self-centered approach to life is such that it is no surprise that they are vocal in accusing God of the mess they make.

Why does God persist with this dysfunctional relationship? Because he is a loving God, who it seems will go to any lengths to save our souls. He is giving us time to make a right choice and many are wasting this time. Meanwhile we all suffer and so does Jesus. Is this persistence of God worth it? Our answer to this question is of course a measure of faith, and God's love in us, on which it is based. I can say it is worth it to me, though sometimes when at the height of anguish or grief, only just. At these times we can be thankful God doesn't press us past our ability to endure and supplies the faith we need. God's perseverance in his purpose of salvation is worth it to me when someone I love suffers because I can pray for them; it is when they die because Jesus is with them; it is when I anticipate the new perfect world we have been promised; it is when I look at all the good things in my life because without God these things would be without flavor; it is when I think about seeing Jesus face to face. Every

Christian has his own reasons for wanting God to persevere with us. In our better moments, like Job when he found himself in the presence of God, we are overwhelmed, speech is inadequate and we can only respond with a "Yes" from our heart. "For no matter how many promises God has made, they are 'Yes' in Christ. And so through him the 'Amen' is spoken by us to the glory of God." (2 Cor. 1:20).

5. "Christians don't practice what they preach; Christianity doesn't work."

For me this is the hardest statement of all to face. The only way to remove this objection is to never act in our own power, but always with Jesus in our heart in the power of God. Only then can we be effective in addressing the urgent need to lift our game. If we don't, as individuals we underperform as does the organized church.

Nevertheless there does seem to be good evidence that those people who attend church do put in a better effort to serve the community and diminish suffering around them than those who don't. The Australian Bureau of Statistics found that of the Australian adults who had participated in church or religious activities within the three months prior to interview in 2002, 52 percent had also done unpaid voluntary work for an organization within the previous twelve months. In comparison, 29 percent of adults who had not participated in church or religious activities had done such voluntary work. These figures just reinforce the fact that the non-believer must realize he cannot avoid his responsibility to respond to God on the grounds of the mistakes Christians are making.

INTOLERANCE

Intolerance in Christians is real and illustrated in huge ways in events like the persecutions of the Spanish Inquisition, and in smaller ways when Christians shout down the beliefs of others and trample on their sensitivities. It is true intolerance and is to be deplored. It is not part of Christian teaching. "Therefore, as God's chosen people, Holy and dearly loved, clothe yourselves with compassion, kindness, humility, gentleness and patience." (Col. 3:12).

However, the irate non-believer is usually not referring to a dogmatic presentation or aggressive manner as being intolerant, so much as to the so-called intolerance of the Christian insisting there is only one true God, the Christian God. This refusal to countenance beliefs other than Christianity is one of the commonest causes of indignation in the non-Christian, but it is not intolerance at all, as born out by the definition of the word itself. True intolerance is defined as "Denial of the right to differ" and "Disposed to persecute those who differ." The word "intolerance" when applied to opinions or beliefs actually refers to how one responds to or treats someone with a different view to one's own; it doesn't refer to a refusal to believe the other person's point of view. As Christians it is vital for us to be tolerant in the true sense of the word, but not in the false sense of the word. This means that we listen respectfully to another's beliefs, but still hold firmly to our own belief that they are in error.

Paul describes himself as the worst of sinners, but saved by grace because of the unlimited patience Jesus extended to him. This patience of Christ is an example for us to follow when we are confronted with any non-believer. Our approach should reflect the fact that God is a God of miracles and the aggressive atheist whose beliefs offend us today could be the Saint Paul of tomorrow. God's plea after the rebellion and consequent exile of the tribe of Ephraim symbolizes God's love and yearning for everyone far from him. "Is not Ephraim my dear son, the child in whom I delight? Though I often speak against him, I still remember him. Therefore my heart yearns for him; I have great compassion for him, declares the Lord. Set up road signs; put up guideposts. Take note of the highway, the road that you take. Return, O Virgin Israel, return to your towns." (Jer. 31:20–21). God is still yearning for those who deny him. Our attitude should be the same and it should infuse all our personal contact with the non-believer.

Whereas gross examples of Christian intolerance in history are sporadic, it is the norm in the non-Christian world. There has been a history of persecution of Christians ever since the apostles were martyred and the Christians were thrown to the lions in ancient Rome. There are many estimates and accurate figures are impossible to obtain. Figures I have found on the net seem to start at the tens of thousands annually. Dangerous countries for Christians today include North Korea, Iran, Saudi Arabia, Somalia, Maldives, Afghanistan, Yemen, Mauritius, and Laos. Without doubt atheism and other religions are more intolerant than Christianity. The current stealthy move towards banning religious teaching in our schools is the same thing. No one should be forced to attend a school Scripture class or a church if they don't want to, but to impose a ban on everyone doing so is more than intolerance, it is persecution.

Christians preach because we have been commanded by Jesus to bring the gospel to other people. We believe that those of us who are adequately informed (and only God knows that), but fail to agree to the pardon Jesus gives, will spend eternity away from God. What sort of love would we have for others if we adopted the false tolerance encompassed in statements like, "Your view that Christianity is invalid is not true for me, but it is true for you, so it is okay"? Truth is never in conflict with itself; two statements that contradict each other cannot both be true. If we say they are, then we have abandoned the absolute truth of God and left the person condemned.

We have to remember though, that people should have the right to choose rather than have a belief forced upon them. Non-believers understandably feel very strongly about this. Coercion is not only counterproductive; it is not God's way. Jesus says he stands at the door of our heart and knocks, and if we open the door he will come in. It is our choice whether or not to open the door and let him in; he never forces his way in. We can't save anyone, we can't drag others protesting into God's presence, we can only tell them he has made salvation available to everyone who chooses to accept it.

ATHEISM AND TRADITION

Tradition is the handing down of statements, beliefs, rules, and customs from person to person or generation to generation. Believers and non-believers alike fall foul of it. It causes Christians to corrupt the teaching of the Scriptures and atheists to give credibility to their disbelief by blending it in with the culture and traditions of the times in which they live.

Family traditions are a particularly important determinant of spiritual beliefs. Those born into Christian families would seem to have an advantage. Maybe they do, and this represents the working of God's many promises to Christians concerning their descendents. Similarly, certain backgrounds lead naturally into atheism.

In a lecture, a proactive atheist said his father had been a good man, a loving father, and a committed atheist. The son attributed his father's atheism to life in the first half of the 1900s where the ruling classes ruled everything including religion and according to this man they took more than their share. As a result, the father was a socialist political leader, and like many others he confused politics and religion.

Atheism often springs from and is tied to some other passionate belief. If it was realized that Christianity may be very compatible with that other passion then maybe there would be fewer atheists. When you define socialism in terms of equality, then Jesus was the greatest socialist of all time. The common confusion of thinking that you can't be both a socialist and a Christian came about because all of us tend "to throw the baby out with the bath water." This father not only wanted to remove the ruling class itself but also the things he considered they had a stranglehold on, like religion, without individual evaluation and rational assessment. Some socialists threw out God along with the upper class, but not fox hunting! Many pursue their brand of atheism with the same sort of obnoxious zeal that some Christians demonstrate in pursuing Christianity. In a similar way, they let their beliefs become unbalanced and then like their unbalanced religious counterparts, they become just as fanatical, intolerant, and unpleasant.

Tragically, although the son telling the story had insight into why his father was an atheist, he was nevertheless an atheist himself. The father's atheism had become part of the family tradition and probably to a large extent defined it, gave it meaning, cohesion, and security. Understandably, rather than thinking for himself, the son held onto this tradition. If only we could see the pitfalls of the blind acceptance of tradition.

WHAT DO NON-BELIEVERS OFFER?

I find the answer to this question most puzzling because the atheists really don't offer anything at all, not in this life or the next. Presumably the main attraction is not what atheism gives us but what it takes away. It takes away all the trappings of religious practice that we could well do without—things like corrupt church practices and false leaders, nepotism, and persecution of minority religious groups. What has to be realized is these evils are of Satan, and although he seems to work with considerable freedom within Christian churches, he is even more powerful outside them. We can't deny though, Satan is not just on the doorstep of the church, he is right inside making himself at home in the pews because we take him in with us. He comes in with our hard, unloving, and hypocritical hearts. Jesus can't stay in a heart like that. A Christian who

Non Believers

doesn't ensure Jesus is always guarding his heart is in greater danger than a non-believer. Jesus told us getting rid of evil within us leaves a void that even greater evil may fill. This can happen in these uncommitted pew-warming "Christians" and then they become the best evangelists for atheism.

Even so, bad as this scene is, we only have to look at Russia where atheism ruled for seventy years to decide we would rather live in a society with flawed Christian practices than one with flawed atheistic practices. Note this bastion of atheism lasted no time at all compared to the approximate 4,500 year history of Christianity. Atheism put into practice is a proven failure.

Doing away with religion removes the obligation to obey a higher power, and we are then free to do what we want and determine our own destiny. No thanks! I freely admit after a lifetime of mistakes that I don't have a clue what I'm doing and I have good reason to believe my efforts are pretty representative of those of everyone else. I am just so grateful God has picked me up and dusted me off after all those forays into independence. The freedom of the atheist is an illusion and it is quite plain the Russian people without religion, like all atheistic regimes, were anything but free, "They promise them freedom, while they themselves are slaves of depravity—for a man is a slave to whatever has mastered him." (2 Pet. 2:19).

The atheists have no solution to the inevitability of death. When he dies, the atheist in his coffin "is all dressed up with nowhere to go." This obviously troubles most of them who search for a way to transcend death. Some say they live on in the genes of their descendents. One of our children might inherit our fingernails; that existence is hardly inspiring. Others say we leave imprints on nature and so become a permanent part of it; one man used the illustration of sitting on grass and leaving an impression on it—that doesn't do it for me. It seems in an effort to fill the void, any fantasy will do, and yet these same people debunk Christianity as fantasy—usually after having made no effort to study the evidence. Theirs is a desperate clutching at straws and the result contrasts starkly with the Christian belief of life and death in the fullest sense with the Creator of the universe. The stories in Christianity are not just stories, but the meaningful stuff of God's truth illustrated. The substitute stories about the life hereafter have no substance and one might as well believe in Santa Claus or Nanny McPhee. It is often implied Christianity is at home in a disorganized mind, but where is the logic of the atheist? How could anyone compile a book of atheistic beliefs, as distinct from disbeliefs, that wouldn't read like boring fairytales? Such a book if put up against the wisdom of the Bible would be laughable if it wasn't so tragic.

Attending the funeral of a loved one who died a non-believer is a very depressing experience and because there is no reference to God and his promises it seems like the ultimate failure. In such gatherings secular songs are sung to the false gods worshipped in life. How would it feel to be standing before the judgment throne to the funeral strains of, "I Did it My Way"? Instead of praise in prayers and hymns to God there is praise of the dead person. In many cases the less said along those lines the better and the truth has to be distorted or embellished to avoid embarrassment. Then after realizing the unrecognizable person being described is actually the departed, there is the further embarrassment of not knowing where to look. A Christian has the comfort of the promise that his Christian friend, no matter how flawed, is safe with God, "For the Lamb at the center of the throne will be their shepherd; he will lead them to springs of living water. And God will wipe away every tear from their eyes." (Rev. 7:17). There is thanksgiving for the dead man's life, but for thanks to be meaningful it has to be directed to someone and for the atheist there isn't anyone—in their case who is being thanked? The deceased may have had an unhappy life or caused much unhappiness to others; a celebration of their life then sounds more than a trifle hollow. Conversely, to celebrate a life marked by many failures, but dedicated to God and showing spiritual progress, really is a time for joy.

Cringe statements are made at non-believers' funerals like, "Dad will be up there playing golf," or "grandma will be up there listening to 'Days of Our Lives,'" or "Johnny will be up there on a cloud barracking for his favorite football team." In other words it will be "the same old, same old." By contrast, our horizon as a Christian expands across our complete consciousness when we think of seeing Jesus.

The funeral service of an atheist is absolutely without hope and merely seems to highlight what is irretrievably lost. No wonder some atheists who recognize this fact refuse to have a funeral ceremony with mourners attending and simply want to be disposed of as quickly and quietly as possible. The tragedy is all the more unbearable if the departed was a much loved and good-living person.

W. H. Auden was regarded by many as one of the greatest writers of the twentieth century. For years he was an atheist, but converted to Christianity in the 1940s. Before then, in 1936, he wrote a most moving poem called, "Funeral Blues",[3] after the death of his friend. In it he captures the utter sadness, and sense of futility, and loss we all feel when a loved one dies. The concluding line is, "for nothing now can ever come to any good." That is the whole picture for the atheist who is left forever in this place of emotional suffering, because only God can lift us up from there. In the weeks after his wife died, C.S. Lewis wrote an account of his feelings in his book, "A Grief Observed".[4] It is just as poignant in describing his emotional desolation as Auden's poem is, but for him because of his hope in the resurrected Jesus, it didn't end there. Thank God, Auden later came to believe in this same redeeming love of Christ, so that it didn't end there for him either.

At his death the atheist has nothing at all, whereas the Christian has nothing but God, and in him has everything. God is not only our hope, he is our only hope. This is illustrated by the following conversation between Jesus and Peter. After some disaffected disciples deserted him, Jesus asked the twelve disciples if they wanted to leave also. Peter answered him: "Lord, to whom shall we go? You have the words of eternal life. We believe and know that you are the Holy One of God." (John 6:68–69).

THE BRILLIANT MIND AND CHRISTIANITY

There is a lot of at best blindness, or at worst, dishonesty in atheism. Christianity is often derided by the non-believer as a sop for the stupid. We see this in well-known quotes, such as religion being described as an "opiate for the masses"; in other words, if you can't cope with life then knock yourself unconscious with religion. It is derided as an easy cop out. The answer to that accusation is to try forgiving someone you really dislike intensely and then follow up with trying to love them just as intensely. Forgetting the whole idea is the far easier option. Christians take the hard road and persevere with forgiveness but atheists simply don't go there.

The atheist ducks many of the hard issues Christians face up to. This approach, plus the belief that as part of humankind he himself is in charge of everything, including his own destiny, can lead the atheist easily into arrogance. The need for humility is a repetitive teaching throughout the Scriptures. When the inevitable major trials of life are unavoidable, the

---

3. Auden, *Tell Me the Truth About Love*, 29.
4. Lewis, *A Grief Observed*.

atheist finds he has painted himself into a corner and either retreats into full denial or is overwhelmed. Yes—that is when the Christian, equally powerless in his own strength throws himself on the mercy, love, and power of God, and even if the atheist sees this as weakness and stupidity, he should try it because he won't be disappointed with the result.

Jesus in his humanity was of course the first and the best example of a brilliant Christian mind. There are countless others. In modern times we have seen C. S. Lewis, both a theologian and an author of children's literature. Most people are familiar with "The Chronicles of Narnia", "The Lion, the Witch and the Wardrobe", and the movie "Shadowlands" that concerned the death of his wife. Many people don't realize he has written many theological books most of which are so erudite one has to study them, rather than read them, in order to understand.

Some of the truly brilliant minds of history had no problem being both scientists and Christians. Johannes Keppler, German mathematician and astronomer, was a key figure in the scientific revolution of the seventeenth century and has been called the father of modern science. In all his scientific discoveries he saw God as the Creator and said so time and again in his writings. After studying the geometry of a snowflake he wrote: "I do not believe that even in a snowflake this ordered pattern exists at random"; he said the person who argues against God as the Creator "joins combat by childish quibbling in a world on paper, and denies the Sun shines because he himself is blind." The brilliant physicist Sir Isaac Newton, famous for his discoveries about gravity, was a Christian. Werner Von Braun who worked in space exploration at NASA recognized God as the Creator of the universe.

Einstein was born into a non-practicing Jewish family and educated in a Catholic school. He was not a Christian, but unlike many of today's worshippers of knowledge, he was clever enough to realize being an eminent scientist still left him with gaps in his knowledge in fields other than his own. He wrote to Freud asking for his advice relevant to avoiding war and said, "The normal objective of my thoughts affords no insight into the dark places of human will and feeling." Not realizing the limits of their brilliance is a mistake many eminent atheistic scientists make and they take their followers, the worshippers of knowledge, into the same confusion. Our knowledge is something God has warned us not to boast about. "I will destroy the wisdom of the wise; the intelligence of the intelligent I will frustrate." (1 Cor. 1:19). He does this so we will realize our faith rests on his power alone.

CREATION AND EVOLUTION

Atheists and some Christians believe one's belief about the origin of Creation determines one's belief in Christianity as a whole. I don't agree with this. However I do agree that if the Christian interpretation of the scriptural account of Creation is false, then the core message of the gospel is very much devalued.

Here are some facts about genetics:[5]

- All life forms have DNA, which forms genes usually arranged on a strand called a chromosome.
- The human has forty six chromosomes, twenty to twenty five thousand genes, and the whole lot is called a genome.
- The DNA in the genes carries information for making all the proteins required by all organisms. It is made up of four similar chemicals (called bases and abbreviated A, T, C, and G) repeated millions or billions of times throughout a genome. The human genome has three billion pairs of bases.
- The particular order of As, Ts, Cs, and Gs is extremely important. The order underlies all of life's diversity, even dictating whether an organism is human or another species such as yeast, rice, or fruit fly. Even a tiny difference in the genes located on DNA can have a big effect if this difference is located in a critical gene; the obvious physical differences between members of the same species result from very small differences in their DNA.

I remember when I started studying zoology how strikingly similar the embryos of different species looked under the microscope early in their development. The science of genetics tells us we have over 99.9 percent of genes in common with other people, 98 percent in common with the chimpanzee—who is our closest living relative, around 90 percent in common with the rat, 36 percent with the fruit fly, 23 percent with yeast and 21 percent with roundworms. [6] Aside from the details, there is a spectrum of genetic complexity with man at the top, and it seems undeniable there is a genetic template on which all living creatures are modeled.

The scientists tell us they have dated the beginning of the earth and the creatures in it. Their calculations as well as the order of the appearance

---

5. United States Dept of Energy, www.Genomics.energy.gov.
6. American Museum of Natural History.

of the various life forms are hugely different to the account in Genesis. Some of their estimates no doubt will change but overall seem undeniable, or at least in the ball park. The layers of the earth containing fossils and archeological clues can be dated by more than a dozen techniques that use the basic principles of physics, chemistry, and earth sciences. Some techniques can even directly estimate the age of ancient teeth and bones. The methods used include measuring the radioactive decay of chemical elements, counting electrons trapped inside rocks or fossils, comparing magnetic particles in sediments with shifts in the earth's magnetic field, and computing genetic changes over time. From these studies scientists have estimated the age of the earth to be about 4.5 billion years; the emergence of primitive life has been traced back to about 3.8 billion years ago; mammals emerged about 200 million years ago;[7] primitive man became recognizable as the ancestor of modern man about 200,000 years ago.[8]

The fundamentalist Christian view based on literal interpretation of Scripture that the earth and its inhabitants were made in days and are six thousand years old is untenable. This shouldn't be a problem to us because the Scriptures tell us several times God's time scale is different to ours.

I can't see what the fuss is all about. We know the Bible is full of symbolism. To me the creation story is symbolic. To take another example of symbolism, Jesus was asked how many times we should forgive each other. On one occasion he said seven times and on another he said seventy-seven. So which is it, how many times is right, seven or seventy-seven? Do we conclude Jesus was unsure of the exact number of times we should forgive so had two different guesses? Could he have been misquoted? The evidence all the words attributed to Jesus recorded in the Bible were actually spoken by him is very strong.[9] We can conclude he gave both answers. However he spoke symbolically and obviously meant we should forgive someone many, many times, in fact so many times that counting at all is irrelevant. That is one of numerous examples of symbolism. Atheists are not interested in arguing that particular point because they are not interested in forgiveness, but they are interested in Creation.

I am quite comfortable believing like the teaching on forgiveness, that the story of Creation is symbolic. I believe the meaning of the

7. Wikipedia, http://en.wikipedia.org/wiki/Timeline_of_evolution.

8. Smithsonian Institute, http://humanorigins.si.edu/resources/intro-human-evolu-tion.

9. McDowell, *The New Evidence that Demands a Verdict*.

account, which is that God made the heavens, the earth, and everything in it is absolutely true, but I think the time frame given in days is symbolic language. The Christian fundamentalists are sincere in their defense of scriptural truth through literal translation of time frames and their motives are to be admired, but by defending their error they are in fact casting doubt on the whole of Scripture, and thus achieving the very opposite effect to that which they intend. The issue has been seized upon by atheists who blow it out of all proportion by giving the impression the fundamentalist view is the mainstream one. The creation controversy is one of the commonest attacks I come under from non-believers and I find it difficult to convince them it is not my view, nor the view of most Christians, and most importantly the truth of Christianity does not hang on this argument. It can be virtually impossible to get the focus of the non-believer off this diversion and onto Jesus, and the life and death things they need to know about. It is also counterproductive when people on both sides of the argument are intolerant in the presentation of their belief. They often state their view in a very aggressive manner and try to force their belief on others. We might expect such an approach from the secular world, but when we see hate, aggression, and control from a professing Christian, we know it is not of God.

Darwin's Theory of Evolution proposed in the eighteen thirties and based on "survival of the fittest" absolutely rocked the Christian world and we are still feeling the shock waves. Again, I don't see it as incompatible with the Scriptures. Whether right or wrong, it is a very logical theory given all the evidence that has accumulated since then. We know changes (mutations) in genes occur for a variety of reasons. In health matters this can result in a defective gene that prejudices survival. Conversely, if a mutation occurs that is favorable for survival, it is logical these offspring are more likely to live to reproduce their genes than those who inherited the defective or more inferior gene. Over millennia a superior being like man could evolve. That is the core of the theory of evolution—the theory of survival of the fittest. As to whether this process is responsible, for example, for a sea creature evolving into a land creature is not proven. There is some suggestive fossil evidence but perhaps not as much as you might expect. As yet we haven't found the "missing link" between man and the chimpanzee, who is closest to us. Given that we have 98 percent of our genes in common with the chimp, maybe there never was another life form closer to us. That there is a basic pattern common to all life is blatantly apparent. The possibility is still open that each life form was derived directly from one pattern, rather than that one life form gradually changed by genetic mutation to the next until the chain to man was complete.

It is intriguing to watch developments. We need to do so with an attitude of healthy skepticism, but our faith in scriptural truth certainly doesn't need to stand or fall on the final outcome. God assures us we have been made in his image. It shouldn't be a problem if it transpires our ancestors originated from primordial slime. We see unattractive clay turned into beautiful artworks, why not slime into primitive life? If so it will be all the more of a miracle that God made us in his image from such unpromising material. The tragedy is people have allowed themselves to be sidetracked on this minor issue even to the point of abandoning their faith. We should not be cowered by the words "science has proven," because all science can prove is the marvel of God's creation.

SUMMARY

People have let themselves be dismayed and browbeaten by science not realizing in its pure form it is of God. We also need to realize not everything is true just because someone labels it "scientifically proven" and not everything is untrue that is not proven. This caption, "scientifically proven", is the buzzword of modern society and is applied to ideas on everything from the origin of the universe to a cure for corns.

While many scientific facts are proven beyond reasonable doubt, the derived belief of atheism cannot be proven any more than the existence of God can be proven; neither belief can be proven or disproven scientifically.

Leading atheists have managed to sound superficially plausible. Many have convinced themselves, and so they are sincere in their belief in man and lack of belief in God. They hold an amazingly naïve view that man unfettered by religion can run his life and the world successfully. Atheism is a belief based on the denial of history—the reality for all to see is that we live for a short time, die, and are forgotten. Atheistic regimes are persecutors not only of religion itself, but they deny many of the things that spring from it and inspire us, such as freedom and basic human rights. The world in rebellion against God hurtles towards destruction.

Non Believers

All this is so obvious that the idea of heaven on earth without God would never have floated at all were it not for the false god of knowledge that dazzles and blinds modern man. This god is the golden calf of modern times and makes just as much sense. Like all the lesser false gods Satan promotes, it is characterized by confusion, false promises, misery, loss of the heights of man's potential, loss of meaning in life, and loss of hope in death. It is a triumph for evil because it preaches a doctrine of loss; by deluding the mind and denying the soul it takes away everything of value, because it denies God. This dismal state of despair is self-imposed, tragic, and unnecessary. It is like a drowning man rejecting a life boat.

By contrast, Christians not only have open and immediate access to God but Jesus will welcome us as brothers and sisters. How easy it is, and how marvelous, that at any time we can call out for our God who loves us, and though spiritual paupers, he will welcome us into his presence and surround us with his love. He has promised us he is accessible to all who seek him. "Call to me and I will answer you and tell you great and unsearchable things you do not know." (Jer. 33:3).

16

Out of Darkness into Light

THE PATH TO BELIEF

WHY IS BELIEF IN God so difficult? The logic of all the evidence should be so convincing, yet for many it isn't. Around us is the witness of Creation and in us is the human psyche with its dependence on love and inspiration.

Underpinning hope for those who are not satisfied with their unbelief and who say, "help me overcome my unbelief!" (Mark 9:24), is Jesus's promise: "For everyone who asks receives; he who seeks finds; and to him who knocks, the door will be opened." (Matt. 7:8).

It is the grace and sovereign power of God that opens the eyes of the most blind, "I will give them an undivided heart and put a new spirit in them; I will remove from them their heart of stone and give them a heart of flesh." (Eze. 11:19). As in everything sometimes God executes his will directly, as he did with Paul, while at other times he works through us. In this we need to partner with Jesus through unceasing prayer for all non-believers and also always be true witnesses to him, so that the love of God flows through us and is seen in everything we do. Mostly we are unaware of the scrutiny of others, which is why our worship has to be whole-hearted. It is only by dwelling in the presence of God and walking with Jesus that we can have a positive effect on the faith of others.

Whenever we have the opportunity, we need to meet the atheist on his ground, because he may be both unwilling and unable to meet us on ours. He can't understand the spiritual life, whereas we do understand exactly what constitutes the life and values of the atheist. Where he is fixated on science and knowledge then that is where we should meet, to show him there is no contradiction between God and truth in any field. Though he can't see it and therefore denies it, God is not only part of his scientific world but he made it and upholds it. The atheist stands as challenged today as Job was three thousand years ago when God asked him if he could set the course of the planets.

Many people are atheists by default. They don't want to be, but they just can't see God as a reality. We need to encourage them to pray. Praying in hope has the potential for the greatest and most marvelous surprise of one's life. God will answer. He is waiting and longing for us to approach him. The idea is not without precedent, the ancient Greeks with the statues of their many gods on display had a statue to the "Unknown God." How that delighted Paul, who was quick to introduce the only true God and many believed. God's answer to the unbeliever's own prayer is the ultimate and undeniable proof they seek. As a Christian we can personally testify it will be a message of the redeeming love of Christ and it captures the soul.

God understands the dilemma, and in order to bring non-believers to belief and believers to the heights of faith, he has given many promises like this one: "My son, if you accept my words and store up my commands within you, turning your ear to wisdom and applying your heart to understanding, and if you call out for insight and cry aloud for understanding, and if you look for it as for silver and search for it as for hidden treasure, then you will understand the fear of the Lord and find the knowledge of God." (Prov. 2:1–5). These verses describe a full-on heart and soul effort. As Thomas found out, Jesus doesn't write the non-believer off as hopeless, rather he will take action to convince the willing but doubting heart. Jesus invited Thomas to touch and explore the scars from his crucifixion wounds and then to stop doubting. Thomas did so and then cried out, "My Lord and my God!" (John 20:28).

THE MORALITY OF CHRISTIAN EVANGELISM

Jesus commanded his followers to spread the gospel across the world. So Christians don't have a problem with the morality of evangelism, but others do and accuse us of intolerance, of a "holier than though" attitude, and of destroying the culture along with the religion of others. We can address the intolerance because that is a matter of our manners not our belief. Jesus was humble himself and humbles us, so the second objection, a superior attitude, doesn't come from him. Both those problems should melt away as he is increasingly expressed in our lives.

The third accusation, that of destroying cultures different from our own, troubles me the most perhaps because I am a fourth generation Australian and a Christian. History records the chaos, disease, and suffering that at least until recently often followed the introduction of Christianity into primitive places. More than two hundred years after white settlement in Australia, the Aboriginal population is still suffering and we don't know what to do to help. When we devalued Aboriginal spirituality and failed to respect their beliefs we destroyed the structure of their society. Now that we have insight and are appalled by what has been done and see their plight, we don't know how to put it right. Apart from Australia's origin as a dumping ground for British jailbirds, the people who soon followed came from the United Kingdom primarily to colonize, and not to preach. As well, evil has always been more newsworthy than good, so recent publicity is not orientated towards recording the positive effects of Christian evangelism. To be fair, it was the colonizing rather than the Christianity that caused many of the problems. Even so, white settlement occurred during the time when religion ruled British society and the religion was overwhelmingly Christian. Although much of what was done to the Indigenous population sprang from human greed, the church was by no means innocent of wrongdoing, and was involved in the stolen generation as recently as forty years ago. If we look to Jesus and his teachings for an explanation of how this happened it is obvious none of this can be laid at his door. The harm was not caused by spreading the gospel itself, but by the evils of community culture at the time, by church tradition, and by political influences, all of which corrupted the understanding of those involved. The destruction of Indigenous culture was unnecessary, the result is appalling. It was yet another assault on Christ. The Mongol hoards did worse, but maybe no worse than we Christians did in Tasmania.

I recently saw on the television the story of Fanny Hamer, who was an African American activist. Her faith and that of the black Christian church flourished against a background of persecution by the white Christian church. It is very comforting that often while some Christians are doing their worst, it is precisely then that God shows us other Christians doing their best. We need to strive to have greater insight, and to overcome the contradiction of the love of God and our own lack of love, that we present to others.

In terms of the morality of evangelism at an individual level, we need to ask whether we have the right to present our beliefs as better than any non-Christian's? Surely we do—providing we really do offer something better. The subject doesn't even have to be studied deeply to see that Jesus is infinitely better than any alternative. Let's be clear—Jesus is better but *we* are not and some aspects of our culture are not. This distinction is something that is often badly presented by the speaker and misheard by the listener. If we can present the true message, then how could we possibly knowingly not do so? Jesus represents the only real hope anyone has in both life and death. We need to present just him, and not ourselves or our cultural or religious habits. To do this we need him with us constantly, then we can give other people his gold without the human dross that without him clings to us and pollutes everything we touch.

Job said, "I know that my Redeemer lives, and that in the end he will stand upon the earth." (Job 19:25). Now Jesus does stand upon the earth and this prophesy of Isaiah has also come to pass. "The people walking in darkness have seen a great light; on those living in the land of the shadow of death a light has dawned." (Isa. 9:2). This must be one of the best descriptions of how a believer sees their life before and after Jesus becomes part of it. Helping to gather everyone we can into this great light is something we are compelled from within ourselves to do, but we have to do it in the company of our Redeemer, and in the power of the love of God. Any other approach will drive people further from the light, and further into the darkness, and we are likely to get lost there ourselves.

METHODS OF EVANGELISM

A few years ago I went for a week to a third-world Buddhist country as part of a medical team. The trip was organized by a world wide ministry and the outreach was both medical and evangelical. I was very impressed by the other members of the team most of whom were there because of a genuine desire to help. They showed selflessness, had great enthusiasm in their faith, and were willing to work as hard as they could and do whatever they could to alleviate the suffering around us. We handed out a month's supply of medication to each person we saw and the least anyone received was a month's supply of vitamins. The dentists did a marvelous job pulling out rotten aching teeth—two teeth per person. As each patient left the makeshift clinic they were directed to the pastors.

I found it depressing and heartbreaking because we could offer no medical follow up. It was "band aid" medicine, what good was a month's worth of high blood pressure tablets, or diabetes tablets, or vitamin tablets? We sent the dying back to their homes to die because the funds were not available to send them to hospital. I felt hypocritical because it seemed as though we were conning them with the false hope of Western medicine and were doing this in order to lure them into Christianity. Interestingly I wasn't aware anyone else had my problem. Jesus went about healing and preaching, but he *really* healed and restored people back to perfect health, whereas we were just knowingly giving the *impression* we were healing; there was no lasting medical benefit in what we did. I wrote a polite but concerned letter to the organizers of the ministry suggesting the money would be better spent building and staffing hospitals. I received no answer and the regular practice of these short term evangelical medical missions has continued. This ministry had started building a hospital when we were there and the program is continuing. It is a ministry I admire for their dedication to spreading the gospel, hard work, and good works. However I really don't have complete peace of mind over the short term medical missions. It is one of the things I have put in my "too hard basket".

On this mission trip there was a marvelous nurse who told us the story of her conversion. She and her family had been living in extreme poverty in the Philippines. One day an evangelical team arrived in her home town, I think from overseas, and offered a free meal together with a sermon. She went along for the free meal and came away a Christian. As a person and as a Christian she was an inspiration to the rest of the team. She now lives in the USA and has worked hard to bring her extended family there. Twice a year she goes on these medical missions around the world. In her case she was offered a meal and received a meal, and probably the advertising that went along with it made it clear the price of it was to listen to a Christian sermon. So that approach seems transparent.

On day one of the mission I went on, I felt very nervous as I hadn't practiced anything but suburban medicine for many years and had been retired for nearly four years. I started to feel totally inadequate and when praying in my room just before leaving, I spoke in garbled panic prayers to God along the lines of desperately needing his help if I was to do anything worthwhile. He broke into this barrage with these words, which I saw written in my head: "and glory shone around." Later on, after I had returned home, I found these words in Luke 2:9. "An angel of the Lord appeared to them, and the glory of the Lord shone around them, and they were terrified." The angel went on to tell the shepherds not to be afraid. At the time it seemed God was saying to me, "relax, my glory is manifested here, that is what is important, there is nothing to stress over." Predictably, receiving this message had an immediate therapeutic effect on me! It is marvelous when God glorifies his name through us and to be told so is fantastic.

What about the validity of mass conversions? Usually the speakers are very dynamic and the atmosphere is highly emotionally charged. Often there is music playing quietly in the background, which can be quite hypnotic. Sometimes one wonders if the scene is deliberately set to allow the campaigners to get control of the minds of their audience. As is the case with hypnosis, some people are more susceptible to atmosphere than others. At the end of the meetings there may be a stampede in response to the altar call, which can closely resemble the audience response to some shows put on by well-known hypnotists.

Jesus was not exclusive about who should spread the gospel. He didn't even require those evangelizing in his day to be on his team, as we learn from the story of the stranger the disciples saw driving out demons in Jesus's name. As he was not one of them they told him to stop but Jesus overruled them for the very reason that the man was using Jesus's name. He also gave this warning: "Many will say to me on that day, 'Lord, Lord, did we not prophesy in your name, and in your name drive out demons and perform many miracles?' Then I will tell them plainly, 'I never knew you. Away from me, you evildoers!'"(Matt. 7:22–23). It seems God can save through anyone, saint or sinner, but this doesn't guarantee the salvation of the person he uses. It means if he enables us to convert people it is to his glory; if we are the instrument he uses then we are on notice to get ourselves right with him.

THE FATE OF THOSE WHO HAVE NEVER HEARD ABOUT JESUS

Occasionally discussed among Christians is the question of how people stand after death if they have never heard the gospel message. If they have never had the chance to accept or reject Jesus will they all go to hell? My answer is an emphatic "No"!

Jesus says a number of times it is only through him we can be with God forever, "No one comes to the Father except by me [Jesus]." (John 14:6). Once we have heard about Jesus we must make a decision for or against him, failing to make a decision at all is taken as a rejection. In that case all the promises of hell, meaning spending eternity without God, will fall on us. The Bible states this view as the clear and unequivocal position of those who have heard the gospel message. On that basis, when we look at other verses as well, we can see how those people fare who have never heard about Jesus. (As an aside only God knows who has heard about Christ in such a way that they have been given an adequate opportunity to accept him. This is one of the reasons it is not up to us to say that an individual is not saved).

We are told Creation has always witnessed to the sovereignty and glory of God and for this reason humankind is without excuse if they do not believe. This is in line with the following parenthetical statement: "(Indeed, when Gentiles, who do not have the law, do by nature things required by the law, they are a law for themselves, even though they do not have the law, since they show that the requirements of the law are written on their hearts, their consciences also bearing witness, and their thoughts now accusing, now even defending them.)" (Rom. 2:14–15). The NIV study notes explain this verse in this way: "The moral nature of pagans, enlightened by conscience (verse 15), functioned for them as the Mosaic Law did for the Jews." It means everyone is made aware of God, whether uninformed about Christ like Abraham and the Israelites in the Old Testament days, or whether informed about him as we are, everyone makes a choice to serve God or to rebel against him. The Israelites were unable to keep God's law as expressed in Mosaic Law and the pagan is unable to keep God's law as expressed in Creation and written on his heart, both need an outside solution to their lack of righteousness.

The Scriptures repeatedly tell us we have no righteousness of ourselves and the only way we can acquire it is through Christ. Hence the righteousness credited to Abraham because of his faith in God, could only come through Christ. Jesus wasn't born for more than two thousand years after Abraham, yet Paul confirmed this retrospective salvation when he told us that the Israelites with Moses in the desert, who were also born before Christ, did in fact have access to the saving grace of God in Christ, "They all ate the same spiritual food and drank the same spiritual drink; for they drank from the spiritual rock that accompanied them, and that rock was Christ." (1 Cor. 10:3–4). This righteousness, which God-fearing ancient people had through the death of Jesus, is reaffirmed here: "God presented him as a sacrifice of atonement, through faith in his blood. He did this to demonstrate his justice, in his forbearance he had left the sins committed beforehand [before Jesus's death] unpunished" (Rom. 3:25). These verses confirm that those who lived before the birth of Christ—those who never knew him, come under his righteousness just as surely as those born after.

Obviously Abraham wasn't the only person who lived too early to know of Jesus, but still went to heaven: Moses and Elijah were seen at the Transfiguration. Jesus spoke of others who were saved: "The men of Nineveh will stand up at the judgment . . . The Queen of the South will rise at the judgment," (Matt. 12:41–42). He said this was so because the men of Nineveh repented and the Queen of the South came to listen to God's wisdom. It means all those people who died before the birth of Christ, and who like Abraham had a heart for God as revealed to them in their culture, and faith in him, would have had their faith credited to them as righteousness in Christ, just like Abraham. Those who lived their life in rebellion against God could not avail themselves of the pardon Christ bought for humankind, and so they remained in their unrighteous state, and were without hope.

We need to rethink the steps to salvation. First we choose God, after that Christ enables our choice. Accepting Christ is not an end in itself, rather he is our way—our only way to God. We have to be righteous to be acceptable to God and Jesus tells us we can only become righteous through him. Christ is outside time and can save all God-fearing people whether born before or after him according to an earthly clock. "Jesus Christ is the same yesterday and today and forever." (Heb. 13:8). All those people who die without ever hearing about Jesus fall into exactly the same category as Abraham and the people mentioned above—they can choose God during their lifetime, and in doing so they drink from the same "spiritual rock" of Christ, just as the ancient Israelites did. Then although unaware of Jesus they go to heaven. Alternatively, they don't choose God and go to hell. Their fate in either case is just as sure as ours is.

In this way there are three groups of people saved to God after death: the first group comprises those God-fearing people born like Abraham, Moses and a host of others before Christ; the second group is those God-fearing people, who though born after Christ have never heard of him;

the third group is those born after Christ, who have heard the gospel message and accepted Jesus as Redeemer. The only difference between these three groups is that we, who are in the third group, know who our Savior is, while those in the first two groups are saved by blind faith in God and his as yet unrevealed purpose for them in Christ. We have been so fortunate because we have been given this further revelation of Jesus.

It is very clear in the Scriptures that Jesus told us to spread the gospel to *all* nations—and note "all" includes our own. This equal geographical emphasis is reflected in this verse, "you will be my witnesses in Jerusalem, and in all Judea and Samaria, and to the ends of the earth." (Acts 1:8). We have tended to put undue emphasis on far flung places and it is interesting to note that Australia would most certainly have been regarded as the "ends of the earth" had it been known to those living in thirty AD. We are now seeing evangelists coming from third-world countries to Australia and this is marvelous. Evangelism is needed wherever there is unbelief. It is what God wants, and in being obedient in this we further his purpose, we show we love him, we reflect his glory, and so we delight him and grow spiritually ourselves. Our efforts should bring the riches of Christ into other lives. We are just incredibly blessed in knowing Jesus and should be thankful for the privilege of making him known— and this is so whether it is talking about Jesus to a non-believing friend in a restaurant in this country, or speaking to a person in the third-world who has rejected God—at an individual level the one is no more urgent than the other.

Those concerned Christians who mistakenly think all those people who have never heard the gospel go to hell understandably place a heavy emphasis on missionary work in third-world countries. We should hold those who work for God overseas in great respect, because it usually involves extreme dedication, deprivation, and often physical danger to bring Christ to dark places in the world. Even so I have noticed thinking often gets out of balance, so we see such service as the ultimate badge of holiness, and pride, and elitism may seep in. At the same time those who serve in other ways at home often feel their service is of lesser value to God. I remember hearing of a person who spent his life doing administrative work in the church, who looked back in his latter years with regret, because he hadn't been a missionary. Maybe he forgot administrative skills are listed in the Scriptures as one of the gifts God gives some people.

Whenever we do what God asks us to do, whatever it is, we delight him and he anoints our efforts, and so we achieve his purpose—it is the very best service we can undertake. In this way we reveal his glory. We need to be grateful and supportive to all God's servants for their example to us. Also, all of us always need to realize God does not need us to do anything for him—we are not doing him any favors. In serving, we are simply trying our best to express our love for him by being obedient to whatever he puts on our heart for us to do. Then we grow spiritually, and benefit at least as much by our efforts as those we serve.

A very important consideration is that those people living in third-world countries who do have faith in God as he has revealed himself, although credited with righteousness and so saved, have much more difficult lives than believers in nominally Christian countries. This is both because they don't know the enormous joy and comfort the knowledge of a personal Savior brings, and also because a non-Christian country is so harsh without Jesus, "the light of the world," (John 8:12). One of the most recent genocides was in Cambodia where the people overwhelmingly follow Buddhism. Many non-Christian nations in Africa and the Middle East are terrifying places to live. Such countries desperately need the good news of great joy that the angels announced at Jesus's birth.

Some Christians also agonize about whether stillborn children, or young children, or the mentally retarded, can go to heaven as they have been unable to make a decision for Christ. Frankly this seems like a "no brainer" to me because it can be answered purely on the basis of everything we know about our loving God— "God *is* love. [my emphasis]" (1 John 4:8). To be reminded of why this is so, we need only consider why we become separated from God—it is because we choose to live in rebellion. Therefore where a person does not have sufficient understanding to be able to make an informed choice, they have not separated themselves from God. This is true even though they have lived long enough to do wrong things, because if their heart is right Jesus covers their sin, as he does for all of us who are reconciled to God. Conversely, those people like the writer and readers of this book have the necessary understanding to make a reasoned choice for or against God as revealed in Christ, and so we need to *ask* for the righteousness of Christ in order to be acceptable to God. We have clearly seen God in nature, and as well we have seen the person of Christ, and so if we reject him, we are all the more without excuse.

Feet on Earth, Head in Heaven

THE POWER OF THE CROSS

After we are reconciled to God through Christ we become a living illustration of the power of the cross. It is only by harnessing this power when we present the testimony of our conversion that others will be able to hear Jesus calling them. If we are willing to open our mouth, he will do the rest.

We are like the demon-possessed man who after Jesus cured him was told to go home to tell what God had done for him. He obeyed and told his story all over town. Jesus gave these instructions to the twelve disciples when he sent them out to preach to the people: "What I tell you in the dark, speak in the daylight; what is whispered in your ear, proclaim from the roofs." (Matt. 10:27). He requires us to hold high the light of the gospel for others to see, "No one lights a lamp and hides it in a jar or puts it under a bed. Instead, he puts it on a stand, so that those who come in can see the light." (Luke 8:16).

There are many ways of doing this and the way God has chosen for one person will be different to another. He is a God of variety and surprises. We only have to look at Creation to see that—consider the camel or the platypus. A friend said at the end of her life that she regretted never having joined in door-knocking evangelism. All I know is that her life as a quiet dedicated Christian was a marvelous witness to me and her faith in her last illness truly inspirational. It requires many types of Christians with different personalities and gifts working in different ways to be effective in helping others to find God. There is no best way overall, only a best way for each of us determined by God, and this may also vary at different times. There are the charismatic TV evangelists, the visiting missionaries, the entertaining speakers, those who visit the outcasts, the people who talk to someone at a bus stop, and those who wash up after outreaches. Note, this list is in order of glamour and therefore not in order of value; there is no value based on category. If we listen to him, God will tell us where we fit and when.

It is not all about getting someone through a church door; it is as much about helping them to stay there. Interestingly, the people best at doing the former are often without skill in the latter, and vice versa. We have to know both our strengths and weaknesses in order to step forward or stand back appropriately, remembering that even working in the way God wants us to at times will take us outside our comfort zone. We have our job to do, but it is God who is in control.

To the unconverted we could say, based on our own experience: "Be warned, God wants you, he is after you. He will never give up trying and with minimal encouragement from you he will get you!—and then he will never let you go"! Unaware of the love of God, they might find this a bit threatening. Anyway, more often we say about someone who exhausts our patience and it gets too hard, "Oh let them go!" God doesn't do that, he saves us despite ourselves. Malcolm Muggeridge in his book, "Conversion,"[1] spoke of this persistence of God and was quoted in the foreword as saying, "God comes padding after me like a hound of heaven."

Of course Satan is pretty persistent too—he managed to keep his grip on the soul of one of the two thieves on the cross. Matthew records that they *both* heaped insults on Jesus. Luke records first Jesus prayed to God asking him to forgive his persecutors. Following on that prayer, Luke says only one of the thieves hurled insults. So it seems likely the repentant thief also hurled insults at first and then later changed his mind, and perhaps this was as a result of hearing Jesus's prayer. This man recognized and bowed to God's sovereign rule when he admonished his fellow thief for not fearing God. He admitted they were guilty and deserved punishment, but said Jesus was innocent. He showed humility and simple faith when he asked, "Jesus, remember me when you come into your kingdom." (Luke 23:42). Convicted by the Holy Spirit, he responded to defend Jesus and the truth, and God was swift to his rescue. Imagine how he must have felt when he heard Jesus say from the cross beside him, "I tell you the truth, today you will be with me in paradise." (Luke 23:43). With these simple words Jesus more than answered the request made by the man to remember him. This side drama on the cross, almost too trivial to mention when compared to the crucifixion of the Son of God, showed although Jesus was down, he was by no means out.

The death of Jesus was seen to be a cosmic event as the attention of heaven was riveted on Golgotha and the power of the cross was unleashed on the earth. The sun was obscured as darkness came over the whole land for three hours, the earth shook, and the rocks split. The temple curtain that had symbolically separated us from the presence of God tore in two from top to bottom. When Jesus hung on the cross it was all heaven on heartbreak hill. I have no way of knowing—yet, but I think the loudest heavenly cry of joy ever over a reclaimed soul may have rung out over

---

1. Muggeridge, *Conversion*, "Foreword," xiii.

the criminal who defended Jesus. Imagine if we had been given the opportunity of speaking up for Jesus on the cross. Would we have done it? To the world he seemed utterly defeated and powerless, and to those who had followed him as the next King of Israel, he was probably a pathetic embarrassment. He was surrounded by mockers who hurled insults and taunted him telling him to come down off the cross. The thief got it right when few others did. When things look bad around us and defy explanation, and others respond by deriding God, we need to remember this thief on the cross. His story is a cliff-hanger, a one-minute-to-midnight rescue. It is one of the most poignant illustrations we have of the timeless battle between God and Satan for the human soul, and of Jesus's victorious role of Redeemer.

THE HOLY SPIRIT

We probably worry too much about how to tell others about the gospel. This can result in our doing nothing at all for fear we will get it wrong, or come on so awkwardly, or so strongly that we drive people away. The disciples apparently also worried about whether they were up to the task because Jesus reassured them the Spirit of God would speak through them.

At times the language of the Holy Spirit is very timely and direct, and the meaning very plain; he is easy to listen to. But there is a catch. If we don't stay tuned to the Holy Spirit by having a close relationship with Jesus, we get it all wrong. We deliver sermons when we should be delivering comfort and become utterly boring and tedious. If the person we are talking to about God is resistant, angry, or politely bored, then we have to wonder if it is us on our soapbox, rather than the Holy Spirit in the pulpit. Total dependence on the Holy Spirit underpins evangelism. It is an impossible task for us on our own. We may either give inappropriate sermons or we may not be direct enough. It is vital every Christian makes every effort to be as close to God as possible. It is the only way he can teach us to be clear about who he is, what we believe, and how to tell others.

To evangelize means to talk about God, and he is love. Anything we say, or any move we make, that does not spring from love, does not come from God. Without love, evangelism is cold, and likely to be fruitless, and it can become a matter of notches on our belt. Without the Holy Spirit, not only are we likely to be less than helpful to others, but we don't benefit ourselves. Anything we do with God is a great blessing to us, anything we do *for* him, but *without* him, may well take us backwards on our spiritual journey.

KNOW THE FACTS

How can we communicate our faith when we don't know what we believe ourselves? How can we talk convincingly about God's promises if we only have a hazy notion of what they are? Some Christians are quite belligerent about other religions when they have only a very vague idea of their own. To make valid comparisons we also need to know the basic facts about all the other major religions. In our ignorance we may trash everything about them. On the contrary, some of the prominent religions in the world have much to recommend them, because they have a vein of altruism and brotherly love running through them. The sentiment of the second greatest commandment, "do to others as you would have them do to you," is present in some form in Judaism, Hinduism, Confucianism and Buddhism. (See Appendix, "Comparison of Buddhism and Christianity"). This leads many people to think differences are inconsequential, and as all the major religions are basically the same, it doesn't matter which one is followed. The crucial point is that an adherent to a religion without reconciliation to God through Christ lacks the power of God to fulfill the ideals of his belief, and has to "pull himself up by his own shoestrings." Such a person believes he can through his own effort perfect himself and bring about a better world. For this reason it is not surprising Buddhism is a religion that attracts academics because it is a religion based on intellectual achievement. At a conference the Dalai Lama is on record as saying, "according to Buddhism, intelligence is considered to be very important in one's spiritual path."[2] By contrast, the Christian knows there is a sovereign God and without him we are nothing and can do nothing. He is the God of the mentally retarded as surely as he is the God of Einstein.

One day at work years ago, a severely mentally retarded woman came along with a sore foot. She sat in a chair and I crouched down so I could examine it closely. When I looked up she was focused on me and looked down into my eyes with the most beautiful loving smile. I can't

---

2. His Holiness The Dalai Lama, *The Good Heart*, 64.

remember another smile quite like it. I feel I came as close as I am likely to come on this earth to seeing the love of God expressed in someone's eyes and smile. I know I have never bestowed a smile like that on anyone. Those who live and work with the mentally retarded know mine was not a unique experience. This woman certainly hadn't used her intelligence to get in touch with God. Christians cannot take intellectual pride in any spiritual progress they make, but can only sit at Jesus's feet with a love and gratitude that is impossible to express, but that he understands.

The aim of the Buddhist is to achieve emptiness,[3] the aim of the Christian is to see God and we do this by looking to Jesus. Some Buddhist sects believe Buddha exists, but in a very nebulous form, while others look only to a stone statue. We need to know the facts about other religions so that we can help those followers to see the riches of Christ, which are missing from these other belief systems. In doing so our own appreciation of the treasures we hold heightens and this is very valuable to us.

PRAYER

Maybe prayer is the best way of all to evangelize, if only because we ask for God's power while we stay out of his way. We can pray directly for the salvation of others, and we can pray for wisdom to know how we should relay the gospel in general, as well as to particular people at particular times. Whenever I find a non-believer talking to me unexpectedly about religion or God, I quickly pray in my mind with these words, "God help me with this." Because I am concentrating on the conversation there isn't time for a more wordy prayer, but there doesn't need to be. Often the person may show by their attitude or words that they are angry, or disappointed with God, or the church, or some Christian; others express disappointment because they have been unable to believe. By praying silently immediately at the time, I hope the conversation will enable them to hear God, and it may be the right time to offer to pray with them.

SUMMARY

It is God alone who saves souls, "No one can come to me unless the Father who sent me draws him, and I will raise him up at the last day." (John

3. His Holiness The Dalai Lama, *The Good Heart*, 172.

6:44). It is one of the great spiritual mysteries that God in his grace and mercy sent Jesus to save the whole world, yet some people are saved and some are not. The individual has the right of veto where God's plan for his salvation is concerned. It is unexplained why one man is willing to give up every earthly thing to ensure his heavenly destiny with his Creator, while another exults in earthly pleasures and doesn't seem to see or care that he is rushing to destruction. As Christians, our role is to guard the gospel by presenting it in its purity so all non-believers will see our great God of love, and choose to walk in his light and goodness.

God will direct his people to spread his gospel in various ways according to the talents he has given each person and according to the needs of the listener. Relevant to all Christians is the personal testimony of our whole life, not just the marvelous time we first felt the presence of God. To ring true we must travel with Jesus, communicate with God constantly in prayer, study the wisdom of his Word, and relate to everyone in practical ways at all times through the power of his love.

Everything about us should speak of Jesus; his light should shine from us. "For God, who said, 'Let light shine out of darkness,' made his light shine in our hearts to give us the light of the knowledge of the glory of God in the face of Christ." (2 Cor. 4:6).

17

Picking Up the Pace with Jesus

I HAVE TOLD THE story of my conversion, which occurred after a friend died of cancer. Then God gave me a revelation of his love, which claimed my soul. This awareness of divine love was in some respects like having all my previous experiences of human love rolled into one, and then being dropped into the depths of it. Simultaneously I was aware it was different because it was an experience of love that conveyed the quality and perfection of its Author. Although it was so personal, I recognized my consciousness had been awakened to the universal love God has for all humankind. One of the characteristics of this love of God is that it is never confined. In contrast with earthly love, divine love never ripples around in the ebb and flow of a backwater, but is a powerful moving torrent carving out its course and flowing on. It is obvious to me it is a love with a purpose, and that purpose is to bring salvation to everyone.

I am running my race with Jesus, which means living life here as he did, fully involved with this earthly existence. At the same time, by sharing my life with him, the Kingdom of God is within me and around me; the Holy Spirit and the love of God is within me; I am surrounded by the hosts of heaven; I am living by the Spirit. With my head in heaven I share God's vision of a perfect world and want to be part of his solution, but this entails keeping my feet on earth and living and working here to promote God's kingdom in Satan's stronghold. These two kingdoms, in which every Christian must live, are locked in deadly combat. Between them there is no peace treaty, no common ground, and no compromise.

In this book I have described how Christ has led me against the enemy in personal skirmishes, in decisive battles marked by victory, and in on-going struggles, as I try to live in these two warring worlds. When I am wrestling with the forces of evil within me and around me, I often think how easy it would be to claim salvation and then immediately move from earth to heaven to be with God for evermore. It doesn't work that way and in my more rational moments I don't want it to. I know it is by involvement here with Jesus that I can be part of things that I don't want to miss. God has given me a set number of days on earth. I have spent much of this time ignoring God and being confused by Satan, so now in my heart where the Holy Spirit dwells, I am filled with a sense of urgency. It is through earthly experiences God is training, molding, and changing me to be more like Jesus; here I can be part of God's unfolding purpose by moving with his Spirit to spread the good news that changes the hearts of others.

I had to go back to the start and realize God had mapped out an ideal spiritual path for me, as for Jeremiah and every individual, even before conception. I found my path when I accepted Jesus as my Redeemer and I can only stay on this path by continually praying to God as Jesus did, "Thy will be done." This needs to be my constant prayer if I am to succeed in my fervent desire to totally submit my heart and mind to God. I am ever aware of our obligation "To act justly and to love mercy and to walk humbly with your God." (Mic. 6:8). Only in this way can I be successful in living, speaking, and defending his Word, and spreading the gospel.

Satan in retreat from the cross is still powerfully hostile to everything of God. It is the duty of every Christian, in the name of Jesus, to move swiftly against evil whenever it surfaces, whether it does so within us, or around us in organized religion or the community. An existence with God is literally worlds apart from "life" without him. We have found the pearl of great price. We have found Jesus Christ the Savior of the world and we must guard his gospel where it sits in our hearts and in our churches. It is the in-dwelling of the Holy Spirit in us who enables us to do so. The results so far of trying to do this, leave me in no doubt that it is highly dangerous to oppose evil and extremely hard to succeed against it. It is not easy to hear the Holy Spirit above the din of Satan's seductive call. When I do hear and act correctly, then despite my best efforts Satan opposes me all the more strongly, and I often find myself in difficulties. There is no formula approach; I cannot second guess the counter move evil will make. I do know what God will do. He will go before me to deal with every challenge and often this takes the form of setting up another milestone for me. Through prayer, serving others, Bible study, regular church attendance, and the companionship of other Christians I stay as close to him as I can. Prayer is paramount and always possible no matter what my circumstances. While I can think, I can pray, and when I can't think, the Holy Spirit prays for me. I wouldn't consider living any other way. To do so would be like sky diving without a parachute.

I have learnt the hard way the need to strive to be steeped in truth, righteousness, peace, and faith, and to hold fast to the Word of God, while praying continuously about everything. It is only these spiritual weapons that can triumph over the worldly weapons of Satan who uses lies, scheming, disloyalty, discord, power coups, and false gods. In the space of five verses in Ephesians chapter 6, we are instructed three times to "stand" our ground, and then to "stand firm"—moving out of the firing line or sitting down on the job is plainly not an option.

As I try to do this, the truth of the following verse is becoming increasingly obvious: "But God chose the foolish things of the world to shame the wise; God chose the weak things of the world to shame the strong." (1 Cor. 1:27). I realize all I can contribute is a love for God and his will, obedience to him, and a willingness to serve when he puts something in my mind and on my heart to do. Anyone can live like this. It doesn't require good health, good looks, charm, high intelligence, or any other particular talent. Even though he does at times select people to whom he has given some outstanding gift, for the most part he works surprisingly through ordinary people with obvious flaws. It seems the more realistic I am about my own weakness and foolishness, the more time I spend in prayer asking for help and guidance. The practical outcome is more intimate time with God, an indescribable blessing in itself, and also I follow instructions better. Satan can't outmaneuver or outwit God, but alone I cannot stand against him. Also, I know even when protected by spiritual armor I can only progress in God's power, and his power is love. My life and behavior should be an ever-changing, ever-more inspiring picture of God's love. All those around me should see me developing increasingly into the likeness of Jesus and becoming a truer channel for this love of God. I don't know if this is so, and I certainly don't have the courage to ask anyone, but I do know as time goes by that I am finding it easier to commit to God's priorities of love and forgiveness of others. His word makes it clear he delights in those who love and obey him. Delighting God and honoring his glory seems very little to give in return for the sacrifice Jesus made for me and all Creation.

The grace of God is like his love and knows no limits. Throughout the Scriptures he has given countless promises to those people whose hearts he holds. The following quote is one of my favorites because the love of God is expressed in his grace, assurance, and faithfulness, and it nourishes my soul whenever I think of it: "A scroll of remembrance was written in his presence concerning those who feared the Lord and honored his name, 'They will be mine,' says the Lord Almighty, 'in the day when I make up my treasured possession. I will spare them, just as in compassion a man spares his son who serves him.'" (Mal. 3:16–17). A disciplined life dedicated to God is full of spiritual riches that unfold before us and envelop us as we journey with Jesus. Obedience is not a burden, it is a great joy. The breathtaking beauty of life with God is there for the taking right now. Already I can see God's hand on the canvas of my life. I see where he has added the rich colors of peace, and hope, and joy, and through them he has infused the light of his love and presence.

It seems to me the reason why many people fail to choose to be with God is because they just can't grasp the depth and quality of his love. I suppose in our humanity no one really can, but we need to actively and urgently seek as much understanding as possible, because it is a love that opens the door to heaven. In closing this account of my journey to date I ask everyone who is reading this last page to pray for yourself, whether you are a believer or not, and for others, as Paul did in this marvelous intercessory prayer of his:

"I kneel before the Father, from whom his whole family in heaven and on earth derives its name. I pray that out of his glorious riches he may strengthen you with power through his Spirit in your inner being, so that Christ may dwell in your hearts through faith. And I pray that you, being rooted and established in love, may have power, together with all the saints, to grasp how wide and long and high and deep is the love of Christ, and to know this love that surpasses knowledge—that you may be filled to the measure of all the fullness of God." (Eph. 3:14–19).

Differences Between Buddhism and Christianity

BUDDHISM	CHRISTIANITY
A very complicated doctrine about the achievement of nothingness which varies in core beliefs between different cultures and schools of Buddhist thought.	A very simple doctrine—man needs to be reconciled to God so must repent and believe that Jesus Christ died for our sin which separates us from God.
No God but an impersonal 'ground of being'.	A personal God who created the world and made man in his own image.
The ultimate nature of truth and reality is emptiness.	The ultimate nature of truth and reality is God.
Buddha is a spontaneous emanation from the timeless expanse of the Truth Body of Buddha; some schools of Buddhist thought also believe he is a historical figure.	God is the truth, the beginning and the ending. Jesus is God but for a brief time was also fully human on earth as a historical figure.
Buddha perfected himself.	God and Jesus were always perfect.
Nirvana (heaven) is a state of perfect enlightenment characterized by true peace and nothingness.	Heaven is being in the presence and fullness of the goodness of God throughout eternity.
The true path to spiritual freedom lies in the development of insight into the absence of permanent self.	The true path to spiritual freedom is in seeking God and thus realizing one's full potential.

BUDDHISM	CHRISTIANITY
Teachers are needed as gateways to develop the spiritual nature	The Holy Spirit leads us to Christ, the only gateway.
The teachings of Buddha lead people to spiritual liberation (salvation).	The teachings of the Bible revealed by the Holy Spirit lead people to salvation.
Nirvana is achieved through the practice of the teachings of Buddha by meditation and good works.	The only gateway to heaven is Jesus Christ; self effort and good works are not adequate.
Intelligence is important in the pursuit of spiritual enlightenment.	Personal acceptance of Christ is all that is necessary for enlightenment.
Emphasis on spiritual enlightenment through personal responsibility which is made effective through personal effort.	Emphasis on spiritual enlightenment through personal responsibility which is made effective only through the power of the Holy Spirit.
The truth of the law of causality is the judge, not a being or a person who is handing out judgments.	God will judge every man for everything ever thought, said or done. Those without pardon through Christ will go to hell.
Hell—there is no hell.	Hell is being out of the presence of God and all his goodness through all eternity and being only in the presence of evil.
Man's nature is innately good.	Man's nature is innately flawed.
There is no evil outside a man's mind; by effort a man can remove this evil from his mind.	Evil is a distinct entity called Satan who relates to man personally; only God can enable man to overcome evil.

BUDDHISM	CHRISTIANITY
Man has no soul; after death the consciousness of a fully enlightened being is reabsorbed into 'the ground of being'.	Man has a spirit which lives after death in either heaven or hell; those who die reconciled to God will dwell with him forever (heaven), those who are not will dwell with Satan (hell).
After death there may be rebirth—not of the person themselves but according to their attachments to earthly things when they died; full enlightenment is the ending of rebirth; a fully enlightened being is able to make the choice to be reborn for the purpose of helping suffering in the world (only some Buddhist schools of thought).	After death there is no rebirth.
Perpetual suffering in the world comes through the deeply ingrained attachment to self and the consequent clinging to earthly things.	Suffering in the world is due to man's sin of breaking the relationship with God by ignoring God and rebelling against him.

Bibliography

Auden, W.H. *Tell Me the Truth About Love*. London: Faber and Faber Limited, 1994.
Chapman, Gary. *The Five Love Languages: The Secret to Love that Lasts*. Chicago: Northfield, 2010.
Dalai Lama. *The Good Heart: A Buddhist Perspective on the Teachings of Jesus*. Massachusetts: Wisdom Publications, 1996.
Kendall, R.T. *Total Forgiveness*. UK: Hodder & Stoughton, 2001.
Lewis, C. S. *Mere Christianity*. UK: HarperCollins, 2001.
———. *A Grief Observed*. New York: Harper & Row, 1961.
———. *The Four Loves*. UK: HarperCollins, 2010.
McDowell, Josh. *The New Evidence that Demands a Verdict*. Nashville: Thomas Nelson, 1999.
Muggeridge, Malcolm. *Conversion*. London: Hodder & Stoughton, 1988.
Strobel, Lee. *The Case for Christ*. Grand Rapids Michigan: Zondervan, 1998.
The New Bible Dictionary. 2nd ed. Edited by J.D. Douglas, et al. Leicester: Inter-varsity Press. Wheaton: Tyndale House Publishers inc., 1982.
The Shorter Oxford English Dictionary. 3rd ed. William Little, H.W Fowler, J.Coulson. Oxford: Clarendon Press, 1970.

www.ingramcontent.com/pod-product-compliance
Lightning Source LLC
Chambersburg PA
CBHW050616300426
44112CB00012B/1535